The IS-LM Model

The IS-LM Model: Its Rise, Fall, and Strange Persistence

Annual Supplement to Volume 36
History of Political Economy

Edited by Michel De Vroey and Kevin D. Hoover

Duke University Press
Durham and London 2004

Contents

Introduction: Seven Decades of the IS-LM Model

Michel De Vroey and Kevin D. Hoover

For some twenty-five years after the end of World War II, the IS-LM model dominated macroeconomics. With the advent of the new classical macroeconomics in the early 1970s, that dominance was at first challenged and then broken. Yet the IS-LM model lives on. While no longer central to the graduate training of most macroeconomists or to cutting-edge macroeconomic research, the IS-LM model continues to be a mainstay of undergraduate textbooks, finds wide application in areas of applied macroeconomics away from the front lines of macroeconomic theory, and lies at the conceptual core of most government and commercial macroeconometric models. What explains the rise, the fall, and the persistence of the IS-LM model? This volume presents essays from the *HOPE* conference held 25–27 April 2003 at Duke University that provide partial answers to this question. In addition to the ten essays from the conference, we are fortunate to be able to reprint an address delivered by Robert Lucas in conjunction with the conference. Professor Lucas made his remarks at a reception celebrating the commitment of his professional papers to Duke University's Rare Book, Manuscript, and Special Collections Library, where they will be housed with the papers of other distinguished economists received through the Economists' Papers Project. As Lucas is one of the central players in the intellectual movement that ultimately dethroned the IS-LM model, his lecture stands

We thank the editors of *HOPE*—Craufurd Goodwin, Neil De Marchi, and E. Roy Weintraub—for giving us the opportunity to organize the conference on the IS-LM model. We also thank Paul Dudenhefer for his unstinting support in helping to organize the conference and in the editorial production of the current volume.

on an altogether different plane than the essays from the conference. It may be regarded reasonably as an eyewitness account by an observant and reflective participant.

The 1930s were years of turmoil for economists concerned with the problems of business cycles. Although macroeconomic questions were among the oldest in economics, macroeconomics as a field was struggling to grow into self-consciousness. The term *macroeconomics* was first coined by Ragnar Frisch in 1933.[1] Economists such as Erik Lindahl, Friedrich Hayek, and John Hicks were struggling with dynamics—time and expectations—and beginning to create formalized models. Frisch and Jan Tinbergen, among others, started to build statistically estimated models. The conceptual basis not only for macroeconomic models, but even for national accounting, was still hotly debated.

History, as is frequently said, is written by the victors. In light of the postwar dominance of "Keynesian" macroeconomics, it would be easy to overlook the fact that John Maynard Keynes's *General Theory of Employment, Interest, and Money* (1936) by no means swept the boards in the macroeconomic debates of the mid-1930s. The *General Theory*, as the essay of Roger Backhouse and David Laidler reminds us, offered a systematic account of the macroeconomy that, on the one hand, built on numerous antecedents and, on the other hand, ignored hard-won theoretical achievements in the areas of economic dynamics. Keynes adopted a Marshallian approach, both in the sense that he deliberately echoed Marshall's microeconomic analysis in a new macroeconomic setting and in the sense that he adopted Marshall's notion that radical simplification is sometimes necessary to achieve a practically applicable analysis (Marshall [1885] 1925; see also Friedman [1949] 1953, 1955). Around the same time that Keynes's *General Theory* provided an account of aggregate general equilibrium, mathematical economics began to make considerable strides in developing the underpinnings for the individually based general equilibrium model that started with Léon Walras and culminated in Kenneth Arrow and Gerard Debreu's proof of the existence of general equilibrium in the early 1950s. The essay in this volume by Michel De Vroey explores the relationships and tensions between these

---

1. Jean-Paul Fitoussi and Kumaraswamy Velupillai (1993) report that Frisch used the term in lectures, whereas Lindahl may have been the first to use it in print. The term *macrodynamic(s)* was, however, already current in the middle to the end of the 1930s. The earliest example in the JSTOR journal archive is in an article by Edward Theiss (1935).

competing visions of general equilibrium and between the Marshallian and Walrasian methodologies. In particular, it claims that the IS-LM model belonged to the Marshallian rather than the Walrasian tradition.

The *General Theory* was immediately seen to be a vitally important book. Keynes used the language of mathematics to articulate elements of the economy: the consumption function, the liquidity preference function, the aggregate supply function, and so forth. But the glue that welded these pieces into a macroeconomic system was Keynes's elegant, but not always transparent, prose. Keynes (1936, v) had addressed the *General Theory* to his fellow economists. And at a meeting of the Econometric Society in Oxford in 1937, his fellow economists gathered to try to work out the meaning of his masterwork. Roy Harrod, James Meade, and John Hicks translated the *General Theory* into mathematical systems.[2] Their accounts have largely been forgotten, except for that of Hicks ([1937] 1967). Cutting through the elegant prose and the many detours, Hicks's IS-LL model proposed to reduce the central theoretical message of Keynes's *General Theory* to a short set of simultaneous equations and a single graph. At the time, Hicks could not have fancied the success that his model was to encounter. In effect, it became the organizing theoretical apparatus of the emerging discipline of macroeconomics.

Knowingly perpetrating a solecism, Keynes conjured up a straw man, "the classics," on page 3 of the *General Theory* in order to have a worthy foe to vanquish over the remaining 409. Hicks's essay, "Mr. Keynes and the 'Classics,'" begins by noting the smell of newly cut hay hanging about Keynes's classics. Nevertheless, Hicks tries to locate the essence of Keynes's approach in an understanding of just what Keynes claims distinguishes himself from the classics. Hicks presents a self-consciously stylized account of the *General Theory* in three equations. But it was the diagram, not the equations, that engendered the enduring fame of the essay.

Figure 1 is Hicks's original diagram. On the vertical axis are interest rates, and on the horizontal axis, aggregate nominal income. The downward-sloping IS curve represents the locus of points for which investment (a function of interest rates) and savings (a function of income) are equal. The upward-sloping LL curve represents the locus of points for which the stock of money (presumed fixed) equals the amount demanded

2. David Champernowne was also present at the meeting. He had previously presented a mathematical and diagrammatic version of the *General Theory* (Champernowne 1936), as had W. Brian Reddaway (1936).

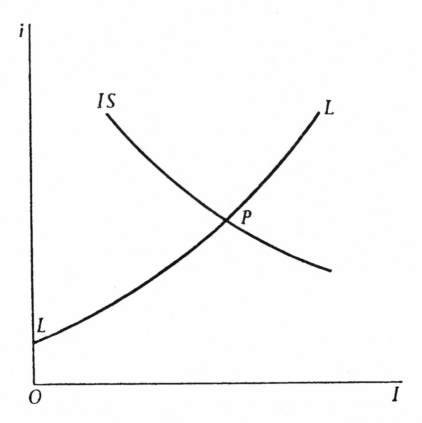

Figure 1 The original IS-LM diagram (Hicks 1937, fig. 3; [1937] 1967, fig. 9)

to satisfy liquidity preference. Hicks saw the essential difference between Keynes and the classics in Keynes's claim that liquidity preference offered a novel account of the determination of interest rates. As a result, Hicks paid special attention to the LL curve. According to him, Keynes's system became "completely out of touch with the classical world" whenever the LL curve exhibited a horizontal section and the intersection between IS and LL occurred on this section (Hicks [1937] 1967, 154). In such an occurrence, the "economics of depression," monetary expansion was unable to increase employment. In contrast, fiscal policy would be effective. With not even an acknowledgment of Keynes's (1936, 207) avowed ignorance of real-world cases of absolute liquidity preference (or, as it came to be known, the *liquidity trap*), Hicks argues that the flat LL curve is *the* characteristically Keynesian case. The essay by Mauro Boianovsky traces the history and analysis of the liquidity trap from Keynes and Hicks through Krugman's analysis of the Japanese economy in the 1990s.

Hicks himself was sensitive to the limitations of his model and his diagram. He anticipated criticisms encapsulated in Joan Robinson's (1975) dismissive phrase "bastard Keynesianism" and in Alan Coddington's (1976, 1263) less pejorative, but accurate, "hydraulic Keynesianism." How then did Hicks's "little apparatus" become canonical? This occurred in two stages. First, recasting Hicks's model (De Vroey 2000), Franco Modigliani (1944) sharpened the contrast between the classical and the Keynesian submodels. The former now referred to a case of flexible wages and market clearing, the latter to downward rigid wages and involuntary unemployment. Modigliani's contribution is analyzed in Goulven Rubin's essay. Rubin also claims that Don Patinkin's (1956) simplified general equilibrium constituted an alternative way of achieving the aim that Hicks and Modigliani had set for themselves. Second, every prophet needs an apostle. Keynes and Hicks found their apostle in Alvin Hansen. Hansen (1949, 1953) reinterpreted Keynes and rewrote elementary macroeconomics using Hicks's model. For reasons that remain somewhat obscure, Hansen relabeled the LL curve "LM." It is a testimony to Hansen's importance in the story that the model has been referred to as IS-LM ever since.

After World War II, the IS-LM model was developed in several directions. It became gradually enriched by the consideration of open economies and by attempts to give microfoundations to the consumption function, portfolio decisions, and the investment schedule. It served as the basis for econometric models. By degrees, standard textbooks—starting with books aimed at graduate students and by the 1960s trickling down to elementary texts—adopted the IS-LM model as their framework.

As the model became more dominant theoretically, it lost its Keynesian character with respect to practical policy issues. That is, non-Keynesians could simply state that only its classical variant was valid, its Keynesian variant being flawed because of its rigid wages assumption. Thus, friends and foes of Keynes alike could use it to promote or confute Keynesian policy prescriptions.

The essay of Warren Young and William Darity is concerned with such an embellishment of the standard IS-LM model. It recounts the story of how the model was broadened to consider the balance of payments and exchange rates—key questions in international finance. The essay by Robert Dimand addresses James Tobin's efforts to introduce more complex, more realistic financial markets into the IS-LM framework.

Throughout the high tide of the IS-LM model in the 1950s and 1960s, Milton Friedman and his fellow travelers (mostly associated in one way or another with the University of Chicago) advocated the superiority of the quantity theory of money over the Keynesian income-expenditure theory. Karl Brunner (1968) coined the term *monetarism* to describe the school of thought that included Friedman, Anna Schwartz, himself, and his frequent coauthor Allan Meltzer, as well as many of their students and colleagues. Drawing on very different paradigms, monetarists and Keynesians often seemed to talk at cross-purposes. When finally he was persuaded to try to articulate the framework of his monetary thinking, Friedman (1974), in an effort to bridge the gap between him and his Keynesian antagonists, turned to the IS-LM model. Friedman was not successful. In their essay, Michael Bordo and Anna Schwartz argue that, because of fundamental methodological differences between the monetarists and Keynesians, the IS-LM model was an inappropriate vehicle for successfully characterizing monetarism and that Friedman's attempt was doomed. They note that other monetarists, such as Brunner and Meltzer, who had argued that a much richer asset structure than was available in the IS-LM model was needed to capture monetarist views of the transmission mechanism for monetary policy, were not tempted to follow Friedman in trying to use the model as a neutral tool of communication with the Keynesians. Keynesians such as Tobin held similar views to Brunner and Meltzer about the need for rich asset structures (see Robert Dimand's essay), but nevertheless saw their position as elaborating rather than contradicting IS-LM (cf. Dornbusch 1976). Scott Sumner's essay argues that the IS-LM model offered an appropriate basis for monetary policy only in the gold standard era that was just ending at the time that Keynes wrote the *General Theory*. Sumner argues that, despite decades of intellectual dominance, the IS-LM model is necessarily an inadequate tool of analysis and communication for the quantity theorist.

The success of the IS-LM model must also be explained by its happy adaptability to econometric modeling. Keynesian economics provided the intellectual foundation of a new theory of economic policy. Although

Keynes himself was deeply skeptical about the new econometrics of the 1930s—expressed particularly in his 1939 review of Tinbergen's early modeling exercises—macroeconometric modeling grew up in tandem with Keynesian macroeconomics. Published as *The Keynesian Revolution* (1947), Lawrence Klein's doctoral dissertation was an interpretation of the *General Theory* in which Klein paid attention to important modeling aspects of Keynesian economics, including microfoundations for, in particular, the consumption function, the money-demand function, and the investment function. Klein went on to become the doyen of macroeconometric modeling in the United States and the United Kingdom. Econometric models became ever more elaborate, but their essential structure was closely related to the conceptual form of the IS-LM model.

Only one key feature of postwar macroeconometric models was not captured in the first generation of the textbook IS-LM model: inflation. The model was conceived in an era in which prices were not expected to trend up or down for long periods. Although the macroeconometric models added lagged variables to capture dynamics in a rough-and-ready way, the IS-LM model itself was essentially static. Soon after the publication of A. W. Phillips's (1958) paper on wage inflation and unemployment in the United Kingdom, the "Phillips curve," now generally estimated for price inflation and unemployment, became the standard way of "closing" the macroeconometric model.

The Phillips curve may have proved to be the undoing of standard Keynesian theory. The Phillips curve was criticized—particularly by Friedman (1968) and Edmund Phelps (1967)—for failing to integrate expectations and for ignoring the long-run neutrality of money. When macroeconometric models appeared to perform badly in the early 1970s, much of the blame attached to the Phillips curve. Robert Lucas (1972a, 1972b) initially turned his fire on his own antecedents, criticizing his old teacher, Milton Friedman, for modeling expectations in a manner that suggested that people made systematic, expensive, and easily correctable errors. Lucas and other "new classicals" such as Thomas Sargent and Robert Barro argued that expectations should be modeled according to the *rational expectations hypothesis* in a manner that did not build in systematic error.

The early new classical models (e.g., Sargent and Wallace 1976) simply added rational expectations to the IS-LM framework. Lucas soon came to see that the failure to model expectations appropriately was part of a larger problem. In his important paper "Econometric Policy Evaluation: A Critique" (1976), he argued that the failure of the macroeconometric models in the early 1970s was attributable to a general failure to model the behavior of the individual, rational, optimizing agents that constitute the economy. In particular, Lucas criticized the practice of assuming that the parameters of aggregate econometric models would maintain stability in the face of changes in the conduct of economic policy. Lucas argued that the parameters themselves were functions of deeper parameters, governing the tastes and constraints of agents, and that these agents would adapt to new economic policies by adapting their behavior in a way that would shift the parameters of aggregate models.

The Lucas critique was widely taken to demand a microeconomic basis for macroeconomics. It is, of course, a difficult problem to model the millions of individual agents in the economy. And, rapidly, the new classicals settled on the representative agent model (and some other highly stylized models) as the basis for macroeconomic theory. This is not the place to go into the successes and failures of this modeling strategy (but see Janssen 1993, Hartley 1997, and Hoover 2001). The important thing in this context is that the widespread acceptance—by new classicals and new Keynesians alike—of the ideal of microfoundations for macroeconomics was a body blow to the aggregative IS-LM model. By 1980, the IS-LM model no longer stood at the forefront of research in macroeconomic theory. Over the next two decades it gradually faded from more and more applied areas of macroeconomics. A graduate student in 2003, having studied no economics as an undergraduate, might obtain a PhD without any acquaintance—much less mastery—of the IS-LM model.

Yet, somehow the model did not die. As Edward Nelson points out in his essay, the pedagogical simplicity of the IS-LM model made it an unparalleled tool of exposition not only to students but also to policymakers. In their pure form, modern dynamic optimization models are difficult to grasp. But with judicious arrangement, policy models used at central banks can be cast as "optimizing IS models." Typically, the LM curve is exchanged for an interest-rate policy rule. Nelson argues that monetary aggregates may, nevertheless, serve as proxies for the wide range of asset prices (beyond the policy rate and a longer bond price often found in these models) affected by policy and affecting the economy. A dynamic optimizing IS model with an important role for monetary aggregate would appear to be another incarnation of Hicks's little apparatus.

In his keynote address, Lucas suggests another reason for the persistence of the IS-LM model—its flexibility and adaptability. He argues that the microfoundational models that he, as the leader of the new classicals, has championed for a quarter century try to capture quite detailed optimization problems. But they are nevertheless more stylized than realistic. They work in environments that suit them. The postwar macroeconomic environment has, he believes, favored them. Central bankers and government policymakers in developed countries have more or less followed sensible policies and have successfully stabilized the economy. In these stable environments, microfoundational models are at home and work well. But in novel and highly disrupted environments—for example, in the Great Depression or in the various crises of the developing countries—they hardly work at all. In contrast, the IS-LM model, although it is unsatisfactory from a purely theoretical point of view, nonetheless provides a framework on which practical empirical analysis can be hung. Lucas still hopes that better models will one day supplant it completely. But that day is not yet at hand.

And, so, the IS-LM model persists. David Colander closes the current volume with an examination of that persistence. No longer at the forefront of research, it remains unsurpassed as a tool of undergraduate pedagogy and communication about macroeconomic policy. A bibliometric study shows only a highly attenuated decline in references to the IS-LM model over the decades. But a greater proportion than ever are in historical or pedagogical contexts and fewer and fewer in pure theory. Textbooks still feature the IS-LM model, but where in Gardner Ackley's 1961 textbook the model itself was a focal point, in N. Gregory Mankiw's popular recent textbook (2003), it is mainly deployed as an instrument for the discussion of economic policy.

References

Ackley, Gardner. 1961. *Macroeconomic Theory*. New York: Macmillan.

Brunner, Karl. 1968. The Role of Money and Monetary Policy. *Federal Reserve Bank of St. Louis Review* 50.7:8–24.

Champernowne, David G. 1936. Unemployment, Basic and Monetary: The Classical Analysis and the Keynesian. *Review of Economic Studies* 3.3:201–16.

Coddington, Alan. 1976. The Search for First Principles. *Journal of Economic Literature* 14.4:1258–73.

De Vroey, Michel. 2000. IS-LM à la Hicks versus IS-LM à la Modigliani. *HOPE* 32.2:293–316.

Dornbusch, Rudiger. 1976. Comments on Brunner and Meltzer. In *Monetarism*, edited by Jerome Stein. Amsterdam: North-Holland.

Fitoussi, Jean-Paul, and Kumaraswamy Velupillai. 1993. Macroeconomic Perspectives. In *Monetary Theory and Thought*, edited by Haim Barkai, Stanley Fischer, and Nissan Liviatan. London: Macmillan.

Friedman, Milton. [1949] 1953. The Marshallian Demand Curve. In *Essays in Positive Economics*. Chicago: University of Chicago Press.

———. 1955. Leon Walras and His Economic System: A Review Article. *American Economic Review* 45.5:900–909.

———. 1968. The Role of Monetary Policy. *American Economic Review* 58.1:1–17.

———. 1974. A Theoretical Framework for Monetary Analysis. In *Milton Friedman's Monetary Framework: A Debate with His Critics*, edited by Robert J. Gordon. Chicago: University of Chicago Press.

Hansen, Alvin. 1949. *Monetary Theory and Fiscal Policy*. New York: McGraw-Hill.

———. 1953. *A Guide to Keynes*. New York: McGraw-Hill.

Hartley, James E. 1997. *The Representative Agent in Macroeconomics*. London: Routledge.

Hicks, John R. 1937. Mr. Keynes and the "Classics." *Econometrica* 5.2:147–59.

———. [1937] 1967. Mr. Keynes and the "Classics." In *Critical Essays in Monetary Theory*. Oxford: Clarendon.

Hoover, Kevin D. 2001. *The Methodology of Empirical Macroeconomics*. Cambridge: Cambridge University Press.

Janssen, Maarten. 1993. *Microfoundations: A Critical Inquiry*. London: Routledge.

Keynes, John Maynard. 1936. *The General Theory of Employment, Interest, and Money*. London: Macmillan.

———. 1939. Professor Tinbergen's Method. *Economic Journal* 49.195:558–68.

Klein, Lawrence R. 1947. *The Keynesian Revolution*. New York: Macmillan.

Lucas Jr., Robert E. 1972a. Econometric Testing of the Natural Rate Hypothesis. In *The Econometrics of Price Determination*, edited by Otto Eckstein. Washington, D.C.: Board of Governors of the Federal Reserve System.

———. 1972b. Expectations and the Neutrality of Money. *Journal of Economic Theory* 4.2:103–24.

———. 1976. Econometric Policy Evaluation: A Critique. In *The Phillips Curve and Labor Markets*, edited by Karl Brunner and Allan H. Meltzer. Carnegie-Rochester Conference Series on Public Policy, vol. 11 (spring). Amsterdam: North-Holland.

Mankiw, N. Gregory. 2003. *Macroeoconomics*. 5th ed. New York: Worth Publishers.

Marshall, Alfred. [1885] 1925. The Present Position of Economics. In *Memorials of Alfred Marshall*, edited by A. C. Pigou. London: Macmillan.

Modigliani, Franco. 1944. Liquidity Preference and the Theory of Interest and Money. *Econometrica* 12.1:45–88.

Patinkin, Don. 1956. *Money, Interest, and Prices*. New York: Harper and Row.

Phelps, Edmund S. 1967. Phillips Curves, Expectations of Inflation, and Optimal Unemployment over Time. *Economica*, n.s., 34.3:254–81.

Phillips, A. W. 1958. The Relation between Unemployment and the Rate of Change of Money Wages in the United Kingdom, 1961–1957. *Economica*, n.s., 25.100:283–99.

Reddaway, W. Brian. 1936. *The General Theory of Employment, Interest, and Money* by J. M. Keynes. *Economic Record* 12 (June): 28–36.

Robinson, Joan. 1975. What Has Become of the Keynesian Revolution? In *Essays on John Maynard Keynes*, edited by Milo Keynes. Cambridge: Cambridge University Press.

Sargent, Thomas J., and Neil Wallace. 1976. Rational Expectations and the Theory of Economic Policy. *Journal of Monetary Economics* 2.2:169–83.

Theiss, Edward. 1935. Dynamics of Saving and Investment. *Econometrica* 3.2:213–24.

Keynote Address to the 2003 *HOPE* Conference: My Keynesian Education

Robert E. Lucas Jr.

I have mixed feelings about Bob Byrd[1] saying he's looking forward to receiving my papers. He's probably only going to get them when I'm gone: I don't seem to be able to give up anything out of my file drawers. But when that does happen, my papers will be in the best library for the history of economic thought they can find anywhere, so they will have a happy home.

Well, I'm not here to tell people in this group about the history of monetary thought. I guess I'm here as a kind of witness from a vanished culture, the heyday of Keynesian economics. It's like historians rushing to interview the last former slaves before they died, or the last of the people who remembered growing up in a Polish shtetl. I am going to tell you what it was like growing up in a day when Keynesian economics was taught as a solid basis on which macroeconomics could proceed.

My credentials? Was I a Keynesian myself? Absolutely. And does my Chicago training disqualify me for that? No, not at all. David Laidler [who was present at the conference] will agree with me on this, and I will explain in some detail when I talk about my education. Our Keynesian credentials, if we wanted to claim them, were as good as could be obtained in any graduate school in the country in 1963.

I thought when I was trying to prepare some notes for this talk that people attending the conference might be arguing about Axel

This address was made on 26 April 2003 in the Rare Book Room of Perkins Library, Duke University.
   1. Director of Duke University's Rare Book, Manuscript, and Special Collections Library.

Leijonhufvud's thesis that IS-LM was a distortion of Keynes, but I didn't really hear any of this in the discussions this afternoon. So I'm going to think about IS-LM and Keynesian economics as being synonyms. I remember when Leijonhufvud's book[2] came out and I asked my colleague Gary Becker if he thought Hicks had got the *General Theory* right with his IS-LM diagram. Gary said, "Well, I don't know, but I hope he did, because if it wasn't for Hicks I never would have made *any* sense out of that damn book." That's kind of the way I feel, too, so I'm hoping Hicks got it right.

Today I'm going to reminisce about my macro courses at Chicago and a little bit about what I learned teaching macroeconomics at Carnegie Mellon, which is where the Keynesian phase of my career ended. And then I would like to talk about what I now think, not as a graduate student but as an adult, about Keynesian economics, both as a political force in the years during and after the Depression and as a scientific influence. But I do think those are two different questions. And then, since I love the reference to the "strange persistence" of IS-LM in the conference title, in the end I'm going to take a crack at that, too. Because it *has* persisted.

I started graduate school in the history department at Berkeley in the fall of 1959. As a Chicago undergraduate in history, I had been excited by writings like Marx and Engels's *Communist Manifesto* and the work of the Belgian historian Henri Pirenne. I was interested in ancient history in those days, and Pirenne had an economic interpretation of the end of the Roman Empire in Western Europe and the advent of the Dark Ages that was exciting for me. So I wanted to learn some economics, but hadn't got around to actually doing so.

In those days, Keynes's standing was kind of like Einstein's—everyone knew he was important—this was among undergraduates, but I suppose it was true everywhere; but no one understood what he meant. In high school, they told us that only six people in the world understood the theory of relativity. So I don't know—the *General Theory* maybe would have had sixteen or something. I remember Alvin Hansen had actually written a watered-down version—you had to have an intermediary to get close to the *General Theory*. Somebody had to help you get at it. But I had no idea what was actually in Keynes's book.

2. *On Keynesian Economics and the Economics of Keynes: A Study in Monetary Theory* (New York, 1968).

At Berkeley, I took economic history courses from Carlo Cipolla and David Landes, which in hindsight was amazing good luck. Landes taught a seminar course for first-year graduate students that was sort of a bibliographical boot camp where you had to pick a topic off a list of his and go to the library and find out everything that was known on this topic and come back and report to the seminar. One student came into the seminar with a single piece of paper that he just unfolded and unfolded until it covered the whole seminar table; we were all lost in admiration for this guy! It was a fun seminar; people were having a lot of fun. For me, history courses had been other people handing me things and saying, "Read this," so it was a new experience to be in a seminar where our job was to find out what was worth reading and to tell other people about it.

One of the topics on Landes's list was nineteenth-century British business cycles. I chose this one, since I wanted an excuse to learn some economics. That's where I met Anna Schwartz, although she doesn't know this. I read the monograph by Gayer, Rostow, and Schwartz[3]—yes, that's *Anna* Schwartz and *W. W.* Rostow—I mean this is really a team, right? And they were the *junior* authors in this book! The senior author was A. D. Gayer at Queen's College. This book was a mix: it went over British economic history in the first part of the nineteenth century. It included a kind of a year-by-year history. There was NBER Mitchell-type stuff, and then there was a sort of Keynesian diagnosis, episode by episode. It was an amazingly ambitious and exciting mix of history and theory. Anna [also at the conference] later told me she was embarrassed by the Keynesian theory in the book, but as a student I thought it was very exciting.

I decided I had to take some real economics courses or I was always going to be on the sideline even of economic history, and Landes encouraged me in this view. But Berkeley wasn't going to support me to study economics. At Christmas break I moved back to Chicago: I had passed an exam as a history undergraduate at a high enough level that I was automatically admitted as a graduate student in social science. So I just showed up at the economics department and said, "Here I am."

I started by taking remedial courses, like undergraduate courses in economics. I took some price theory. At Chicago price theory—micro— is always at the center, but my first macro course was from Carl Christ, who introduced me to Patinkin's work. We never used Patinkin in a

3. *The Growth and Fluctuation of the British Economy, 1790–1850: An Historical, Statistical, and Theoretical Study of Britain's Economic Development* (Oxford, 1953).

course. And then I had a fabulous course from Martin Bailey. Christ's course was a step-by-step model-building course, making sure you had the same number of equations and unknowns. Just what I needed. We read some of the Keynesian classics. That's where I first read Hicks's "Mr. Keynes and the 'Classics'" and Modigliani's 1944 paper.[4] I think this was the basis for IS-LM theory, those two papers. Christ also assigned us Klein's book *The Keynesian Revolution*, which is a pretty nice little book.[5] Another book that influenced me a lot was Samuelson's *Foundations*—I'm part of the Samuelson generation that Mark Blaug [who had been mentioned in the introduction to this talk] talked about— which I started reading on my own.

After class one day, I asked Christ about what Hicks thought was going on in labor markets, because there's not much on it in "Mr. Keynes and the 'Classics.'" That's when Christ told me to read Patinkin's *Money, Interest, and Prices*,[6] and I tried to do it. It's such a beautiful book physically, even the pictures. I just loved looking at that book. It made me feel like I was in touch with something elevated. Also, Patinkin's scholarly style, his erudition, I liked that, too. I still do. But the main thing I liked about Patinkin's book was that it was full of supply and demand, of people maximizing, of markets. There's a lot of micro in the book. That was the objective Patinkin had stated in his subtitle: to unify value theory and monetary theory. I liked his high aspirations. They were inspiring to me. But the book doesn't quite come off, does it? I mean, the theory is never really solved. What are the predictions of Patinkin's model? The model is too complicated to work them out. All the dynamics are the mechanical auctioneer dynamics that Samuelson introduced, where *anything* can happen.

There's an interesting footnote in Patinkin's book. Milton Friedman had told him that the rate of change of price in any one market ought to depend on excess demand and supply in all markets in the system. Patinkin is happy about this suggestion because he loves more generality, but if you think about Friedman's review of Lange, of Lange's book,[7]

4. "Liquidity Preference and the Theory of Interest and Money," which appeared in the January 1944 issue of *Econometrica*. Hicks's article appeared in the April 1937 issue of that same journal.

5. Published in 1947 by Macmillan.

6. Published in 1956 by Row, Peterson of Evanston, Ill. The book was subtitled *An Integration of Monetary and Value Theory*.

7. *Price Flexibility and Employment* (Bloomington, Ind., 1944). Friedman's review appeared in the September 1946 regular issue of the *American Economic Review*.

what Friedman must have been trying to tell Patinkin is that he thinks the theory is empty, that anything can happen in this model. And I think he's got a point.

If you look at Rapping's and my paper on labor markets[8]—which I'll come back to, because that's a Keynesian paper—we have a cleared labor market at every point in time, and we were a little self-conscious about that because people didn't think that was the right way to do things. Going back to Patinkin's book, and even though Patinkin says that all the dynamics is some auctioneer moving prices, you can see from his verbal discussion that he's reading a lot of economics into these dynamics. What are people thinking? What are they expecting? He's too good an economist to take the Samuelsonian dynamics literally. He's really thinking about intertemporal substitution. He doesn't know *how* to think about it well, but he's trying to. So in some sense Patinkin's book is less mechanical than it looks.

I think Patinkin was absolutely right to try and use general equilibrium theory to think about macroeconomic problems. Patinkin and I are both Walrasians, whatever that means. I don't see how anybody can not be. It's pure hindsight, but now I think that Patinkin's problem was that he was a student of Lange's, and Lange's version of the Walrasian model was already archaic by the end of the 1950s. Arrow and Debreu and McKenzie had redone the whole theory in a clearer, more rigorous, and more flexible way. Patinkin's book was a reworking of his Chicago thesis from the middle 1940s and had not benefited from this more recent work.

In the spring quarter that year, I took Martin Bailey's course. He was then writing his book *National Income and the Price Level*.[9] It wasn't out then, but it was in draft and this was the basis for the course. Bailey's book moves right along. He's got a Keynesian cross in nine pages. He's got a well-motivated IS-LM diagram by page 20. He's got a production sector and a labor market by page 35. It took Patinkin to page 343 to get to that point! So, Bailey is speeding things up by a factor of ten. And he's getting the mathematical structure of the model clear. You can count equations and unknowns. You can see what the predictions of Bailey's model are. You have to make some assumptions, but you can work with the model.

8. "Real Wages, Employment, and Inflation," which appeared in the September-October issue of the *Journal of Political Economy*.

9. Published in 1962 by McGraw-Hill.

When I think of IS-LM, I think of what I learned from Bailey, where you have IS-LM and then this production sector that he took from Modigliani's paper and put them all together with some additions. For example, Bailey put us on to the fact that it's a *nominal* interest rate in the LM curve and a *real* interest rate in the IS curve. You are making use of the vertical axis for two different things. You have to do something about that. So Bailey's book was good training and was the basis for preparing for the core exam at Chicago and Carnegie Mellon for ten or fifteen more years after that.

I mentioned Samuelson's book [*Foundations*]. You'll see the IS-LM model in Samuelson's chapter when he introduces the correspondence principle: the idea that you can learn about comparative statics by looking at the stability properties of a model. Example 1 is the IS-LM model. (Maybe that's example 2. Maybe supply and demand is example 1.) That's an example of how standard IS-LM was at that point.

So that's my first year [1959–60] of graduate school, as an unsuccessful history student and then as a student in remedial courses in economics. And then by the next fall, I was ready to take Friedman's course, which was the high point of everyone's education at Chicago.

But in my day, Friedman taught price theory; he didn't teach macro. I don't know if Mike Bordo [also at the conference] may have had him— ["I had him for money and macro," Bordo said]. I had a neighbor in Chicago, Sue Freehling, who was an MBA student at Chicago and had taken Friedman's course in money and macro. Sue was an active liberal Democrat, and I wondered how she liked the course. She said, "Oh, I loved Friedman. He's such a wonderful guy. But he had us read this awful book by Keynes." I don't know if that's how it was for you [speaking to Bordo], but Sue thought Friedman took that book way too seriously and she wished he'd just talked more about his own ideas.

Anyway, I didn't have any macro from Friedman. What I had that was exciting in macro in my first year was Harry Johnson's first course at Chicago. He had just arrived in Chicago, and he was full of the controversy stemming from Patinkin's book, Archibald and Lipsey's criticism,[10] and so on. This stuff was *way* over the heads of anyone in the class as far as I could tell. Except for Neil Wallace. I remember Neil asking him—I can't imitate his voice but he just calls out without raising his hand: "Wait a minute, Harry! *That's* not what you want to say."

10. "Monetary and Value Theory: A Critique of Lange and Patinkin," published in the October 1958 issue of the *Review of Economic Studies*.

Things didn't happen this way in England, and nobody called him Harry. [*Laughter.*] Somehow I got nothing out of the course. Too much detail. I think I thought I knew everything after Bailey's class, so I basically bailed out and got a C in the course. Which was probably an overstatement of what I actually learned. And Harry never really had a high opinion of me after that.

Johnson's heyday as a teacher at Chicago came when Mundell arrived a few years later, and then he and Mundell trained Frenkel, Dornbusch, Mussa, Razin—people who just transformed and kind of Keynesianized international macro. That was a great period, but it hadn't even started when we were students, and I missed out on that.

Johnson's was the last macro class I took at Chicago. My fields were econometrics and public finance, so I didn't take any advanced macro, I just took the core courses. But public finance in those days was half macro. If you remember, Musgrave's book[11] was divided about equally into a macro part and a micro part. Sort of a Ramsey part and a Keynesian part. Arnold Harberger taught a course—a public finance course on macro policy, and this was really a nice thing. It was based on a multiplier-accelerator model he had calibrated to U.S. national income and product accounts. He really got into the nitty-gritty of all the leakages and the multipliers. It was the only place at Chicago where I saw a dynamic model, I mean with time subscripts, and he actually ran a system of difference equations out, trying to see what kind of shocks it would take to produce a recession. That was an exciting course. In terms of dynamics, until Uzawa showed up—again, after I left—Chicago was a backwater then. The growth theory that was starting at MIT and Stanford and Yale at that point had not yet got under way at Chicago, even though all the students had read Solow's paper[12] and were excited about it.

So what about Milton Friedman and the monetarist counterrevolution? That's what you think of when you think of Chicago in the 1960s. I was even the draftsman for Friedman and Meiselman's paper for the Commission on Money and Credit where they criticized Keynesian models.[13] But I thought of it as just drafting—it was a job. I didn't really

11. *The Theory of Public Finance: A Study in Public Economy* (New York, 1959).

12. "A Contribution to the Theory of Economic Growth," which appeared in the February 1956 issue of the *Quarterly Journal of Economics*.

13. "The Relative Stability of Monetary Velocity and the Investment Multiplier in the United States, 1897–1958," which was published in the commission's *Stabilization Policies* (Englewood Cliffs, N.J., 1963).

know what was going on in the paper. His consumption book was published in 1957.[14] His project with Anna Schwartz on monetary history was just getting going.[15] There were a lot of things that Friedman was doing in macroeconomics in my day, but he didn't talk about any of this in his price theory courses. In fact, Friedman didn't spend much time plugging his past work or talking about it. The only way you would have been in on this monetarist counterrevolution was to be writing your thesis with Friedman and be a member of the money and banking workshop, but that was an invitation-only thing. I was not working with him. The first money and banking workshop I went to was in 1974 when I was a visiting faculty member. I remember learning about the consumption study from my classmate Glen Cain, who was using it in his thesis and saw how important it was going to be, but I can't remember Friedman mentioning that book. It would not have been out of place to talk about it in his price theory course, but I can't remember his doing it. Maybe David's memory differs from mine. He was there.

["I'm trying to remember; I don't remember," said Laidler.

"You were probably more with it than I was," said Lucas.

"He did Archibald and Lipseyian price theory, though," said Laidler.

"He did?" asked Lucas.

"Yeah, he did," said Laidler.

"God, I missed it. I had two shots at Archibald and Lipsey and whiffed both times," said Lucas.]

Everyone from Chicago is a Friedman student in some very basic sense, but in terms of macro, I claim that the credentials I'm describing are true-blue Keynesian.

When I was done with my graduate education, how did I think of Keynesian economics? I didn't think about it very deeply, to tell you the truth. It wasn't my field. I didn't picture myself as doing research in the area. But I certainly thought of myself as a Keynesian. Kennedy was elected in 1960. I remember the Kennedy tax cut. We, meaning students, were excited with the Council of Economic Advisors that Kennedy appointed, the tax cut—it seemed like the theory we were learning about in class was being put in place. We were definitely excited about that. I also remember that the cost-benefit analysis was explicitly introduced in the Department of Defense back in the Kennedy administration when

14. *A Theory of the Consumption Function* (Princeton, N.J., 1957).

15. The results of which were published in 1963 by Princeton University Press as *A Monetary History of the United States, 1867–1960*.

McNamara became secretary—and that was another exciting thing for economics. It seemed like everything we were learning in class, micro and macro, was being put to work in U.S. economic policy. It all went down the drain in Vietnam, so all we remember now about McNamara is how he got us into that awful war, but, at the beginning, it was much more promising.

When I began to teach at Carnegie, I took Bailey's book [*National Income and the Price Level*], his version of IS-LM, as kind of standard stuff. This is the theory, the accepted theory that everyone should know, that it was my job to teach to graduate students, and did. I also held on to Patinkin's ambition somehow, that the theory ought to be microeconomically founded, unified with price theory. I think this was a very common view. Ed Burmeister. [Burmeister attended the talk.] Where's Ed? Ed can remember this, I'm sure. Nobody was satisfied with IS-LM as the end of macroeconomic theorizing. The idea was we were going to tie it together with microeconomics and that was the job of our generation. Or to continue doing that. That wasn't an *anti*-Keynesian view. You can see the same ambition in Klein's work or Modigliani's.

The first macroeconomics work I ever did was my work with Leonard Rapping on Phillips curves and labor markets.[16] This was an ambitious move for us. We wanted to contribute to Keynesian economics, and in particular to the econometric models that were being based on Keynesian economics. Our models—the examples we wanted to follow—were Friedman and Modigliani's work on consumption or Jorgensen and Eisner's work on investment or Meltzer's and Friedman's work on money demand.[17] These were the people who staked out an important equation for macroeconomics and were trying to estimate its parameters. We were going to go after the production and labor side of that model. There was a lot of really bad work being done on labor unions: people regressing wages in this industry on wages in some other industry and getting

16. See Lucas and Rapping, "Real Wages" (cited in footnote 8) and "Price Expectations and the Phillips Curve," published in the June 1969 issue of the *American Economic Review*.

17. See Friedman, *A Theory of the Consumption Function*; Modigliani and Richard Brumberg, "Utility Analysis and the Consumption Function: An Interpretation of Cross-Section Data," in *Post-Keynesian Economics*, edited by Kenneth K. Kurihara (New Brunswick, N.J., 1954); Dale W. Jorgenson, "Capital Theory and Investment Behavior," in the May 1963 "Papers and Proceedings" issue of the *American Economic Review*; Robert Eisner and Robert H. Strotz, "Determinants of Business Investment," in *Impacts of Monetary Policy* (Englewood Cliffs, N.J., 1963); Allan H. Meltzer, "The Demand for Money: The Evidence from the Time Series," in the June 1963 issue of the *Journal of Political Economy*; and Friedman and Schwartz, *A Monetary History of the United States*.

R-squares of .99. Really junk. There was a paper by George Perry that had a respectable theory of wage determination with a Phillips curve in it, but it was all based on labor unions.[18] Rapping and I knew that something like a fifth of the U.S. labor force was in labor unions. It didn't make any sense to have a model of the whole labor market that pretended everybody was a union member. So we thought we'd write down a competitive model.

If you look back at Rapping's and my *JPE* paper, the introduction to that paper, it's a Keynesian introduction, very much so. It's an IS-LM introduction, not that we have an IS-LM sector—somebody else had worked that stuff out—but we were going to try and work out a compatible production side and then put it all together. That was the general idea. Remember the Brookings model from those days? It was like a church supper, the way I think about it, where somebody's bringing the consumption function and somebody else is bringing the investment function. It's like Mrs. Smith is bringing the potato salad and Mrs. Jones is bringing the ribs. Somehow—you just trusted dumb luck that there was going to be the right balance of desserts and salads and God knows what. It's not a good way to design a menu, and it's a completely crazy way to put together a general equilibrium model of the whole economy. Nobody's thinking about the whole thing.

Well, that takes me up to the end of the Keynesian phase of my career. What went wrong? I'm not going to talk about this. It's a complicated story, the story of what's happened in macroeconomics since the late 1960s. It's pretty interesting. I've written about it elsewhere and so have lots of other people. So I'm just going to fast forward. This is complete hindsight. It has nothing to do with what I thought in '63 or '68, but how I think about it now. What happened? What did in Keynesian economics? I'm just going to sketch an outrageously simple view of how I think economic thought evolves, and then I'm going to try and apply it to the models that I've been talking about.

I think the basic view of economics that Hume and Smith and Ricardo introduced, taking people as basically alike, pursuing simple goals in a pretty direct way, given their preferences, where you are trying to explain differences in behavior by differences in the situation people are finding themselves in rather than differences in their culture, their inner wiring, inner workings, their race, whatever, their class, just thinking

18. "The Determinants of Wage Rate Changes and the Inflation-Unemployment Trade-Off for the United States," published in the October 1964 issue of the *Review of Economic Studies*.

about people as people and then trying to account for their behavior in terms of how they are responding to their environment, that this is it for economics. We got that view from Smith and Ricardo, and there have never been any new paradigms or paradigm changes or shifts. Maybe there will be, but in two hundred years it hasn't happened yet. So you've got this kind of basic line of economic theory.

And then I see the progressive—I don't want to say that everything is in Smith and Ricardo—the progressive element in economics as entirely technical: better mathematics, better mathematical formulation, better data, better data-processing methods, better statistical methods, better computational methods. I think of all progress in economic thinking, in the kind of basic core of economic theory, as developing entirely as learning how to do what Hume and Smith and Ricardo wanted to do, only better: more empirically founded, more powerful solution methods, and so on. So I don't think there *was* a Keynesian revolution in a scientific sense, in the sense of a new paradigm or a bifurcation of economic theory into two different directions. I'll tell you what I think did happen, but it wasn't that.

In the twentieth century, which I think was a pretty good century for economics, important technical developments included mathematically rigorous general equilibrium theory, which can be analyzed in modern mathematical terms in a rigorous and clear way, and a language for talking about dynamics, difference equations, differential equations, shocks. The latter tradition I think of as due to Slutsky, Frisch, Tinbergen. It's sort of a statistical language, not an economic language. You think of Slutsky's paper on stochastic difference equations, it's just a purely statistical model that he simulates using results from some Russian lottery and then generates a time series and says, "Hey, this thing looks like pictures I saw in Mitchell's book."[19] People started putting the economics into it, and I think of Keynesian theory as having this excitement because it breathes some economic life into these difference equation systems. So when I think of Keynesian economics or at least the Keynesian economics *I* signed on for, it was part of this econometric model-building tradition. We didn't really treat much of this when I was a student at Chicago, but I certainly moved into it at Carnegie Mellon.

Now what happened is that this statistical way of thinking about dynamics failed. It got replaced by the Arrow-Debreu model, which shows

19. Slutsky's paper, "The Summation of Random Causes as the Source of Cyclic Processes," appeared in the April 1937 issue of *Econometrica*.

how you can take what seems to be a static general equilibrium model and talk about markets for contingent claims, talk about any kind of dynamics you'd like, coming right out of the economics. No auctioneer, or the auctioneer works very quickly. Everything is accounted for in terms of preferences and technology in this model, and everything can include as much dynamics as you can get from a Tinbergen model or Slutsky's model. Patinkin or Bailey or their students, we didn't know this theory existed back in 1960, although it did. But now its potential is getting realized. It has completely succeeded in taking over growth theory, most of public finance, financial economics. Now it's coming in use in macroeconomics with real business cycle theory; certain kinds of monetary variations have been introduced with success. So when I teach macro now, that's all that I teach: variations on these models. Of course, I specialize them and try to apply them to particular economic questions: I'm not a mathematician. But I don't teach any IS-LM. I don't even mention it. I tell them to go somewhere else. Take the course from somebody else. In that sense, for me, it's over.

But I want to come to this persistence of the IS-LM model, because it *isn't* over.

The problem is that the new theories, the theories embedded in general equilibrium dynamics of the sort that we know how to use pretty well now—there's a residue of things they don't let us think about. They don't let us think about the U.S. experience in the 1930s or about financial crises and their real consequences in Asia and Latin America. They don't let us think, I don't think, very well about Japan in the 1990s. We may be disillusioned with the Keynesian apparatus for thinking about these things, but it doesn't mean that this replacement apparatus can do it either. It can't. In terms of the theory that researchers are developing as a cumulative body of knowledge—no one has figured out how to take that theory to successful answers to the real effects of monetary instability. Some people just deny that there are real effects of monetary instability, but I think that is just a mistake. I don't think that argument can be sustained. I do think that most of the post–World War II fluctuations of GDP about trend can be accounted for in real terms. I've estimated that would be something on the order of 80 percent. People can argue with that. But that's not because money doesn't matter. That's because monetary policy in the postwar United States has been so good.

So that's I think where Keynes's real contribution is. It's not Einstein-level theory, new paradigm, all this. I am in agreement with my neighbor

Sue Freehling, that's just so much hot air. I think that in writing the *General Theory*, Keynes was viewing himself as a spokesman for a discredited profession. That's why he doesn't cite anyone but crazies like Hobson. He knows about Wicksell and all the "classics," but he is at pains to disassociate his views from theirs, to overemphasize the differences. He's writing in a situation where people are ready to throw in the towel on capitalism and liberal democracy and go with fascism or corporatism, protectionism, socialist planning. Keynes's first objective is to say, "Look, there's got to be a way to respond to depressions that's consistent with capitalist democracy." What he hits on is that the government should take some new responsibilities, but the responsibilities are for stabilizing overall spending flows. You don't have to plan the economy in detail in order to meet this objective. And in that sense, I think for everybody in the postwar period—I'm talking about Keynesians and monetarists both—that's the agreed-upon view: We should stabilize spending flows, and the question is really one of the details about how best to do it. Friedman's approach involved slightly less government involvement than a Keynesian approach, but I say slightly.

So I think this was a great political achievement. It gave us a lasting image of what we need economists for. I've been talking about the internal mainstream of economics, that's what we researchers live on, but as a group we have to earn our living by helping people diagnose situations that arise and helping them understand what is going on and what we can do about it. That was Keynes's whole life. He was a political activist from beginning to end. What he was concerned about when he wrote the *General Theory* was convincing people that there was a way to deal with the Depression that was forceful and effective but didn't involve scrapping the capitalist system. Maybe we could have done it without him, but I'm glad we didn't have to try. Thank you.

What Was Lost with IS-LM

Roger E. Backhouse and David Laidler

In the third quarter of the twentieth century, the IS-LM model became the basis of what James Tobin called "the trained intuition" of the great majority of economists working in macroeconomics, and this had important effects on the subsequent evolution of the area.[1] Insights that were easy to formulate as applications or extensions of IS-LM flourished, but lines of inquiry that were harder to fit into it atrophied to the point at which some important ideas came close to being lost altogether. Some of these losses were temporary and have already been reversed, but others were longer lasting. This is not to say that other approaches to macroeconomics vanished without trace. To give some examples: Perry Mehrling (1998) has reminded us that Edward Shaw kept an earlier American institutionalist tradition alive well into the 1960s; such émigré economists as Fritz Machlup, William Fellner, and Adolph Lowe gave continuing life to disparate Continental traditions in business cycle theory; and Maurice Allais and Clark Warburton, not to mention Milton Friedman, preserved and developed ideas derived from the quantity theory of money, which had flourished long before 1936. Even so, though their work, and that of others too numerous to mention here, certainly formed part of the profession's discourse in the 1950s and 1960s,

We are grateful to two anonymous referees, other participants in the 2003 *HOPE* conference, and Perry Mehrling for helpful comments on an earlier draft of this essay. Each author nevertheless reserves the right to pin the blame for all errors and omissions on the other. Laidler gratefully acknowledges the Bank of Montreal's support.

1. See Tobin 1982, 172; cf. Dimand, this volume.

all of it catered to minority tastes. At that time, IS-LM dominated macro-economics.

Many commentators have pointed out that important elements of the *General Theory* itself were lost with IS-LM, a judgment well summed up in Joan Robinson's famous gibe at this framework as "bastard Keynesianism." There is much to be said for such arguments, but the publication of the *General Theory*, and the development of IS-LM as a means of conveying what many took to be its central message, can also be seen as representing two stages in a longer process whereby a number of questions that had been prominent in monetary and business cycle theory before 1936 were moved down economists' agendas, or pushed off them altogether. The issues in question all had a common element. From the late 1930s onward, the fact that economic activity takes place in time began to lose its central place in what by then had come to be called macroeconomics. Neglected in IS-LM, some of the implications of this fact have now reemerged, but only gradually, and in an intellectual climate very different from that of the 1930s.

The Keynesian Revolution and the Rise of Static Equilibrium Macroeconomic Theory

The IS-LM model provided the lens through which economists, from the 1940s up to at least the 1960s, viewed not only Keynesian economics but the theories that preceded it. If the "classical economics" described in John Maynard Keynes's *General Theory*, the IS-LM model, and post-war macroeconomics textbooks had been an accurate and complete summary of the pre-1936 literature, this essay would hardly need to be written.[2] The story of the Keynesian revolution and the role of IS-LM in it would be both simple and already well known. However, the development of macroeconomics before 1936 was both more complicated and more interesting than is generally appreciated, and the intellectual revolution that began in that year marked the climax of over a quarter century of intensive theorizing about the causes and structure of the business cycle. This work followed a wide variety of paths, by no means all of which led in the same direction. What happened after 1936 was that an important and rather specific subset of ideas that had been developed by a large community of economists during the 1920s and 1930s

2. Likewise for many history of economic thought textbooks (e.g., the first four editions of Blaug 1962).

was summed up and formalized, first in the *General Theory* and then in a small number of models, of which the IS-LM model was by far the most important.[3]

The simplest way to establish this point is to recall, first, that Keynes himself argued that his theory rested on three relationships—the propensity to consume, the marginal efficiency of capital, and the liquidity preference function, which in turn interacted to determine the level of effective demand; and second, that none of these ideas was original to the *General Theory*. The idea of a propensity to consume arose out of work in the 1920s in which economists began to separate and define the concepts of saving and investment, and Jens Warming's (1932) deployment of the idea is identical to that used by Keynes from 1933 onward. The marginal efficiency of capital, whose crucial feature is that the rate of return on investment is determined by forward-looking expectations, rather than by some physical productivity of capital, was, as Keynes acknowledged, simply Irving Fisher's (1907) rate of return over cost under another name. The concept of liquidity preference derived from Frederick Lavington's (1921) extension of the Cambridge theory of the demand for money had already been developed in detail in Keynes's *Treatise on Money* (1930) and John Hicks's "Suggestion for Simplifying the Theory of Money" (1935). As to the concept of effective demand, this had been deployed, under that name, by Ralph Hawtrey as early as 1913 and had played a central role in his work thereafter.

It was no accident that these concepts had evolved before 1936. Monetary theory had been shifting away from analyzing the quantity of money's effects on the price level and toward understanding the influence of the rate of interest on saving and investment, at least since the appearance of Knut Wicksell's cumulative process analysis in 1898. Subsequent developments as different from each other as Austrian business cycle theory and Swedish dynamic process analysis can be traced directly to this common origin. Wicksell's work also exerted an explicitly acknowledged influence on *The Treatise on Money*, and elements of it were certainly known to Irving Fisher (see 1911, 59–60).[4]

---

3. Other important macroeconomic models that also originated at about the same time, for example the multiplier-accelerator business cycle model and the Harrod-Domar growth model, remained in specialized niches, rather than vying with IS-LM for pride of place in the discipline. We discuss this point at greater length below.

4. Fisher (1907, 59 n. 2) noted his analysis of "the connection between the rate of interest on bank loans and changes in the level of prices due to the resulting expansion and contraction

When the *General Theory*, and a little later IS-LM, synthesized and formalized earlier developments to create a "Keynesian revolution," some previously important ideas were simplified and others simply dropped from sight, in a process that was far from random. As economists came increasingly to use formal models to analyze macroeconomic questions, ideas that could be fitted into them flourished, while those that could not began to seem unimportant. Crucially, the IS-LM model was a comparative-static device, and this meant that issues related to the fact that economic activity happens in time could not find a comfortable place within it. Only ideas that seemed relevant to the equilibrium features of the economic system and its comparative-static properties received careful attention from those who used IS-LM, but that was the vast majority of economists working on macroeconomic issues between the 1940s and the 1970s.

It is uncontroversial that the *General Theory* contained many arguments, about money-wage movements, the role of expectations, the interest inelasticity of investment demand, own rates of interest, capital satiation, the falling rate of profit, and so on, that could not be brought into the heart of the IS-LM model.[5] It selected and formalized only those parts of the book that could be fitted into a static equilibrium framework, which could in turn be manipulated to derive propositions believed to be characteristically "Keynesian" and "classical." However, as we argue here, the loss of ideas from the broader interwar literature on monetary economics and the business cycle, which began with the *General Theory* itself and was accentuated by the development of IS-LM, was more widespread, and therefore more important for the subsequent development of macroeconomics, than the mislaying of some insights from that book during the transformation of "Keynesian economics" into IS-LM. When all is said and done, IS-LM did sum up a critical and central subset of the ideas expounded in the *General Theory*. This is why it is legitimate to refer to a Keynesian rather than a Hicksian revolution.

---

of such loans." Wicksell's earlier influence on English monetary economics is problematic. A paper setting out the essential features of his "cumulative process" appeared in the *Economic Journal* in 1907, but such important contributors as Hawtrey and Dennis Robertson did not cite him in the 1920s and subsequently claimed that they were unaware of his work at that time.

5. Note that we are here discussing what could be incorporated into the formal geometric and algebraic structures on which the intuitions of future generations of economists were trained. We do not intend to deny that these ideas often found a place in the verbal discussions with which the textbooks of the 1950s onward accompanied their formal analysis.

In the *General Theory*, Keynes not only expounded his own ideas, he also rewrote the macroeconomics that had come before and labeled the result "classical economics." In the process he presented a theoretical critique of propositions that were entirely static and atemporal. In the absence of this distortion of what macroeconomics was like before the *General Theory*, Keynes's own contribution would have been perceived very differently, and it would have been much more difficult for such early exponents of IS-LM as Roy Harrod (1937) and John Hicks (1937) to present this model as capable of capturing the fundamental issues at stake between Keynes and his predecessors. As it was, none of the functional relationships that lay at the heart of IS-LM, in either its "Keynesian" or its "classical" form, explicitly modeled issues having to do with time, nor did the framework itself permit time to be brought into the analysis of their interaction. In that model the implications of economic activity taking place in time were kept in the background, and those whose intuitions were trained on its manipulation came to view the macroeconomics that had existed before 1936 as being just as amenable to characterization in comparative-static terms as Keynes's own.

Some examples will help make clear just how many ideas were thus rendered inaccessible to a younger generation of economists. Hawtrey, following a tradition that dated back at least to the currency school–banking school controversies of the 1830s and 1840s, had argued that the monetary transmission mechanism during the cycle involved the continual creation and destruction of credit. For him, and for Irving Fisher, too, not to mention the many economists whom these two influenced, the interest rate set by the banking system was therefore considered to be a critical variable for swings in the price level, and in output, too, because Hawtrey placed increasing emphasis on wage and price stickiness in the 1920s and 1930s. Others, notably the Austrian and Swedish followers of Wicksell, but also Dennis Robertson, carried this line of analysis further and stressed the capacity of interest rate swings to generate variations in output that often involved "forced saving." The Austrians in particular had argued that the market mechanisms that existed in a monetary economy were likely to fail in fully coordinating the choices of individual agents, notably with regard to the allocation of resources over time; this because the banking system's activities would interfere with the interest rate's capacity to induce a time structure of production compatible with households' plans for future consumption. Those Swedish economists known as the "Stockholm school" focused on how *ex ante* disequilibria were turned into *ex post* equilibria. They therefore paid careful attention to the role of expectations and their evolution over time in conditioning behavior. And so on.

The neglect of ideas such as these under the influence of IS-LM profoundly affected not only macroeconomic theory but also economists' conceptions of macroeconomic policy, which came to be analyzed in terms of comparative-static diagrams. Monetary policy, for example, began to be seen in terms of discretionary shifts in variables, designed to offset the effects of disturbances to the private sector of the economy. These disturbances were typically characterized as once and for all shifts in the investment function that underlay the IS curve, to which an ad hoc offsetting shift in the LM curve was the appropriate monetary response. As they became accustomed to thinking in these terms, economists began to lose sight of the idea that in the actual economy, such measures would always be deployed in the context of a specific policy regime, and that the nature of the regime itself might affect the type of shocks hitting the economy, the menu of responses available to the authorities, as well as the transmission mechanism through which the private sector would respond to policy.[6]

It might seem paradoxical to argue that macroeconomics began to neglect time, just when economists were starting to construct formal dynamic models of economic growth and were learning how to deploy systematically the interaction of the multiplier and the accelerator to analyze the business cycle. However, though these developments preserved some aspects of economists' earlier concerns with economic processes that happened in time, where those concerns had once been of the very essence of macroeconomics, by the 1960s they were confined to these specialized areas, which were treated as distinct from the main body of macroeconomics, which was built around the comparative-static IS-LM model.[7]

6. Though it is important not to read too much currently available wisdom into the earlier literature, it is nevertheless the case that such contributors as Keynes (1923), Young (1927), and Robertson (1928) always focused on the characteristics of alternative policy regimes and their implications for the economy's behavior, rather than the details of stabilization policy per se.

7. It is worth noting that, even within business cycle theory, a process of formalization and forgetting took place. Despite the bewilderingly wide variety of approaches that had existed in the interwar literature, by the 1950s and 1960s, business cycle theory was dominated by the analysis of multiplier-accelerator interaction, and the models to which students were exposed were almost invariably ones whose properties could be understood by analyzing a second- or higher-order difference equation.

It is also true that economists never altogether forgot that consumption and investment decisions had something to do with the allocation of resources over time, and that, by the 1960s, economists were once again becoming aware that these decisions might fruitfully be analyzed, along the lines pioneered by Irving Fisher (1907), as the outcome of maximizing intertemporal choices. Thus theories of the consumption and investment functions began to acquire well-articulated microeconomic foundations that involved paying explicit attention to expectations. Even so, the proper macroeconomic application of such ideas was still thought of as being the derivation of essentially static consumption and investment functions, for example, a consumption function with permanent income or wealth as an argument instead of current income.[8] No doubt these relationships were better formulated than the ones they replaced, but time in their derivation played only a minor role in theoretical macro models. In empirical applications, however, time did become more important because these theories provided a rationale for the use of distributed lags in econometric estimation.

In what follows, we discuss four overlapping sets of problems associated with the passage of time from which IS-LM distracted attention. The first involves the simplest kind of dynamics: economic changes take time to happen, which means that variables need to be dated and that adjustment paths between equilibria need to be examined. The second arises because current decisions are always taken with reference to some time horizon or other, which means that expectations are always relevant when maximizing behavior is analyzed. The third is significant because economic policy also involves forward-looking decisions, and this insight suggests that policy is better thought of in terms of regimes and how they function, rather than as a series of isolated interventions. Finally, to take explicit note of the temporal dimension inherent in all aspects of economic activity draws attention to important coordination problems, having to do with the allocation of resources over time, that are invisible in a static world.

All of these matters had received widespread attention in the interwar literature, but the wholesale adoption of the static IS-LM framework from the 1940s onward led to their falling into neglect. When some of these problems were rediscovered, they were approached using theories

---

8. The work on the consumption function that we have in mind here is, of course, that of Friedman (1957) and Modigliani and Brumberg (1954). On investment see, for example, Jorgenson 1967.

whose own development had been profoundly affected by the dominance of IS-LM, as we shall now see; and, as we shall also see, some of them have yet to reclaim a place on the agenda of modern macroeconomics.

The Loss and Rediscovery of Dynamics

IS-LM is a static model in the simplest sense of the term. Variables are not dated, and lags are not modeled formally. They are arguably implicit in those stories about the stability of the IS-LM equilibrium that Victoria Chick (1973) felicitously labeled "the pseudo-dynamics of IS-LM," but even here the dynamic structure of the world plays no role in determining the equilibrium toward which the economy converges, in the delineation of differences between alternative theoretical positions, or in the analysis of policy choices. This is a major reason why wage rigidity seemed to play a crucial role in explaining persistent unemployment and, also, perhaps why monetary theory and the theory of inflation became estranged from one another in the 1950s. Economists knew, of course, that wages and prices did change, but in an IS-LM framework such change had to be viewed, formally speaking, as an exogenous factor shifting the LM curve, not as an endogenous response to anything, even to variations in the nominal quantity of money, which themselves also appear simply as exogenous influences that shift the LM curve.[9]

There is no doubt that the static nature of IS-LM constitutes a considerable simplification of the analysis presented in Keynes's *General Theory*. As an example, consider Keynes's discussion (in chapter 19) of how cuts in money wages might raise employment. Some of the mechanisms he describes there can be fitted into a static equilibrium framework (the effects of lower money wages on the demand for money and on distribution), but others make sense only in a dynamic setting (the reduction of present money wages relative to money wages expected in the future; the possibility that a general reduction in wages might be mistaken for a reduction specific to individual firms). Even so, not too much should be made of these dynamic elements in Keynes's account in the current context, because, although he made many remarks that could be (and in some cases were later) turned into dynamic models, the emphasis of the *General Theory* was nevertheless on unemployment as an *equilibrium*

---

9. It is true that the price level was an endogenous variable in aggregate demand–aggregate supply elaborations of IS-LM, but these models treated money wages as exogenous and were not a satisfactory vehicle for analyzing inflation.

phenomenon. Dynamic accounts of how money wages might affect employment were only a little more integrated into Keynes's formal analysis than they later were into IS-LM.

Far more significant for the development of macroeconomics than IS-LM's neglect of the dynamic element in Keynes's thought is how Keynes himself systematically neglected dynamic factors that had been discussed in previous explanations of unemployment. This was a feature of the *General Theory* remarked on by Bertil Ohlin (1937, 235–36):

> Keynes's theoretical system . . . is equally "old fashioned" in the second respect which characterizes recent economic theory—namely, the attempt to break away from an explanation of economic events by means of orthodox equilibrium constructions. No other analysis of trade fluctuations in recent years—with the possible exception of the Mises-Hayek school—follows such conservative lines in this respect. In fact, Keynes is much more an "equilibrium theorist" than such economists as Cassel and, I think, Marshall.

Another way to make the same point is to observe that, though the 1920s in particular generated a substantial literature on the microeconomics of unemployment that used Marshallian comparative statics as its principal tool, in the pre-1936 macroeconomics literature, with some notable exceptions such as Pigou 1933, aggregate employment was analyzed specifically in the context of the cycle, with shocks, lags, and dynamic adjustment processes being the order of the day.[10] As Ohlin pointed out, such ideas were pervasive in macroeconomics before 1936—so pervasive that it is possible to provide no more than a few illustrations of the point in this essay.

The clearest example of the use of explicitly dynamic analysis before 1936 was to be found in the work of the Stockholm school, which formed the basis of Ohlin's critique of Keynes. As Bjorn Hansson (1982) has shown, this group developed an explicit method, using the idea of a succession of "unit periods," in which each period began with agents having plans based on newly formed expectations about the outcome of executing them, and ended with the economy in some new situation that was the outcome of market processes set in motion by the incompatibility of those plans, and in which expectations had been reformulated, too, in the light of experience. They applied this method to the construction of a wide variety of what they called "model sequences," many of which

---

10. See Laidler 1999, chap. 7, for a brief survey of this literature.

involved downward spirals in economic activity at whose very heart lay rising unemployment. This is not the place to discuss the vexed question of the extent to which some of this work anticipated the Keynesian multiplier process, but it should be noted that, in IS-LM, it is the limit to which such processes move, rather than the time path they follow to get there, that is emphasized.

The Swedes may have taken explicitly dynamic analysis further than anyone else, but they were far from alone in putting it at the center of their endeavors. Ralph Hawtrey, one of the most influential cycle theorists of the 1920s, made dynamics central to his explanation of how unemployment emerged (Backhouse 1985, 184–86; Laidler 1999, 112–18). Though he started his analysis from the quantity theory of money, he nevertheless criticized it for emphasizing an equilibrium relationship between money and prices that did not apply when the money supply was changing. Rather than analyzing the demand and supply of money as static schedules, therefore, he emphasized the continual creation and repayment of credit (bank deposits), as banks and firms interacted over time. New loans were taken out in order to be spent, generating income in a process that involved purchasing power returning to the banks to cancel old loans and constantly being returned to circulation as new loans were created.

Explicit, albeit informal, dynamics were central to Hawtrey's story of how a cycle emerged. The process of credit creation was unstable: there were lags between credit creation and spending; lags between the credit-financed investment in inventories and the production of goods to meet that investment; and, at turning points in the cycle, lags between variations in output and money wages, the nonbank public's demand for currency, and the banking system's interest rate response. Hawtrey relied on wage and price stickiness to explain why fluctuations in effective demand brought about by swings in the money supply caused fluctuations in employment. Because he did not allow for the possibility that velocity might vary systematically with the nominal interest rate, he argued that expansionary fiscal policy not financed by money creation would be ineffective in countering unemployment, and this particular idea can, *ex post*, be captured in a vertical LM curve special case of IS-LM.[11] Hawtrey himself, however, always explained fluctuations in effective demand as manifestations of the workings of an inherently dynamic

11. As indeed Hicks noted in 1937, with his oblique reference to the "Treasury view" (152 n. 4).

system, and these essential features of his analysis could not be captured by this model. Virtually all of the subtlety of Hawtrey's story lay in its systematic analysis of what can be thought of as the factors that would keep the LM curve moving back and forth in an ongoing cycle, and such swings can only be treated as exogenous shifts in the IS-LM model.

Robertson's analysis of the cycle was also intrinsically dynamic, and it may, in the 1920s, have provided some inspiration to the Swedes as they began their own work. In *Industrial Fluctuation* (1915), he proposed a real theory of the cycle. Innovations could start an upswing in business activity that, because of the lag between investment and the resulting increase in output, would eventually lead to a surplus of specific capital goods and a shortage of saving. This emphasis on real dynamics was part of a tradition going back at least to Marx, about which Robertson seems to have learned from his reading of Albert Aftalion (1913) and Mikhail Tugan-Baranovksy (1913). When he later (e.g., Robertson 1926) extended his analysis to take account of monetary factors, he continued to pay close attention to dynamics. Because consumers build up cash balances by spending less than they receive as income, an increase in the transactions demand for money that arises in the process of a real expansion will cause expenditure to lag behind income, with consequent effects on the time path of aggregate demand. This effect, which is also relevant to how the economy adjusts to an increase in the money supply, is missing from the standard static IS-LM model, though it was later revealed by the Phillips machine, whose very nature prevented questions about the economy's time path between equilibria from being evaded (Leeson 2000, 45, 48–49).

Economists of the IS-LM generations were, of course, aware of time lags. In the 1950s and 1960s it was part of an economist's specialized training to learn about the various lags that might be brought in when creating a theory of the cycle or an empirical model. There were also formal dynamic analyses of the stability of the equilibria that underlay the comparative statics of income determination, such as are present in Don Patinkin's *Money, Interest, and Prices* ([1956] 1965). Patinkin's model, though somewhat broader, shared many features with IS-LM, and in his work, dynamics usually described explicit adjustment paths around static equilibria. He analyzed a limited range of transitional stock-flow links and the *tâtonnement* process, but it was the comparative-static equilibrium properties of his model that dominated his exposition. Indeed, when Patinkin concluded that, formally speaking, unemployment was a disequilibrium phenomenon when viewed in the context of his system, he was considered by many Keynesians to have sold out to "classical economics."[12]

The extent to which dynamics had become marginalized and effectively forgotten by a profession accustomed to thinking in terms of IS-LM is well illustrated by the dispute between Friedman and the Keynesians in the 1960s and early 1970s. In his attempt to reinstate the quantity theory of money, Friedman, who had been trained before the *General Theory* or IS-LM came on the scene, chose to focus on the dynamic effects of monetary changes on money income. He refused to play the static game laid down by "Keynes and the classics" and the "neoclassical synthesis," and he was accused by many of his colleagues not of having an erroneous theory but of having no theory at all to justify his claims about the important role played by the quantity of money in the economy. He had failed, or so it was said, to provide a satisfactory account of the transmission mechanism whereby money had its effects.

In fact, an elaborate account of the dynamics of the interaction of money, real income, and prices had been presented in Friedman and Schwartz 1963b, so much of the criticism leveled at Friedman in the 1960s and early 1970s was unfair, but Friedman nevertheless tried to address it in the critics' own terms in his "Theoretical Framework for Monetary Analysis" (Gordon 1974). There, he deployed an IS-LM framework to explain the differences among Keynesian economics, the simple quantity theory, and the sophisticated quantity theory that he espoused. The first two were described in purely static terms, but the sophisticated quantity theory was described as involving a lagged adjustment of nominal income to changes in the money supply, and as being short of one equation, which was needed to determine how nominal income variations were broken down over time between output and the price level.[13] To economists trained on IS-LM, where the central problem was the determination of a static equilibrium, Friedman's 1974 framework revealed him either as having the same theory as them, if they concentrated on its first part, and hence as having nothing to teach them, or as having

12. The reader's attention is drawn to our use of quotation marks here. The classical economics that these critics had in mind would more accurately be described as Keynes's caricature of that body of doctrine.

13. This aspect of Friedman's work is described in more detail by Bordo and Schwartz (this volume) and Nelson (this volume). Both essays stress the inadequacy, from a monetarist standpoint, of IS-LM-based accounts of monetary policy's transmission mechanisms that run exclusively through a narrow range of market interest rates.

yet again failed to answer their questions about the theoretical basis for his claims. What they seemed to want from him was a formal model that differed from IS-LM but remained comparative static in nature, but what they got was an account of monetary dynamics that had much in common with the interwar analysis of the interactions among money, inflation, the business cycle, and, crucially, expectations that IS-LM had temporarily superseded.

The centrality of dynamics for macroeconomics was arguably "rediscovered" by the majority of economists working on macro theory only later in the 1970s when they became concerned with inflation and had to confront the above-mentioned interactions. For example, they were forced to deal with the coexistence of high inflation and high interest rates and turned to the Fisher effect to do so. This effect, which was common in the pre-1936 literature, relied on the influence of inflation expectations on nominal interest rates, and the influence of actual inflation on those expectations, and both of these factors were absent from the static monetary theory that underlay the LM curve. Once the importance of the Fisher effect was recognized, it became clear that a real rate of interest was relevant to the IS curve, but a nominal rate to the LM curve; and because inflation expectations thus had to become part of the IS-LM model, it also became harder to preserve it as a fundamentally static construction.[14]

However, the real breakthrough in dynamizing IS-LM came when it was supplemented by a Phillips curve augmented with endogenous expectations of inflation. The original Phillips curve, which had the advantage that it could be reinterpreted as deriving from the familiar *tatônnement* process (Lipsey 1960), had sometimes been used "to close" IS-LM models from the 1960s onward (Lipsey 2000, 61–63). In this form, however, it was a dynamic adjunct to a static system whose only equilibrium was at full employment with a constant price level, and, with benefit of hindsight, it amounted to little more than a particular way of characterizing the price level changes that underlay Patinkin's real balance effect. By the 1970s, though, the coexistence of rising unemployment with high inflation began to pose an empirical problem that, it turned out, could be addressed using Friedman's (1968) and Edmund Phelps's (1967) extensions of the Phillips curve to accommodate endogenous

---

14. The explicit introduction of the Fisher effect into an IS-LM model seems to have been pioneered by Martin Bailey (1962, 49–54) and Robert Mundell (1963). Needless to say, Friedman's dynamic framework had always had ample room for this effect.

inflation expectations and the idea of an equilibrium unemployment rate whose value was independent of the conduct of monetary policy. This relationship was quickly recognized as providing one solution to Friedman's "missing equation" problem (though Friedman himself seems to have remained skeptical about this application), and its addition to the IS-LM model turned out to be sufficient to render the whole system properly dynamic, in the sense that it became capable of analyzing the interactions of output and inflation over time in response to changes in the rate of growth of nominal money.

The Loss and Rediscovery of
Intertemporal Choice and Expectations

Decisions to save and invest are clearly about the allocation of resources over time, for they concern the timing of consumption and production. However, this intertemporal dimension of aggregate demand was neglected in IS-LM analysis and also in the *General Theory*. The marginal propensity to consume was presented by Keynes as "a fundamental psychological law" whose foundations, however, he did not investigate, and in practice he treated it as a behavioral regularity that could be justified empirically. Similarly, though all economists understood that the marginal efficiency of capital depended on expectations, and though Keynes himself, following A. C. Pigou (e.g., 1929) and Lavington (1922), had stressed this factor, under the label "animal spirits," and had emphasized the influence on those spirits of moods of pessimism and optimism, the marginal efficiency of capital was often treated in subsequent literature as easily derived from a static production function exhibiting diminishing marginal productivity of capital.

Questions about capital theory that had seemed of great importance in the 1920s and 1930s, when economists were accustomed to treating matters of intertemporal choice as central, were reduced to side issues, or at least to the status of exogenous shift parameters lying behind the IS curve. Though there were debates about capital theory in the 1950s, these arose not in the context of core short-run macroeconomics but in the context of growth theory and were largely concerned with the properties of steady state growth paths. Even in this context, formal modeling of intertemporal choice in consumption was minority taste, most growth models using, despite Ramsey's example, exogenous propensities to save to anchor their analysis.

Economists rediscovered the analysis of expectations and their bearing on intertemporal choice in two stages, the first of which involved attempts to seek better theoretical bases for the individual relationships that underlay the IS curve and to refine formulations of these relationships. The intertemporal dimension of consumption decisions received a new emphasis with the work of Friedman, and Franco Modigliani and Richard Brumberg, in the 1950s. They showed, building on an essentially Fisherian (1907) foundation, that it was not possible to understand consumption behavior without taking this matter into account. However, though the permanent income hypothesis and its life-cycle variant became a part of the established curriculum in the 1960s, along with theories of investment that paid attention to adjustment costs, their foundations in the explicit modeling of intertemporal choice remained peripheral. The empirical implementation of the permanent income–life cycle theory required that consumption depend not on current income alone but on current income and a geometrically weighted average of lagged incomes, often captured in a lagged dependent variable. This formulation distracted attention from the forward-looking nature of the consumption decision. The same applied to investment: the static IS-LM model required no more than an investment function that sloped downward with respect to the rate of interest and in its econometric implementation the addition of a few exogenous shift parameters, and, once more, a suitable pattern of distributed lags seemed to suffice to cope with its dynamics.

An important corollary of this neglect of the explicit analysis of intertemporal choice was a relative neglect of theorizing about expectations. In the late 1920s, some Swedish economists had begun to struggle with the idea that the current configuration of an economy inhabited by forward-looking agents would have to depend on their expectations about its future configuration (see Lindahl 1929). But forward-looking expectations seemed impossible to handle, so, as the 1930s progressed, these Swedish economists and their colleagues began to investigate the endogenous evolution of expectations formed by extrapolating from past observations using mechanical rules (often called "backward-looking" expectations) as an integral part of the dynamic method whose salient characteristics we have discussed above. Even this approach, however, which had also been Robertson's, and was not dissimilar to the above-mentioned later deployment of distributed lags in econometric consumption and investment functions, led to clumsy and unwieldy theoretical analysis. Keynes's "solution" to this problem had been to force expectations into only two categories: long-term, relevant to investment decisions, which he treated as exogenous, and short-term, relevant to firms' output decisions, which he assumed were always correct (cf. Kregel 1976). This in turn enabled him to reduce the macroeconomic modeling of processes in which expectations were fundamental to a matter of comparative statics. Perhaps Keynes was well aware of what he was doing here, but those who came after him were not always as careful, so his approach was a crucial step toward the explicit modeling of expectations being pushed into the background.

Even Hicks, whose concern with expectations in *Value and Capital* (1939) surely derived from his knowledge of the Swedish literature, was one of those who extracted a set of equations from the *General Theory* in which expectations were completely in the background. To be sure, the location of his curves, and shifts of them, could be interpreted as reflecting particular expectations, and changes therein, but there was no necessity to do this.

Until the late 1960s, none of this seemed to present a problem, and even when the Phillips curve was introduced, and economists became aware that wage and price changes might depend on expectations of inflation, this factor was not treated as central to the analysis (e.g., Samuelson and Solow 1960). Indeed, Richard Lipsey (2000) has argued that, when he tried to model expectations empirically, he could find no sign of their being important in the data. To cite another example, the general disequilibrium macroeconomics that Robert Clower and Axel Leijonhufvud espoused at the end of the 1960s might have provided the basis of an analysis that focused on the effects of *expected* constraints on sales, perhaps developing into an approach akin to Robertsonian or Swedish dynamics, but it did not: instead, largely in other hands, it analyzed the constraints imposed on *current* decisions by *realized* sales and purchases and elaborated the microfoundations of a fixed-price comparative-static macro model that bore more than a passing resemblance to IS-LM.[15]

It was, therefore, left to Friedman (1968) and Phelps (1967) to draw attention to the crucial importance of expectations in macroeconomics, using arguments that were in due course developed by Robert Lucas (e.g., 1972) and others. The rediscovery of the role of expectations in

15. See especially Barro and Grossman 1976 and Malinvaud 1977. For applications of this analysis to the derivation of the comparative statics of the rate of interest, output, and employment, see Barro and Grossman 1976, chap. 3, and Malinvaud 1977, lecture 2.

macroeconomics then took its second step. Instead of modeling their role in particular relationships in isolation from the system as a whole, as had been done from the 1950s onward, the new classicals stressed that agents' decisions about all aspects of their own behavior would be conditioned by expectations about how the system as a whole was likely to evolve. The analysis of expectations then became linked to the exploration of the macroeconomic implications of assuming the existence of continuously clearing competitive markets, and "rational expectations" economics came to signify, for many economists, a theoretical package in which the rational expectations hypothesis itself was only one, and arguably not the most important, component.

The Loss and Rediscovery of Policy Regimes

A specific view of economic policy went along with IS-LM's neglect of intertemporal choice and forward-looking behavior. The model's logic can accommodate a wide variety of views, but it was typically used to show how real fluctuations might originate in real variables, notably investment, and how ad hoc fiscal and monetary responses could be deployed to iron them out. This way of looking at things descended from that strand in the older literature, associated in particular with Frederick Lavington and A. C. Pigou, which focused on the role of errors of optimism and pessimism as sources of the cycle, and its policy implications can be regarded as spelling out some of the details of the activist policy agenda that usually went with this approach in the 1920s. However, when formulated in IS-LM terms, the significance of the time element in policy design that permeated the earlier literature was lost.

The point here is *not* that policy has to take account of lags and dynamic effects on the stability of the economy's response to policy measures, for there was surprisingly little said about such problems in the pre–*General Theory* literature, even by such exponents of explicit dynamics as Robertson or the Stockholm school; it was left to A. W. (Bill) Phillips (1954) and Friedman (1953b) to take up these issues in a serious way in their early and crucial contributions to the reintroduction of explicit dynamics into macroeconomic analysis.[16] Rather, it is that economic activity takes place over time, that shocks are unpredictable, and,

16. Unlike Friedman, Phillips did not owe his dynamic vision of macroeconomic issues to a training in economics that predated IS-LM but to training as an electrical engineer that had conditioned him to think about the problems inherent in trying to control systems in which responses of variables are subject to delays and lags. On all this, see Leeson 2000.

crucially, that monetary stability over time, including but hardly confined to price level stability, is vital for the efficient working of a market economy.

This way of posing policy issues permeated the literature of the 1920s and 1930s. It inevitably pointed to the importance of questions about the appropriate policy regime and whether, given the "right" policy regime, a market economy displays inherent stability in the longer run. Keynes himself paid constant attention to such questions. They were central to his analysis of the choice between domestic price level stability and the fixity of the exchange rate in the *Tract on Monetary Reform*, played a role in his analysis of Britain's return to gold in "The Economic Consequences of Mr. Churchill" (1925), lay behind his emphasis on the role of the long rate of interest as an influence on investment behavior in the *Treatise on Money*, and even appeared in those passages of the *General Theory* that expressed doubts about the desirability of encouraging wage-price flexibility as a way to improve the economy's performance. It is also the case that policy rules were an important element in the American literature, following the establishment of the Federal Reserve System in 1913. Unlike the Bank of England, the Fed could not draw on any long-established tradition to inform its policy actions and give them credibility with private sector agents, and economists both inside and outside the system were fully conscious of the problems this posed. The monetary policy rule proposed in Friedman's *Program for Monetary Stability* (1960) falls squarely into a tradition that runs from Irving Fisher's frequent proposals in the 1920s that Congress should subject the Federal Reserve to a legislated price stability rule, through Henry Simons's ([1933] 1994, 1936) advocacy of legislated monetary policy rules.[17]

These proposals were one important element in a lively and continuous debate that went on throughout the interwar period. Pitted against the idea of a price level rule, whose incompatibility with the maintenance of the gold standard Fisher proposed to remedy with his "compensated dollar" scheme, which would see the gold content of the currency varying with the price of gold relative to that of goods in general, were two alternatives. The first of these supplemented a commitment to the gold standard with a version of the "real bills doctrine" that derived from

17. The reader's attention is drawn to the fact that the word *rule* was, and still is, used in two distinct senses in the literature we are here discussing: first, to describe a stable rule of thumb that might be adopted by policymakers as the basis for a systematic policy reaction function; and second, to describe the imposition of legislated or even constitutional constraints on their behavior.

the work of the nineteenth-century British banking school, by way of the work of Fisher's leading intellectual opponent, J. Laurence Laughlin (e.g., 1903).[18] The latter doctrine had it that, if the Federal Reserve system followed the practice of providing credit elastically to a banking system that made only good quality short-term commercial loans, it would be doing all that it could to stabilize the monetary system, and elements of it were actually written into the Federal Reserve Act in whose preparation Laughlin's student Henry Parker Willis played a crucial role. The second alternative to a price stability regime was one in which "credit control," what nowadays would be called discretionary stabilization policy, was to be cautiously undertaken, again against the background of a firm commitment to the gold standard. American advocates of this approach, such as Allyn Young (1927), were heavily influenced by Ralph Hawtrey. Despite the fact that his monetary explanation of the cycle is closest to Friedman's among the interwar writers, Hawtrey was perhaps the period's leading advocate of such a regime and even, as the principal author of the 1923 Genoa Resolutions, saw a reformed gold standard as forming the basis for its implementation on an international scale.[19]

Though the price stability rule attracted considerable academic support, it made little headway in political or policymaking circles, where opinion became divided between the other two alternatives. As is well known, this division of opinion also appeared within the Federal Reserve System and, in the view of Friedman and Schwartz (1963a), helped ensure that the response of monetary policy to the onset of the Great Depression was sluggish, timid, and ultimately ineffective.

This essay is not the place to debate the latter point, however. What is important here is that before IS-LM, monetary policy debates were about alternative regimes, and not just in the United States, as, for example, Robertson's remarkable 1928 paper, "Theories of Banking Policy," makes so clear. After IS-LM, the debates were concerned with the likely effectiveness of specific measures that might be taken in the context of an atrophied version of the "credit control" option and with the possibility that fiscal policy, conceived of in terms of ad hoc changes in taxes

18. Laughlin was the founding head of the economics department at the University of Chicago. Fisher's celebrated exposition of the quantity theory, *The Purchasing Power of Money* (1911), may be read as an extended critique of Laughlin's monetary theory.

19. Keynes's advocacy of a heavily managed floating exchange rate, coupled with a commitment to domestic price stability, as set out in the *Tract*, is a direct response to the Genoa Resolutions, whose origins in Hawtrey's work go back to the latter's pre–World War I book *Good and Bad Trade* (1913).

and government expenditures designed to shift the IS curve, might be more reliable. It was only as explicit dynamics began to come back into the picture that the idea of consistent-over-time policies conceived of within a specific regime began to reemerge as a central concern. At first this reemergence took the form of discussions of built-in stabilizers and later came to be cast in terms of stochastic versions of the IS-LM framework.[20] After the establishment of rational expectations as a critical element in economic thinking, questions about policy credibility became central and merged with Friedman's earlier (1960) advocacy of rule-guided policy to generate the still-lively contemporary literature that revolves around inflation targeting and supranational monetary unions as alternative monetary orders.

Even so, contemporary policy debates in open economies are still frequently cast in terms of the choice between flexible and fixed exchange rates, a habit inherited from the style of short-run open economy macroeconomics surveyed by Warren Young and William Darity Jr. (this volume). From a longer-run perspective, this approach is deeply flawed, since a flexible exchange rate is merely a permissive device that makes it possible for the authorities to choose among a wide variety of domestically oriented policy regimes, and it has no intrinsic merits or drawbacks that exist independently of the regime that is in fact selected. Before IS-LM, economists knew better. For example, Alfred Marshall ([1887] 1925) and Keynes (1923) posed the policy choice as lying between domestic monetary stability and exchange rate stability, in the full understanding that to choose the former would require that the exchange rate be permitted to vary, but they treated a stable price level, not a flexible exchange rate, as the alternative policy goal to which a fixed exchange rate should be compared.

The Loss and Aborted Rediscovery of Intertemporal Coordination Failures

When contemporary economists think of the allocation of resources over time, they probably think first of Irving Fisher's (1907) diagram showing how the rate of interest might coordinate the intertemporal choices of consumers and producers. For Fisher, moreover, the cycle was a "dance of the dollar," and he believed that, were it not for monetary instability

20. See, for example, Poole 1970 for a crucial paper dealing with alternative monetary rules within such a framework.

originating in the banking system and manifesting itself in price level fluctuations, the allocation of resources over time would present no special problems and that there would be no business cycle. Hawtrey differed from Fisher in understanding that wage and price stickiness could translate the "inherent instability of credit" directly into output fluctuations without major price level swings, but he too largely took it for granted that variations in the rate of interest would suffice to coordinate saving and investment at whatever level of output was ruling.

However, Fisher and Hawtrey were in the minority in holding these opinions, for others saw the matter very differently. Cambridge economists, such as Pigou and Lavington, were convinced that markets failed to coordinate saving and investment decisions because of the ubiquity of error among investors. The monetary system might have trouble mediating between them and savers when prices fluctuated, but even if such disturbances were eliminated, output instability would still occur. Pigou (1929, 219) speculated that a monetary policy that successfully stabilized the price level would no more than halve the amplitude of fluctuations. Dennis Robertson (1926) went further, arguing that some fluctuations—those that represented the effects of an uneven pattern of technical progress—were "appropriate." He saw the task of monetary policy as being to aid and abet these, even at the cost of occasional bouts of inflation, while preventing them from being overlaid by "inappropriate" fluctuations that would involve investment running ahead of savings as a result of the same types of errors that his Cambridge colleagues emphasized, and fed by forced saving made possible by too much credit creation.

The clearest exponents of the view that intertemporal coordination failures lay at the root of macroeconomic instability were undoubtedly the so-called Austrians—Ludwig von Mises, Friedrich Hayek, Lionel Robbins, et al. For them, the crucial role of the rate of interest in a market economy was to harmonize the intertemporal choices of producers and consumers. In their view any net creation of credit by the banking system in an already fully employed economy, even if it did not provoke price level changes, would lead to trouble.[21] Firms would be encouraged by

21. The full-employment assumption is crucial here, but the Austrians made it as a matter of methodological principle. To explain unemployment one had to start without it and show how it came about. The Stockholm school in particular was less rigid about this matter; a willingness to assume unemployment to begin with, and then to ask the simpler question of what factors might cause its level to change, underlay many of their model sequences. One sympathetic

such an absence of "monetary neutrality" to invest in processes of production that were longer than was appropriate given households' preferences vis-à-vis the time path to be followed by consumption. This, they believed, was what had happened in the United States in the 1920s. With nonneutral money, the resulting excess of investment over voluntary saving was financed by forced saving, and as soon as the authorities attempted to restore monetary policy to a neutral stance, the associated boom would become unsustainable. As a result of this imbalance between the time structures of production and consumption, the ensuing crisis would see long processes of production being closed down. Because time was required to start up new, shorter processes, there would inevitably be a period of unemployment whose severity and duration would depend on the length and strength of the preceding expansion, which in turn would have determined the extent of overinvestment in inappropriately long processes of production.

With the eclipse of Austrian economics in the 1930s, a key perspective on the importance of economy's supply side in economic fluctuations was lost. Keynes's polemical criticism of *Prices and Production* (1931) occurred during a debate with Hayek that had been prompted by the latter's (1931–32) review of *The Treatise on Money*. This criticism showed that Keynes (1931, 394–96) did not believe that the Austrian theory of capital was acceptable or that such a theory was needed to explain output fluctuations and unemployment. He emphasized the effects of discrepancies between the Wicksellian market and natural rates of interest on savings and investment, just as did the Austrians, but, unlike them, only to the extent that such discrepancies affected the level of aggregate demand in what we would now call the short run. Keynes simply ignored the fact that the volume of current investment had implications for the size of the capital stock and hence for the economy's capacity to produce goods and services in the future. Crucially, this neglect also led him to overlook another fact: namely, that mistaken investment decisions made in the present had the capacity to disrupt future equilibria between supply and demand, perhaps at the level of the economy as a whole, as the Austrians argued, but even in particular sectors of the economy, as his Cambridge colleague Robertson had frequently insisted.

---

modern commentator, Roger Garrison (2001), suggests that the crucial role played by the full-employment assumption in Austrian theory means that it should be regarded as a theory of the unsustainable boom, rather than a complete account of the cycle.

In the *General Theory*, Keynes moved even further from these views. The rate of interest was there said to depend on liquidity preference, to be determined on the margin between money and bonds as the outcome of a decision about how wealth was to be held. Keynes emphatically denied that it was a price with a crucial role to play in coordinating saving and investment decisions, a matter about which Robertson among others would, hardly coincidentally, take him strongly to task. Not only this, but saving was assumed to depend on a "fundamental psychological law" rather than being the outcome of a utility maximizing intertemporal choice. As to investment, Keynes's emphasis on exogenous "animal spirits" as a key factor driving expected profits distracted attention from the fact that his theory, like Fisher's, presumed that firms sought to maximize the present value of a stream of future returns.

All of the above factors, along with Keynes's use of a terminology in which saving and investment were always identically equal to one another, and his downplaying of the importance of price changes, helped ensure that ideas about forced saving were pushed aside, and with them any consideration of the possibility that the current mistakes in investment decisions might lay up problems for the future on the economy's supply side. As the post–*General Theory* debate evolved, economists became aware of the Swedish *ex ante–ex post* terminology, and this might have, but did not, create scope for further exploration of such ideas. Paradoxically, Keynes himself would use ideas about forced saving, apparently derived from his 1920s collaboration with Robertson, to great effect in *How to Pay for the War* (1940), and this work exerted considerable, albeit indirect, influence on Milton Friedman, who took it up in the work on the "Inflationary Gap" (1953a), from which many of his later ideas on monetary theory would evolve.[22] But mainstream macroeconomists ignored this development, perhaps because many of them were unaware of it or perhaps because it could not be fitted into an analytic framework dominated by IS-LM.

Whatever the reason, however, it is a fact that when economists began to rediscover the intertemporal dimensions of consumption and

22. The crucial evidence on this matter is to be found in a little-known paper by Friedman (1943), in which he praises the methods of coping with the inflationary pressures inherent in wartime spending adopted in the 1941 U.K. budget, apparently unaware of Keynes's influence on this document. The monetary analysis that was added to his discussion of this approach in the 1953 version of the paper on the "Inflationary Gap" is essentially that deployed by Keynes (1923) to analyze inflation as a tax, and by Robertson (1926), under the label "induced lacking," to show how forced saving might, in some circumstances, be transformed into one of voluntary saving, as agents attempted to adapt their money holdings to rising prices.

investment theory in the late 1940s and 1950s, they did not also immediately recover the idea that unemployment might be the result of an
intertemporal coordination failure that had the capacity to disrupt the
economy's supply side. This idea was partially resurrected by Leijonhufvud (1968), who argued that unemployment in Keynes's own analysis should be thought of as representing such a disequilibrium associated
with relative price distortions, which in turn arose from the inelastic expectations that were a natural feature of markets characterized by limited
information. These ideas, which Leijonhufvud attributed to the *General
Theory*, are all to be found in the pre-1936 literature, as his 1981 paper,
"The Wicksell Connection," would in due course begin to make clear.[23]

However, despite Leijonhufvud's emphasis on the importance of see-
ing unemployment as the outcome of an intertemporal coordination failure, and despite the large immediate effect that his work had on his
colleagues, his insights became bracketed with Clower's (1965) dual-
decision hypothesis and the concept of quantity constraints, and began
to be viewed as part of the "general equilibrium under fixed prices" approach to macroeconomics discussed above. Even while this was hap-
pening, moreover, Lucas and his associates were beginning to provide
an alternative set of microfoundations for macroeconomics that, in stark
contrast to Leijonhufvud's, insisted that markets were always cleared by
completely flexible prices. As we know, for good or ill, it was this new
classical approach that caught on, and mainstream economics nowadays
takes for granted the smooth coordination of choices made by savers
and investors about the allocation of resources over time, as it does the
smooth coordination of all other choices. Thus what had been treated
as a fundamental problem in interwar discussions of the consequences
of economic activity taking place in time is nowadays habitually solved
by assumption, notwithstanding the efforts of a few commentators, for
example Roger Garrison (2002), to draw attention to its significance.

The Significance of the Losses

Many economists and some philosophers of science share what could le-
gitimately be called a Panglossian view of the losses that accompany the

---

23. The main difference between our argument and Leijonhufvud's is that whereas he sees
the loss of insights about intertemporal coordination as occurring between the *General Theory*
and IS-LM, we see the *General Theory* itself, along with IS-LM, as an important contribution
to the suppression of these ideas about time.

move toward more formal models. Philip Kitcher (1993), for example, has argued, in the context of natural science, that although science may drop ideas that cannot be expressed with the required degree of rigor, if the problems are important, scientists will eventually return to them. When they do so, the problems will be analyzed in greater depth than would previously have been possible, and the result is progress. Referring to the transitions from Aristotelian to Newtonian physics, and from Priestley's chemistry to that of Lavoisier, Kitcher (1993, 117) has said:

> The losses (if any) were vague insights that could not be articulated at that stage in the development of science; the gains, in both instances, were correct explanatory schemata that generated significant, *tractable*, questions, and the process of addressing these questions ultimately led to a recapturing of what was lost.

This view of progress is similar to the one articulated by Paul Krugman (1995) in the context of theories of location and economic development. He argues that economists ignored theories of location other than that of Johann Heinrich von Thünen, because they all relied on forms of increasing returns that they were not able to model formally. Krugman also suggests that they turned their back on the "high" development theories developed by Paul Rosenstein-Rodan, Albert O. Hirschman, et al. during the 1950s for similar reasons. In both cases economists chose to confine their work to what could be modeled formally, even though this meant ignoring what were believed to be important aspects of reality, but once they found the techniques that enabled them to deal with increasing returns, some of the insights that they had set aside in order to indulge in formal modeling were regained.

In a similar vein, it could be suggested that the loss of the time dimension of economic activity and all that went with it in the move to IS-LM was only temporary. Thus, we have seen that, as modeling strategies developed and the range of techniques available to economists increased, dynamic problems were rediscovered and in due course understood better than would ever have been possible using the methods available to economists such as Hawtrey, Myrdal, Robertson, etc. It is indeed now technically possible to construct models in which intertemporal choice is central and expectations are truly forward-looking, in which policy changes have dynamic effects on the economy, and in which it is natural to analyze policy problems in terms of choices among alternative regimes. The creation of formal models along these lines was undoubtedly beyond the mathematical capacities of the economists of the interwar years.

However, to argue along these lines is to beg some important questions—in particular about the extent to which post-IS-LM discussions have recovered not just the approaches but also the insights yielded by pre-IS-LM theories. In particular, as we have seen, though contemporary macroeconomic models do allow us to address some of the questions that concerned writers in the 1920s and 1930s, they nevertheless rest on preconceptions about the problems that the area should deal with that differ markedly from those of this earlier period, preconceptions that seem to rule out even thinking about certain other issues. In particular, where IS-LM analysis merely distracted attention from the possibility that certain phenomena, such as systematic failures in intertemporal coordination, might be important, newer approaches seem to rule out the analysis of such failures as a matter of analytic principle. Attractive though it is, therefore, there is at least one serious flaw in the Panglossian argument; namely, that it is possible that more than one route to theoretical progress in macroeconomics was available and could have been taken, after the 1930s, and that a different route or perhaps routes could have led to radically different destinations.

When at last the importance of time was rediscovered in the 1970s, economists had come to take for granted general competitive equilibrium as a framework for economic analysis.[24] When markets are assumed to be competitive, and the only "imperfections" permitted to affect them arise from agents' failures to anticipate changes that cannot be forecast, it is perhaps inevitable that markets will also appear to operate efficiently and natural to take it for granted that systematic coordination failures will not occur. In contrast, it is possible to conceive of a route whereby, starting from Swedish dynamic analysis, naive of competitive equilibrium theory, economists might have explored lines of inquiry about which we can currently say little. In a world such as the Swedes analyzed, coordination failures were common, and we might know much more about them than we did in the 1930s, had economists persevered in investigating such a world. The point here is not to argue that this would inevitably have happened—counterfactuals are always hypothetical—but that it could conceivably have done so. This possibility is enough to warn us of the dangers inherent in presuming, as a methodological principle, that losses do not matter.

24. Game theory, which in any case came later, does not alter the conclusions significantly.

There is the further argument to be made here, particularly important for macroeconomics, that, whether its academic practitioners like it or not, economic theory is always available to be pressed into service by policymakers.[25] Because policy problems require attention as and when they arise, it is not always possible to wait for a theory to be fully developed before applying it, and whatever is at hand is what is going to be used. For example, we have pointed out above that the dominance of IS-LM led to the temporary loss of what had once been commonplace insights about the monetary nature of inflation and about the intrinsically dynamic nature of inflation that stems from the role that expectations play in determining its course. Even though macroeconomics had largely regained its understanding of money and inflation by the mid-1970s, so that these were not permanent losses of scientific knowledge, that still leaves two decades during which policymakers used the "naive" IS-LM model to guide them, possibly into making some of the mistakes that created the inflation of the 1970s and 1980s. That inflation had serious consequences for the economic well-being of agents in numerous countries, and it is arguable that policymakers with intuitions informed by some serious study of Fisher and Hawtrey (or even David Ricardo and Henry Thornton), in addition to IS-LM, would have had a better chance of avoiding at least its worst aspects.

While some dismiss this example as a one-off phenomenon, as did Robert Lucas and Thomas Sargent ([1978] 1981) in their indictment of Keynesian economics, it seems more plausible that the danger is a recurrent one. Consider, for example, the monetary problems faced by the Japanese economy in the last decade. As Mauro Boianovsky (this volume) accurately records, it is taken for granted by many commentators that Japan has encountered a "liquidity trap." This is hardly surprising, because within IS-LM, the interest rate is the only channel through which monetary policy can work, and the liquidity trap—in the form of an interest elasticity of demand for money that approaches infinity at some low level—is the only financial market factor that can block this channel. But, as Boianovsky also notes, students of Hawtrey would know that a "credit deadlock"—a situation in which money creation is inhibited by the unwillingness of pessimistic firms to borrow from the banks at any interest rate—can also render monetary policy ineffective. They would also know, however, that sufficiently aggressive open market operations or money-financed budget deficits could be used to break such

25. See Lucas, this volume.

a deadlock, and that if, as Hawtrey believed (and as Edward Nelson reminds us in his article in this volume, monetarists still believe) money creation can have effects through a much wider range of channels than market interest rates, this might be enough to revive a depressed economy. The fact that none of this has been tried in Japan, and that monetary policy was declared impotent there the moment short interest rates began to meet their zero lower bound, suggests that we might here have another example of serious policy consequences flowing from the loss of an idea that didn't fit into IS-LM.[26]

Finally, we come back to the question of intertemporal coordination failures, whose analysis has been ruled out by methodological fiat in modern macroeconomics. Recent financial crises in many countries (including the collapse of the Japanese "bubble economy" in 1991) have ended not just with stock market crashes and bank failures but with the sudden emergence of large stocks of unwanted capital goods—so-called see-through buildings or, more recently, large stocks of unwanted computing equipment and fiber-optic cable, and so on—and these are precisely the symptoms that the Austrians and Dennis Robertson highlighted as consequences of forced saving financed by excessive credit growth. But modern macroeconomics seems to leave policymakers without any insight into the problems that these phenomena create. In a few years' time, then, we may look back on the late twentieth century with a sense of incredulity similar to that with which Lucas and Sargent viewed the Keynesian era. We may wonder how economists could ever have thought that differences among agents would not matter for the workings of the economy, and how they could have failed to see that coordination failures are endemic in complex systems.

Conclusion

In view of these considerations, it is hard to portray the development of macroeconomics after 1936 as involving steady progress at the cost of no

26. Brunner and Meltzer's (e.g., 1993) long-standing insistence that the IS-LM model contains an inadequate account of what they termed "the money supply process," referred to by Michael Bordo and Anna Schwartz (this volume), is highly relevant here, since it bolstered their efforts to analyze explicitly the same set of interactions among the central bank, the commercial banks, and the nonbank public that underlay Hawtrey's analysis. However, their attempt to force these interactions into the formal comparative-static framework that monetary economics inherited from IS-LM, rather than into an informal dynamic framework such as that used by Hawtrey himself, made their analysis hard for their readers to appreciate.

significant losses. A more accurate verdict of what went on would be that the subdiscipline's formalization involved desirable gains to be sure, but regrettable losses as well as (cf. Backhouse 1998). This in turn raises the question of whether it is important for economics to ensure that its practitioners retain familiarity with older ways of thinking as new ideas develop. The discipline must certainly remain open to new ideas, but also, to a much greater extent than currently seems to be the case, it needs to retain a healthy skepticism about the extent to which these describe all relevant aspects of the macroeconomic world better than do older approaches. The evidence from the development of macroeconomics during the era of IS-LM suggests that a failure to keep track of already existing ideas extracted a price from the discipline, one that it continues to pay.

References

Aftalion, Albert. 1913. *Les crises périodiques du surproduction*. Paris: Marcel Rivière.

Backhouse, Roger E. 1985. *A History of Modern Economic Analysis*. Oxford: Basil Blackwell.

————. 1998. If Mathematics Is Informal, Then Perhaps We Should Accept That Economics Must Be Informal Too. *Economic Journal* 108 (November): 1848–58.

Bailey, Martin J. 1962. *National Income and the Price Level*. New York: McGraw-Hill.

Barro, Robert J., and Herschel I. Grossman. 1976. *Money, Employment, and Inflation*. Cambridge: Cambridge University Press.

Blaug, Mark. 1962. *Economic Theory in Retrospect*. Homewood, Ill.: Irwin.

Brunner, Karl, and Allan H. Meltzer. 1993. *Money and the Economy: Issues in Monetary Analysis*. Cambridge: Cambridge University Press for the Raffaele Mattioli Foundation.

Chick, Victoria. 1973. *The Theory of Monetary Policy*. London: Gray-Mills.

Clower, Robert W. 1965. The Keynesian Counter-revolution: A Reappraisal. In *The Theory of Interest Rates*, edited by Frank R. P. Brechling and Frank H. Hahn. London: Macmillan for the International Economic Association.

Fisher, Irving. 1907. *The Rate of Interest: Its Nature, Determination, and Relation to Economic Phenomena*. New York: Macmillan.

————. 1911. *The Purchasing Power of Money*. New York: Macmillan.

Friedman, Milton. 1943. Methods of Forecasting Inflation. In *Taxing to Prevent Inflation: Techniques for Estimating Revenue Requirements*, by Carl Shoup, Milton Friedman, and Ruth Mack. New York: Columbia University Press.

————. 1953a. The Inflationary Gap. In *Essays in Positive Economics*. Chicago: University of Chicago Press.

————. 1953b. The Effects of a Full Employment Policy on Economic Stability: A Formal Analysis. In *Essays in Positive Economics*. Chicago: University of Chicago Press.

————. 1957. *A Theory of the Consumption Function*. Princeton, N.J.: Princeton University Press.

————. 1960. *A Program for Monetary Stability*. New York: Fordham University Press.

————. 1968. The Role of Monetary Policy. *American Economic Review* 58:1–19.

Friedman, Milton, and Anna J. Schwartz. 1963a. *A Monetary History of the United States, 1867–1960*. Princeton, N.J.: Princeton University Press.

————. 1963b. Money and Business Cycles. *Review of Economics and Statistics* 45 (February): 32–64.

Garrison, Roger W. 2001. *Time and Money*. London: Routledge.

Gordon, Robert J., ed. 1974. *Milton Friedman's Monetary Framework*. Chicago: University of Chicago Press.

Hansson, Bjorn A. 1982. *The Stockholm School and the Development of Dynamic Method*. London: Croom Helm.

Harrod, Roy F. 1937. Mr Keynes and Traditional Theory. *Econometrica* 5 (January): 74–86.

Hawtrey, Ralph G. 1913. *Good and Bad Trade*. London: Constable.

Hayek, Friedrich A. 1931. *Prices and Production*. London: Routledge.

————. 1931–32. Reflections on the Pure Theory of Money of Mr. J. M. Keynes. Pts. 1 and 2. *Economica*, no. 33:270–95; no. 35:22–44.

Hicks, John R. 1935. A Suggestion for Simplifying the Theory of Money. *Economica*, n.s., 1 (November): 479–83.

————. 1937. Mr. Keynes and the "Classics": A Suggested Interpretation. *Econometrica* 5 (April): 147–59.

————. 1939. *Value and Capital*. Oxford: Clarendon.

Jorgenson, Dale. 1967. The Theory of Investment Behavior. In *The Determinants of Business Behavior*, edited by Robert Ferber. New York: National Bureau of Economic Research.

Keynes, John Maynard. 1923. *A Tract on Monetary Reform*. London: Macmillan.

————. 1925. The Economic Consequences of Mr. Churchill. In *Essays in Persuasion*, vol. 9 of *The Collected Writings of John Maynard Keynes*. London: Macmillan.

————. 1930. *A Treatise on Money*. London: Macmillan.

————. 1931. The Pure Theory of Money: A Reply to Dr Hayek. *Economica* 34 (November): 387–97.

————. 1933. *The Means to Prosperity*. London: Macmillan.

————. 1936. *The General Theory of Employment, Interest, and Money*. London: Macmillan.

———. 1940. *How to Pay for the War: A Radical Plan for the Chancellor of the Exchequer*. London: Macmillan.

Kitcher, Philip. 1993. *The Advancement of Science: Science without Legend, Objectivity without Illusions*. New York: Oxford University Press.

Kregel, Jan A. 1976. Economic Methodology in the Face of Uncertainty: The Modelling Methods of Keynes and the Post-Keynesians. *Economic Journal* 86 (June): 209–25.

Krugman, Paul. 1995. *Development, Geography, and Economic Theory*. Cambridge: MIT Press.

Laidler, David. 1999. *Fabricating the Keynesian Revolution*. Cambridge: Cambridge University Press.

Laughlin, J. Laurence. 1903. *The Principles of Money*. New York: Charles Scribner's.

Lavington, Frederick. 1921. *The English Capital Market*. London: Methuen.

———. 1922. *The Trade Cycle*. London: P. S. King.

Leeson, Robert. 2000. *A. W. Phillips: Collected Works in Contemporary Perspective*. Cambridge: Cambridge University Press.

Leijonhufvud, Axel. 1968. *On Keynesian Economics and the Economics of Keynes*. Oxford: Oxford University Press.

———. 1981. The Wicksell Connection: Variations on a Theme. In *Information and Co-ordination*. Oxford: Oxford University Press.

Lindahl, Erik. 1929. Review of *Dynamic Prices*, by G. Myrdal. *Economic Journal* 39 (March): 89–91.

Lipsey, Richard G. 1960. The Relationship between Unemployment and the Rate of Change of Money Wage Rates in the United Kingdom, 1862–1957: A Further Analysis. *Economica* 27 (February): 1–31.

———. 2000. IS–LM, Keynesianism, and the New Classicism. In vol. 2 of *Macroeconomics and the Real World*, edited by Roger E. Backhouse and Andrea Salanti. Oxford: Oxford University Press.

Lucas, Robert E., Jr. 1972. Expectations and the Neutrality of Money. *Journal of Economic Theory* 4.2:103–24.

Lucas, Robert E., and Thomas J. Sargent. [1978] 1981. After Keynesian Macroeconomics. In *Rational Expectations and Econometric Practice*, edited by Robert E. Lucas and Thomas J. Sargent. London: Allen and Unwin.

Malinvaud, Edmond. 1977. *The Theory of Unemployment Reconsidered*. Oxford: Blackwell.

Marshall, Alfred. [1887] 1925. Remedies for Fluctuations in General Prices. In *Memorials of Alfred Marshall*, edited by A. C. Pigou. London: Macmillan.

Mehrling, Perry G. 1998. *The Money Interest and the Public Interest*. Cambridge: Harvard University Press.

Modigliani, Franco, and Richard Brumberg. 1954. Utility Analysis and the Consumption Function: An Interpretation of the Cross-section Data. In *Post Keynesian Economics*, edited by Kenneth Kurihara. New Brunswick, N.J.: Rutgers University Press.

Mundell, Robert. 1963. Inflation and Real Interest. *Journal of Political Economy* 71.3:280–83.

Ohlin, Bertil. 1937. Some Notes on the Stockholm Theory of Saving and Investment. *Economic Journal* 47 (March, June): 53–69, 221–40.

Patinkin, Don. [1956] 1965. *Money, Interest, and Prices*. Rev. ed. New York: Harper Bros.

Phelps, Edmund H. 1967. Phillips Curves, Expectations of Inflation, and Optimal Unemployment over Time. *Economica*, n.s., 34 (August): 254–81.

Phillips, A. W. H. 1954. Stabilisation in a Closed Economy. *Economic Journal* 64 (June): 290–323.

Pigou, A. C. 1929. *Industrial Fluctuations*. 2nd ed. London: Macmillan.

———. 1933. *The Theory of Unemployment*. London: Macmillan.

Poole, William. 1970. Optimal Choice of Monetary Policy Instruments in a Simple Stochastic Model. *Quarterly Journal of Economics* 84 (May): 197–216.

Robertson, Dennis H. 1915. *A Study of Industrial Fluctuation*. London: P. S. King.

———. 1926. *Banking Policy and the Price Level*. London: Macmillan.

———. 1928. Theories of Banking Policy. *Economica* 8 (June): 131–46.

Samuelson, Paul A., and Robert M. Solow. 1960. Analytical Aspects of Anti-inflation Policy. *American Economic Review* 50.2:177–94.

Simons, Henry. 1936. Rule versus Authorities in Monetary Policy. *Journal of Political Economy* 44 (February): 1–30.

Simons, Henry, et al. [1933] 1994. Banking and Currency Reform. Unpublished manuscript, University of Chicago. In *Research in the History of Economic Thought and Methodology* (archival supplement) 4.

Tobin, James. 1982. Money and Finance in the Macroeconomic Process. *Journal of Money, Credit, and Banking* 14 (May): 171–204.

Tugan-Baronovsky, Mikhail. 1913. *Les crises industrielles en Angleterre*. Paris: M. Giard & É. Brière.

Warming, Jens. 1932. International Difficulties Arising out of the Financing of Public Works during Depression. *Economic Journal* 42 (June): 211–24.

Wicksell, Knut. [1898] 1936. *Interest and Prices*. Translated by R. F. Kahn. London: Macmillan for the Royal Economic Society.

———. 1907. The Influence of the Rate of Interest on Prices. *Economic Journal* 17 (June): 213–20.

Young, Allyn A. 1927. The Structure and Policies of the Federal Reserve System. In *Economic Problems New and Old*. Boston: Houghton Mifflin.

The History of Macroeconomics Viewed against the Background of the Marshall-Walras Divide

Michel De Vroey

The demise of the line of thought embodied in the IS-LM model and its replacement by stochastic intertemporal equilibrium models is probably the most salient change that occurred in macroeconomics during the last quarter of the twentieth century.[1] My aim in this essay is to analyze this demise against the background of what I call the Marshall-Walras divide. According to the defenders of this divide, the contributions of Alfred Marshall and Léon Walras to economic theory are less complementary than usually believed, and the Marshallian and the Walrasian approaches should rather be considered alternative research programs. The underlying reason is their being based on radically different trade technology assumptions. This divide has a direct bearing on the unfolding of macroeconomics: the change that took place about two decades ago is the substitution of Walrasian macroeconomics for Marshallian macroeconomics.[2]

Comments by David Colander and Kevin Hoover on an earlier version of this article are gratefully acknowledged. This work was supported by the Belgian French-Speaking Community (grant ARC 03/08-302) and the Belgian Federal Government (grant PAI P5/10).

1. Several interesting papers on this subject have been published recently: Blanchard 2000, Blinder [1988] 1997, Drèze 2001, Danthine 1997, Hairault 1999, Lipsey 2000, Snowdon and Vane 1996, and Woodford 1999.

2. This claim was voiced by some authors who studied what at the time was called "Monetarism Mark I" and "Monetarism Mark II," associated respectively with Friedman's (1968) and Lucas's (1972) Phillips curve models. For example, Kevin Hoover ([1984] 1990, 528) noted that "Friedman, as one important monetarist, differs from the new classicals on a fundamental point of methodology: he is a Marshallian; they are Walrasians."

Before going further, I must clarify two things. First, I need to make clear what I mean by the terms *general equilibrium model*, *macroeconomics*, *Keynesian approach*, and *neoclassical synthesis*. Second, I must spell out how I understand the Marshall-Walras divide.

1. Terminology

1.1 General Equilibrium Models and Macroeconomics

Usually a general equilibrium model is associated with Walrasian or neo-Walrasian theory, that is, Walras's own theory as expounded in his *Elements of Pure Economics* (1954) or the Arrow-Debreu model.[3] The implication is that there exists only one way to do general equilibrium analysis, the Walrasian. Instead, I suggest a broader conception, that general equilibrium analysis exists as soon as two criteria are met. First, the object of analysis must be an economy as a whole rather than a subsection of it. Second, the analysis must deal with a formalized, or mathematical, model.[4]

The point to be underlined, because it goes against the grain, is that the Walrasian approach has no monopoly over general equilibrium theory. It is true that most general equilibrium models belong to the Walrasian approach, but this actual hegemony cannot be viewed as a matter of principle. Alternative programs cannot be excluded.

My next step is to see how the categories of general equilibrium model and macroeconomic model fit together. What exactly is macroeconomics? In their recent accounts of the unfolding of macroeconomics, written at the occasion of the millennium, Olivier Blanchard and Michael Woodford concur in stating that macroeconomics consists of the study of fluctuations (Blanchard 2000, 2; Woodford 1999, 1). It is, of course, true that present macroeconomics deals with fluctuations, yet it should not be inferred that any study of fluctuations is macroeconomics. For example, if this definitional stance is taken, it turns out that the IS-LM model does not belong to macroeconomics.

---

3. Henceforth the term *Walrasian* will be understood in a broad sense as encompassing neo-Walrasian models (the Arrow-Debreu model and its followers) or even models that are often misleadingly called non-Walrasian, such as the Barro-Grossman model.

4. The rationale for this second condition is that, in its absence, I should always need to distinguish between earlier general equilibrium theories, reasoning in prose, and formalized general equilibrium models.

The term *macroeconomics* is usually ascribed to Ragnar Frisch, who coined it in his essay "Propagation Problems and Impulse Problems in Dynamic Economics" (1933, 172). To him, its concern was "the whole economic system in its entirety," while microeconomics focused on individual behavior. Unfortunately, this cogent conception has not been followed, and the meaning of macroeconomics has become messy. What is now called macroeconomics deals with a whole economy, yet not every analysis bearing on such an object is usually considered macroeconomics. Take Walrasian theory. Beyond a doubt, it studies the economy as a whole, yet it is ranked as microeconomics. In contrast, why count real business cycle models, which claim a Walrasian heritage, as macroeconomics?

To solve this puzzle, we should return to Frisch's viewpoint and consider that macroeconomics belongs to the domain of general equilibrium.[5] In effect, it meets the two criteria posited above. However, it should be viewed as a subcategory of general equilibrium analysis rather than being equated with it. In other words, different types of general equilibrium analysis must be separated. My suggestion is to distinguish between complex and simplified general equilibrium models.

Macroeconomics then deals with simplified general equilibrium models. They comprise a small number of variables. They study a few markets, named after those markets deemed to be the most important real-world markets. They deal at once with aggregates, by reasoning in terms of representative firms or agents. They embed a few institutions, such as the government and the central bank. They are geared toward addressing policy issues, such as the level of employment, national output, inflation, government deficit, effects of changes in money supply, etc. Finally, they claim to be empirically relevant and to give results that can be tested against reality. In contrast, Walras's model or the Arrow-Debreu model involves a great number of agents and commodities. They are geared toward more abstract purposes, like demonstrating the logical existence of equilibrium, stability, etc. Therefore, what is usually "general equilibrium analysis" can be recast as "complex general equilibrium analysis."

If macroeconomics belongs to the general equilibrium line of research, it is concerned with mathematical models. If reasoning in prose is not a model *strictu sensu*, the rise of macroeconomics should be ascribed

---

5. Patinkin ([1956] 1965) has already expressed this viewpoint. It is also to be found in Woodford 1999, 8; Farmer 1993, 1; and Young and Zilberfarb 2000, 1.

Table 1

	Complex general equilibrium models	Simplified general equilibrium models (i.e., macroeconomics)
The Walrasian approach	—	—
The Marshallian approach	—	—

not to John Maynard Keynes's *General Theory* but to the subsequent models that tried to translate Keynes's blurred message into a precise model. Here the IS-LM model stands out. Thus, if my definitional stance is taken, macroeconomics started with the IS-LM model.[6]

To summarize, general equilibrium analysis can be subdivided along two lines. First, a distinction must be drawn between Walrasian general equilibrium, the Walrasian modifier being understood in its broadest sense, and what could be called "non-Walrasian" general equilibrium models, had this modifier not been preempted by models that actually belong to the Walrasian line. The contending alternative line is general equilibrium in the Marshallian approach.[7] The second divide relates to the division between complex and simplified general equilibrium models. By crossing the two criteria, one gets table 1.

The story to be told in part 3 of my essay is that of the gradual filling in of the diagram. The first research program to be implemented corresponded to the upper-left box, concomitant to the publication of Walras's *Elements of Pure Economics* (the first edition was published

6. Several passages of Laidler's book on the Keynesian revolution (1999) hint at my viewpoint, although this is not its main thrust. Let me quote one of them: "Nevertheless, the impression of continuity in the development of macroeconomics which one might get from the very selective survey of reactions to the *General Theory* presented in the foregoing chapters would be misleadingly incomplete. A break did occur around 1936, and it did center on the *General Theory*. The break in question, however, arose not directly from that book itself, but from the IS-LM model, which a number of younger commentators found in it and used to expound not just what they took to be its main message, but that of an earlier classical tradition too" (303). Other passages are on pages 318 and 324.

7. As is well known, Marshall is an author who can be pulled into opposed directions. There is Marshall the evolutionary-institutionalist economist, often associated with book 4 of the *Principles*, and Marshall the value theorist, associated with book 5. Although the first Marshall has become more popular than the second, my interest here lies with the latter. Thus, when speaking of Marshallian theory, I have in mind the reconstruction of his "great fifth book on 'General Relations of Demand, Supply, and Value,'" to borrow Hicks's characterization ([1939] 1946, 119).

Table 2

	Complex general equilibrium models	Simplified general equilibrium models (i.e., macroeconomics)
The Walrasian approach	*The Walrasian model (1874–77)*	— *First attempts: Patinkin [1956] 1965, Barro and Grossman 1971* — *Full-scale emergence: real business cycle models*
The Marshallian approach	*Imperfectly competitive general equilibrium models (e.g., Hart 1979)*	*The IS-LM model: Hicks [1937] 1967, Modigliani 1944*

in two installments in 1874–77). The second step was the invention of macroeconomics with John Hicks's IS-LM model later recast by Franco Modigliani (1944).[8] This model, I will claim, belongs to the Marshallian approach. The third step, the establishment of Walrasian macroeconomics, has been a more protracted phenomenon. Don Patinkin can be considered the first modern author having constructed a simplified Walrasian general equilibrium model in his *Money, Interest, and Prices* ([1956] 1965). It was later revived by Robert Barro and Herschel Grossman in their disequilibrium model. Although Patinkin's book exerted an important influence, the model it contained was never viewed as an alternative to IS-LM base camp for macroeconomics. Nor did Patinkin campaign to this effect (see Rubin, this volume). As far as the disequilibrium à la Barro and Grossman is concerned, its vogue has been short-lived. The age of Walrasian macroeconomics had to await the emergence of real business cycle models, themselves the offspring of Robert Lucas's "Expectations and the Neutrality of Money" paper ([1972] 1981). Finally, I associate the creation of Marshallian complex general equilibrium theory with imperfectly competitive general equilibrium models. In sum, while Marshallian macroeconomics predates Walrasian macroeconomics, the contrary is true for what concerns complex general equilibrium modelization. See table 2.

8. Cf. De Vroey 2000.

1.2 Elucidating the "Keynesian" Modifier

In his paper criticizing the new classical approach, A. Blinder ([1988] 1997, 112–13) draws the following distinction between normative and positive Keynesianism.

> The division of Keynesian economics into positive and normative components is central to understanding both the academic debate and its relevance to policy. Positive Keynesianism is a matter of scientific judgement. A positive Keynesian believes that both monetary and fiscal policy can change aggregate demand, that fluctuations in aggregate demand have real effects, and that prices and wages do not move rapidly to clear markets. No policy prescriptions follow from these beliefs alone. . . . Normative Keynesians add both value judgement and political judgement to the preceding list. A normative Keynesian believes that government should use its leverage over aggregate demand to reduce the amplitude of business cycles. He or she is probably far more interested in filling in cyclical troughs than in shaving off peaks. These normative propositions are based on judgements that (a) macroeconomic fluctuations significantly reduce social welfare, (b) the government is knowledgeable and capable enough to improve upon free-market outcomes, and (c) unemployment is a more important problem than inflation.

Blinder's insight can be cast differently by drawing a distinction between a theoretical framework or apparatus, on the one hand, and the "policy cause" that it may serve, on the other. The *Keynesian apparatus* term then refers to what Blinder calls "positive Keynesianism," the *Keynesian policy cause* label to his "normative Keynesianism."

Most commentators agree that the IS-LM model is the Keynesian theoretical framework par excellence—for sure, it has been the most influential translation of Keynes's prose reasoning into a model. But the "Keynesian" modifier can also be used in reference to what motivated Keynes to write the *General Theory*. In this line, it can be viewed as a catchword for regrouping authors who think that, for all its virtues, the market economy can exhibit market failures, which state interventions, in particular demand stimulation, are able to remedy. The laissez-faire policy cause, which pleads against such interventions, can then be viewed as the non-Keynesian or anti-Keynesian policy cause.

In an interview with Duncan Foley, Wassily Leontief (1998, 122) remarked that in his opinion Keynes developed his theory essentially as an instrument to support his policy advice. Put crudely, my viewpoint is that this observation extends beyond Keynes's person and applies to Keynesians and anti-Keynesians (in the policy cause sense) alike. Moreover, I think that there is nothing blameworthy about such an attitude.

To further compound the matter, no one-to-one relationship exists between the Keynesian theoretical framework and the Keynesian policy cause or between the non-Keynesian theoretical framework and the anti-Keynesian policy cause. While the launching of the Keynesian apparatus was motivated by the will to support the Keynesian policy cause, authors who were anti-Keynesian from a policy perspective—Milton Friedman being the emblematic example—were able to subvert it and use it as a weapon for the laissez-faire cause. Thus Friedman, although being anti-Keynesian from the policy cause perspective, must be considered a Keynesian author methodologically speaking—that is, insofar as the modifier refers to the theoretical apparatus dimension. Likewise, while the non-Keynesian conceptual apparatus, to be associated with new classical economics, was initiated by authors wanting to defend the anti-Keynesian policy cause, this does not exclude the possibility of it becoming subverted in its turn. This is the very task that new Keynesian economists set for themselves. Against my distinction, they are non-Keynesian from the theoretical framework viewpoint yet Keynesian from the policy cause perspective.

2. The Marshall-Walras Divide

The standard view about the Marshallian and the Walrasian approaches, the former being narrowed down to book 5 of the *Principles*, is that they are complementary.[9] They share the same subjective theory of value grounding market supply and demand functions in agents' optimizing behavior. Moreover, a division of labor seems to exist between them, with Marshallian theory focusing on the study of isolated parts of the economy and Walrasian theory on the study of the economy as a whole. The latter then appears to be the generalization of the former.[10]

---

9. It is, for example, expressed in Hicks [1934] 1983, 86.

10. Marshall's only foray into the study of general equilibrium was in his Mathematical Notes 14 and 21 (on this, see Dimand 1990). Why did he not try harder to develop a theory as to the functioning of the economy as a whole? Two possible answers come to mind. First, he might have considered that this subject matter was not concrete enough. Second, he might have been aware that the tools for such a study were unavailable.

Following Robert Clower and Axel Leijonhufvud (Clower and Leijonhufvud [1975] 1984; Leijonhufvud 1999), I dissent from this view. I share their belief that there is room for a Marshallian general equilibrium approach distinct from the Walrasian. Moreover, like them, I am of the opinion that the possible emergence of alternatives to Walrasian general equilibrium theory is a matter of trade technology, that is, the institutional setup enabling equilibrium outcomes to be arrived at.

If it were accepted that the logical existence of equilibrium is the exclusive issue that economic theory needs to address, then the matter would be sealed: no need for an alternative theoretical construction exists. Walras paved the way to solving it, and Kenneth Arrow and Gérard Debreu finalized the job by constructing the benchmark general equilibrium model. For all intents and purposes, most economists have no qualms with such a restricted approach. Yet economic theory cannot limit itself to the issues of the logical existence and stability of equilibrium. Trade technology must be taken in earnest.

2.1 The Walrasian Trade Technology

One of Walras's strokes of genius was to have started his analysis with considering an entire economy at once, rather than a section of it. A Walrasian economy constitutes a single centralized market, encompassing every agent and every good and service. The auctioneer, though not explicitly introduced by Walras in the *Elements of Pure Economics*, is the cornerstone of the Walrasian trade technology (De Vroey 1998). His main task consists of using the price system to make individual trade offers compatible. To this end, he announces price vectors to which agents react by expressing the optimal quantity they offer to trade. Prices are changed until general equilibrium is reached—that is, whenever every market excess demand is nil or negative, the price being equal to zero in the latter case. Most general equilibrium theorists only grudgingly recognize the auctioneer's role and openly declare their disliking. In contrast, I think that it is integral to the neo-Walrasian research program. To say it bluntly and at the risk of raising the eyebrows of important commentators of Walras, such as Walker (1996), as well as of many present-day Walrasian theorists—yet not Lucas (see Lucas 1986)—the Walrasian approach cannot dispense with the auctioneer, because it is the only working trade technology assumption on stock.

This being granted, the need for making explicit the whereabouts of the auctioneer-led *tâtonnement* process cannot be sidestepped. On top of what I already stated, other characteristics are worth mentioning. The formation of equilibrium proceeds in one stroke, involving all goods and agents. At each trade round everything occurs simultaneously. Actual transactions remain suspended until the equilibrium price vector is arrived at. Although there is less consensus on this point, I am of the opinion that a Walrasian economy is basically nonmonetary, in spite of the existence of a *numéraire*-good.[11] Another point that needs to be clarified is the information structure. In the canonical Walrasian or neo-Walrasian model, agents are supposed to hold perfect information over the prices announced by the auctioneer, the quality of goods and services, and the states of the world. However, because of the presence of the auctioneer, they are not supposed to be knowledgeable about other agents' demand and supply functions, or about the factors underpinning them. All this still makes for a quite heroic information assumption, yet, as will be seen, it is less heroic than the informational assumption underpinning Marshallian theory. Finally, consider the communication structure of an auctioneer-led system. The auctioneer economy is a set of bilateral relationships between the auctioneer and isolated individual agents. Before the attainment of equilibrium, agents' exclusive social link is with the auctioneer. They do not interact and communicate between themselves. Nor, as stated, are they cognizant about excess demand functions and the data that underpin them. An important implication ensues. Whenever a given agent makes a trading offer by responding to the prices announced by the auctioneer, he or she ignores how many other agents are making a similar offer. This means that an agent can be in a monopolistic position while being totally unaware and hence incapable of taking advantage of it. In other words, the *tâtonnement* setup itself guarantees the "perfectness" of competition, whatever the possible monopolistic factors that may be present in the economy. Agents cannot influence prices because the institutional device is such as to preclude it.[12] The auctioneer hypothesis and imperfect competition, it turns out, are incompatible bedfellows.

11. This is clear for what concerns the Arrow-Debreu model. It is likewise so for Walras's *Elements* insofar as it is accepted that Walras's introduction of money in his model of circulation and money does not stand up to scrutiny (cf. Bridel 1997). On the other hand, starting with Patinkin ([1956] 1965), several authors have claimed to have successfully introduced money in Walrasian theory, yet Hahn ([1965] 1969) has refuted this claim (cf. Bridel 2002). Turning to present-day theory, money is present under the form of cash in advance in some new classical models, yet again it can be argued that its introduction is contrived.

12. De Vroey (1998) argues that they are unable to manipulate the auctioneer.

2.2 Extending the Marshallian Trade
Technology to the Economy as a Whole

Imagine that Walras never wrote his *Elements*, and that only Marshall's writings were available for economists wanting to build a general equilibrium theory.[13]

Marshall implicitly gave a clue on how to proceed. Walras's decision to study an entire economy from the onset was counterintuitive. Intuitively, one would rather take a step-by-step approach consisting of studying the functioning of an isolated typical market in the first stage of the enterprise while relegating the study of the interrelationship of markets, the piecing together of the results of partial analysis, for its second stage. This two-tier general equilibrium methodology can be considered typically Marshallian in contrast to the one-shot Walrasian methodology. Its gist is well encapsulated in Hicks's following observation—a statement that Walras would not have uttered: "If a model of the whole economy is to be securely based, it must be grounded in an intelligible account of how a single market is supposed to work" (Hicks 1965, 78).[14]

Extrapolating from the institutional setup on which Marshall's partial equilibrium analysis is based, we can reconstruct the trade technology that would have underpinned his general equilibrium analysis had he been able to construct it, thereby defining the contours of a Marshallian economy to be contrasted with the Walrasian economy. A first feature is that the economy is depicted as composed of separate markets of different subtypes (factors, final goods, etc.). Each of them is an autonomous locus of formation of equilibrium. Another of its features is its monetary character, each market witnessing an exchange between one given good and money. Contrary to what is the case for Walrasian theory, a nonmonetary Marshallian model can hardly be conceived of. As far as price setting is concerned, no auctioneer is assumed to be present. Agents are price makers. Finally, all this goes along with a stronger information assumption, a point that requires more elaboration.

As in the Walrasian setup, perfect information is supposedly present, yet it receives a stronger content. Insofar as the auctioneer is absent from the Marshallian scenario, the burden of the formation of equilibrium now lies on economic agents. They need to assess relevant market supply and

13. In fact, this was the position Keynes was facing because of the wide ignorance of Walrasian theory among Cambridge economists.

14. The following other statement is in the same vein: "What we have to do now is to generalize his [Marshall's] framework, so that it can be used for the discussion of the problems of a whole economic system" (Hicks 1965, 121).

demand functions on their own. Therefore, they must be informed about the relevant private data. Perfect information in this stronger meaning turns out to be the linchpin of the equilibrium formation process. In short, the agents participating in the market are supposed to be as omniscient about it as the outside model-builder economist.[15]

Once this omniscience feature is brought to the forefront, which is scarcely the case, the conclusion must be drawn that the Marshallian trade technology fares hardly better than the Walrasian in terms of realism. Both are based on a deus ex machina, perfect information in one case, the auctioneer in the other. Perfect information is no less a betrayal of the alleged theoretical *explanandum*, a decentralized trading system, than the auctioneer, because the hallmark of a decentralized economy is that private data will not become public. Methodologically, the underlying flaw is that two levels of knowledge, which should have been kept separate—the knowledge of the outside omniscient economist and that of the economic agent—have become blurred.[16]

The result obtained up to now is as follows. Assume a Marshallian theorist, endowed with the conceptual toolbox to be found in book 5 of the *Principles* and wanting to study the economy as a whole. He would face the need to put forward some scenario as to the functioning of the economy. What I have done is to spell it out. Clearly enough, the Marshallian trade technology is different from the Walrasian. Five differences stand out.

1. A single all-encompassing market characterizes the Walrasian approach, versus a juxtaposition of separate markets in the Marshallian approach.
2. Prices are formed by the auctioneer in the Walrasian approach while agents are price makers in the Marshallian approach.
3. Money is absent from the Walrasian approach (if present, it is introduced in a contrived way), while it is an essential ingredient of the Marshallian; put differently, the Marshallian economy, unlike the Walrasian, is necessarily monetary.
4. In the Walrasian approach perfect information does not include agents' ability to reconstruct market supply and demand function, while this requirement is needed for the formation of equilibrium in the Marshallian approach.

15. Cf. De Vroey 2003.
16. This is a point that Hayek underlined more than half a century ago, unfortunately with little impact. Cf. Hayek [1937] 1948, 45.

5. The Walrasian trade technology excludes imperfect competition (i.e., the possibility of monopolistic or oligopolistic behavior), while there is no reason for this exclusion in the Marshallian approach.[17]

3. The Unfolding of Macroeconomics Viewed against the Background of the Marshall-Walras Divide

3.1 The Overall Picture

I am now able to address the issue of the relevance of the Marshall-Walras divide for explaining the history of macroeconomics. My claim is that macroeconomics started as Marshallian but became Walrasian after the new classical revolution. To make my point, let me confront the state of development of general equilibrium theory, including macroeconomics as its simplified subtype, at two points in time: first, in the heyday of the IS-LM tradition, say in the 1950s and 1960s; and second, at the turn of the century. Figures 1 and 2, which display a few potential lines of development of general equilibrium theory in a tree form, serve this purpose. Four nodes are separated. The first is a bifurcation between Marshallian and Walrasian general equilibrium; the second separates complex from simplified models. A further distinction, which is relevant only for the Marshallian approach, is between perfectly and imperfectly competitive models. Finally, a last node is between static and dynamic models, dynamics meaning here intertemporal.

Figure 1 shows that during the first period the Marshallian and the Walrasian research programs were in an inverse position. I argue that the IS-LM model is Marshallian. This being granted, it turns out that the Marshallian program successfully constructed simplified general equilibrium models (macroeconomics), yet no Marshallian complex general equilibrium models existed. The inverse is true for the Walrasian program: no Walrasian macroeconomics existed, except for Patinkin and the disequilibrium approach, yet the complex part of the Walrasian program was alive and well.

Figure 2 reflects the present situation. The difference with the earlier situation is that most of the empty slots have been filled up. The IS-LM

---

17. Perfect competition should not be equated with price-taking behavior. It can also be associated with price-making behavior. Hence my criteria (2) and (5) are not identical.

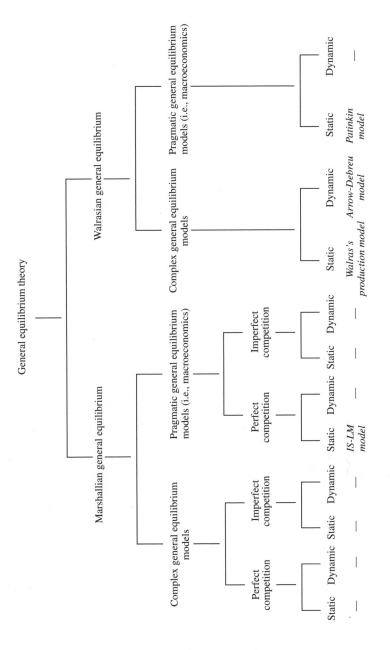

Figure 1 General equilibrium and macroeconomics in the heyday of the IS-LM tradition

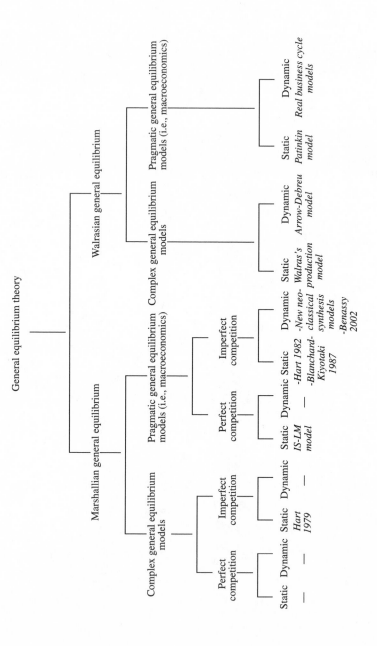

Figure 2 General equilibrium and macroeconomics at the turn of the twenty-first century

model has been supplemented with important developments in the imperfect competition branch. For example, I take the model in Hart 1979 as a fine example of a complex Marshallian general equilibrium model with imperfect competition. Moreover, dynamic imperfect competition models have emerged.[18] As far as the Walrasian branch is concerned, the salient feature is the breakthrough of Walrasian macroeconomics with real business cycle models.

3.2 The IS-LM Model

The IS-LM model is often, yet offhandedly, characterized as Walrasian.[19] This judgment is mistaken. Two possible reasons may have led economists to adhere to such a characterization. One is that general equilibrium is equated with Walrasian theory. This was, for example, Patinkin's stance. He rightly perceived that Keynes's project amounted to a study of the interdependency across markets. Since he did not conceive of any alternative to the Walrasian route, he concluded that Keynes had unwittingly followed Walras's footsteps.[20] I have shown that such a stance is inappropriate. As soon as it is admitted that the Walrasian approach is not the exclusive way of doing general equilibrium analysis, Patinkin's conclusion falls.

A second reason is that Hicks, the initiator of the IS-LM tradition ([1937] 1967), is considered a Walrasian economist—at least, he supposedly was when writing his "Mr. Keynes and the 'Classics.'" This was also the period during which he was working on *Value and Capital* ([1939] 1946), which is often credited for having revived Walrasian theory. Hence the conclusion that IS-LM must be Walrasian as well. The snag, however, is that *Value and Capital* is less Walrasian than is usually claimed. In my opinion, Hicks was never more than a halfhearted Walrasian. He may well have considered that Walrasian theory opened

18. See, for example, Benassy 2002.

19. See, for example, Vercelli 2000. This view is also taken for granted in several of the contributions to the Young-Zilberfarb volume on IS-LM (2000).

20. "Thus a basic contribution of the *General Theory* is that it is in effect the first practical application of the Walrasian theory of general equilibrium: 'practical' not in the sense of empirical . . . but in the sense of reducing Walras' formal model of n simultaneous equations in n unknowns to a manageable model from which implications for the real world could be drawn" (Patinkin 1987, 27). "The analysis of the *General Theory* is essentially that of general equilibrium. The voice is that of Marshall, but the hands are those of Walras. And in his IS-LM interpretation of the *General Theory*, Hicks quite rightly and quite effectively concentrated on the hands" (35).

a window on new horizons ([1979] 1983, 358), yet he always read Walras through Marshallian glasses. Contrary to subsequent Walrasians, he did not want to limit his analysis to the study of the logical existence of equilibrium. Following Marshall's lead, he confined mathematical developments to the appendixes of his book. Nor was he ready to adopt the auctioneer hypothesis. Marshall was to him a better reference for studying the working of markets than Walras. Finally, as seen, his general equilibrium methodology was different from the Walrasian. All in all, Hicks's mistake lies in his failure to have envisaged that Marshall and Walras were in a relationship of discontinuity. Unfortunately, most of the profession followed suit.

To assess whether the IS-LM model belongs to the Marshallian or the Walrasian approach, we must see how it fares with respect to the criteria adopted above to differentiate the Marshallian and the Walrasian trade technologies—the structure of the economy, the price-making process, the role of money, the information assumption, and the admissibility of imperfect competition.[21]

As far as the first criterion is concerned, the matter is clear. The economy that the IS-LM model analyzes is composed of markets that function separately, each of them being an autonomous locus of equilibrium. Likewise, for what concerns the second criterion, no auctioneer is supposedly present. The monetary character of an IS-LM economy is also undeniable. In regard to the information assumption, it is true that accounts of the IS-LM model scarcely evoke the possibility that it might rest on the assumption that agents are omniscient. But then nobody seems to have raised the issue of how equilibrium is arrived at in this model.[22] The IS curve describes every combination of income and interest at which the goods market is clearing, and the same is true about the LM curve with respect to the money market. Nothing is stated about how these market-clearing results are arrived at.[23] What is even more perplexing is how the intersection of the IS-LM curves can be obtained.

21. As the last criterion is irrelevant here, this leaves us with the first four.

22. This issue was dodged because it was believed, certainly by Hicks, that Marshall's haggling and bargaining mechanism would do the job. In De Vroey 2003, I have claimed that this argumentation is hollow.

23. In his study of Modigliani's 1944 IS-LM model, Goulven Rubin (this volume) shows that Modigliani was concerned with the formation of equilibrium. However, the fact that in Modigliani's reasoning the adjustment took place exclusively in the money market, requiring no across-market changes, is further testimony to the Marshallian character of the IS-LM model.

I see no other explanation than assuming agents' abilities to reconstruct the equilibrium values of the economy, that is, their being omniscient.[24]

Two supplementary factors point to a Marshallian belonging. First, it has often been remarked that the IS-LM model has little room for expectations.[25] To me, this lack is due to the stationary equilibrium conception underpinning the Marshallian approach and centered on the distinction between market prices and normal prices, with normal equilibrium serving as a center of gravitation.[26] This conception of equilibrium is based on a central yet unnoticed assumption, namely, that the economic data remain constant over the period of analysis, except for shocks that are supposed to be accidental, reversible, and unpredictable. Now if shocks cannot be predicted (although once they have occurred, agents are supposed to be able to assess their effect and length correctly) and if, moreover, their impact is supposedly well circumscribed, so that all the other data of economy remain unchanged, why on earth would one bother about expectations? In order for these to become important, economic data must be constantly changing over time. In regard to the second factor, different enrichments were brought to the initial IS-LM model, pertaining to consumption, portfolio choice, investment, and the labor market. All of them consisted of analyzing one sector of the economy viewed in isolation from the others, thereby witnessing to the Marshallian two-step general equilibrium methodology evoked above.

The conclusion to be drawn is that the IS-LM model is a simplified Marshallian general equilibrium model. This conclusion accords with the implicit view taken by most defenders of IS-LM macroeconomists. In spite of their unawareness of the Marshall-Walras divide, they firmly believe that their approach is poles apart from Walrasian microeconomics.[27]

24. One might claim that the equilibrium can alternatively be attained by adopting the auctioneer assumption, in which case the IS-LM could be viewed as based, at least in this respect, on the Walrasian trade technology. On reflection it turns out that this will not do. It may be accepted that markets function separately, in which case an auctioneer per market would be present. Yet how will one of the local auctioneers, say, the auctioneer in charge of the goods markets, be able to determine which among the possible equilibria between savings and investment will be the "true" one? To this end, he or she should come in touch with the other auctioneer, which makes the story too contrived. Alternatively, it can be assumed that a single auctioneer takes care of the economy as a whole. But then the idea of separate markets ceases to make sense.

25. See, for example, King 1993.

26. Cf. De Vroey 1999.

27. See, for example, Lipsey 2000, 69.

3.3 Patinkin's Macroeconomics

According to Leijonhufvud (1994, 148), the development of economic theory can be thought of as forming a decision tree.

> It is useful to think of our subject as forming a decision tree. Major economists force their contemporaries to face choices—choices of what to ask, what to assume, what to regard as evidence and what methods and models to employ—and persuade the profession or some faction of it to follow the choice they make. The path that any particular school has followed traces a sequence of such decisions. Many of the choices faced in such a sequence were not anticipated by the founder to which we trace the development in question, but were created by subsequent contributors; some of the decisions made we may judge to have been "wrong" in hindsight.

These remarks are apposite for reflecting on the place of Patinkin's *Money, Interest, and Prices* ([1956] 1965) in the history of macroeconomics. This book, which aimed at integrating value analysis and money theory, comprised a simplified general equilibrium model with two variants, a classical and a Keynesian, that can be put on the same footing as the IS-LM model. Arguably, Patinkin's model is superior to the IS-LM model in several respects—its composing markets are better defined, it has stronger microfoundations, its adjustment process involves all the commodities forming the economy.[28] When Patinkin's model is gauged against my criteria for separating the Marshallian from the Walrasian trade technology, its Walrasian belonging stands out, except for money. Yet Patinkin hardly pushed it that way. Not that he was unaware of the Walrasian character of his model. The contrary is true. But he missed the un-Walrasian nature of the IS-LM model and hence the deep-seated contrast between the two models. Although his book exerted an important influence, it was considered as a contribution to monetary theory rather than to macroeconomics. As a result, the fact that it might constitute an alternative to the IS-LM model was disregarded. Patinkin's insights were rediscovered a few decades later by the authors of the so-called disequilibrium approach (Barro and Grossman 1971, 1976). Yet its success was short-lived, and many of its practitioners ended up admitting to the validity of the criticism leveled against it—that its cornerstone, the idea of price rigidity, was ill grounded.

---

28. Cf. Rubin, this volume. Small wonder then that Patinkin's model was hailed by Lucas in his contribution to this volume.

To conclude, Walrasian macroeconomics could have emerged as an alternative to the IS-LM way of modeling, first in the 1950s with Patinkin's model and later with the disequilibrium line of research, yet this possibility failed to be realized.

3.4 The Neoclassical Synthesis

Several authors, in particular Marvin Goodfriend and Robert King (1997), have claimed that the unfolding of macroeconomics has led to the emergence of a new neoclassical synthesis close in spirit to the neoclassical synthesis that prevailed in the 1960s. Hence the need to clarify the contents of the "old" synthesis.

The term *neoclassical synthesis* is often traced back to Paul Samuelson's 1955 edition of his *Economics* textbook, yet what he writes there is hardly instructive.[29] For a more substantive explanation, we may turn to Peter Howitt's or Blanchard's entries in the *New Palgrave Dictionary* or to Woodford 1999. All of them hold the same viewpoint well summarized in the following quotation from Howitt (1987, 274):

> Since it was widely believed that wages were less than fully flexible in the short run, it seemed natural to see Keynesian theory as applying to short-run fluctuations and general equilibrium theory as applying to long-run questions in which adjustment problems could safely be ignored. This view came to be known as the "neoclassical synthesis."[30]

The problem lies in what should be understood by the term *synthesis*. Strictly speaking, a synthesis refers to the process by which two theoretical analytic frameworks that at a certain stage were considered as antagonistic eventually turn out to be congruent. Hence a merger between them proves possible.[31]

The neoclassical synthesis as understood by Howitt et al. does not stand up to this strict understanding of the notion of synthesis. Actually,

---

29. "In recent years 90 per cent of American economists have stopped being 'Keynesian economists' or 'anti-Keynesian economists.' Instead they have worked toward a synthesis of whatever is valuable in older economics and in modern theories of income determination. The result might be called neo-classical economics and is accepted in its broad outlines by all but about 5 per cent of extreme left-wing and right-wing writers" (Samuelson 1955, 212).

30. See also Blanchard 1987, 634–35.

31. The identity of the involved streams should be made clear. Thus one should speak of the synthesis between theories A and B. In this respect the neoclassical synthesis appellation is wanting.

their conception expresses a Keynesian viewpoint, which "classicists" have no reason to endorse. The classical model has as much to say about the short period as does the Keynesian—actually, it has a rival theory to propose about it. Therefore, classicists should have refused the territorial partition that Keynesians were proposing.[32] In short, the so-called neo-classical synthesis was a metatheoretical compromise between two approaches that did not want to enter into an open intellectual fight rather than a synthesis in the strict sense of the term.

3.5 Monetarism

Monetarism is associated with the work of Milton Friedman and his criticism of Keynesian activist policy. At a certain juncture, it was believed that monetarism could become a new paradigm, a rival to the Keynesian.[33] At present, a different view prevails. For example, Woodford (1999, 18) thinks that monetarism has won the day in bringing monetary policy and expectations to the forefront, yet he considers that, from a methodological viewpoint, it has been absorbed within the Keynesian paradigm. Likewise, Brian Snowdon and Howard Vane (1996, 386) write that "monetarist influences were absorbed *within* the existing framework leading to a Keynesian-monetarist synthesis." Finally, R. Lipsey (2000, 68) views the difference between monetarists and Keynesian as being mainly rhetorical.

Although making this point would require an article on its own, Friedman's contribution should not be viewed as a rejection of Keynes's methodology. Let me just evoke three elements of justification. First, Keynes and Friedman shared the same style of theorizing and a common belonging to the Marshallian connection.[34] Friedman praised Keynes for being "a true Marshallian in method" and for adopting the Marshallian instead of the Walrasian framework (Gordon 1974, 18).[35] Second, when asked

32. The point that it is logically inconsistent to be a "Keynesian" in the short period and a "new classicist" in the long period was made by Lucas in his *Tobin and Monetarism* review article (1981).

33. Cf. Johnson 1971.

34. On this, see Hirsch and De Marchi 1990, chap. 9; Dostaler 1998; and Hammond 1992.

35. The following excerpt from his "Marshallian Demand Curve" illustrates: "Of course, it would be an overstatement to characterise all modern economic theory as 'Walrasian' in this sense. For example, Keynes' theory of employment, whatever its merits or demerits on other grounds, is Marshallian in method. It is a general equilibrium theory containing important empirical content and constructed to facilitate meaningful predictions" (Friedman [1949] 1953, 92).

to put his claim in a broader theoretical perspective, Friedman chose the IS-LM model. Third, as claimed in De Vroey 2001, Friedman's conception of expectation in his expectations-augmented Phillips curve model must be characterized as Marshallian rather than as Walrasian.

The distinction between Keynesianism as a theoretical apparatus and Keynesianism as a defense of policy activism must come into play at this juncture. Friedman's aim was to reverse Keynesian policy conclusions. Yet he did not feel it necessary to overthrow the Keynesian theoretical apparatus, contrary to what Lucas and Sargent ([1978] 1994) had in mind ten years later. In short, Friedman should be considered as Keynesian from the methodological viewpoint and as anti-Keynesian from the policy viewpoint. In Blinder's ([1988] 1997, 112–13) words:

> The long and to some extent continuing battle between Keynesians and monetarists, you will note, has been primarily fought over the *normative issues*. . . . Thus, by my definition, most monetarists are positive Keynesians, but not normative Keynesians. . . . The briefer, but more intense, debate between Keynesians and new classicals had, by contrast, been fought primarily over the tenets of positive Keynesianism.

Above, I have argued that what was called the neoclassical synthesis should not be considered a real synthesis. In contrast, it can be claimed that such an integration has taken place for what concerns the relationship between monetarism and the IS-LM model.[36] No deep conceptual opposition divides the IS-LM framework and monetarism. The irony of this state of affairs, however, should not go unnoticed. On the one hand, the reconciliation between Keynesians and monetarists had to wait for the emergence of a common foe, the new classical paradigm. On the other, its counterpart has been a split between "old" and "new" Chicago, the former being Marshallian, the latter Walrasian.[37] In this light, the

---

36. The well-known Laidler-Tobin debate in the *Economic Journal* (Laidler 1981; Tobin 1981) illustrates this.

37. Snowdon and Vane's interviews of Friedman and Lucas are enlightening in this respect. "Question [to Lucas]: *You acknowledge that Friedman has had a great influence on you, yet his methodological approach is completely different [from] your own approach to macroeconomics. Why did his methodological approach not appeal to you?* Answer: I like mathematics and general equilibrium theory. Friedman didn't. . . . Question: *His methodological approach seems more in keeping with Keynes and Marshall.* Answer: He describes himself as Marshallian, although I don't know quite what it means. Whatever it is, it's not what I think of myself" (1998, 132). "Question [to Friedman]: *Kevin Hoover has drawn a methodological distinction between your work as Marshallian and that of Robert Lucas as Walrasian. Is that distinction*

terminology that was used at the time, separating "Monetarism I" (à la Friedman) from "Monetarism II" (à la Lucas), reveals itself as inappropriate. The use of the same substantive suggests that these two models belong to a same program. If my interpretation is accepted, the contrary is true, Friedman's work belonging to the Marshallian approach while Lucas's is Walrasian.

3.6 The Unnoticed Emergence of Marshallian General Equilibrium Theory

Has the Marshallian general equilibrium line ever been pursued? The quick answer to this question is "No." Evidently, no well-established Marshallian general equilibrium theory has seen the day. Yet this should not be the last word. First of all, attention should be given to programs that exist only in an inchoate way. The first name to be mentioned here is that of Keynes. He had a reason for making the step of studying the economy as a whole that Marshall did not have, that is, his interest in mass unemployment and the insight that, although the problem manifested itself in the labor market, its origin was to be looked for in other parts of the economy. Such an insight required studying the interdependency across apparently unrelated markets (the labor market and the money market) and thus engaging in general equilibrium analysis. Therefore the *General Theory* (1936) can be viewed as an attempt to build a Marshallian general equilibrium theory. Other authors who set forth the task of building a Marshallian general equilibrium theory are Clower and Leijonhufvud ([1975] 1984). They had in mind a radically different way of studying the coordination of economic activities, abandoning the study of the logical existence of equilibrium to concentrate on economic processes and institutions. They also suggested abandoning optimizing behavior. Yet, for all its appeal, Clower and Leijonhufvud's program has had trouble taking off.[38]

Moreover and somewhat oddly, we must consider the possibility that Marshallian general equilibrium theory exists, yet only in disguise. What

---

valid? Answer: There is a great deal to that. On the whole I believe that is probably true. I have always distinguished between the Marshallian approach and the Walrasian approach. I have always been personally a Marshallian" (1997, 202).

38. Their program recently received a new impulse in the works of a group of economists centered on David Colander (1996). Oddly enough, these authors call their approach "post-Walrasian," while in terms of methods it is poles apart from Walras. "Neo-Marshallian" would have been a better brand, reference being then made to "Marshall the evolutionist."

needs to be envisaged is that models, which are presented as amending the canonical Walrasian model, are in fact built on a radically different trade technology. This might occur with neither their builders nor their users being aware of it, because of their focus on problems of logical existence of equilibrium and their neglect of the trade technology dimension. I have in mind here imperfect competition general equilibrium models.[39]

Authors developing such models have rightly noted that the equilibriums they obtain are non-Walrasian, differing from the equilibriums that would be arrived at if perfect competition had been prevailing. However, the question to be raised is that of the trade technology on which their models are based. Is it Walrasian—one can get a non-Walrasian equilibrium outcome within a Walrasian trade technology, to wit Drèze 1975—or non-Walrasian in the radical sense, pointed out above in section 1.1, of a trade technology radically distinct from the Walrasian? Unfortunately, imperfect competition theorists have hardly reflected on this issue.

The Walrasian perfect competition model has served as the benchmark for several types of developments, the latter proceeding usually through the introduction of imperfections. Missing markets, externalities, information imperfections, price rigidities are all lines that have been taken. All of them have proven compatible with the auctioneer trade technology. Would imperfect competition then be just another such departure? No! All imperfections cannot be put on the same footing. My above remark on the working of an auctioneer economy, stating that Walrasian models necessarily are perfectly competitive models, points to the contrary. Now, if general equilibrium models exist that cannot be considered as belonging to the Walrasian approach, this means that another way of doing general equilibrium is possible. Hence my claim that imperfectly competitive general equilibrium models belong to the Marshallian rather than to the Walrasian approach. They are based on the Marshallian representation of the working of the economy. Take the models in Hart 1979, [1982] 1991, Blanchard and Kyotaki [1987] 1991, and Benassy 2002 and look at them against the grid of my opposition between the two types of trade technology. They all feature the Marshallian traits instead of the Walrasian ones. In short, while most models that are called non-Walrasian should better be called "quasi-Walrasian," imperfect competition models are really non-Walrasian.

39. Pioneering works in this line were Negishi 1961 and Gabszewicz and Vial 1972. Cf. De Vroey 2003.

As soon as it is accepted that trade technology matters, the view that
Walrasian perfect competition theory is the base camp for imperfectly
competitive general equilibrium models must be abandoned.[40] Admittedly, it looks odd to claim that these models are a departure from the
Marshallian perfectly competitive general equilibrium model if the latter
is nonexisting. The way out is to consider that the builders of these models have constructed a Marshallian perfectly competitive general equilibrium result inadvertently. It is to be found in those passages of their papers where they substitute the assumption of a great number of agents to
that of a monopolistic or of oligopolistic agents. Then, one falls back on
a Walrasian equilibrium, that is, the array of prices and quantities that the
auctioneer would have made emerge. However, here these equilibrium
values result from the Marshallian trade technology rather than from the
Walrasian.

3.7 The New Classical Revolution

Like everybody, I consider that Lucas's work, especially his "Expectations and the Neutrality of Money" paper ([1972] 1981), caused a radical
breach. Interpreting it as having started a Kuhnian scientific revolution
seems to be no exaggeration. His motivation for writing this article was
to strengthen Friedman's policy ineffectiveness claim by giving it stronger microfoundations and casting it in an explicit general equilibrium
framework. Yet the end result was a methodological revolution blazing
the trail for real business cycle theory and dynamic macroeconomics
(Sargent 1996). The shift from IS-LM to real business cycle models is
twofold: a move from a static to a dynamic approach, on the one hand,
and a shift from the Marshallian to the Walrasian side of the tree, on the
other.

Some commentators draw a divide between new classical and real
business cycle models. I consider them as representing two stages in
the development of the same paradigm, centered on stochastic dynamic
equilibrium models. However, they differ in that Lucas's model is a para-
ble with no claim to direct empirical confrontation, while real business
cycle models claim to explain the real world.[41]

40. Cf. Pignol 1999.

41. In Woodford's terms, "The real business cycle literature offered a new methodology,
both for theoretical analysis and for empirical testing. . . . It showed how such models [of the
Lucas type] could be made *quantitative*, emphasising the assignment of realistic numerical

The novelty of the new classical approach (defined broadly to encompass both Lucas's initial models and real business cycle models) can be accounted for in several ways. Mine is as follows. Its distinctive feature lies in its having extended the scope of relevance of value theory (i.e., the theory of equilibrium price) to a domain that before was believed to be beyond its grasp.[42] Thereby it bridged a gulf that had marked economic theory for more than a century, its split in two distinct branches, value or price theory, on the one hand, and business cycle theory, on the other. Evolving at a high level of abstraction and concentrating on the logical existence of equilibrium, the first branch was based on trade technology assumptions that necessarily led to market clearing. The second consisted of qualitative, descriptive accounts of the evolution of economies over time with only vague references to equilibrium, what allowed it to integrate phenomena such as market rationing that had no room in value theory.[43] Underlying this evolution is the abandonment of what was the initial motivation of macroeconomics, that is, bringing to the fore some malfunctioning of the market system—after all, it was born in the aftermath of the Great Depression.[44]

Real business cycle theoreticians insist that their models belong to the Walrasian general equilibrium approach. This is not to be denied. Yet a sharp contrast exists between Walrasian models as they were existing before the rise of the new classical paradigm, pertaining to an economy

---

parameters values and the computation of numerical solutions to the equations of the model, rather than being content with merely qualitative conclusions derived from more general assumptions. The 'equilibrium business cycle models' of Lucas had really only been parables; they could not be regarded as literal descriptions of an economy, even allowing for the sort of idealisation that all models of reality have. . . . Real business cycle models are instead quantitative models, that are intended to be taken seriously as literal depictions of the economy, even if many details are abstracted from. The literature emphasises the numerical predictions of the models, when parameter values are assigned on the basis of measurement of the relevant aspects of an actual economy" (Woodford 1999, 25–26).

42. Critics might say it has brought the imperialism of value theory to a new height.

43. A tempting way of putting the issue is to state that price theory was concerned with equilibrium and business cycle theory with disequilibrium. Yet this is misleading insofar as equilibrium and disequilibrium are part and parcel. The truth is rather that these linked categories played only a marginal role in business cycle theory. The latter, it was believed, was too complex a field of inquiry to be accounted for with the tools of price theory.

44. As aptly perceived by Hahn and Solow (1995, 2–3), "The irony is that macroeconomics began as the study of large-scale economic pathologies: prolonged depressions, mass unemployment, persistent inflation, etc. This focus was not invented by Keynes (although the Depression of the 1930s did not pass without notice). After all, most of Gottfried Haberler's classic *Prosperity and Depression* is about ideas that were in circulation before the *General Theory*. Now, at last, macroeconomic theory has as its central conception a model in which such pathologies are, strictly speaking, unmentionable. There is no legal way to talk about them."

comprising a large number of agents and goods, and the new models based on the assumption of a representative agent and the existence of a single good traded over time. This evolution should be interpreted as a return to square one of Walras's construction dealing with the two-good exchange economy.[45] But then, this is exactly what macroeconomics is all about, to work with simple rather than complex models. Hence my claim that real business cycle models mark the start of Walrasian macroeconomics or, more precisely, its coming to predominance, in view of the existence of earlier attempts.

This being stated, it may be wondered whether Walras himself would have endorsed the move made by real business cycle theorists. When he started to write his *Elements of Pure Economics* (which appeared in English in 1954), his intention was to construct a theory able to account for the working of the competitive process in decentralized economies. However, he gradually became aware of a conflict between the requirements of demonstrating the logical existence of equilibrium states and any realistic account of the competitive process. Facing such a dilemma, Walras opted for rigor over realism and consequently refrained from claiming any straightforward empirical relevance for his model, thereby forgoing his initial ambition.[46] The methodological implication was far-reaching. In particular, Walras came to believe that the validity of his theory was not a matter of empirical relevance. The following extract, drawn from an unpublished note written by Walras and criticizing Pareto, is enlightening: "Pareto believes that the aim of science is to ever come closer to reality through successive approximations. I, for one, believe that the eventual aim of science is to bring reality close to a certain ideal. This is why I formulate this ideal" (Walras 2000, 567; my translation).[47]

Subsequent neo-Walrasian economists have for all intents and purposes followed suit.[48] Authors such as Kenneth Arrow, Gérard Debreu,

45. For a more detailed analysis, see De Vroey 2002.

46. As William Jaffé ([1980] 1983, 345) put it, "The *Elements* was intended to be and is, in all but the name, a realistic utopia, i.e. a delineation of a state of affairs nowhere to be found in the actual world, independent of time and place, ideally perfect in certain respects, and yet composed of realistic psychological and material ingredients."

47. Walras's note is undated. Pascal Bridel's conjecture is it was written between 1896 and 1906. A similar testimony is Walras's annotation on page 17 of his copy of Cournot's *Principes de la théorie de la richesse*, held at the Centre Walras-Pareto of the Université de Lausanne, where he wrote that "pure theory requires no confirmation from reality" ("la théorie pure n'attend aucune confirmation de la réalité"), quoted in Baranzani and Bridel 2003.

48. This assertion is true only for mathematical Walrasian economists. Other economists who also claim a Walrasian affiliation, for example neo-Austrians or Donald Walker (1996), pull Walras toward the stationary equilibrium perspective.

and Frank Hahn have repeatedly insisted that neo-Walrasian general equilibrium theory is an abstract construction, the strength of which lies in the ability to posit issues rigorously. Its main interest with respect to reality, they argue, it to provide a negative benchmark. In short, they admit to no bridge between their theoretical construct and real-world market economies.

Real business cycle models mark a radical change in this respect by adopting Friedman's methodological standpoint according to which models ought to be evaluated in terms of their predictive capacity.[49] The validity of their models, they argue, ought to be assessed by gauging their capacity to mimic real-world time series.

The oddity, however, is that the gist of Friedman's criticism of Walrasian economics was that one could not jointly take into account the total set of interdependency across agents and goods and have a tractable model allowing for predictions. The preference of many economists for the Marshallian approach was probably based on their readiness to trade rigorous general equilibrium perspective for empirical measurability. In other words, Friedman and lucid Walrasian authors at least concurred on one point, that one should not turn to the general equilibrium methodology whenever aiming to explain concrete phenomena. Why is it that what was true for the earlier Walrasian models—that higher rigor had to be paid for by an admission to a lack of empirical relevance of the model—is no longer so for even more rudimentary Walrasian models? Now, outwardly, there is no longer a price to be paid for engaging in Walrasian theory: one can have the cake (Walrasian rigor) and eat it (engaging empirical work) at the same time.

3.8 A New Neoclassical Synthesis?

Initially, dynamic macroeconomics was entirely non-Keynesian. This was true for both the conceptual framework and the policy cause. Not surprisingly, the new classical attack on Keynesian economics stirred up a revival of Keynesian thought, known as "new Keynesian economics."

49. Although Lucas's neutrality of money model still belongs to the "old" Walrasian tradition, since it has no empirical counterpart, Lucas nonetheless endorses the real business cycle viewpoint. In their interview, Snowdon and Vane (1998, 132) asked him whether he "would agree that the appropriate criterion for establishing the fruitfulness of a theory is the degree of empirical corroboration attained by its predictions?" Lucas's answer was, "Something like that. Yes," and to the next question—"You are Friedmanite on that issue of methodology?"—his answer was affirmative.

This label does not cover a unified theoretical program. For example, efficiency wage models are partial equilibrium models (or at least they started this way), coordination failure models can be Walrasian yet are not necessarily so, imperfect competition models are Marshallian, etc. Moreover, the "new Keynesian" label is ambiguous in that the Keynesian modifier should be understood exclusively in reference to the policy cause dimension. It is inappropriate as far the theoretical framework is concerned.

Without commenting on new Keynesian models any further, I want now to address the issue of the new synthesis. The particular branch of new Keynesian models of concern here is imperfectly competitive general equilibrium models, which I have characterized as unwittingly belonging to the Marshallian research program. Their hallmark is to combine imperfect competition with price and wage stickiness in order to refute the Friedman-Lucas ineffectiveness of monetary policy claim.[50] The idea of a merger between these models and real business cycle models has been wholeheartedly endorsed by new Keynesians, as the following excerpt from Gregory Mankiw's interview by Snowdon and Vane (1994, 340) illustrates:

> I'm delighted that some of the people who previously worked closely with the real business cycle models are now trying to incorporate monetary effects in those models. That provides a hope that somewhere down the line the new Keynesian models and the real business cycle models are going to merge to some grand synthesis that incorporates the strengths of both approaches.

Many new Keynesians share Mankiw's viewpoint. Olivier Blanchard is among them. Rejecting any view of the evolution of macroeconomics in terms of scientific revolution, he claims that the passage from the IS-LM model to real business cycle models must be viewed as a smooth evolutionary process. "On the surface, the history of macroeconomics appears as a series of battles, revolutions and counterrevolutions. . . . But this would be the wrong image. The right one is of a surprisingly steady accumulation of knowledge" (Blanchard 2000, 2). To Blanchard, the clash between new Keynesians and new classicists in the 1970s was short-lived and based on a misunderstanding (39).

In the early 1980s, macroeconomic research seemed divided in two camps, with sharp ideological and methodological differences. Real

50. See, for example, Blanchard and Kiyotaki [1987] 1991.

business cycle theorists argued that fluctuations could be explained in a fully competitive model, with technological shocks. New Keynesians argued that imperfections were of the essence. Real business cycle theorists used fully specified general equilibrium models based on equilibrium and optimization under uncertainty. New Keynesians used small models, capturing what they saw as the essence of their arguments, without the paraphernalia of fully specified models.

Today, the ideological divide is gone. Not in the sense that underlying ideological differences are gone, but in the sense that trying to organise recent contributions along ideological lines would not work well. As I argued earlier, most macroeconomic research today focuses on the macroeconomic implications of some imperfection or another. At the frontier of macroeconomic research, the field is surprisingly a-ideological.[51]

Interestingly enough, some economists coming from what was earlier viewed as the opposite camp hold the same viewpoint. In particular, Goodfriend and King (1997, 231) claim that in the last ten years "macroeconomics is moving toward a New Neoclassical Synthesis." Like Blanchard and Woodford, they praise the real business cycle program for its microfoundations and its allowing a comparison of alternative policies on the basis of measures of utility benefits or costs. Like them, Goodfriend and King argue that it must be enriched with the considerations of imperfections, such as imperfect competition and sticky prices, the very purpose of new neoclassical synthesis models. Under this heading, they put models that "range from the flexible, small models of academic research to the new rational-expectations policy model of the Federal Reserve Board" (232). These models, which Goodfriend and King view as close in spirit to the neoclassical synthesis that prevailed in the 1960s, combine Keynesian elements—the above-mentioned imperfections—and real business cycle elements—intertemporal optimization, rational expectations, and their integration in the stochastic dynamic model (232). These two components, they claim, are compatible because of their shared reliance on microeconomics (256). As far as policy is concerned, they concur with new Keynesians in believing that "aggregate

---

51. Contrary to Blanchard, Woodford (1999, 29) finds it useful to account for the history of macroeconomics in terms of a succession of revolutions and counterrevolutions. However, he shares Blanchard's and Mankiw's opinion that the future of macroeconomics lies in incorporating Keynesian features into real business cycle models.

demand must be managed by monetary policy in order to deliver efficient macroeconomics outcomes" (255–56).[52]

Has the so-called new synthesis the attributes of a real theoretical merger? At the present juncture, this remains an open question. A positive answer would be appealing because it would reveal that the reigns of the IS-LM paradigm and that of the new classical paradigm have witnessed a similar evolution. On the score of the theoretical dimension, a two-step evolution would have taken place, where two frameworks that used to be considered rivals turn out to be compatible. On the score of the policy cause dimension, a shift would have occurred from a situation where the policy cause and the theoretical framework seemed part and parcel of a more open state of affairs in which the same conceptual framework proves able to justify either the Keynesian or the laissez-faire policy cause.

It is not to be denied that most macroeconomists have rallied around the real business cycle methodology. New Keynesian authors have admitted that macroeconomics should study the dynamic evolution of the economy in a stochastic context, rational expectations and intertemporal substitution being furthermore considered sine qua non ingredients of the analysis. Likewise, most of these authors have abandoned the aim of demonstrating involuntary unemployment. Nonetheless, two arguments point against the achievement of the proposed synthesis. First, will the quid pro quo that the new Keynesians are offering to new classicists— the rallying to their methodology against the introduction of the assumptions of imperfect competition and sticky prices—be accepted? In other words, would prominent real business cycle theoreticians—say Lucas or Edward Prescott—be ready to sign any manifesto as to a merger between the two approaches along the terms proposed by Goodfriend and King? I, for one, doubt it. "Chicago" (and for that matter, Minnesota) may well have shifted from Marshall to Walras, yet, as well documented by Robert Leeson (2000), its resistance to imperfect competition is deep-rooted. Second, if my above analysis is accepted, the perfectly competitive and imperfectly competitive models must be viewed as rooted in incompatible trade technologies, the Walrasian and the Marshallian. Therefore a merger between them is hard to envisage. The picture that then emerges is rather one of two rival macroeconomic paradigms, a Marshallian (i.e., imperfect competition) and a Walrasian (i.e., perfect competition), existing side by side.

52. Jean-Olivier Hairault (1999, 616) makes the same point.

4. Conclusion

The starting point of this essay is my insight that any valid critical analysis of economic theories must take into account the trade technology assumptions on which they are based. Interesting conclusions ensue. First, it turns out that the Marshallian and the Walrasian approaches ought to be viewed as alternative research programs because they rest on radically different trade technologies. Second, the Marshall-Walras divide provides an interesting angle of attack for reflecting on the history of macroeconomics, allowing for an original interpretation of its recent unfolding. To wit, the new classical revolution, that is, the replacement of the IS-LM paradigm by stochastic dynamic models, can be interpreted as a shift from Marshallian to Walrasian macroeconomics. Finally, against the background of the Marshall-Walras divide, the possibility of constructing a real theoretical synthesis between new Keynesians and new classicists looks doubtful.

References

Backhouse, R., and A. Salanti, eds. 2000. *Macroeconomics and the Real World*. Vol. 2 of *Keynesian Economics, Unemployment, and Policy*. Oxford: Oxford University Press.

Baranzini, R., and P. Bridel. 2003. Echange et utilité: Walras, versus Pareto. Paper presented at the Communication au X Colloque de l'Association Charles Gide pour l'Étude de la Pensée Économique, Grenoble, September.

Barro, R., and H. Grossman. 1971. A General Disequilibrium Model of Income and Employment. *American Economic Review* 61:82–93.

———. 1976. *Money, Employment, and Inflation*. Cambridge: Cambridge University Press.

Benassy, J.-P. 2002. *The Macroeconomics of Imperfect Competition and Nonclearing Markets*. Cambridge: MIT Press.

Blanchard, O. 1987. Neoclassical Synthesis. In vol. 3 of *The New Palgrave: A Dictionary of Economics*, edited by John Eatwell, Murray Milgate, and Peter Newman. London: Macmillan.

———. 2000. What Do We Know about Macroeconomics That Fisher and Wicksell Did Not? NBER Working Paper no. 7550.

Blanchard, O., and N. Kiyotaki. [1987] 1991. Monopolistic Competition and the Effects of Aggregate Demand. In *Imperfect Competition and Sticky Prices*, vol. 1 of *New Keynesian Economics*, edited by G. Mankiw and D. Romer. Cambridge: MIT Press.

Blinder, A. [1988] 1997. The Fall and Rise of Keynesian Economics. In *A Macroeconomics Reader*, edited by B. Snowdon and H. Vane. London: Routledge.

Bridel, P. 1997. *Money and General Equilibrium Theory: From Walras to Pareto (1870–1923)*. Cheltenham, U.K.: Edward Elgar.

———. 2002. Patinkin, Walras, and the "Money-in-the-Utility-Function" Tradition. *European Journal of the History of Economic Thought* 9:268–92.

Clower, R., and A. Leijonhufvud. [1975] 1984. The Coordination of Economic Activities: A Keynesian Perspective. In *Money and Markets: Essays by Robert Clower*, edited by D. Walker. Cambridge: Cambridge University Press.

Colander, D., ed. 1996. *Beyond Micro-Foundations: Post-Walrasian Macroeconomics*. Cambridge: Cambridge University Press.

Danthine, J.-P. 1997. In Search of a Successor to IS-LM. *Oxford Review of Economic Policy* 13:135–44.

De Vroey, M. 1998. Is the Tâtonnement Hypothesis a Good Caricature of Market Forces? *Journal of Economic Methodology* 5:201–21.

———. 1999. Equilibrium and Disequilibrium in Economic Theory: A Confrontation of the Classical, Marshallian, and Walras-Hicksian Conceptions. *Economics and Philosophy* 15:161–85.

———. 2000. IS-LM à la Hicks versus IS-LM à la Modigliani. *HOPE* 32:293–316.

———. 2001. Friedman and Lucas on the Phillips Curve: From a Disequilibrium to an Equilibrium Approach. *Eastern Economic Journal* 27:127–48.

———. 2002. Equilibrium and Disequilibrium in Walrasian and Neo-Walrasian Economics. *Journal of the History of Economic Thought* 24:405–26.

———. 2003. Perfect Information à la Marshall versus Perfect Information à la Walras. *Journal of Economic Methodology* 10:465–92.

Dimand, R. W. 1990. Alfred Marshall and the General Equilibrium Theory of Value and Distribution: An Examination of Notes XIV and XXI. In *Alfred Marshall in Retrospect*, edited by R. McWilliams Tullberg. Aldershot, U.K.: Edward Elgar.

Dostaler, Gilles. 1998. Friedman and Keynes: Divergences and Convergences. *European Journal of the History of Economic Thought* 5:317–47.

Drèze, J. 1975. Existence of Equilibrium under Price Rigidities. *International Economic Review* 16:301–20.

———. 2001. Advances and Challenges in Macroeconomics. In *Advances in Macroeconomic Theory*, edited by J. Drèze. IEA conference volume, no. 133. Houndmills, U.K.: Palgrave, in association with the International Economic Association.

Farmer, R. 1993. *The Macroeconomics of Self-Fulfilling Prophecies*. Cambridge: MIT Press.

Friedman, M. [1949] 1953. The Marshallian Demand Curve. In *Essays in Positive Economics*. Chicago: University of Chicago Press.

———. 1968. The Role of Monetary Policy. *American Economic Review* 58:1–17.

Frisch, R. 1933. Propagation Problems and Impulse Problems in Dynamic Economics. In *Economic Essays in Honour of Gustav Cassel*. London: Allen and Unwin.

Gabszewicz, J., and J. P. Vial. 1972. Oligopoly "à la Cournot" in a General Equilibrium Analysis. *Journal of Economic Theory* 4:381–400.

Goodfriend, M., and R. King. 1997. The New Neoclassical Synthesis and the Role of Monetary Policy. In *NBER Macroeconomics Annual 1997*, edited by B. Bernanke and J. Rotenberg. Cambridge: MIT Press.

Gordon, R. J., ed. 1974. *Milton Friedman's Monetary Framework: A Debate with His Critics*. Chicago: University of Chicago Press.

Hahn, F. [1965] 1969. On Some Problems of Proving the Existence of Equilibrium in a Monetary Economy. In *Monetary Theory*, edited by R. Clower. London: Penguin Education.

Hahn, F., and R. Solow. 1995. *A Critical Essay on Modern Macroeconomic Theory*. Oxford: Basil Blackwell.

Hairault, J.-O. 1999. Vers une nouvelle synthèse néoclassique? *Revue d'économie politique* 109:613–69.

Hammond, J. D. 1992. An Interview with Milton Friedman on Methodology. In vol. 1 of *The Philosophy and Methodology of Economics*, edited by B. Caldwell. Aldershot, U.K.: Edward Elgar.

Hart, O. 1979. Monopolistic Competition in a Large Economy with Differentiated Commodities. *Review of Economic Studies* 46:1–30.

———. [1982] 1991. A Model of Imperfect Competition with Keynesian Features. In *Imperfect Competition and Sticky Prices*, vol. 1 of *New Keynesian Economics*, edited by G. Mankiw and D. Romer. Cambridge: MIT Press.

Hayek, F. [1937] 1948. Economics and Knowledge. In *Individualism and Economic Order*. Chicago: University of Chicago Press.

Hicks, J. [1937] 1967. Mr. Keynes and the "Classics." In *Critical Essays in Monetary Theory*. Oxford: Clarendon.

———. [1934] 1983. Léon Walras. In vol. 3 of *Classics and Moderns: Collected Essays on Economic Theory*. Oxford: Basil Blackwell.

———. [1939] 1946. *Value and Capital*. 2nd ed. Oxford: Clarendon.

———. 1965. *Capital and Growth*. Oxford: Clarendon.

———. [1979] 1983. The Formation of an Economist. In vol. 3 of *Classics and Moderns: Collected Essays on Economic Theory*. Oxford: Basil Blackwell.

Hirsch, A., and N. De Marchi. 1990. *Milton Friedman: Economics in Theory and Practice*. New York: Harvester Wheatsheaf.

Hoover, K. [1984] 1990. Two Types of Monetarism. In vol. 3 of *Milton Friedman: Critical Assessments*, edited by J. Cunningham Wood and R. N. Woods. London: Routledge.

Howitt, P. 1987. Macroeconomics: Relations with Microeconomics. In vol. 3 of *The New Palgrave: A Dictionary of Economics*, edited by John Eatwell, Murray Milgate, and Peter Newman. London: Macmillan.

Jaffé, W. 1954. Translator's Notes. In Walras 1954.

———. [1980] 1983. Walras's Economics as Others See It. In *William Jaffé's Essays on Walras*, edited by D. Walker. Cambridge: Cambridge University Press.

Johnson, H. 1971. The Keynesian Revolution and the Monetarist Counterrevolution. *American Economic Review* 61:91–106.

Keynes, J. M. 1936. *The General Theory of Employment, Interest, and Money.* London: Macmillan.

King, R. 1993. Will the New Keynesian Macroeconomics Resurrect the IS-LM Model? *Journal of Economic Perspectives* 7:67–82.

Laidler, D. 1981. Monetarism: An Interpretation and an Assessment. *Economic Journal* 91:1–28.

——— . 1999. *Fabricating the Keynesian Revolution: Studies of the Inter-war Literature on Money, the Cycle, and Unemployment.* Cambridge: Cambridge University Press.

Leeson, R. 2000. *The Eclipse of Keynesianism: The Political Economy of the Chicago Counter-revolution.* Basingstoke, Hampshire, U.K.: Palgrave.

Leijonhufvud, A. 1994. Hicks, Keynes, and Marshall. In *The Legacy of Hicks: His Contributions to Economic Analysis*, edited by H. Hageman and O. Hamadou. London: Routledge.

——— . 1999. Mr. Keynes and the Moderns. In *The Impact of Keynes on Economics in the Twentieth Century*, edited by L. Pasinetti and B. Schefold. Cheltenham, U.K.: Edward Elgar.

Leontief, W. 1998. An Interview with Wassily Leontief by Duncan Foley. *Macroeconomic Dynamics* 2:116–40.

Lipsey, R. 2000. IS-LM, Keynesianism, and the New Classicism. In Backhouse and Salanti 2000.

Lucas, R. E., Jr. [1972] 1981. Expectations and the Neutrality of Money. In *Studies in Business Cycle Theory*. Cambridge: MIT Press.

——— . 1981. Tobin and Monetarism: A Review Article. *Journal of Economic Literature* 19:558–67.

——— . 1986. Adaptative Behavior and Economic Theory. *Journal of Business* 59:S401–S426.

Lucas, R. E., Jr., and T. Sargent. [1978] 1994. After Keynesian Macroeconomics. In *The Rational Expectations Revolution: Readings from the Front Line*, edited by R. Miller Preston. Cambridge: MIT Press.

Marshall, A. 1920. *Principles of Economics.* 8th ed. London: Macmillan.

Modigliani, F. 1944. Liquidity Preference and the Theory of Interest and Money. *Econometrica* 12:45–88.

Negishi, T. [1961] 1994. Monopolistic Competition and General Equilibrium. In *General Equilibrium Theory*, vol. 1 of *The Collected Essays of Takashi Negishi*. London: Edward Elgar.

Patinkin, D. [1956] 1965. *Money, Interest, and Prices.* 2nd ed. New York: Harper and Row.

——— . 1987. Keynes, John Maynard. In vol. 3 of *The New Palgrave: A Dictionary of Economics*, edited by John Eatwell, Murray Milgate, and Peter Newman. London: Macmillan.

Pignol, C. 1999. Le statut des modèles de concurrence imparfaite: De l'amendement des hypothèses de la concurrence parfaite à la représentation d'agents price-makers. PhD diss., Université Paris-I.

Samuelson, P. 1955. *Economics: An Introductory Analysis*. 5th ed. New York: McGraw-Hill.

Sargent, T. J. 1996. Expectations and the Nonneutrality of Money. *Journal of Monetary Economics* 37:535–48.

Snowdon, B., and H. Vane. 1994. *A Modern Guide to Macroeconomics: An Introduction to Competing Schools of Thought*. Aldershot, U.K.: Edward Elgar.

————. 1996. The Development of Modern Macroeconomics: Reflections in the Light of Johnson's Analysis after Twenty-Five Years. *Journal of Macroeconomics* 18:381–401.

————. 1997. Modern Macroeconomics and Its Evolution from a Monetarist Perspective: An Interview with Professor Milton Friedman. *Journal of Economic Studies* 24:192–221.

————. 1998. Transforming Macroeconomics: An Interview with Robert E. Lucas Jr. *Journal of Economic Methodology* 5:115–45.

Tobin, J. 1981. The Monetarist Counter-revolution Today—An Appraisal. *Economic Journal* 91:29–42.

Vercelli, A. 2000. The Evolution of IS-LM Models: Empirical Evidence and Theoretical Presuppositions. In Backhouse and Salanti 2000.

Walker, D. 1996. *Walras's Market Models*. Cambridge: Cambridge University Press.

Walras, L. 1954. *Elements of Pure Economics*. Translated by W. Jaffé. London: Allen and Unwin.

————. 2000. *Oeuvres diverses*. Vol. 13 of *Auguste et Léon Walras: Oeuvres économiques complètes*, edited by P. Dockès, C. Mouchot, and J-P. Potier. Paris: Economica.

Woodford, M. 1999. Revolution and Evolution in Twentieth-Century Macroeconomics. In *Frontiers of the Mind in the Twenty-First Century*, edited by P. Gifford. Cambridge: Harvard University Press.

Young, W., and B. Z. Zilberfarb, eds. 2000. *IS-LM and Modern Macroeconomics*. Boston: Kluwer Academic Publishers.

The IS-LM Model and the Liquidity Trap Concept: From Hicks to Krugman

Mauro Boianovsky

> The General Theory of Employment is the Economics of Depression.
> —John Hicks, "Mr. Keynes and the 'Classics':
> A Suggested Interpretation" (1937)

> Depression economics is back.
> —Paul Krugman, *The Return of Depression Economics* (2000)

One main feature of John Hicks's 1937 "Mr. Keynes and the 'Classics'" is the identification of the assumption that there is a floor to the rate of interest on the left part of the LM curve as the central difference between John Maynard Keynes's 1936 *General Theory* and "classical" economics, a judgment that Hicks repeated on other occasions ([1939] 1946, 1950, 1957). The notion of a "liquidity trap"—a phrase coined by Dennis Robertson (1936, 1940), albeit in a different context, as discussed below—was conspicuous in macroeconomic textbooks of the 1950s and 1960s (see, e.g., Hansen 1953, Ackley 1961, and Bailey 1962), but it gradually receded into the background until it came to the fore again in the recent literature triggered by the Japanese depression and the experience of low inflation and low nominal interest rates in the United States and Europe in the late 1990s (see, e.g., McKinnon and Ohno 1997, chap. 5; Fuhrer and Madigan 1997; Krugman 1998, [1999] 2000; special

I would like to thank Craufurd Goodwin, Geoff Harcourt, Don Moggridge, Paul Samuelson, Hans-Michael Trautwein, and participants at the *HOPE* 2003 conference for helpful comments on an earlier version of this essay. I am also indebted to two anonymous referees for useful suggestions. Michel Rocha provided efficient research assistance. Financial support from CNPq (Brazilian Research Council) is gratefully acknowledged. A longer version of this essay is available from the author upon request.

issues of the *Journal of Money, Credit, and Banking*, November 2000, and of the *Journal of the Japanese and International Economies*, December 2000; Benhabib et al. 2002; Walsh 2003, chap. 10; Woodford 2003, chap. 2). The revival of interest in the notion of a liquidity trap as a constraint on the effectiveness of monetary policy is also visible in connection with references by modern textbooks to the Japanese depression (see, e.g., Gordon [1978] 2000, Froyen 2002, Gärtner 2003, Mankiw 2003, and Krugman and Obstfeld 2003).

Whereas the liquidity trap literature traditionally associated with Keynes 1936 and Hicks 1937 concerned the existence of a positive floor to the interest rate, a more recent approach investigates the possibility of a zero lower bound on interest rates. This is in part explained by the shift from Keynes's model—where the long-term interest rate is the relevant opportunity cost in money demand, and expectations about the future values of that long rate are assumed to be regressive or inelastic—to the formulation of money demand in terms of the short-term nominal interest rate, which affects the long rate through the expectations theory of the term structure of interest rates. However, it should be noted that the textbook IS-LM approach to the liquidity trap set off by Alvin Hansen (1949, 1953) is closer to Keynes's 1936 original exposition than to Hicks's 1937 reformulation, which is in some aspects similar to the modern discussion. As pointed out by Don Patinkin (1976, 113 n. 9), Hicks (1937) formulated the liquidity trap "in a notably less extreme form than that which later became the standard one of macroeconomic textbooks." Hicks based his formulation of the liquidity trap on the notion that the short-run nominal interest rate cannot be negative and that the long rate is formed by expectations about the future value of the short rate plus a risk premium. These ideas were fully developed in his 1939 classic *Value and Capital*, which Hicks was writing when he published the IS-LM article.

The purpose of the present essay is to examine how the development of the liquidity trap concept is associated with the interpretation of the IS-LM model in general and the LM curve in particular, with emphasis on the original formulation by Hicks and the new interpretation put forward by Paul Krugman and others. The 1937 article—and the liquidity trap concept in particular—is interpreted against the background of the notion of "elasticity of price expectations" developed in *Value and Capital*. Oskar Lange (1938) was the only author, besides Hicks, to stress the form of the LM curve as the dividing line between Keynes and the "classics," but in a form quite different from Hicks. The recent literature shares with Hicks ([1939] 1946) the view that under liquidity trap conditions the central bank loses its ability to control the price level. Furthermore, the modern optimizing approach brings into the picture the notion of expectations of economic policy (with its consequences for the interpretation of the liquidity trap idea and for the IS-LM model), which Hicks ([1936] 1982, [1939] 1946, 1969) mentioned only briefly.

1. Hicks on the Rate of Interest Minimum

Hicks himself pointed out the importance of *Value and Capital* for an understanding of the framework of the 1937 IS-LM article. In correspondence with Warren Young (1987, 98), Hicks recalled that "during those years (34–38 inclusive) my thought was mainly directed to the writing of *Value and Capital* (to be published in early '39); anything else was a side-line." The IS-LM article, together with Hicks [1936] 1982, "were, from my point of view, just applications of *Value and Capital* methods."

In part 3 of *Value and Capital* Hicks introduced the method of "temporary equilibrium" in order to discuss economic dynamics. Equilibrium is defined over a period of time when supply and demand in the various markets are adjusted to price expectations held at the start of the period. It was in that context that Hicks introduced the notion'of elasticity of price expectations to study the effect of actual prices on price expectations. Hicks ([1939] 1946, 205) defined the elasticity of a "person's expectations of the price of commodity X as the ratio of the proportional rise in expected future prices of X to the proportional rise in its current price." As long as elasticities of price expectations are zero, any change in current prices will bring about large substitution effects over time in markets for inputs and outputs, which will stabilize the economic system. But, if changes in current prices are expected to be permanent, there will be no opportunities left for substitution over time. As pointed out by Hicks ([1939] 1946, 251), the case of unit elasticities of expectations was at the time implicitly taken for granted by most economists, without realizing its implications for stability analysis.[1] In particular, if the expected future price level is given, an excess supply in the market for goods will cause a reduction in current prices and, by that, a fall in the

1. Knut Wicksell ([1898] 1936) advanced the association between instability and unit elasticity of price expectations. After Hicks, the assumption of unit elasticity of price expectations became widespread (see, e.g., Modigliani 1944, 45; Patinkin [1956] 1965, 61).

expected real rate of interest (since individuals expect a return to the previous price level), which will increase aggregate demand for goods and stabilize the price level. However, if elasticities of expectation are 1.0 (or higher), the expected future price level changes together with current prices, which precludes stabilization and leads to cumulative falling prices. Hicks claimed that "the proposition which we have thus established is perhaps the most important proposition in economic dynamics" (255).

Under the (provisional) assumption that nominal interest rates are given, downward instability of the price level in the case of unit elasticity of expectation can be only checked if money wages are rigid, as in Keynes's *General Theory* (until chap. 19) and in Hicks's IS-LM model. In that case, stability is achieved through unemployment and a contraction of output. However, changes in current prices (expected to be permanent) will affect the demand for money and therefore, for a given money supply, will bring about changes in the interest rate required to equilibrate the market for money. An increase of the interest rate is effective to check a rise in prices, but in the case of falling prices the interest rate mechanism may be unable to stabilize the economy because of the floor to the rate of interest. "In this case, the system does not merely suffer from imperfect stability; it is absolutely unstable. Adequate control over the money supply can always prevent prices rising indefinitely, but it cannot necessarily prevent them from falling indefinitely" (259).

Hicks's notion that the central bank cannot avoid falling prices once the interest rate hits its minimum level is based on his hypothesis that the short-term rate of interest is determined by transaction costs, that is, by the lack of general acceptability or imperfect "moneyness" of very short bills (166). Long rates are then determined by expectations about the future course of the short rate according to the theory of the term structure introduced in chapter 11 of *Value and Capital*. Hicks's theory of interest was developed as a reaction against Keynes's (1936, chap. 13) view that the current rate of interest is determined by risk and uncertainty about its future value. In a famous passage, Hicks ([1939] 1946, 164) pointed out that "to say that the rate of interest on perfectly safe securities is determined by nothing else but uncertainty of future interest rates seems to leave interest hanging by its own bootstraps." Hicks's solution is that while the current long rate depends on the expected short rates, the current short rate is not dependent on expectations but on the current supply and demand for money. Hicks's approach to the determination of the interest rate was followed by Keynesian economists such as Nicholas Kaldor (1939, 13–14) and Michal Kalecki ([1943] 1991, 138–39).[2] Hicks concluded that securities normally stand at a discount relative to money, since the storage costs associated with money are usually negligible ([1939] 1946, 167 n. 1; 1950, 142). It is as part of that framework that Hicks's explanation of the liquidity trap in the 1937 IS-LM article should be read. According to Hicks (1937, 154), the demonstration of the interest rate minimum is "so important that I shall venture to paraphrase the proof, setting it out in a rather different way from that adopted by Mr. Keynes."

> If the costs of holding money can be neglected, it will always be profitable to hold money rather than lend it out, if the rate of interest is not greater than zero. Consequently the rate of interest must always be positive. In an extreme case, the shortest short-term rate may perhaps be nearly zero. But if so, the long-term rate must lie above it, for the long rate has to allow for the risk that the short rate may rise during the currency of the loan, and it should be observed that the short rate can only rise, it cannot fall. This does not only mean that the long rate must be a sort of average of the probable short rates over its duration, and that this average must lie above the current short rate. There is also the more important risk to be considered, that the lender on long term may desire to have cash before the agreed date of repayment, and then, if the short rate has risen meanwhile, he may be involved in a substantial capital loss. It is this last risk which provides Mr. Keynes' "speculative motive" and which ensures that the rate for loans of infinite duration (which he always has in mind as *the* rate of interest) cannot fall very near zero. (154–55; emphasis in the original)[3]

---

2. Modigliani (1944, 82–86) and Patinkin ([1956] 1965, 109–10) rejected Hicks's notion that the short-term nominal interest rate would become zero in the absence of transaction frictions, on the grounds that the consequence of an increased liquidity of securities is not a lowered rate of interest but a decreased use of money as a medium of exchange. See, however, Walsh 2003, chaps. 2 and 3.

3. Gottfried Haberler (1946, 220) has been one of the few commentators to notice the similarity between that passage and chapter 11 of *Value and Capital*. See also Hicks 1950, 141–42. As suggested by Patinkin ([1956] 1965, 352 n. 27), in the 1950 passage Hicks deduced the liquidity trap as the result of a "market experiment" (the effect of an increase of money supply on the rate of interest) instead of an "individual experiment" (the effect of a reduction of the interest rate on the demand for money). Patinkin claimed that the liquidity trap is a property of the market for securities, not of the money demand function (see also Grandmont and Laroque 1976).

Hicks deployed in his 1937 demonstration of the floor to the rate of interest the two main elements later developed in his theory of the term structure ([1939] 1946, chap. 11): the notion that the long rate is an average of current and expected short rates (the so-called expectations theory of the term structure); and the view that, under the assumption that speculators are averse to risk, they must be paid a liquidity or risk premium to induce them to hold long-term securities (the so-called liquidity preference theory of the term structure; see also Malkiel 1966, chap. 2). Hicks added two important footnotes to the passage quoted above. The first note (1937, 155 n. 6) argues that it is unlikely that individuals might interpret the very low short rate as permanent. Instead, they will interpret it as part of the business cycle and, therefore, be aware that it may possibly rise whether the economy improves (which would increase transactions demand for money) or gets worse (which would increase liquidity preference). Hence the size of the difference between the long and the short rates is a business cycle phenomenon in Hicks's IS-LM. The second note (155 n. 7) claims that the "speculative motive" alone cannot account for the system of interest rates, anticipating some elements of his 1939 criticism of Keynes's theory of interest. Hicks explained that "the shortest of all short rates must equal the relative valuation, at the margin, of money and such a bill." The prospective terms of rediscounting are relevant, however, for the determination of the "*difference* between short and long rates" (emphasis in the original). Hicks's comments can be read as an implicit criticism of the aggregative structure of the *General Theory*, with its simplified two-asset structure comprising "money" (representing short-term assets) and "non-money assets."

The rate of interest assumed in the IS-LM diagrams and equations is the long-term rate, as implied by Hicks at the end of that passage. In correspondence with Young, Hicks recalled that IS-LM did not appear in his Cambridge lectures in the late 1930s, which were based on *Value and Capital*. The reason is that the "heavy emphasis on the long-term rate of interest in the *General Theory* (followed by IS-LM) was not in my line. My theory of interest (in *Value and Capital*) was a theory of the structure of interest rates" (Young 1987, 99). Toward the end of the IS-LM article, Hicks (1937, 158) pointed out that the schedules express a relation between the price system and the system of interest rates, and "you cannot get that into a curve." Nevertheless, as shown by Hicks ([1939] 1946, 147–52), it is possible to reduce the system of interest rates for various maturities to a single short or long rate, which he called a "spot economy" (i.e., with no forward trading) with short lending only or long lending only, respectively.

Hicks (1950, 142) clarified later on that "the exact position of the [interest rate] minimum depends on the method we adopt of choosing a single rate of interest to represent the whole interest-structure." Furthermore, the elasticity of the IS and LM functions is affected by the choice of the representative rate. The short rate is more sensitive to monetary changes than the long rate, but its effect on investment decisions is smaller. Hence both the IS and LM curves will appear more elastic if a long rate is used as the representative rate. The upshot is that, since the choice of a short or long rate as the single representative rate affects the IS and LM schedules in the same way, the relation between the two curves will be the same (151–52). Moreover, Keynes's use of the long rate as "the" rate of interest in the *General Theory* did not mean a representative rate but a particular rate, which would raise Hicks's (1974, 32–33) criticism.

Although Hicks's 1937 demonstration of the interest rate minimum differed from the one found in the *General Theory* (1936, 201–3), he made clear that it was an elaboration of an original idea by Keynes. The relation between Keynes's and Hicks's formulations is better appreciated with the help of the concept of "elasticity of interest-expectations" introduced in *Value and Capital* (Hicks [1939] 1946, 260). Like the concept of elasticity of price expectations, it expresses the effect of changes in current short or long rates on their expected values. Two cases must be distinguished, depending on whether interest expectations mean expectations of short rates or long rates. In the first case, if interest expectations are rigidly inelastic, a change in the short rate will have almost no effect on the long rate. Hence the whole adjustment must be made through major changes in the short rate, and "it becomes very easily conceivable that downward adjustments may be necessary on a scale which would involve a negative rate of interest, if interest changes are to restore equilibrium" (Hicks [1939] 1946, 260). Hicks also made the argument in terms of expectations of long rates, which is closer to Keynes (261). If these expectations are inelastic—that is, if individuals interpret a fall in the long rate as temporary—the current long rate can be reduced only very slightly, since it cannot fall by more than the expected value (at the end of the period) of the long rate multiplied by itself.[4] The

---

4. This comes from Hicks's ([1939] 1946, 149, 261 n. 2) formula that the net yield obtainable by investing in long-term securities for a given period is $R + (R/R') - 1$, where R is

general conclusion is that a large fall in the demand for money (caused by falling money income) will be effective in reducing short rates as far as they can be reduced, but long rates will be affected significantly only if interest expectations are elastic enough.

As pointed out by Kaldor (1939, 15) in a critical comment on Keynes (1936, 218–19), it is the inelasticity of interest expectations, not the uncertainty concerning future interest rates, that explains why the demand for liquid funds is highly elastic with respect to the long-term rate, making the long rate stable relative to the short rate. As mentioned above, Hicks (1937, 155 n. 6) assumed implicitly inelastic interest expectations in his demonstration of a positive floor to the long-term rate, above the near zero floor to the short rate. The main reason for the inelasticity of the interest expectations assumption is that the long rate is governed mainly by "fairly long-run prospects; by the danger of credit restriction in the future rather than by current credit policy," so that if individuals do not believe that the decline is permanent, the long rate will not come down significantly (Hicks [1939] 1946, 282).

2. Keynes versus the "Classics"

The main reason why Hicks was so careful in his discussion of the existence of a floor to the rate of interest was that he considered it to be "the most important thing in Mr. Keynes' book" (Hicks 1937, 254), a judgment that he repeated in *Value and Capital* (259) as part of his treatment of absolute instability downward when prices are falling continuously. Hicks (1950, 141) was convinced that the nearly horizontal stretch at the left of the LM curve was "an essential part of Keynes's argument." He later reaffirmed that the individuality of Keynes's theory vis-à-vis "classical" economics is based on the assumption that there are conditions in which "the interest-mechanism will not work" (Hicks 1957, 279). The IS-LM diagram, according to Hicks (1979, 990), shows that Keynes and the "classics" are "both of them special cases of something *more* general. . . . Keynes's model, though an extreme case of the *general* IS-LM model, is an extreme case that is outstandingly important."

---

the current long-term rate and R' stands for the rate expected to rule at the end of the period. Since that expression is necessarily positive, R must be higher than $R'(1 + R')$, or approximately, $R > R'(1 - R')$, which gives the maximum possible fall in the current long rate. It corresponds to Keynes's (1936, 202) well-known proposition that a liquidity trap will occur if investors expect long-term rates to rise by more than the square of the current long interest rate.

Hicks (1957) realized that such a judgment depends a great deal on how one describes "classical" economics. As is well known, Hicks's IS-LM is a short-run model built under the assumptions of a fixed amount of capital and given money wages (1937, 148, 158; 1957, 280). The assumption of given money wages was applied in the 1937 article to both Keynes and the "classics," since Hicks was concerned with a comparison between their respective approaches to short-run economic fluctuations when employment is below its full level (see Coddington 1979). The assumption about the behavior of money wages is a "special assumption that can be incorporated into any theory . . . in response to changing facts" (Hicks 1957, 281). Among pre-Keynesian economics, Hicks (1937, 152–53) distinguished between classical orthodox and the "revised and qualified Marshallian" theories—the former corresponds to the Cambridge quantity theory of money with a given proportion k between money and nominal income, while the latter acknowledges that the demand for money depends on the rate of interest (see also Laidler 1999, 310–13). The relevant comparison, according to Hicks, should be between Keynes and the revised theory of later Marshallians that prevailed when the *General Theory* was written, not between Keynes and the orthodox quantity theory of money. "Mr. Keynes in 1936 is not the first Cambridge economist to have a temperate faith in Public Works" (Hicks 1937, 154).

Hicks's suggested clarification of the difference between Keynes and the qualified classical theory is based on an analysis of the shape of his (Hicks's) LL curve (renamed LM by Hansen [1949]). The curve will tend to be "nearly horizontal" on the left (because of the floor to the rate of interest) and "nearly vertical" on the right, because there is an upper limit to the velocity of money (Hicks 1937, 154). This is illustrated in figure 1, where, as pointed out by Hicks, the LL curve approaches these limits asymptotically. Keynes's theory becomes relevant if, because of a weak inducement to invest or a high propensity to save, equilibrium lies on the left of the LL curve, since, on the one hand, the rate of interest is not influenced by real factors, and, on the other, income is not affected by changes in money supply. As stressed by Hicks, an increase in money supply cannot bring the interest rate down any further—the LL curve shifts to the right, but "the horizontal parts are almost the same" (155), as shown in figure 1. Therefore Keynes's theory is the "Economics of Depression" (155), a judgment that Hicks would repeat on other occasions: "The *General Theory* . . . is the book of the Great Depression

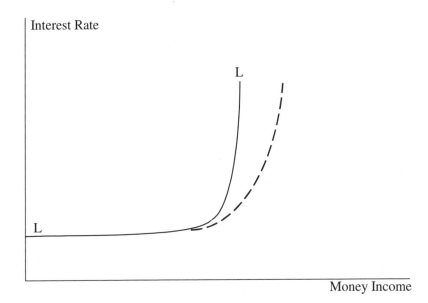

Figure 1   Hicks's LL curve with exogenous money supply (Hicks 1937, 153)

of the nineteen-thirties. . . . [Keynes's] practical problem was emergence from Depression; he looked at the world from a Depression point of view" (Hicks 1967a, 156, 169).[5]

Hicks's description of the *General Theory* in terms of the left section of the LL curve was motivated not only by the ineffectiveness of monetary policy in the Depression but also by his attempt to discuss Keynes's "startling conclusion" that an increase in the inducement to invest will not affect the rate of interest, but only employment (Hicks 1937, 152; cf. Keynes 1936, 165, 184). Dennis Robertson (1936, 182–83) discussed the point, arguing that Keynes's claim would be valid only if either "the liquidity schedule proper is perfectly elastic (the curve representing it a horizontal straight line)" or the monetary authority expands the money supply and holds the rate of interest down in the face of upward shifts of investment. Hicks had discussed the issue in his 1936 review of the *General Theory*, but he then focused the argument on the conditions for

5. Robert Skidelsky (1992, 440–41; 1996) argued for the notion that Keynes's *General Theory* was designed to supply a theory for the Great Depression, despite the absence of explicit references to that episode in the book.

the operation of the multiplier mechanism, which would bring about an increase in saving and, by that, in the supply of loanable funds (Hicks [1936] 1982, 90–91).[6] In the book review, he had not taken into account the increase of the interest rate caused by the effect of a higher income level on money demand, which is central to the 1937 IS-LM model.

Although Hicks finished writing his IS-LM paper in August 1936 (for presentation at the September 1936 conference of the Econometric Society; see Young 1987), before the publication of Robertson's 1936 article, he had access to preliminary drafts, as indicated by Robertson's (1936, 168) acknowledgment. Hence the shift in the argument between the 1936 review and the 1937 IS-LM article may in part reflect Robertson's influence, but Robertson's description of Keynes's argument in terms of a horizontal LM curve with perfectly elastic demand for money is much closer to Lange's (1938) later formulation than to Hicks's careful discussion of a floor to the rate of interest as the left part of the LM curve (see section 3). Furthermore, Robertson (1936, 183) decided to put aside the case of a horizontal liquidity schedule quoting a passage from the *General Theory* in which Keynes wrote that "whilst this limiting case might become practically important in the future, I know of no example of it hitherto" (207). This is in contrast with Hicks (1937, 1950, 1957), who, despite Keynes's ambiguity on the relevance of the interest rate minimum (see Patinkin 1976, 111–13; Laidler 1999, 258–59), had no doubts about its importance for Keynes's theory.

Regardless of whether Robertson had an influence on Hicks's discussion of the interest rate minimum in 1937, there is clear evidence that Hicks's description of the "qualified classical theory" was in great part a result of their correspondence about the first draft of Hicks's 1937 article (see Mizen and Presley 1998). However, Robertson did not share Hicks's implicit interpretation that the neo-Marshallians realized the full implications of the relation between money demand and interest for the analysis of the investment-saving process in general equilibrium. In particular, according to Robertson (1936, 188–90; 1940, 19, 34, 36), the pre-Keynesian literature did not take into account that an increase in the

---

6. Kregel (2000, 42–47) wrongly imputes to Hicks (1937) the argument that the horizontal stretch of the LM curve is based on the assumption of a high elasticity of supply of consumption goods or of money. The relation between Keynes's theory of the multiplier and the theory of interest rates was clarified by Kaldor (1939, sec. 3), who showed that the finance of long-term investment in the multiplier process depends on the stabilization of the long-term rate by speculators owing to a shortage of savings, not on the supply of cash by the banking system.

desire to save, even if it is spent on a purchase of securities, will not bring about an increase in investment in the same proportion. Pre-Keynesian economists overlooked the effect of a fall in the rate of interest (caused by an increase in the demand for securities) on money demand, which interrupts the fall in the rate of interest.

> Some part of the additional savings devoted by individuals to the purchase of securities will come to rest in the banking accounts of those who, at the higher price of securities, desire to hold an increased quantity of money. Thus the fall in the rate of interest and the stimulus to the formation of capital will be less than if the [liquidity schedule] were a vertical straight line, and the stream of money income will tend to contract. . . . Liquidity [is] a trap for savings. (Robertson 1936, 188–90)

> Thus owing to the existence of this sliding or trap, my act of thrift does not succeed, as "classical" theory asserts that it will, in creating incomes and money balances [in the capital goods sector] equal to those which it has destroyed [in the consumption goods sector]. (Robertson 1940, 19)

In terms of Hicks's 1937 model, Robertson's (1940, 34, 36) phrase "liquidity trap" describes a leftward shift of the IS curve along an upward-sloping LM schedule. Hicks (1957, 279, 285), however, was not convinced by Robertson's point that the argument about the general equilibrium effects of an increase in the propensity to save was not part of the pre-Keynesian tradition. According to Hicks, a "properly equipped 'classical' economist . . . *can* go so far" as recognizing that real shifts will have monetary effects if the interest rate elasticity of money demand is assumed.[7] In the same way—in contrast with Kaldor 1937, the first article to refer to Hicks's IS-LM diagram—Hicks (1957, 286–88) would not identify as originally Keynesian the notion that a reduction in money wages can only bring about an increase in income and employment through its effect on the position of the LM curve (cf. Keynes 1936, chap. 19).

However, Hicks would later change his interpretation of the relation between Keynesian and "classical" monetary theories. In his contribution to the *Chambers's Encyclopaedia*, Hicks (1967b, 621) pointed out that

---

7. It was in his review of Robertson's 1940 *Essays* that Hicks (1942, 56) used for the first time Robertson's phrase "liquidity trap for savings."

the "novelty" of the Keynesian theory of interest was that the long-term rate of interest, not just the short rate, is subjected to monetary influences. The "classical" tradition of Marshall and Hawtrey used to treat the money (or bill) market and the bond market as almost completely separate entities. Hence, although the "classics" had a theory of the short rate of a "liquidity preference type," they proposed a different theory for the long-term market as determined by real forces (see also Hicks 1989, chap. 9). Hicks's 1967 account differs from his 1937 minimization of the differences between Keynes and the neo-Marshallians, but it is not inconsistent with his discussion of the Keynesian floor to the long rate.

The notion that the short-term nominal interest rate cannot fall below zero was occasionally mentioned in the pre-Keynesian literature, usually in connection with the discussion of a deflationary process. This led "classical" authors to recognize the limitations of monetary policy in the Depression: "What if the rate of depreciation of prices is actually *greater* than the natural rate of interest? If that is so nothing that the bankers can do will make borrowing sufficiently attractive. . . . This phenomenon of stagnation will only be possible where the *expected* rate of depreciation of the prices of commodities happens to be high" (Hawtrey [1913] 1962, 186–87; emphasis in the original). The problem, then, from Ralph Hawtrey's point of view, is that the (Fisherian) expected real rate of interest is negative, but the bank rate cannot be lower than zero. Similar comments can be found in the second edition (1928) of Robertson's *Money* ([1922] 1948, 177) and in Pigou 1933, 213.

Hawtrey also introduced the related notion of a "credit deadlock." It may be impossible in a depression to expand the money supply through the banking system because of a crisis of confidence that affects both the demand and supply sides of the credit market (Hawtrey 1932, 172). Under these circumstances, open market operations are not able to increase money supply because banks are willing to hold excess reserves rather than lending. As indicated by Paul Wonnacott (1978, 193–94; see also Laidler 1999, 123, 286), the "excess reserve trap" argument advanced by Hawtrey is consistent with the quantity theory of money, since it is not about the ineffectiveness of changes in money supply (as in Hicks's 1937 liquidity trap discussion) but about the difficulty of increasing the money supply through the banking system in a depression. Despite the recognition in the pre-Keynesian literature of limits to monetary policy in a slump, those authors acknowledged that Keynes's (1936, 207) suggestion of the possibility that "liquidity preference may become virtually absolute" at a low but positive long rate introduced a new element into the discussion. As pointed out by Hawtrey ([1937] 1952, 205), "Keynes rendered a service to economics in pointing out that [this problem] may occur at a stage when the long-term rate of interest is still some way above zero." From this point of view, Hicks's 1937 emphasis on the floor to the long-term rate as a Keynesian contribution is not contradicted by previous discussions of the zero lower bound in the "classical" literature. It does not reflect a "glut of capital" (since the capital stock is constant in the IS-LM model), but a reduction in aggregate demand. Also, in contrast with most of that literature, it is not based on the assumption of deflationary expectations.[8]

Hicks's 1937 formulation of the floor to the interest rate makes no reference to the banking system, which is also true of the basic version of his IS-LM model as a whole. Nevertheless, Hicks (1937, 157) did try to incorporate some features of a banking system by replacing the assumption of a given supply of money by a given "monetary system." As Hicks (1950, 142–43) pointed out later on, this becomes particularly important if under "money supply" one includes bank deposits, since the supply of deposits by the banking system is responsive to interest and income. The new LL curve will not feature in its right part a nearly vertical segment. The left part of the curve will remain the same, which is not clear in Hicks's (1937, 157) figure 3. Hicks (1950, 141) would provide the correct construction of the new LL curve under the assumption of endogenous money supply; it is reproduced as figure 2. If the monetary system is elastic—meaning that a rise in the rate of interest increases the supply of money—the economy will move from point P_1 on curve L to P_2' on L' (with a larger money supply) instead of P_2 on the old LL curve. The new LL curve is formed by connecting the dotted points, each one corresponding to a different money supply for a given elasticity of the monetary system (see also Bailey 1962, chap. 2). In the case of a perfectly elastic monetary system, the adjusted curve would become horizontal at the level of the interest rate minimum, corresponding to a mix of the Keynesian liquidity trap and the Wicksellian pure credit economy (cf. Hicks 1937, 158; 1957, 286).

---

8. The deflationary process is important, however, to explain what Hicks ([1939] 1946, 264–65) called "depression psychology," provoked by the impact of unexpected falling prices on the real value of debt.

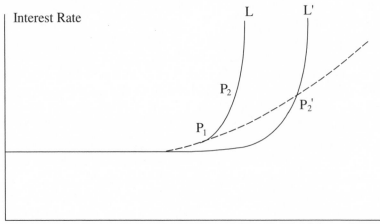

Figure 2   Hicks's LL curve with endogenous money supply (Hicks 1951, 141)

3. Hansen, Lange, and the Textbook IS-LM

Hicks's IS-LM analysis attracted the attention of the profession (Kaldor 1937; Modigliani 1944; Klein 1947; Hansen 1949, 1953) until it became the standard representation of "Keynesian economics." Before that, Oskar Lange (1938, 12 n. 1) put forward independently of Hicks (1937) an alternative diagrammatic analysis that also focused on the form of the LM function, which Lange (1938, 28) called the "isoliquidity curve." Like Hicks, Lange discussed under what conditions Keynes's claim— that the rate of interest does not react to changes in investment or saving—holds. Lange argued that Keynes "obviously . . . must have in mind" the limiting case when the "interest-elasticity of the demand for liquidity is infinite," and the isoliquidity curve "degenerates into a horizontal straight line"(19, 28, 31). The other special case is the traditional quantity theory of money, with a corresponding vertical isoliquidity curve.

Despite apparent similarities with Hicks (1937), their respective treatments are quite different. In Lange the issue is not the logical existence of a floor to the rate of interest created by a nearly zero short-term rate, but the empirical matter of the value of the interest elasticity of the demand for money, without any mention of the speculative demand for money (or of the term structure of interest rates, for that matter). In Hicks's approach, money and securities necessarily become perfect substitutes when the short-term rate hits its lower bound. Accordingly, while Lange described Keynes's case as a completely horizontal LM curve, Hicks distinguished between the different parts of the LM curve. As shown in section 2, Hicks's LM can become completely horizontal only if the monetary system is perfectly elastic. Lange's approach has been adopted by several textbooks, especially when a linear formulation of the IS-LM model is deployed (see, e.g., Dornbusch and Fischer 1978, Gordon 2000, and Hall and Taylor 1986).

With Franco Modigliani (1944), the Keynes versus "classics" issue changed from the discussion of the specification of the money demand function to the determination of money wages in the labor market (see De Vroey 2000).[9] Modigliani used the long-period version of the general classical model with perfectly flexible wages as a benchmark for comparison with Keynes. The floor to the rate of interest is still relevant, but only if the assumption of rigid money wages is removed from Keynesian theory—as shown by Modigliani (1944, 74–75), if the interest rate is at its minimum level, a reduction of money wages will affect only the price level, with no effect on employment and real wages. Modigliani's (59) LL curve has the same shape as Hicks's original LL, with horizontal and vertical stretches on its left and right parts. He followed Hicks's *Value and Capital* closely in the explanation of the lower bound to the rate of interest by transaction costs (Modigliani 1944, 50–53, 83; but see note 2 above). Although Modigliani subscribed to Hicks's theory of the term structure, he did not apply it to the determination of a floor to the long-term rate of interest above the lower bound of the short rate (56).

Lawrence Klein (1947) moved the discussion to an econometric level. Instead of resorting to Keynes's hypothesis of infinite elasticity for money at some low interest rate (for which there was "not sufficient evidence"), Klein (1947, 72, 85) claimed that the data indicated that the saving and investment functions are interest inelastic. Accordingly, from Klein's point of view, the core of Keynesian economics is the proposition that there is no positive value of the rate of interest able to equilibrate saving and investment at full-employment income. This is illustrated in

9. David Champernowne (1936) anticipated Modigliani's (1944) emphasis on the labor market as the dividing line between Keynes and the classics (see Boianovsky 2005). Instead of Hicks's general equilibrium with simultaneous equations, Champernowne stressed the distinct causality structures of Keynes's and classical theories.

figure 3, which shows the saving and investment schedules (continuous lines) at full-employment income Y_0. Excess saving will be eliminated by a reduction of income to Y_1. Klein did not claim that the assumption of interest inelasticity of the investment function could be found in the *General Theory*—it pertained to Keynesian economics, not necessarily to the economics of Keynes. Klein (1947, 88) next argued that wage flexibility does not bring the economy to full employment if the IS function is very steep and the LM schedule features a horizontal stretch. Klein's discussion, however, was marred by his imprecise interpretation that a reduction in money wages shifts the whole LM schedule down, including its horizontal stretch. Although Klein distinguished sharply between the interest inelasticity and the liquidity trap arguments, it is clear enough that they are not entirely disconnected, since, as first stressed by James Tobin (1947, 127–28), the inconsistency between saving and investment arises from the impossibility of reducing the nominal rate of interest below its zero bound (see also Smith [1956] 1966, 42; Ackley 1961, 194–95; Bailey 1962, 48–49).

Klein's notion of a steep IS function was adapted by Hansen (1949, 79), with the suggestion that it becomes interest inelastic at low income levels only.[10] As shown in figure 4 (where income levels, as in Klein, are expressed in real, not nominal, terms; this makes no difference for the diagrammatic representation of a liquidity trap), the shape of Hansen's LM is very similar to Hicks's original LL (see also Hansen 1953, 146). At the point of intersection of the IS_1 curve and the LM_0 curve "monetary policy is ineffective" (Hansen 1949, 80). However, Hansen's explanation of the floor to the rate of interest differs from Hicks's (1937), as well as from Modigliani's (1944). According to Hansen (1949, 64–65; 78; 1953, 152), the floor to the rate of interest is explained by the fact that the compensation for bearing the risk of a change in (long-term) interest rates approaches zero as the interest rate declines.

Hansen's 1949 interpretation of the liquidity trap was not based on Keynes's (1936, 201) analysis of the behavior of speculators when the current long-term rate is below what they consider its normal, or "safe," value. Instead, Hansen built on another element mentioned by Keynes (1936, 169, 202), that is, the notion that every fall in the interest rate reduces the "insurance premium to offset the risk of loss on capital

10. Hansen (1949, 79–80) sometimes associated the interest inelasticity of the IS curve in a depression to capital saturation, but this is imprecise, since the capital stock is constant in the IS-LM model.

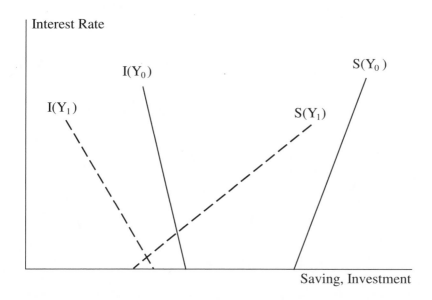

Figure 3 Klein's saving-investment inconsistency (Klein 1947, 85)

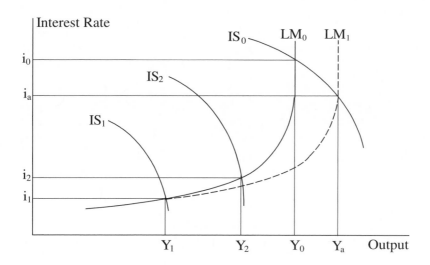

Figure 4 Hansen's IS-LM (Hansen 1949, 79)

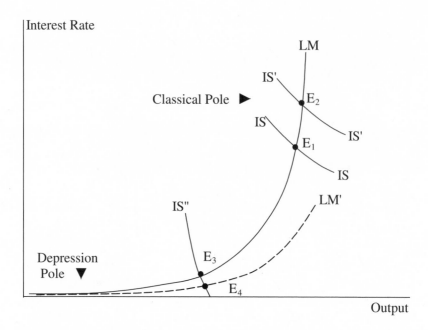

Figure 5 Samuelson's classical and depression poles (Samuelson 1967, 331)

account." Hansen's discussion is consistent with the argument developed by Tobin ([1958] 1966, 191) that, under the assumption of risk aversion, the interest elasticity of the demand for money increases as the rate approaches zero. Hicks ([1936] 1982, 96) had used the same argument in his review of the *General Theory*. Paul Samuelson reproduced Hansen's diagram in the seventh edition of his *Economics* (1967, 331; it was first introduced in the third edition [1955], without the "depression" and "classical" poles; see Pearce and Hoover 1995), with the difference that the left stretch of the LM curve approaches zero, instead of a positive interest rate. Samuelson probably had in mind a short-term rate, as suggested by his explanation that an increase in money supply (M) "by open-market purchases which involved swapping a close-money substitute Treasury bill for M itself" would leave the horizontal part of the LM curve "virtually unchanged."

Both Hansen and Samuelson dismissed the association of Keynesian economics with a liquidity trap, though. The notion that the IS-LM model (not just the liquidity trap region) represents "Keynesian economics" as a whole is quite clear in Hansen's (1953, 147–48) assessment that Hicks provided the correct general equilibrium formulation by putting together Keynes and Robertson in the IS-LM model. The question remained, however, whether money wage flexibility could bring the economy to its full-employment output. It was in that context that the liquidity trap concept continued to attract attention in macroeconomic textbooks.

Gardner Ackley (1961, chap. 9) provided a careful textbook discussion of the speculative demand for money and of the liquidity trap as an obstacle to full employment. Although Ackley (1961, 363) used the Hicks-Hansen IS-LM model, his presentation of the liquidity trap was based on Keynes's hypothesis of regressive expectations, instead of Hicks's (1937) term structure formulation or Hansen's (1949) risk aversion argument. Ackley was probably influenced by Joan Robinson's ([1951] 1952) and Tobin's ([1958] 1966) reexamination of Keynes's theory of liquidity preference. Keynes's (1936, chap. 15) discussion of the circumstances in which liquidity preference becomes "virtually absolute" was marred by his tendency to interpret that phenomenon as a generalization of his speculative demand for money because of uncertainty as to the future of the rate of interest. As explained by Kaldor (1939) and by Robinson ([1951] 1952), Keynes's argument about the floor to the long rate of interest does not depend on uncertainty, since it is the very confidence with which speculators believe in the normal price of bonds that makes it difficult to reduce the rate of interest. "In the limit, if the market confidently believes that from tomorrow the rate of interest will be at its past average value, the long and the short rate will be equal to that value today. In this case liquidity preference in Keynes' sense is absolute" (Robinson [1951] 1952, 17–18).

Keynes's model of regressive interest expectations, as elaborated by Robinson, does not lead to a gap between the short and long rates of interest in the liquidity trap, in contrast with Hicks's 1937 formulation. Furthermore, the "normal" rate is not a constant magnitude, but it falls if the current long rate is continuously lower than the expected rate and if bear speculators are convinced that "the new low rate has come to stay," which may shift downward the whole LM curve over time (Robinson [1951] 1952, 30; Ackley 1961, 198–201).[11]

11. Hicks (1967a, 96–97) explained the fall in the long-term interest rate in Great Britain in the mid-1930s along similar lines. According to Hicks, "the basic thing that was needed was a continuation of monetary ease, and an expectation that this ease would go on. . . . So long as the pattern of expectations remained as I have been describing it, a 2 per cent Bank rate was bound to press down the long-term rate, even to fairly low levels." As pointed out by Hicks, in the

By 1957, when Hicks reexamined his IS-LM framework, he added another factor that could also prevent the working of the interest mechanism: interest inelasticity of the IS curve à la Klein (Hicks 1957, 288). Hicks's (1937, 153) original IS schedule was drawn as an elastic curve, to represent Keynes's view that the effect of changes in the long rate on investment "was of major importance" (Hicks 1967a, 54). Furthermore, Hicks (1967a, 57–58) criticized Keynes for confusing two different issues that should be kept apart: the short-period question about the effectiveness of monetary policy in the Depression and the ability of the financial system to adjust to a condition in which the marginal productivity of capital has fallen permanently (cf. Friedman 1970, 212–15; and Laidler 1999, 263–65). Hicks's 1937 IS-LM discussion of the liquidity trap applied to a cyclical, not permanent, change of the marginal productivity of capital. "The long-period question, I now hold, is rather different. While one can understand that large balances may be held idle for considerable periods, for a speculative motive, it is harder to grant that they can be so held indefinitely" (Hicks 1967a, 58). Hicks suggested that the idea of a floor to the long-term rate of interest in long-period equilibrium could still be used, but it should be interpreted as a result of the fact that even if the rate set by the central bank is reduced to zero, the marginal cost of capital to industry will not be so reduced because of costs of financial intermediation associated with information problems and risk evaluation of potential borrowers—a supply side phenomenon, instead of the usual short-period liquidity trap.

4. The Recent Approach to the Liquidity Trap

The Keynesian liquidity trap argument gradually receded into the background in the macroeconomic literature of the 1970s and 1980s.[12] The increasing attention devoted to the microfoundations of price and wage rigidity was one reason behind the relative marginalization of IS-LM analysis (see Dixon and Gerrard 2000). Hicks himself was part of that shift with his contributions to the fixprice literature (see his 1979 account

---

mid-1930s the Bank of England started to target the interest rate instead of the exchange rate. See also Roberts 1995 for a discussion of the relation between the gold standard and Keynes's treatment of the liquidity trap.

12. Tobin 1980, 5, was an exception. Tobin then explained a liquidity trap along Hicksian lines, that is, by the fact that "the absolute floor for nominal interest rates is zero," together with the notion that "long term rates . . . would be held above zero by expectations . . . that short rates will rise from rock bottom in future."

of how he moved beyond "IS-LM Keynesianism" after the late 1950s). Another reason was the long experience with significant inflation rates in Europe, Japan, and the United States, accompanied by high nominal interest rates. Hicks (1979, 994) remarked that "one can see why [the liquidity trap] appeared, in the thirties, to be such an important matter; in the inflationary conditions to which we have now become accustomed, it is irrelevant." Hicks's (1982, 263; 1989, 79) discussion in the 1980s of the determination of the interest rate indicates that inflation had moved the old liquidity trap idea out of his research agenda, which helps explain why the floor to the rate of interest is absent from his 1980–81 "explanation" of IS-LM.

Furthermore, the traditional notion of a liquidity trap suffered from the growing criticism of the concept of a speculative demand for money— whether in its Keynesian or Tobinian formulations—and from Patinkin's ([1956] 1965, 1959) real balance effect. Already in the second edition of his *Value and Capital* ([1939] 1946, 335), Hicks realized that his demonstration of the absolute instability of the economy, under the assumption of unit elasticity of price expectations and a floor to the rate of interest, was valid only if the "income effect" of price changes was disregarded. However, in his 1957 review of Patinkin, Hicks wrongly interpreted the real balance effect as shifting the LM curve only, which led to Patinkin's (1959) critical reaction. The lack of empirical support for a liquidity trap (in the Hansen-Tobin sense) in econometric studies of the demand for money carried out in the 1960s also contributed to the criticism of that concept (Laidler 1969, chap. 9).

The return of the liquidity trap concept to the research agenda of monetary macroeconomics in the late 1990s is not explained by new econometric evidence on the interest elasticity of money demand (Miyao 2002; Hondroyiannis, Swamy, and Tavlas 2000). Instead, it reflects changes in the economic environment, with deflationary tendencies in Japan and near price stability in the United States and Europe. Moreover, the criticism of the traditional Keynesian approach to the demand for money, as well as the focus on an economy with multiple financial assets, has brought monetary theory closer to Hicks's (1935, [1939] 1946) treatment. This was already visible in Ackley's (1978, 715–31) detailed discussion of the term structure of interest rates. The term structure is also prominent in Olivier Blanchard's (1997, chap. 9) treatment of the IS-LM model.

The new generation of optimizing IS-LM models (McCallum 1989, 102–7; Krugman 1998, 142–49; McCallum and Nelson 1999; Walsh 2003, 230–40) approaches the money demand function in terms of a model of money as a medium of exchange (money-in-the-utility-function, shopping time, or cash-in-advance models), with the general result that the (short-term) nominal interest rate is positive only if money yields liquidity services (Walsh 2003, 49, 107). This is a formalization of Hicks's insight in chapter 13 of *Value and Capital*. If money has no storage costs and there is a finite level of money balances at which there is satiation with the transaction services of money, it will be possible to reduce the nominal rate all the way to zero (McCallum 2000, 875–76). Otherwise, there will be a liquidity trap at a low positive short-term nominal interest rate. As discussed above, Hicks and his followers assumed that the lower bound to the short nominal rate was generally slightly above zero, but this makes no real difference for the analysis of a liquidity trap.

Allan Meltzer (1995, 1999) has criticized the transmission mechanism of the IS-LM model and its implications for the interpretation of a liquidity trap. According to Meltzer, the IS-LM approach does not take into account the positive effect of an increase in money supply on the price of securities and, by that, on the value of financial wealth, explained by the imperfect substitutability between alternative financial assets. Meltzer claims that monetary policy remains effective even if the short rate hits its lower bound, since the central bank may buy or sell long-term assets that are not perfect substitutes for money and do not have a zero yield. Meltzer's interpretation of the transmission mechanism is reminiscent of Hicks's (1967a, 51–53; 1974, 52–53) "liquidity pressure effect" on investment. Such a liquidity effect will be stronger the larger the proportion of reserves held in relatively "long" assets. However, in contrast with Meltzer, Hicks (1967a, 52; 1974, 53) was skeptical of the general effectiveness of a "liquidity pressure effect" in a depression, since an increase in money supply should only be able to reduce longer-term interest rates if such action is interpreted as a change in the central bank's commitment regarding the future path of short-term rates (see also Eggertsson and Woodford 2003, sec. 2; and note 11 above).

Apart from the specification of the LM curve as a function of the (short-term) nominal rate of interest, another important feature of optimizing IS-LM models is the assumption that the IS curve is a function of the expected (long-term) real interest rate. The notion that nominal rates matter for money demand, while real rates are relevant for investment, was advanced by William Vickrey (1954, 92–93) and applied to the IS-LM model by Martin Bailey (1962, 50–51). Vickrey's essay became well known for introducing the notion of programmed inflation to counteract the limits imposed by the interest rate lower bound on the effectiveness of monetary policy. Hicks ([1939] 1946) was aware of the distinction between real and nominal interest rates, which had been introduced by Irving Fisher (1896).[13] However, in the framework of *Value and Capital*, the assumption of an elasticity of 1.0 of price-expectations was enough to yield Hicks's instability results. The crucial issue, from the perspective of the modern literature, is that expected deflation puts a floor to real interest rates and limits the effectiveness of monetary policy (see, e.g., Blanchard 1997, 573). If the central bank follows a Wicksell-Taylor interest rate feedback rule—whereby the short-term nominal rate is set as an increasing and nonnegative function of the inflation rate—it can be shown that deflationary expectations, together with a lower bound to the nominal interest rate, may lead to a self-fulfilling deflationary spiral that cannot be avoided by monetary policy (see Benhabib, Schmitt-Grohé, and Uribe 2002; Walsh 2003, 484–87).[14]

Another factor that may bring about a liquidity trap in recent discussion is the possibility that the Wicksellian "natural rate of interest" is negative (Krugman 1998, 2000a). As discussed above, Klein (1947) associated that possibility with the interest inelasticity of saving and investment. In the modern literature, the natural rate of interest, as decided by the rate of time preference à la Ramsey, will be negative if the marginal utility of consumption in the next period is greater than in the current period, which will happen if people expect their income to fall in the future (cf. Krugman 1998, 150). Alfred Marshall ([1890] 1990, 192–93) had entertained the possibility of a negative natural rate on those grounds, but did not realize that, in a monetary economy, the actual rate of interest could never be lower than zero. Krugman's scenario has some similarities with A. C. Pigou's famous 1943 article. However, while for Pigou the

13. See Hicks [1939] 1946, 119, 160. After Wicksell, Hicks called the rate of interest in terms of goods the "natural" rate. It should be noted that Hicks's proposition about zero interest rate in the absence of transaction frictions applies to the nominal, not the natural, rate.

14. The modern notion of a liquidity trap can also be applied if the usual LM curve is replaced by the assumption that the central bank follows an interest rate rule (see Romer 2000). It is worth noting that Romer's curve differs from Hicks's suggestion of an elastic LM curve, since Hicks had in mind reactions by the private banking system to changes in the interest rate, not an interest rate rule set by a central bank.

economy will eventually converge to its full-employment growth path through the effect of falling prices on shifting the saving function, Krugman argues that a fall in current prices will bring the economy back to full-employment equilibrium only if it represents an increase in the ratio between the expected future and the current price levels and, by that, a reduction in the expected real rate of interest to the level of the negative natural rate of interest.

The real balance effect is not generally part of the Euler condition used in deriving the IS function in recent optimizing IS-LM models. A real balance effect would arise if real balances entered the representative agent's utility function and this function was nonseparable with a positive cross-derivative between consumption and real balances (McCallum 2000, 882–83; Woodford 2003, 102–4). However, even if a real balance effect is present in the IS function, this effect vanishes when the short-term nominal interest rate falls to its lower bound. As pointed out by Michael Woodford (131–35), additional real balances affect the marginal utility of expenditure only to the extent they can reduce the short-term nominal rate, which indicates the value of further reduction in transaction frictions from holding more wealth in money form. Hence the real balance effect, as a liquidity effect, will not work under liquidity trap conditions (see also Rabin and Keilany 1986–87). Nevertheless, the real balance effect might still work as a wealth effect if consumption is a function of permanent income and population is growing, so that money can be treated as net wealth outside the standard representative agent framework (see Ireland 2001; Walsh 2003, 487–88).[15]

5. Krugman, Expectations, and the IS-LM Model

Krugman's (1998, 2000a) discussion of the liquidity trap concept is particularly relevant for the purposes of the present essay, since he presents it as part of an intended reformulation of Hicks's original IS-LM model (on Krugman's argument, see also Wilson 1999, Kregel 2000, Sumner

15. Before the revival of interest in the liquidity trap, the notion of a zero interest rate was usually associated in monetary economics with Milton Friedman's (1969, chap. 1) proposition that only deflationary monetary policies that generate a zero nominal interest rate will lead to satiation in money demand and, therefore, to optimality. Uhlig (2000) discussed the contrast between Friedman's framework and the depression scenario of the recent liquidity trap literature.

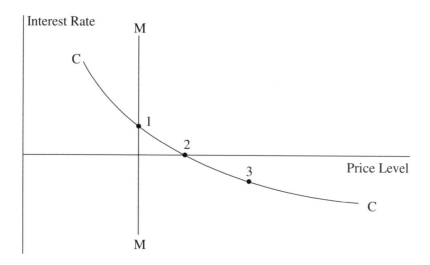

Figure 6   Krugman's IS-LM with flexible price level (Krugman 1998, 145)

2002, and Eggertsson and Woodford 2003). Krugman (1998, 138–39, 142–45; 2000a, 224–27) put forward a simple rational expectation model of a representative agent that maximizes its intertemporal utility function and demands money according to a cash-in-advance constraint in an endowment economy. Under the assumption that there is no uncertainty and that the nominal rate of interest on one-period bonds is positive, the cash-in-advance constraint is binding and the quantity theory of money applies: $P = M/y$, where y is the output level (see also Boianovsky 2002). This relationship is represented by the line MM in figure 6, which describes equilibrium in the market for money. The IS curve is obtained from the equilibrium in the market for goods, derived by Krugman from the Euler equation for consumption: $(1 + i)(P_t/P_{t+1}) = (1/D)(y_{t+1}/y_t)^\rho$, where D and ρ stand for the discount factor and relative risk aversion, respectively. The price level in the next period (P_{t+1}) is determined by M_{t+1} and y_{t+1}, which are assumed to be given constants. Hence a rise in the current price level generates expected deflation and a lower nominal rate of interest, for a given real (or "natural") interest rate, which explains the inverse relation illustrated by the curve CC.

Patinkin ([1956] 1965, 233) advanced the representation of equilibrium in the markets for money and for goods in a flexible price economy in (i, P) space (see also Krugman 2000b). It is implicit in chapter 22 of

Hicks's *Value and Capital*. In terms of Hicks's framework, Krugman's assumption that the future expected price level (P_{t+1}) remains constant when the current price level (P_t) changes means that the elasticity of price expectations is zero. As discussed above, this implies, according to Hicks, that the system can be stabilized through intertemporal substitution, which is exactly Krugman's conclusion.

Any increase in the current money supply—for a given long-run money supply and expected price level in future periods—past point 2 has no effect on the price level, since, at zero nominal interest rates, the cash-in-advance demand for real money balances is indeterminate because money is also held as a store of value. Money and bonds become perfect substitutes, and the cash-in-advance constraint is no longer binding at the zero lower bound. In this context, a liquidity trap arises if the economy is beset by deflationary expectations that shift the CC curve to the left or if the natural interest rate is negative because of the time preferences of individuals. Krugman (1998, [1999] 2000, 2000a) discusses mainly the last factor, which he applies to the Japanese economy in the late 1990s (see also Kuttner and Posen 2001). Under these circumstances, the current price level will fall in relation to the expected future price level, with an ensuing reduction of the Fisherian real expected rate of interest to the negative equilibrium level of the Wicksellian natural rate of interest. Again, it is Krugman's assumption that the expected price level is given—in contrast with Hicks's unit elasticity of price expectations—that is behind the equilibration mechanism that prevents a cumulative price fall in the liquidity trap. Hicks ([1939] 1946, 271, 298) mentioned that "people's sense of normal prices" might counteract the initial effects of the unit elasticity of price expectations and stabilize the economy in a depression.

Krugman next investigates the role of monetary policy in a liquidity trap under the assumption that the price level in the current period is predetermined and that the consumption good is produced. The equation for the IS curve is now given by $y = y_{t+1}(P_{t+1}/DP_t)^{1/\rho}(1 + i)^{-1/\rho}$, which is drawn as curve CC in the (i, y) space in figure 7. Once again, expansionary money supply will not be able to increase output beyond point 2. Nevertheless, in Krugman's framework, this is true only if individuals see monetary expansion as transitory, that is, if the future money supply is held constant. Even if the nominal rate of interest is zero, an increase in the money supply perceived to be permanent will raise current prices in the flexprice model, or output in the sticky price model.

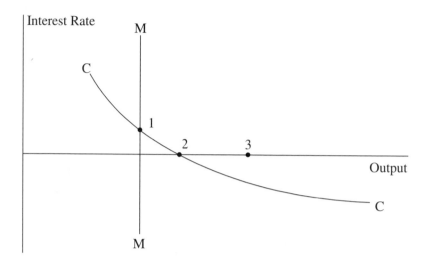

Figure 7   Krugman's IS-LM with predetermined price level (Krugman 1998, 149)

The upshot is that the liquidity trap concept now involves a "credibility problem": monetary policy is ineffective only if people do not believe that monetary expansion will be kept in the future (Krugman 1998, 142, 161).

The notion that expected inflation could provide a way out of the impasse posed by a negative natural rate of interest could be found already in Vickrey 1954 and Bailey 1962, 101. Bailey dismissed its practical relevance on the grounds that "there is nothing to assure that such expectations will develop." Krugman, though, has claimed that inflationary expectations can be generated by the perception by forward-looking consumers of the future path of money supply. The assumption of forward-looking expectations has implications not just for the liquidity trap concept but for the interpretation of the IS-LM model as a whole. Indeed, as pointed out by Axel Leijonhufvud (1983, 1987), traditional IS-LM analysis is based on the notion that disturbances that shift one of the curves will not at the same time affect the position of the other curve, which is not true under a rational expectations equilibrium. In particular, an anticipated monetary impulse will shift both IS and LM schedules, with the implication that the interest elasticity of the two curves is largely irrelevant for the monetary transmission mechanism in general and for the liquidity trap in particular (see also Christiano 2000; Krugman and

Obstfeld 1994, 392, 456, 474; Krugman and Obstfeld 2003, 499–501; Gordon 2000, 135–38; Mankiw 2003, 303).

Although Hicks ([1936] 1982, 88) hailed Keynes's notion that short-period equilibrium depends on the state of expectations, he was critical of the assumption that such expectations could be treated as given when economic policy changes. In *Value and Capital*, expectations of price are determined by autonomous changes in the state of the "news" and by the elasticity of price expectations (204). Hicks ([1939] 1946, 277–79) showed how an autonomous rise in price expectations will shift demand in favor of current commodities at the expense of securities or money, with an ensuing increase in current prices. He did not apply that to the discussion of the liquidity trap concept, though. Later on Hicks (1969, 315; see also Hicks 1989, chap. 11) would point out that "expectations of the future (entirely rational expectations) are based upon the data that are available in the present." Although that passage indicates that Hicks could be aware of some of the issues that would be raised by Leijonhufvud (1983) concerning the interdependence of the IS and LM curves under forward-looking expectations, there is no recorded reaction by Hicks (who died in 1989) to Leijonhufvud's comments and to their implications for the analysis of the liquidity trap concept.

6. Conclusion

Hicks's formulation of a long-term interest rate minimum in the 1937 IS-LM article was based on his theory of the determination of the short-term rate by the marginal value of liquidity and of the long rate by the term structure, plus the double assumption of elastic price expectations and inelastic interest expectations. The theory of interest developed in *Value and Capital* has provided the foundation for much of the modern approach to the determination of interest rates, which explains why Hicks's 1937 presentation of the liquidity trap argument is in many ways closer to the recent discussion than Keynes's or the traditional textbook version built on Hansen or Lange. Despite similarities between Hicks's original treatment and recent literature, it should be noted that Hicks's 1937 emphasis on a positive floor to the long-term rate of interest has not been shared in the theoretical discussion triggered by the Japanese depression of the late 1990s. Instead, the focus is on the lower bound to the short-term interest rate used as an instrument of monetary policy by the central bank. Accordingly, the rate of interest determined in recent optimizing IS-LM models is the rate on a one-period bond. This is reminiscent of Hicks's ([1939] 1946) discussion of a spot economy with short loans only. Although it is occasionally mentioned (see, e.g., Krugman 1998, 146) that in a liquidity trap the interest rate is zero (or nearly so) on short-period bonds only, this is not generally incorporated into recent models. In any event, the implicit justification for such an approach is that long-term interest rates are also bound as soon as the short rates have hit their (near) zero lower bound, which is consistent with Hicks's 1937 insight.

As noted by Hicks (1969, 314), the "famous trouble of the 'floor' to the rate of interest" is "one of the legacies to 'modern' Keynesian economics of Keynes's preoccupation with the long rate." However, a liquidity trap may also arise in IS-LM models where the short rate is used as the representative interest rate; in this case the floor will be (near) zero. By focusing analytically on the short-rate minimum, the recent literature is led to stress deflationary expectations (just like some pre-Keynesian authors) or a negative natural rate of interest as necessary conditions for the emergence of a liquidity trap. Both elements are sufficient but not necessary conditions for the 1937 demonstration of a Hicksian liquidity trap. In the same vein, the possibility of a liquidity trap in recent discussion is not related to the interest elasticity of money demand or to the slope of the LM curve, since, by definition, money and bonds become perfect substitutes when the short rate hits its (near) zero lower bound. This is illustrated by Krugman's formulation of a vertical LM curve to investigate the liquidity trap concept.

The revival of interest in the notion of a liquidity trap has not been generally motivated—in contrast with the discussion by Hicks, Lange, and (to a lesser degree) Modigliani and Hansen—by an attempt to use the IS-LM model to distinguish between Keynesian and classical economics. We have seen that the liquidity trap concept played a key role in Hicks's IS-LM exercise in part because of his encompassing description of neo-Marshallian monetary theory. Hicks's suggestion that the *General Theory* is the economics of depression has been controversial in macroeconomic theory, but it did bring to the fore the idea of demand failures that cannot be corrected by cutting the interest rate all the way to its lower bound. This is the aspect of the liquidity trap concept that has attracted most attention recently (see, e.g., Krugman [1999] 2000, chap. 9), together with the possibility of deflationary spirals if the central bank follows a Wicksell-Taylor rule for the interest rate (Benhabib,

Schmitt-Grohé, and Uribe 2002). Hicks was aware that the notion of a liquidity trap—and of aggregate instability in general—depends heavily on the assumption about price expectations. The instability results of his classic 1939 book and of the 1937 article are built on the assumption of unit (or higher) elasticity of price expectations. The notion of elasticity of price expectations (adaptative expectations) has been replaced in the new generation of IS-LM models by forward-looking expectations, which has led to further developments of Hicks's original liquidity trap concept.

References

Ackley, G. 1961. *Macroeconomic Theory*. New York: Macmillan.

———. 1978. *Macroeconomics: Theory and Policy*. New York: Macmillan.

Bailey, M. J. 1962. *National Income and the Price Level*. New York: McGraw-Hill.

Benhabib, J., S. Schmitt-Grohé, and M. Uribe. 2002. Avoiding Liquidity Traps. *Journal of Political Economy* 110.3:535–63.

Blanchard, O. 1997. *Macroeconomics*. Upper Saddle River, N.J.: Prentice Hall.

Boianovsky, M. 2002. Simonsen and the Early History of the Cash-in-Advance Approach. *European Journal of the History of Economic Thought* 9.1:57–71.

———. 2005. Some Cambridge Reactions to the *General Theory*: David Champernowne and Joan Robinson on Full Employment. *Cambridge Journal of Economics* 29.1.

Champernowne, D. G. 1936. Unemployment, Basic and Monetary: The Classical Analysis and the Keynesian. *Review of Economic Studies* 3:201–16.

Christiano, L. 2000. Comment on Theoretical Analysis Regarding a Zero Lower Bound on Nominal Interest Rates. *Journal of Money, Credit, and Banking* 32.4:905–30.

Coddington, A. 1979. Hicks's Contribution to Keynesian Economics. *Journal of Economic Literature* 17:970–88.

De Vroey, M. 2000. IS-LM à la Hicks versus IS-LM à la Modigliani. *HOPE* 32.2:293–316.

Dixon, H., and B. Gerrard. 2000. Old, New, and Post Keynesian IS-LM Framework: A Contrast and Evaluation. In *IS-LM and Modern Macroeconomics*, edited by W. Young and B. Zilberfarb. Boston: Kluwer.

Dornbusch, R., and S. Fischer. 1978. *Macroeconomics*. Tokyo: McGraw-Hill.

Eggertsson, G., and M. Woodford. 2003. The Zero Bound on Interest Rates and Optimal Monetary Policy. *Brookings Papers on Economic Activity*, no. 1:139–233.

Fisher, I. 1896. *Appreciation and Interest*. New York: Macmillan.

Friedman, M. 1969. *The Optimum Quantity of Money and Other Essays*. Chicago: Aldine.

———. 1970. A Theoretical Framework for Monetary Analysis. *Journal of Political Economy* 78.2:193–238.

Froyen, R. 2002. *Macroeconomics: Theories and Policies*. 7th ed. Upper Saddle River, N.J.: Prentice Hall.

Fuhrer, J., and B. Madigan. 1997. Monetary Policy When Interest Rates Are Bound at Zero. *Review of Economics and Statistics* 79.4:573–85.

Gärtner, M. 2003. *Macroeconomics*. Harlow, U.K.: Financial Times/Prentice Hall.

Gordon, R. 2000. *Macroeconomics*. 8th ed. Boston: Addison-Wesley.

Grandmont, J.-M., and G. Laroque. 1976. The Liquidity Trap. *Econometrica* 44.1:129–35.

Haberler, G. 1946. *Prosperity and Depression*. 3rd ed. New York: United Nations.

Hall, R., and Taylor, J. 1986. *Macroeconomics: Theory, Performance, and Policy*. New York: Norton.

Hansen, A. 1949. *Monetary Theory and Fiscal Policy*. New York: McGraw-Hill.

———. 1953. *A Guide to Keynes*. New York: McGraw-Hill.

Hawtrey, R. G. 1932. *The Art of Central Banking*. London: Longman.

———. [1937] 1952. *Capital and Employment*. 2nd ed. London: Longmans, Green.

———. [1913] 1962. *Good and Bad Trade*. New York: A. M. Kelley.

Hicks, J. 1935. A Suggestion for Simplifying the Theory of Money. *Economica* 2:1–19.

———. 1937. Mr. Keynes and the "Classics": A Suggested Interpretation. *Econometrica* 5:147–59.

———. 1942. The Monetary Theory of D. H. Robertson. *Economica* 9:53–57.

———. [1939] 1946. *Value and Capital*. 2nd ed. Oxford: Clarendon.

———. 1950. *A Contribution to the Theory of the Trade Cycle*. Oxford: Clarendon.

———. 1957. A Rehabilitation of "Classical" Economics? *Economic Journal* 67:278–89.

———. 1967a. *Critical Essays in Monetary Theory*. Oxford: Clarendon.

———. 1967b. Interest. In vol. 7 of *Chambers's Encyclopaedia*. London: Pergamon.

———. 1969. Automatists, Hawtreyans, and Keynesians. *Journal of Money, Credit, and Banking* 1:307–17.

———. 1974. *The Crisis in Keynesian Economics*. Oxford: Basil Blackwell.

———. 1979. On Coddington's Interpretation: A Reply. *Journal of Economic Literature* 17:989–95.

———. [1936] 1982. Mr. Keynes' Theory of Employment. In Hicks 1982.

———. [1980–81] 1982. IS-LM: An Explanation. In Hicks 1982.

———. 1982. *Money, Interest, and Wages*. Cambridge: Harvard University Press.

———. 1989. *A Market Theory of Money*. Oxford: Clarendon.

Hondroyiannis, G., P. Swamy, and G. Tavlas. 2000. Is the Japanese Economy in a Liquidity Trap? *Economics Letters* 66:17–23.

Ireland, P. 2001. The Real Balance Effect. NBER Working Paper no. 8136.

Kaldor, N. 1937. Prof. Pigou on Money Wages in Relation to Unemployment. *Economic Journal* 47:745–53.

———. 1939. Speculation and Economic Stability. *Review of Economic Studies* 7:1–27.

Kalecki, M. [1943] 1991. *Studies in Economic Dynamics*. In vol. 2 of *Collected Works of Michal Kalecki*, edited by J. Osiatynsky. Oxford: Clarendon.

Keynes, J. M. 1936. *The General Theory of Employment, Interest, and Money*. London: Macmillan.

Klein, L. R. 1947. *The Keynesian Revolution*. New York: Macmillan.

Kregel, J. 2000. Krugman on the Liquidity Trap: Why Inflation Won't Bring Recovery to Japan. *Economia* 1.1:39–58.

Krugman, P. 1998. It's Baaack: Japan's Slump and the Return of the Liquidity Trap. *Brookings Papers on Economic Activity*, no. 2:137–205.

———. [1999] 2000. *The Return of Depression Economics*. 2nd ed. London: Penguin.

———. 2000a. Thinking about the Liquidity Trap. *Journal of the Japanese and International Economies* 14:221–37.

———. 2000b. How Complicated Does the Model Have to Be? *Oxford Review of Economic Policy* 16:33–42.

Krugman, P., and M. Obstfeld. 1994. *International Economics*. 3rd ed. New York: Harper Collins.

———. 2003. *International Economics*. 6th ed. Boston: Addison-Wesley.

Kuttner, K., and A. Posen. 2001. The Great Recession: Lessons for Macroeconomic Policy from Japan. *Brookings Papers on Economic Activity*, no. 2:93–185.

Laidler, D. 1969. *The Demand for Money: Theories and Evidence*. Scranton, Pa.: International Textbook Company.

———. 1999. *Fabricating the Keynesian Revolution*. Cambridge: Cambridge University Press.

Lange, O. 1938. The Rate of Interest and the Optimum Propensity to Consume. *Economica* 5:12–32.

Leijonhufvud, A. 1983. What Was the Matter with IS-LM? In *Modern Macroeconomic Theory: An Overview*, edited by J.-P. Fitoussi. Oxford: Basil Blackwell.

———. 1987. IS-LM Analysis. In vol. 2 of *The New Palgrave: A Dictionary of Economics*, edited by J. Eatwell, M. Milgate, and P. Newman. London: Macmillan.

Malkiel, B. 1966. *The Term Structure of Interest Rates*. Princeton, N.J.: Princeton University Press.

Mankiw, N. G. 2003. *Macroeconomics*. 5th ed. New York: Worth.

Marshall, A. [1890] 1990. *Principles of Economics*. London: Macmillan.

McCallum, B. T. 1989. *Monetary Economics*. New York: Macmillan.

———. 2000. Theoretical Analysis Regarding a Zero Lower Bound on Nominal Interest Rates. *Journal of Money, Credit, and Banking* 32:870–904.

McCallum, B. T., and E. Nelson. 1999. An Optimizing IS-LM Specification for Monetary Policy and Business Cycle Analysis. *Journal of Money, Credit, and Banking* 31:296–316.

McKinnon, R., and K. Ohno. 1997. *Dollar and Yen: Resolving Economic Conflict between the United States and Japan*. Cambridge: MIT Press.

Meltzer, A. 1995. Monetary, Credit, and (Other) Transmission Processes: A Monetarist Perspective. *Journal of Economic Perspectives* 9.4:49–72.

————. 1999. Commentary: Monetary Policy at Zero Inflation. In *New Challenges for Monetary Policy*. Kansas City, Mo.: Federal Reserve Bank.

Miyao, R. 2002. Liquidity Traps and the Stability of Money Demand: Is Japan Really Trapped at the Zero Bound? RIEB Discussion Paper Series, no. 127, Kobe University.

Mizen, P., and J. Presley. 1998. Keynes, Hicks, and the Cambridge School. *HOPE* 30.1:1–16.

Modigliani, F. 1944. Liquidity Preference and the Theory of Interest and Money. *Econometrica* 12:45–88.

Patinkin, D. 1959. Keynesian Economics Rehabilitated: A Rejoinder to Professor Hicks. *Economic Journal* 69:582–87.

————. [1956] 1965. *Money, Interest, and Prices*. 2nd ed. New York: Harper & Row.

————. 1976. Keynes' Monetary Thought: A Study of Its Development. *HOPE* 8.1:1–150.

Pearce, K., and K. Hoover. 1995. After the Revolution: Paul Samuelson and the Textbook Keynesian Model. In *New Perspectives on Keynes*, edited by A. Cottrell and M. Lawlor. *HOPE* 27 (supplement): 183–216.

Pigou, A. C. 1933. *The Theory of Unemployment*. London: Macmillan.

————. 1943. The Classical Stationary State. *Economic Journal* 53:343–51.

Rabin, A., and Z. Keilany. 1986–87. A Note on the Incompatibility of the Pigou Effect and a Liquidity Trap. *Journal of Post Keynesian Economics* 9:291–96.

Roberts, M. 1995. Keynes, the Liquidity Trap, and the Gold Standard: A Possible Application of the Rational Expectations Hypothesis. *Manchester School* 43:82–92.

Robertson, D. H. 1936. Some Notes on Mr. Keynes' General Theory of Interest. *Quarterly Journal of Economics* 51:168–91.

————. 1940. *Essays in Monetary Theory*. London: P. S. King.

————. [1922] 1948. *Money*. London: Nisbet.

Robinson, J. [1951] 1952. The Rate of Interest. In *The Rate of Interest*. London: Macmillan.

Romer, D. 2000. Keynesian Macroeconomics without the LM Curve. *Journal of Economic Perspectives* 14:149–69.

Samuelson, P. A. 1967. *Economics*. 7th ed. New York: McGraw-Hill.

Skidelsky, R. 1992. *John Maynard Keynes: The Economist as Saviour, 1920–1937*. London: Penguin.

————. 1996. The Influence of the Great Depression on Keynes's *General Theory*. *History of Economics Review* 25:78–87.

Smith, W. [1956] 1966. A Graphical Exposition of the Complete Keynesian System. In *Readings in Macroeconomics*, edited by M. Mueller. New York: Holt, Rinehart and Winston.

Sumner, S. 2002. Some Observations on the Return of the Liquidity Trap. *Cato Journal* 21:481–90.

Tobin, J. 1947. Liquidity Preference and Monetary Policy. *Review of Economics and Statistics* 29:124–31.

———. [1958] 1966. Liquidity Preference as Behavior towards Risk. In *Readings in Macroeconomics*, edited by M. Mueller. New York: Holt, Rinehart and Winston.

———. 1980. *Asset Accumulation and Economic Activity*. Oxford: Basil Blackwell.

Uhlig, H. 2000. Should We Be Afraid of Friedman's Rule? *Journal of the Japanese and International Economies* 14:261–303.

Vickrey, W. 1954. Stability through Inflation. In *Post Keynesian Economics*, edited by K. Kurihara. New Brunswick, N.J.: Rutgers University Press.

Walsh, C. E. 2003. *Monetary Theory and Policy*. 2nd ed. Cambridge: MIT Press.

Wicksell, K. [1898] 1936. *Interest and Prices*. Translated by R. F. Kahn. London: Macmillan.

Wilson, D. 1999. Is Shutting Krugman's Liquidity Trap the Answer to Japan's Problems? *Pacific Economic Papers*, no. 297.

Wonnacott, P. 1978. *Macroeconomics*. Homewood, Ill.: Irwin.

Woodford, M. 2003. *Interest and Prices: Foundations of a Theory of Monetary Policy*. Princeton, N.J.: Princeton University Press.

Young, W. 1987. *Interpreting Mr Keynes: The IS-LM Enigma*. Cambridge: Polity.

IS-LM-BP: An Inquest

Warren Young and William Darity Jr.

Open economy macroeconomics is not a new field of theoretical inquiry. Its origins can be traced back to mercantilist and classical notions of the impact of the trade balance, gold flows, and exchange rate mechanisms (e.g., Hume [1752] 1970). But formal mathematical and geometric models of trade and capital flows and exchange rate movements are a much more recent development, emerging only over the past seventy years. Roy Harrod and James Meade published early works, parts of which dealt with floating exchange rates and "free capital movements" (Harrod 1933, 1936; Meade 1936). This and subsequent work of Meade and Lloyd Metzler, among others, stimulated a generation of theorists to develop what Robert Mundell (2002) calls the "international macroeconomic model."

In previous work, we examined the development of the early mathematical models of IS-LM closed economy vintage (Darity and Young 1995). Here, we attempt to do the same for the open economy version of IS-LM. There are a number of general accounts of the evolution of the open economy model, including Kenen 1985, Flanders 1989, and Isard 1995, and specific accounts of the evolution of the "Mundell-Fleming model" (Blejer, Kahn, and Masson 1995; Boyer 2002; Boughton 2003),

The authors would like to thank Robert Mundell, Peter Kenen, Max Corden, Richard Cooper, June Flanders, and especially Russell Boyer for insightful comments on earlier versions of this paper. David Laidler, Mike Bordo, and other participants at the conference also stimulated the present improved version. Although they are not cited in the text, the following works were important in the composition of this article: Dornbusch 2000, Fleming 1968, Haberler, Metzler, and Triffin 1947, Kindleberger 1937, Maclup 1943, Metzler 1968, and Modigliani 1987.

and Mundell himself (1999, 2001, 2002). But up to now, the specific development of IS-LM-BP (balance of payments) as distinct from the Mundell-Fleming story as told by Mundell, among others, has not been dealt with. Indeed, IS-LM-BP has a history parallel to that of Mundell's models and J. Marcus Fleming's model as told by Mundell, R. Boyer, and J. Boughton. In this context we must distinguish between the Mundell-Fleming model synthesized by Rudiger Dornbusch, that is, with flexible exchange rates and perfect capital mobility only (Dornbusch 1980b, 193–94), and the more general IS-LM-BP framework, which encompasses both fixed and flexible exchange rates and all degrees of capital mobility. Recently Mundell has told his side of the story (1999, 2001, 2002), and this will not be repeated at length here. The full story of Fleming's contribution has never been told, despite some recent work in this direction (Boyer 2002; Boughton 2003), and a serious attempt is currently being made to rectify this (Boyer and Young forthcoming). It must also be recalled that at least three alternate models of the open economy—the Swan-Salter-Meade-Corden framework, the Polak-IMF framework, and the Johnsonian-monetary approach framework—were developed immediately prior to the IS-LM-BP framework. But IS-LM-BP, and its Mundell-Fleming "special case," became the model of preference for both policy analysis and pedagogy.

The essay is divided into three sections. Section 1 deals with the early mathematical and geometric models of the open economy, including Metzler's pioneering 1942 model and the Laursen-Metzler model (1950); Metzler's 1951 model is also briefly discussed as it influenced Mundell, on Mundell's own account. This section also deals with the impact of Meade's 1951 model and Metzler's models on Mundell's work. In this context, we integrate the relevant parts of Mundell's accounts of the development of his models (1999, 2001, 2002). Section 1 also briefly surveys the early alternatives to IS-LM-BP, that is, the Swan-Salter-Meade-Corden framework, on the one hand, and the Polak-IMF and Johnsonian-monetary balance approach frameworks, on the other. Section 2 surveys the characteristics of Mundell's models from 1960 to 1964 and compares them with Fleming's 1962 model. Section 3 deals with the diagrammatic development of IS-LM-BP as it emanated from the important generalized model of Anne Krueger (1965); the "overlooked" linkage of Krueger's model to the "Hicksian IS-LL construct" made by Michael Michaely (1968); Akira Takayama's 1969 "general equilibrium model" based on the open economy extension, that is, "straightforward use," of IS-LM; the somewhat forgotten "IS-LM-EE" approach of Dwayne Wrightsman (1970); and the appearance, in William Branson's widely used 1972 textbook, of IS-LM-BP with fixed exchange rates; all this before Dornbusch's synthesis of Mundell's models and Fleming's model into what he called the Mundell-Fleming model (1976–80). This section also deals with Dornbusch's contribution to the IS-LM-BP story, that is, his Mundell-Fleming synthesis and its extensions. Finally, this section attempts to answer the question of why IS-LM-BP came to "rule the roost," at the pedagogical level at least.

Early Mathematical and Geometric Models

Meade, Metzler, and Samuelsonian Methods:
Metzler and Laursen-Metzler, 1942–51

Metzler's 1942 *Econometrica* paper, "Underemployment Equilibrium in International Trade," is a pioneer among the early mathematical models of the open economy after the publication of John Maynard Keynes's *General Theory* (1936) and Harrod's *Trade Cycle* (1936). In the initial footnote to his 1942 paper, Metzler wrote that he had "confined" his "analysis" to the "real income approach" to the balance of trade (97 n. 1), as set out by Harrod (1933, 1936). Metzler's "*static* scheme" (1942, 99; emphasis in the original) is based on national accounts equations for an open economy, albeit extended to the two-country case. But the object of Metzler's model was not simply to analyze investment-consumption relations. For, as he wrote, "if certain stability conditions . . . are satisfied, this fundamental system determines the equilibrium of investment and consumption in each country, and hence total incomes and the balance of trade" (99), or in other words, the general equilibrium of the two-country system.

Metzler then turned his "static scheme" into a "dynamic system" by dating the variables and analyzing the stability and equilibrium of the system he proposed (100). By doing this, he departed from Harrod's methodological approach and adopted that of John Hicks's *Value and Capital* and Paul Samuelson's *Foundations* (see Young 1989, 1991). But more is involved here, for Metzler was among the first to utilize the Samuelsonian "Correspondence Principle" (Samuelson 1941; 1947, 258, 262); and this was based on Samuelson's then unpublished book, which Metzler (1942, 100 n. 6) cited as "the foundations of analytical economics." This is readily seen in Metzler's summary of Samuelson's view that "stability depends not only upon the characteristics of the static equations . . . but also upon the nature of the assumed dynamic system" (100).

Metzler's 1942 model is a two-country model, with domestic prices, interest rate, and exchange rate fixed and no capital movements. His dynamic system consists of "linear difference equations with constant coefficients" (98, 101). Using Samuelson's methods, Metzler is able to analyze "four types" of parametric variation as they affect total consumption, investment, and income, in the respective countries, and the trade balance, dependent on whether one or both of the countries are stable or unstable "in isolation." For example, as he writes, "domestic expansion will lead to a drain on foreign balances only if the country with which the expanding country deals is stable in isolation." Thus, Metzler continues,

> one should always specify which of the countries is assumed to be unstable in isolation and which stable. Many economists will probably prefer to assume that all countries are stable in isolation. . . . With stability conditions specified, directions of change may be determined for all variables except investment in one of the two countries. This remaining ambiguity is attributable to the dual nature of such investment. That is, whenever the balance of trade of a country declines while domestic investment rises (or conversely), the direction of change of total investment cannot be determined without further information. . . . the final outcome under these circumstances depends . . . upon such nonstability conditions as the relation between marginal propensity to invest and marginal propensity to import. (110–12)

Interestingly enough, Metzler's paper antedates Franco Modigliani's *Econometrica* paper by two years, but while the latter is recognized as the apex of the "neoclassical synthesis" of IS-LM closed economy vintage (Fischer 1987), the former is not recognized as one of the key starting points of the general equilibrium IS-LM-BP approach to the open economy. For example, Peter Isard (1995) does not mention Metzler's 1942 paper, nor do M. Blejer, M. Kahn, and P. Masson (1995).

In their 1950 *Review of Economics and Statistics* paper, Svend Laursen and Metzler extended the analysis of Metzler's 1942 paper to the case of flexible exchange rates. Indeed, as they indicated in their mathematical appendix (which greatly influenced Mundell, among others, as will be seen below), similar questions had been addressed in Metzler's 1942 paper (Laursen and Metzler 1950, 297–98; 298 n. 6). The 1950 model is a two-country model with fixed interest rate and no capital movements but with the possibility of price flexibility (292) under a flexible exchange rate regime. As Laursen and Metzler wrote, if "the exchange rate is [a] flexible rate . . . it accordingly takes on a value at which the international payments and receipts between the two countries are equalized. If capital movements are prohibited, the equilibrium exchange rate will be that rate at which each country's exports are equal to its imports" (293). Based on this, they then presented an equation system that "with given expenditure functions and price levels in both countries" indicated "the equilibrium levels of income as well as the equilibrium exchange rate" (293). The Samuelsonian "Correspondence Principle" method was also used by Laursen and Metzler; that is, they examined the conditions of stability and dynamic behavior of their proposed equation system before evaluating their "static equations" (295). But the main thing to remember here is that the Laursen-Metzler model does not flow from "Keynesian headwaters." Rather, "the fundamental problem" the paper tries to address—"the degree of economic insulation that can be achieved by a system of flexible exchange rates" (291)—emanated from issues raised a decade earlier by Gottfried Haberler in the "revised edition" of *Prosperity and Depression* (Laursen and Metzler 1950, 284 n. 10).

Metzler's 1951 paper "Wealth, Saving, and the Rate of Interest"— while a closed economy model—also emanated from what Metzler called "the remodeled classical theory," or general equilibrium approach of Haberler ([1937] 1941), among others (Metzler 1951, 93 n. 3; 98). The formal model, as presented in the mathematical appendix to the paper, consists of two markets: goods and services, and securities, and a system of equations determining the equilibrium values of variables. Metzler first presents a static system (113) and then goes on to present two "dynamic" postulates, that is to say, "equations of adjustment" (115), which "are the dynamic counterpart" of two of his static equations. He then presents his "complete dynamic system" by utilizing the "definitional equations" of the static system (115). He goes on to analyze the stability of the system and its "approach toward equilibrium," in addition to the possibility of cyclical fluctuations, by means of Samuelsonian methods—that is, analysis of the roots of his dynamical equations—in a manner similar to the 1950 Laursen-Metzler paper (1951, 115–16; see also 1950, 295–97). And, as will be seen below, it is this paper that stimulated Mundell into extending Metzler's approach to the open economy, according to Mundell himself.

Meade, Metzler, and Mundell:
Meade's *Mathematical Supplement* (1951)

According to Mundell's accounts, there were three major influences on his work: Meade, Metzler, and Samuelson. After completing his doctoral exams at MIT, where he was "especially influenced by Samuelson and Kindleberger" (Mundell 2001, 216), Mundell chose to visit the London School of Economics from mid-1955 for a year and work on completing his thesis under the supervision of Meade (Mundell 1999; 2001, 216; 2002, 1–2), because he "was fascinated" with, as he put it, Meade's 1952 "Geometry of International Trade" (1999). While at LSE, Mundell met Meade weekly, but Mundell focused on trade theory and not macroeconomics (1999, 2001, 2002).

In his 1999 letter to one of the present authors—which became the basis for his 2001 *IMF Staff Papers* article and his subsequent "Notes on the Development of the International Macroeconomic Model" (Mundell 2002, 15–16 n. 1)—Mundell assessed the mathematical supplement (MS) to Meade's 1951 volume *The Balance of Payments*, which he did not include in his published accounts (Mundell 2001, 2002). In his letter, Mundell talks about his "own methods" of solving mathematical problems involving equational systems. And, as he writes, "it is almost true to say that I didn't get any of my international macroeconomics from Meade's MS" (1999). Mundell goes on to say, "My interest in macroeconomics was very much below the surface that year 1955–56 in London, which was taken up with a thesis that had an entirely classical flavor" (3). He repeated this more or less verbatim in his subsequent accounts. With regard to Meade's indirect influence on his work, however, Mundell said, "I was able to develop his work in some new areas, develop some of the dynamics, and generalize the model, following up on Mosak, in a multi-country framework" (2001, 217; Mosak 1944).

Now, according to Mundell (2001, 217), Meade's MS does contain "the equations of an international macroeconomic model." Mundell (2002, 3) goes on to say, "But when I was doing my work on this subject a few years later, I never made any connections to it, although it must have influenced me at least subconsciously. The reason, I think, is that my approach came through a Walrasian-like general equilibrium theory, which was at best only implicit in Meade's analysis." Mundell then distinguishes his approach from that of Meade by citing Meade's effort to bring about, in his model, "a marriage of the Keynesian and Hicksian type of analysis" for "balance of payments theory" (Meade 1951b, 2–3), something that, as Mundell states, "was *not*, however, what I was trying to do in my international macroeconomic model" (1999; 2001, 217; 2002, 3; emphasis in the original). Indeed, Mundell's own treatment of balance of payments problems may have been catalyzed by Meade's footnote in the MS. For, as Meade noted, "the Hicksian type of analysis has been applied to international trade problems in J. L. Mosak's *General Equilibrium Theory in International Trade. . . .* But that work does not deal at all directly with problems of disequilibrium in the balance of payments" (Meade 1951b, 3 n. 1). What was still missing, however, in Mundell's thought was a systematic way to enable him to approach the international economy within a general equilibrium framework; and it is this Metzler supplied, according to Mundell himself.

Metzler's "Architectonic Paradigm"

One of the most important questions regarding Mundell's accounts of the development of his models relates to the influence of Metzler's models. This is because in a key paper, "Flexible Exchange Rates and Employment Policy," Mundell based his model "on the work of Laursen and Metzler" (1961b, 510 n. 3; Laursen and Metzler 1950). This model became the basis for his subsequent analysis in perhaps his best-known paper, "Capital Mobility and Stabilization Policy under Fixed and Flexible Exchange Rates" (1963, 481–82 n. 5), in which he assumed "perfect capital mobility."

But Metzler influenced Mundell some five years before he even published his 1961 *Canadian Journal of Economics* paper. This is seen in his 1961 *Kyklos* paper, "The International Disequilibrium System" (1961a, 155 n. 5), in which Mundell writes, "at this point I should like to record my indebtedness to Professor Lloyd Metzler for stimulating discussion at Chicago in 1956 on the subject of the conditions of general equilibrium in an open economy." Indeed, as Mundell recalled, he spent the year 1956–57 as a postdoctoral fellow in political economy at the University of Chicago and, as he put it, "became especially interested in the work of Lloyd Metzler in theory and Milton Friedman in policy. Metzler's architectonic 'Wealth, Saving, and the Rate of Interest' in the *JPE . . .* started me thinking about that model as a more suitable paradigm for macroeconomics than the Keynesian model and worth developing in an international framework. By 1955 [actually, 1956], Patinkin's work had appeared and the Metzler-Patinkin general equilibrium approach to the closed macroeconomy provided a more classical full-employment counterpart to the standard IS-LM framework" (Mundell 2001, 4). In his 1999 letter to one of the present authors, Mundell also wrote that reading Metzler's "'Wealth, Saving, and the Rate of Interest' started me thinking about it in [an] international context. . . . This general equilibrium approach to the closed macroeconomy got me thinking about the way to write down the general equilibrium equations for the international economy. In retrospect I'm surprised I didn't think about it earlier! . . . I remember conversations I had with Metzler in that year [1956–57] and, even though after his brain operation, he was only 50%, I'm sure that wonderful man helped me getting my thinking straight. My personal view is that if Metzler had stayed healthy . . . he would have done the work I did, in some ways better. As an architect of original economic systems, he was peerless in his generation." Mundell (2002, 4) subsequently repeated his opinion regarding Metzler's potential contribution by writing that "had he remained healthy, he would surely have pioneered the international macroeconomic model. His 1950 article with Laursen was an important step along the way."

The influence of Metzler's work of the early 1950s on Mundell is clear. The question that must be asked, however, is: Why did Mundell overlook the model presented in Metzler's 1942 paper "Underemployment Equilibrium in International Trade" in his various accounts of the development of his own models? At this point, suffice it to say that Mundell does not refer to it at all, and in view of the fact that it is mentioned in the appendix to the Laursen-Metzler paper—the model of which is the basis for Mundell's 1961 *Canadian Journal* paper—that Mundell would overlook it deliberately is surprising indeed. The most plausible explanation would be that since Metzler's 1942 model is characterized by fixed prices, interest rates, and exchange rates (1942, 98), Mundell did not consider it to be as general as either the 1950 Laursen-Metzler model or Metzler's 1951 model, both of which he subsequently utilized. Mundell himself (2003) has recently offered another explanation: "I fixed upon the Laursen-Metzler article because it integrated the early Metzler-Machlup works with an adjustment system (the exchange rate) to correct the balance of trade. Of course there were no monetary equations in the system so the exchange rate had to be the real exchange rate (or the terms of trade). For me to give credits to those earlier articles [e.g., Metzler 1942] would be like hand-waving to the General Theory of Hicks' IS-LM paper."

Samuelsonian Methods and Economic Policy Alternatives

Mundell's approach—that is to say, the conflation of Meade's complex three-market model, Metzler's mechanism for general equilibrium, and Mundell's special emphasis on the importance of capital movements—enabled Mundell to create, as Dornbusch (1980b, 5) noted, simple albeit powerful models that served as analytic frameworks, not only for thought and policy but for posing new questions. In other words, Mundell "did a Hicks" (Young 1987).

The "methods" that Mundell refers to in his 1999 letter relate to what can be called the "Stability Analysis and the Correspondence Principle" (Samuelson [1947] 1958), which enabled Mundell to "reduce" the "Central Message" of a Meade-type (static) model to five equations and then to three equations (markets) by focusing on the dynamics involved in the adjustment process (Mundell 1968, 219–21). For, as Samuelson ([1947] 1958, 262) noted,

the equations of comparative statics are . . . a special case of the general dynamic analysis. They can indeed be discussed abstracting completely from dynamical analysis. . . . But the problem of stability of equilibrium cannot be discussed except with reference to dynamical considerations. . . . in order for the comparative-statics analysis to yield fruitful results, we must first develop a theory of dynamics.

He goes on to note that

indeed, the correspondence principle, enunciating the relationship between the stability conditions of dynamics and the evaluation of displacements in comparative statics, provides the second great weapon in the arsenal of the economist interested in deriving definite, meaningful theorems. (350)

And, on Samuelson's criterion, it was Mundell, using the methodology of the correspondence principle, and not Meade, who developed the "meaningful" models that yielded "fruitful results."

In his 1999 letter, Mundell first gave his account of how his dynamic approach developed. As he put it,

The first and in some respects my most important international macroeconomic model was not the Hicks-Keynes IS-LM internationalized, but the QJE 1960 model "The Monetary Dynamics of International Adjustment Under Fixed and Flexible Exchange Rates." . . . The purpose of this article was not to introduce a new model but to find a way to analyze the difference between fixed exchange rates with flexible prices, and flexible exchange rates with fixed prices. I needed a coherent and plausible international macroeconomic model that was at least consistent with a full-employment economy or at least one in which full employment policy was being pursued by the government. There did not as yet exist such a model in the literature. The macroeconomic model I used employed an internal balance and a foreign balance schedule (for the first time in the literature) and the variables were the interest rate (representing monetary policy) and the real exchange rate (or the relative prices of home and foreign goods). These defined four zones of disequilibrium and made possible an examination of the different dynamics relevant to a fixed exchange rate system (such as the gold standard) compared to a flexible system in which monetary policy is directed at price-level stabilization.

Mundell then went into detail about how he had developed his dynamic approach, linking it with the analytic methodology of Samuelsonian dynamic stability analysis, and recalled how he discovered that the dynamic stability conditions of variant exchange rate regimes differed (1999), a "four-zone" result that he called the "principle . . . of effective market classification" (1960, 250). Mundell's results impressed Johnson so much that Mundell (1999) received "a nice letter from Harry Johnson complimenting me on it, saying something to the effect that it carried the subject to a different level." However, as will be seen below, Swan and Corden had also been developing a "four-zone" model from 1955 onward, which provided an alternate basis for policy analysis and pedagogy to that of Mundell's 1960 *Quarterly Journal of Economics* (*QJE*) model, on the one hand, and IS-LM-BP, on the other.

Early Alternatives to IS-LM-BP:
The Swan-Salter-Meade-Corden Framework

Meade's work inspired the development of a framework of analysis encompassing both equations (Meade 1951b; Hemming and Corden 1958; Swan 1960) and diagrams (Meade 1949; Swan [1955] 1968, [1950]

1963; Hemming and Corden 1958; Salter 1959; Corden 1960), albeit with special emphasis on "geometrical representation" (Meade 1949; Corden 1960). "Alternative diagrams" were presented by Meade (1949), Swan ([1955] 1968, [1950] 1960), and Salter (1959), respectively (Corden 1960, 19–22). Meade's 1949 diagrammatic system was complicated, taking "into account not only the policies in one country but in the rest of the world" (Corden 1960, 21). The original "Swan diagram" of 1955 vintage depicted "in four zones" (20) the internal-external balance approach, which had its predecessors in Harrod 1933, Nurkse 1947, and Meade 1951a. It had the level of "real expenditure" on its horizontal axis, while its vertical axis was what Swan called the "cost ratio," that is, "the ratio of an index . . . of prices of imports and exports" to "an index of local wages" (Corden 1960, 19–20). Swan revised his approach somewhat and presented, in 1960, the core of his model in equational and diagrammatic form. Salter (1959) built on Swan's earlier approach and also combined it with the earlier "Australian model" of Wilson on "capital imports and the terms of trade," bringing about the development, with Corden (1960), of what Swan first called the "dependent economy" model (Wilson 1931; Swan 1960; Dornbusch 1980b, chap. 6). In Salter's original diagram, "the quantity of traded goods is measured on the horizontal axis; and the quantity of non-traded goods on the vertical axis." The "total expenditure" line cuts both vertical and horizontal axes, thereby setting "the amount of traded" and "non-traded" goods that "could be purchased with this expenditure," given their respective prices. The slope of the expenditure line, "therefore, represents the relative price of non-traded goods compared to traded goods" (Salter 1959, 227).

However, the so-called Swan-Salter diagram, based on Swan [1955] 1968, [1950] 1960, 1963, and Salter 1959 and popularized by Corden (1960), which is the major graphic tool of the "dependent economy model," was never standardized and has appeared in numerous forms since its original presentation. For example, Dornbusch's (1980b, 101) version of the Swan-Salter-Corden diagram has real expenditure, output, and employment on the horizontal axis, and the "relative price of traded goods in terms of home goods" on its vertical axis. But only one year afterward, in an influential *Journal of Economic Literature* article, McKinnon (1981, 534) had already given a new twist to what he called "the famous Swan diagram," which he presented in government expenditure–price of foreign exchange space (534, fig. 1). By 1985, then, Kenen (1985, 650) had not only reversed the axes but also revised them for his analytic purpose, with "expenditure policy (monetary or fiscal)" on the vertical axis, and nominal and real exchange rates on the horizontal axis, respectively. Salvatore (1987, 463), in his widely used textbook, also had different axes from those of Dornbusch, with "domestic expenditure" on the horizontal and "exchange rate" on the vertical axes. Thus, while Dornbusch (1980b, 100–102) tried to present the "dependent economy model" with "three schedules" (YY-BB-NN) he set out for it as a complement to the "Mundell-Fleming model" he presented in his 1980 book, *Open Economy Macroeconomics*, his approach to the "Swan-Salter diagram," as will be seen below, simply never caught on.

The Polak-IMF and Johnsonian-Monetary Approach Frameworks

In a retrospective paper, Polak noted that he had utilized "a version" of the "IMF model" as early as 1950, although it was "first published" in 1957 (Polak 1957; 1998, 396). In his view (1998, 396–97), the "simplicity" of the model, based only on "banking and trade data," in combination with its focus on one control variable, "domestic credit creation," was its important characteristic. But, as Polak noted, "over the years" there had been "different formulations of the model" (Argy 1969; Polak and Argy 1971), so that there is no single "Polak-IMF" framework (Polak 1998, 398). Moreover, the fact that modern policy-relevant "extensions"—such as inclusion of "flexibility of international capital movements," "domestic interest rate," and variant "exchange rate policies"— would "essentially" render the model "useless" has limited its efficacy to "ad-hoc" institutional analysis (Polak 1998, 406).

What Polak has called the "Johnsonian," or "monetary," approach to the balance of payments framework emanates from Johnson's 1958 paper (Polak 2002, 27; Johnson [1958] 1968). As the model is well known, it will not be described here. The formal model, which reached its apex in *The Monetary Approach to the Balance of Payments* (Frenkel and Johnson 1976), however, is limited in its usefulness, as Plessner has recently noted, because it is expressed in a fixed price–fixed exchange rate regime (Plessner 2002, 46).

Capital Mobility in Meade and Mundell

Before proceeding, one issue remains: the reason for Mundell's emphasis on capital mobility in his best-known paper, and the one most often cited, the 1963 *Canadian Journal* paper. Here Mundell (1963, 475, 484) stressed the importance of capital movements and capital mobility. At first glance, Mundell's approach could be attributed to the influence of Meade (1951b, 3), who over a decade earlier had written, "Our model also allows for movements of capital in the balance of payments and not only for current payments for visible and invisible trade." However, while capital movements had already appeared in Meade's 1951 model, their role in his model was minimal, in comparison to the role they attained in Mundell's models. Indeed, as Kenen (1985, 636) noted, "Meade was careful to include them, but they could be deleted without altering his argument." The central role played by capital movements in Mundell's approach emanated from the passage of a decade between Meade (1951a, 1951b) and Mundell, who was working in the early 1960s, when international capital movements had grown to such a significant extent that they were seen by economists as an important factor in influencing economic activity.

But there was also a "hidden agenda" in Mundell's stress on capital mobility. This emanated from his defense of his 1962 *IMF Staff Papers* article against critics at the Federal Reserve, on the one hand, and what Mundell called the "Samuelson-Tobin 'neo-classical synthesis'" view that he took strong issue with, on the other. As Mundell (1999; 2001, 222; 2002, 9) recalled,

> I decided to reply to my critics by writing an even more extreme piece, assuming complete capital mobility, which made the Samuelson-Tobin view even more absurd, because it showed that under fixed rates and perfect capital mobility, monetary policy was completely impotent. Open market operations to buy Treasuries would result in equivalent gold losses or build-up of dollar balances. This led to the . . . 1963 paper that has been so frequently reproduced . . . [and] that is usually cited as the locus classicus of my half of the Mundell-Fleming model.

Mundell's Models and Fleming's Model in Comparative Perspective

Mundell's 1960 Model

The importance of Mundell's 1960 *QJE* model (Mundell 1960) cannot be overstated. Despite this, J. Flanders (1989, 329) does not deal at all with Mundell's 1960 *QJE* paper, preferring to focus on Mundell's 1961 *Kyklos* paper, which she asserted "flows naturally . . . out of the Metzler headwaters, and it is an elegant statement of what the other models are about." It should be recalled at this point that Mundell (1999) himself placed his *Kyklos* paper (1961a) in the "group of articles" of "Mundell-Fleming," that is, "Hicks-Keynes IS-LM internationalized" vintage. Moreover, as he put it, "the first and in some respects my most important international macroeconomic model was not the [static] Hicks-Keynes IS-LM internationalized, but the [macrodynamic] 1960 *QJE* model" (1999). In light of this, specific treatment of Mundell's 1960 model is, in our view, warranted here.

The first thing to recognize is that in his 1960 paper, Mundell separated his analysis into what he called "the static system" (229–32) and "the dynamic systems" (232–36) in order to deal with both fixed and flexible exchange rate regimes according to Samuelsonian methodology. His model consists of two markets—domestic goods and services, and foreign exchange. These markets are influenced by two factors, the domestic interest rate—determined by the central bank's monetary policy—and what Mundell (1960, 229–30) calls the "terms of trade," that is, the ratio of domestic to foreign prices. He assumes flexible domestic prices and also assumes foreign prices, incomes, and interest rates constant, meaning that changes in the ratio of domestic to foreign prices emanate only from changes in the rate of exchange or in the domestic price level.

Mundell (1960, 230–32) then presents a "simple geometric interpretation of the forces governing the rate of interest [r] and the terms of trade [P]" by constructing what he calls the "foreign-balance schedule" for the foreign exchange market (FF) and the "internal balance schedule" for the goods and services market (XX) accordingly. It is clear from the text of his paper that FF is what we now call the BP schedule with imperfect capital mobility, whereas XX is the IS schedule. This is illustrated in figure 1 (231).

But Mundell proceeded in a different manner from that of the conventional approach. Rather than developing the comparative statics of the model, he followed Samuelsonian methodology to develop its comparative macrodynamics, which consisted of the adjustment processes and paths of adjustment, and not only an analysis of the equilibrium states after the processes were completed. This was to answer some of the key questions he posed at the beginning of the paper (1960, 228), which related to stability conditions of fixed as against flexible exchange

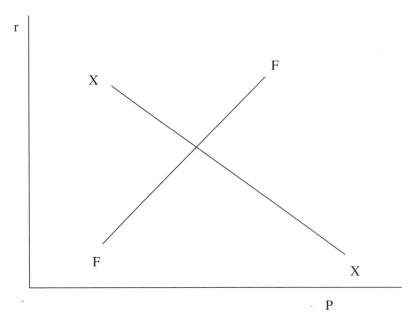

Figure 1   Mundell's 1960 *QJE* model

rate systems and the nature of the paths to equilibrium and their relation to the extent of capital mobility, among other issues.

Mundell's 1961 Vintage Models:
The 1961 *Kyklos* Model—the IS-LM-BP Prototype

According to Flanders (1989, 329), this one-country model flows "naturally" from Metzlerian "headwaters." Mundell (1999), on the other hand, saw the model as what he called an "internationalized" version of "Hicks-Keynes IS-LM." In any event, Mundell assumes general equilibrium in three markets—goods, money, and foreign exchange—and develops two systems of "excess demand" equations: a static system and a generalized system. In the static system, the excess demand for goods and services, and the balance of payments surplus, are functions of money income and rate of interest; while the excess demand for money is a function of money income, the rate of interest, and the quantity of money. In the generalized system, all three equations include money income, the rate of interest, and the quantity of money. Mundell goes on to "assume also that the conditions of balance in each of the . . . markets depend only on the level of money, the rate of interest and the quantity of money." He says that "for simplicity, however, and also to show that the results are not dependent on the Quantity Theory of Money, I assume that a change in the money supply affects the level of effective demand and the balance of payments only insofar as it first affects the rate of interest" (1961a, 155).

Mundell defines "F," the balance of payments surplus, as the "trade balance + net capital imports." He also has included a money market in his model and has excluded the quantity theory of money (1961a, 155). These are crucial distinguishing features between Mundell's "prototype" IS-LM-BP model as it appears in his 1961 *Kyklos* paper and Fleming's 1962 model, as will be seen below.

The diagrammatic representation Mundell uses in this paper is in interest rate and *money income* space (*r-y*), with three markets: goods (*XX*), foreign exchange (*FF*), and money market (*LL*). As Mundell (1961a, 155–56) puts it,

> The curve XX traces the locus of interest rates and money incomes along which there is equilibrium in the goods market. . . . The curve FF traces the locus of interest rates and money incomes along which there is equilibrium in the balance of payments; this *foreign balance* schedule has a positive slope because an increase in the rate of interest improves the balance of payments (by attracting capital) while an increase in money income worsens the balance of payments (by worsening the trade balance). The LL curve, on the other hand, requires a slightly different interpretation: it gives the pairs of interest rates and money incomes at which there is equilibrium in the money market *for any given quantity of money*, and it occupies a different position as a quantity of money varies, moving downward and to the right as the supply of money increases, and upward and to the left as the supply of money decreases. General equilibrium of the system is determined at the point Q common to both the XX and FF schedules, with a supply of money such to make the LL curve pass through Q. (emphasis in the original)

The IS-LM-BP model with imperfect capital mobility, therefore, flows directly out of Mundell's 1961 *Kyklos* paper. In this model, general equilibrium is based on equilibrium in three markets: the foreign exchange and balance of payments (FF schedule), the goods and services market (XX schedule), and the money market (LL schedule), all

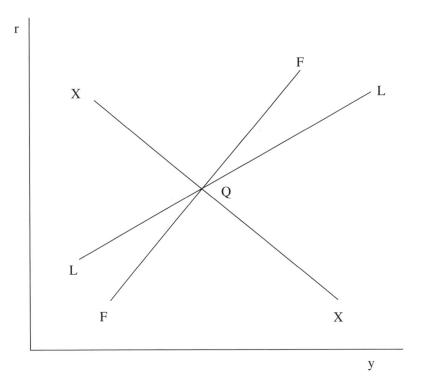

Figure 2   Mundell's 1961 *Kyklos* model

in income–interest rate space. Below the LL schedule there is excess demand for money; above it, excess supply. The equilibrium point is at Q, as illustrated in figure 2.

Mundell's 1961 *Canadian Journal* Model

Mundell develops his 1961 *Canadian Journal* model in exchange rate (y) and output space (x). The model consists of two markets, domestic goods and services, and foreign exchange and balance of payments, represented by the XX-FF schedules of 1960 *QJE* vintage. In (x-y) space, the slope of the XX schedule must be larger than that of FF in order to ensure systemic equilibrium, as illustrated in figure 3.

On the basis of his 1961 *Canadian Journal* model, Mundell developed the comparative statics regarding fiscal and monetary policy under alternate exchange rate regimes. According to this model, expansionary

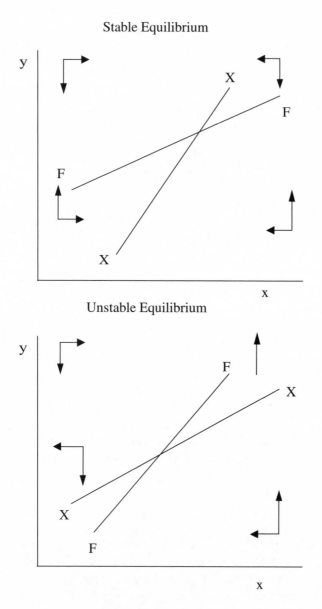

Figure 3 Mundell's 1961 *Canadian Journal* model

fiscal policy would shift the XX schedule down and to the right (1961b, 512). The intermediate increment is that which results from the simple multiplier. The final increment is that which results from the fiscal policy itself and from the increment to domestic product that results from the devaluation fiscal policy brings about. According to Mundell, it follows from this that fiscal policy is more effective in increasing domestic product and employment under a flexible exchange regime than under a fixed rate regime (512–13).

According to the model, expansionary monetary policy increases the money supply and decreases the interest rate and thus increases investment shifting the XX curve to the right. In addition, capital inflow will decrease and thus a deficit in the balance of payments will result, that is, the FF curve will shift up and to the left accordingly, reaching a new equilibrium (513). From this, Mundell concluded that monetary policy under a flexible exchange rate regime is more effective than one under a fixed rate regime, under which the deficit in the balance of payments would bring about a loss of foreign exchange reserves, and not a change in the exchange rate (513–14).

Mundell also analyzed import restrictions and export incentives that did not have direct effects on saving or investment. Import restrictions or export incentives would shift the XX schedule downward and to the right, and the FF schedule to the right and downward, that is, both shift in the same direction (514). In this case, what exactly would happen to the domestic product could not be ascertained, as the outcome of such policies would depend on the relative movement of each schedule in relation to the other. However, it is clear that FF would have to move rightward more than XX, as the initial outcome of the simple multiplier on the level of domestic product would not be enough to eliminate the surplus in the balance of payments. For there may still be a surplus in the balance of payments, which can be eliminated only by an increase in the domestic product, and thus the exchange rate must fall. To ascertain if the domestic product has declined or increased, it is necessary to see whether XX has moved vertically more than FF (514–15).

The conclusions that Mundell draws are as follows. First, if capital mobility is imperfect, then fiscal policy is more effective under a flexible exchange rate regime than a fixed rate regime, but is not effective under a flexible rate regime when capital mobility is perfect. Second, monetary policy is more effective under a flexible rate than fixed rate regime. Third, trade policies such as import restrictions or export incentives are less effective under flexible than fixed rate regimes and may even bring

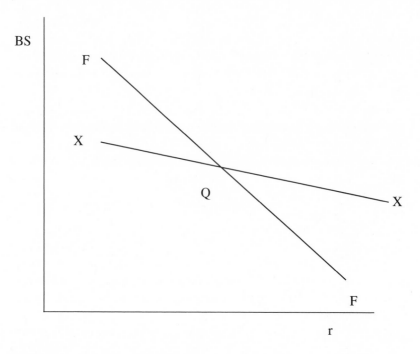

Figure 4   Mundell's 1962 *IMF Staff Papers* model

about deflationary results and have a negative impact on domestic product (515–16).

Mundell's 1962 *IMF Staff Papers* Model

In this model, there are two markets in budget surplus (*BS*) and interest rate (*r*) space, the goods and services market and the foreign exchange market. Once again, Mundell utilizes his FF and XX schedules, but this time both slope downward from left to right as illustrated in figure 4 (1962, 72).

In his 1962 approach, Mundell also developed the notion of "the proper policy mix," or "the assignment problem." Mundell showed that every policy instrument should be assigned to a policy objective on which it had the greatest impact. According to his approach (1962, 76–77), this meant that monetary policy should be directed toward external targets, while fiscal policy directed toward internal targets. Interestingly enough, Meade (1951a, 108–14) had made the same points a decade earlier.

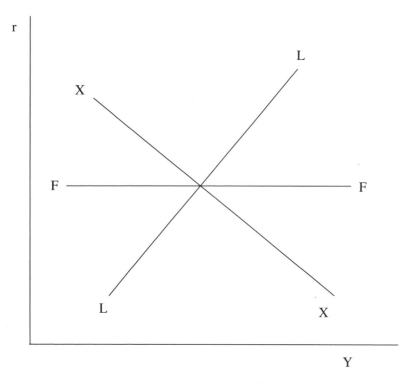

Figure 5   Mundell's 1963 *Canadian Journal* model

Mundell's 1963 *Canadian Journal* Model

The IS-LM-BP model with perfect capital mobility flows directly out of Mundell's 1963 *Canadian Journal* paper. In this model, general equilibrium is based on equilibrium in three markets: the foreign exchange and balance of payments (FF schedule), the goods and services market (XX schedule), and the money market (LL schedule), with all schedules in income-interest rate space. In this paper, Mundell returns to the diagrammatic exposition of his 1961 *Kyklos* paper and his 1961 *Canadian Journal* paper by presenting a combination of diagrams: one in income–interest rate space, and a mapping of the results of the comparative statics of monetary and fiscal policy under fixed and flexible exchange; that is, he also gives the results by plotting the internal (XX) and external (FF) balance lines in exchange rate and income space. However, despite its importance, the combined diagram is not the one that "caught on";

rather, the one illustrated in figure 5 came to "rule the roost" because of the influence of one of its main expositors, namely, Dornbusch, as we will show.

Mundell's 1964 *Canadian Journal* Model

As Mundell noted (1999; 2001, 223; 2002, 10), it was a critical comment on his 1963 *Canadian Journal* model that "provoked" him "into extending the model to the two-country global context." This model is perhaps the most sophisticated of his early models and, indeed, because of "complicating features," Mundell (1964, 424) presented the model "in the form of an explicit mathematical system" only and did not use diagrammatic exposition, which limited its utilization; this was in contrast to his previous models that, for the most part, used both equations and diagrams. The main results of his analysis, however, were subsequently co-opted into the Mundell-Dornbusch-Krugman two-country model with diagrammatic exposition (Dornbusch and Krugman 1976, 543–48; Dornbusch 1980b, 199–202).

Fleming's 1962 *IMF Staff Papers* Model versus
Mundell's 1961 *Kyklos* Model

Fleming (1962, 369) assumes "a simple Keynesian model" with fixed prices. He presents "a mathematical formulation" of the model in his appendix (377). These equations include one relating income velocity to the ratio of national income to the stock of money. The rate of interest in Fleming's model is a function of the velocity of money, but there is no demand for money function. In other words, in Fleming's (1962, 377) model money demand is set equal to supply, and he uses a modified quantity theory equation to determine the interest rate.

More important, however, Fleming has no balance of payments function per se. Rather, he deals with the balance of trade and net capital imports in separate equations, with the result that the adjustment in the balance of payments cannot be determined. This can be seen in the example of the impact of a change in "budgetary policy" given by Fleming (1962, 370–71), with divergent outcomes regarding the trade balance and net capital imports, and indeterminacy regarding the balance of payments as a whole.

In addition, under fixed rates, as Mundell has asserted, the money supply must be endogenous, so as to enable adjustment, and not constant, as Fleming (1962, 370) would have it. Under Fleming's assumption, there would be no adjustment of LM, that is to say, "accommodating monetary policy," in the case of the "budgetary expansion" he is talking about. The money stock cannot be "held constant" if adjustment is to take place. Thus, under fixed rates, according to Fleming's model, not only would "budgetary expansion" be ineffective, it would have no effect on the outcome at all. In other words, Fleming's 1962 model generates an outcome contrary to the conventional "Mundell-Fleming" result.

Briefly put, an attempt to analytically link Mundell's 1961 *Kyklos* paper—with its IS-LM-BP prototype model and sophisticated general equilibrium equational-diagrammatic system and market adjustment processes—to Fleming's 1962 "simple Keynesian model" is problematic, to say the least.

Fleming's 1962 *IMF Staff Papers*
Model versus Mundell's 1961 and 1963
Canadian Journal Models

To reiterate, in his 1962 paper, Fleming deals with a small country under both a fixed and flexible exchange rate regime, and tries to assess the relative efficacy of fiscal versus monetary policy. In his analysis of an increase in government expenditure under a fixed rate regime, he held the stock of money constant and then assessed under what conditions the balance of payments would improve. But, as Kuska (1978, 665–66) noted in his critique of "Keynesian balance-of-payments theory," Fleming seemed to be "unaware that his money market assumption requires the balance of payments to be zero." Moreover, as Kuska went on to say, in Fleming's "consideration of the effects of an increase in the supply of money under fixed exchange rates, he continues to require equilibrium in the money market, and then deduces that the equilibrium balance of payments decreases, which is another contradiction." Mundell (1999) later called the indeterminacy described above, and the results Kuska criticized, Fleming's "fatal error."

There is a problem, however, in that in his 1961 paper, Mundell also obtained an indeterminate result, while in his 1963 paper he made a similar assumption to that of Fleming regarding fiscal policy. For example, in the former paper (1961b, 512–13), the magnitude of the increase in output resulting from expansionary fiscal policy under fixed rates is a function of the magnitude of devaluation because of the resultant balance of payments deficit, that is, if devaluation is adopted as a policy option under the "constant exchange rate" Mundell initially assumed. Moreover, in his figure illustrating "the effect of fiscal policy on employment," Mundell (1961b, 513, fig. 3) is essentially comparing a point of flexible rate equilibrium with a situation of fixed rates, where the balance of payments is not in equilibrium (Boyer 2003); and this, without advising the reader that he has "conflated" his diagrammatic analysis, to use Hicks's methodological terminology (Young 1987).

In his 1963 paper, Mundell made an identical assumption to that of Fleming, when he wrote, "I have defined fiscal policy as an increase in government spending financed by government bond issues with *no* change in the money supply" (481 n. 5; emphasis in the original). What saves Mundell's 1963 model, however, is his more significant assumption of perfect capital mobility and the change in his definitions of both fiscal and monetary policy, so as to get around the "apparent conflict" with the results in his previous papers (481–82 n. 5). Once again, to link Mundell's 1961 and 1963 results with Fleming's 1962 results is problematic.

Mundell's Models versus
Fleming's Model, 1960–64

Up to now, it has been customary to refer to the open economy equilibrium macro model as the Mundell-Fleming model. We have dealt with Mundell's own view of Fleming's work above. It should be stressed that Mundell's interests were different than those of Fleming. Mundell emphasized the theory of the equilibrium open market model and the "policy-mix"; Fleming emphasized what he took to be the concerns of the central bank. Their respective methods of economic analysis and presentation differed greatly. Mundell preferred an integration of static and dynamic analysis, based on Samuelsonian *Foundations* methodology and, for the most part, both equational and diagrammatic representations of his models. Fleming (1962, 369) preferred the comparative statics of "a simple Keynesian model" with fixed prices, without any extraneous dynamic analysis or diagrammatic exposition.

Moreover, in his 1960 *QJE* paper, both Mundell's static and dynamic models are based on flexible prices (1960, 232–33). His 1961 *Kyklos* static and dynamic models are based on money income, and his stated purpose "is to show the *existence* of an adjustment process under both classical and Keynesian assumptions" (1961a, 158; emphasis in the original). It is only in his 1963 *Canadian Journal* paper that he makes the explicit assumption of fixed prices (1963, 476), enabling his model to be linked by later observers, such as Dornbusch, as will be seen below, to that of Fleming. Mundell's 1964 extension of his analysis to the two-country case also distinguishes his approach from that of Fleming. In addition, Mundell and Fleming disagreed on several important points. In a 1963 *IMF Staff Papers* article, Fleming actually took issue with one cornerstone of the Mundell-Fleming model, that is, the principle of the policy-mix, which was also a basic element in Mundell's 1962 vintage model. Mundell had asserted that monetary policy should be directed toward attaining external balance, and fiscal policy toward internal balance. But Fleming maintained that in most nations the state budget was too "rigid," and thus it was impossible to rely on it as the "sole means" for attaining internal stability. Fleming suggested an alternative based on the following logic. If all nations set their interest rate with respect to their balance of payments position, without reference to saving and investment considerations, a situation would arise where the interest rates would be too high, and the countries would be forced to adopt expansionary deficit fiscal policies to maintain full employment. Fleming proposed a solution to the problem that differed from that of the Mundell-Fleming model when he suggested "cooperative" action on the part of the countries involved to regulate the interest rate structure.

Moreover, Fleming had always been in favor of flexible exchange rates (see Polak 1978, xxiii), in contrast to Mundell. Fleming's (1978, 138–39) justification for his support for flexible exchange rates was twofold. First, fixed exchange rates caused speculative capital movements in periods of disequilibrium in the foreign exchange markets without bringing about actual adjustments in the exchange rates in order to attain stable equilibrium. Second, countries with balance of payments deficits chose the option of import restrictions and not devaluation in order to regain equilibrium.

To sum up, Fleming's 1962 model was based on "a simple Keynesian representation" of the open economy, without any dynamics or diagrams. Mundell's critique of that "fatal error" has been presented above, insofar as in Mundell's view, Fleming examined "a system that has no mechanism of adjustment" (Mundell 1999). But this is only to be expected, as

Fleming's 1962 model did not "flow most naturally" out of the Mundell "headwaters" of the 1960 *QJE* or 1961 *Kyklos* vintages.

The "Mundell-Fleming" Synthesis: Dornbusch "Did a Hansen"

Because Mundell attributes the coining of the term "Mundell-Fleming model" to Dornbusch (Mundell 2002, 6, 11), we must now turn to Dornbusch's contributions to ascertain what he actually meant when he referred to the Mundell-Fleming model in his writings, and how his exposition of what he called "the Mundell-Fleming approach" developed. In addition, some possible influences on Dornbusch's linking of Mundell and Fleming, such as the approaches of Anne Krueger (1965), Michael Michaely (1968), and J. Niehans (1975), must be taken into account.

Dornbusch without "Mundell-Fleming": 1971–75

The members of Dornbusch's 1971 PhD thesis committee at the University of Chicago were Harry Johnson, Stanley Fischer, and Robert Mundell. The title of his dissertation was "Aspects of a Monetary Theory of Currency Depreciation." It was the basis for his two major 1973 papers in the *Journal of Political Economy* (*JPE*) and *American Economic Review* (*AER*), respectively (1973a, 893; 1973b, 871), both of which made no mention of Fleming's work, although the *JPE* paper did refer to Mundell's 1968 volume *International Economics*, which contained his early papers (1973a, 915). Dornbusch's early interest in Mundell's approach can readily be seen in his short 1971 *Canadian Journal* paper, "Notes on Growth and the Balance of Payments"—which he based on chapter 9 of Mundell's 1968 volume (1971, 389)—but no mention of Fleming's 1962 paper appears there either. In addition, in his 1974 paper "Real and Monetary Aspects of the Effects of Exchange Rate Changes," Dornbusch does not mention Fleming's 1962 paper, although he does cite Mundell's 1971 volume *Monetary Policy*. Neither Dornbusch's *Manchester School* paper, "Exchange Rates and Stabilization Rules" (1975a), nor his *AER* paper, "Exchange Rates and Fiscal Policy in a Popular Model of International Trade" (1975b), mentions Fleming's work. Briefly put, then, up to the end of 1975 at least, Fleming's model had no influence on Dornbusch's ideas.

From Krueger to Niehans, 1965–75:
Krueger's 1965 Model and Michaely's 1968
"IS-LL-BP" Adaptation

In her May 1965 paper "The Impact of Alternative Government Policies under Varying Exchange Rates," Krueger set out a "general" model to deal with the "special cases" and "apparently conflicting results" of Mundell 1961b, 1963, Fleming 1962, and Rhomberg 1964. As she put it (Krueger 1965, 195–96, 198), her object was to specify a model that "provides a satisfactory framework for analysis of all the cases" considered by Mundell, Fleming, and Rhomberg. Krueger was, therefore, the first to provide a generalized equational system linking Mundell's "analysis" with that of Fleming and Rhomberg.

Krueger initially dealt with the special case of "fiscal policy" under fixed rates as analyzed by Fleming and Rhomberg. As she wrote (1965, 203),

> The Rhomberg-Fleming result hinges on the assumption that government expenditures are not accompanied by any issuance of money. This in turn results in an increase in the interest rate. If capital flows are sufficiently responsive to interest-rate changes, and if the government did not issue any money as the level of income rose, this particular form of "fiscal policy" could generate a balance-of-payments improvement, but it is attributable to the rising interest rate, and not to government expenditures per se.

She went on to say that

> by contrast, Mundell's analysis of fiscal policy assumes no change in the interest rate. . . . In the limiting case pointed out by Mundell, if capital flows were perfectly elastic with respect to the interest-rate, it would be impossible for the monetary authority to raise the interest rate, since foreign purchasers would be willing to purchase all bonds offered at the prevailing price. (203)

Krueger then proceeded to the case of flexible exchange rates and focused on "the special case considered by Fleming and Rhomberg" under a flexible rate regime, which concerned "the utilization of fiscal policy with no money creation" (205). She wrote, "Indeed, any interest rate-expenditure policy that would lead to an improved payments position and rising incomes under fixed rates would lead to a currency appreciation under flexible rates. . . . The 'ineffectiveness' of fiscal policy results from a rising interest rate, rather than from government expenditures themselves" (205).

Now, this is not the place for detailed consideration of Krueger's significant contribution and the conclusions that she draws from her "general" model. Suffice it to say, however, that her *QJE* paper has, until now, been overlooked by most observers—including Dornbusch—who did not cite it in his papers or his 1980 text, *Open Economy Macroeconomics*. Moreover, the paper is not even cited by Isard (1995) in his ostensibly comprehensive review of the literature.

In his comment on Krueger, Michaely (1968, 508–10) was perhaps the first to make the transition from the original diagrammatic framework of earlier analyses—such as those that appeared in Mundell's works between 1961 and 1963—to one based on what he called "the Hicksian IS-LL construct"; and this in order to analyze both Krueger's "general" model and "the analysis advanced by Fleming and Rhomberg." As he wrote (1968, 508), the Hicksian construct "may easily be adapted to deal with an open economy." His IS-LL-BP diagram (1968, 509) illustrates the case of imperfect capital mobility (an upward-sloping BP cutting LL from below at the equilibrium rate of interest). Michaely (1965, 510) utilized his IS-LL-BP framework "to provide a convenient and graphic demonstration of the analyses advanced by Fleming and Rhomberg" regarding "expansionary budgetary policy" under fixed rates. It is not surprising that Michaely associated the "Hicksian IS-LL construct" with Fleming's result, as Fleming's 1962 model was based only on comparative statics, as we have already shown above. When Krueger's 1965 *QJE* generalized model of the Mundell and Rhomberg-Fleming results is combined with Michaely's IS-LL-BP diagram, however, we obtain exactly the same Mundell-Fleming analytic framework put forward by Dornbusch a decade later.

Takayama, Wrightsman, and Branson:
General Equilibrium, Four-Quadrant Analysis,
and Textbook IS-LM-BP, 1969–72

In his 1969 paper, "The Effects of Fiscal and Monetary Policies under Flexible and Fixed Exchange Rates," Takayama first surveyed the "state of play" of the models extant that dealt with the question of the relative efficacy of alternative policies under alternative exchange rate regimes.

He placed special emphasis on what he called the "Mundellian assumption" of perfect capital mobility and its related "model" and "conclusion," as against that of Johnson (what he called the "Johnson effect," and Johnson's assumption of imperfect mobility), utilizing, at the beginning of his paper, a standard IS-LM diagram without BP for the purpose of his analyses (1969, 192–93, figs. 1 and 2). Indeed, when referring to Mundell's 1963 diagrammatic analysis, he wrote (1969, 190 n. 1), "I believe that we do not need diagrams as complicated as the ones he used, rather straightforward use of the IS and LM diagram appears to be sufficient." Takayama goes on to say that the purpose of his "paper is to construct a general equilibrium model which will include both of the" approaches of Mundell and Johnson "as special cases and point out their special assumptions," adding, "we shall focus on Mundell and Johnson, but shall always be aware of other works on the topic" (194). And, interestingly enough, in his 1969 paper, Takayama mentions Fleming's 1962 paper only in a footnote (191 n. 1). But this is not surprising, in light of the fact that in the influential AEA *Readings in International Economics* volume edited by Caves and Johnson, and published a year before, Fleming's 1962 paper was not mentioned at all.

Wrightsman's 1970 *AER* article, "IS, LM, and External Equilibrium: A Graphical Analysis," has been overlooked until now. He provided the following rationale for his approach: "The IS-LM exposition of general equilibrium in the domestic money and goods markets excludes the problem of balance of payments equilibrium when the economy engages in foreign trade under the conditions of fixed foreign exchange rates. This expositional shortcoming is easily rectified by superimposing an external equilibrium condition onto the IS-LM framework" (203). He proposed "a new external equilibrium curve, called the EE curve," which he "derived geometrically" in a "four-section diagram" where the "EE curve shows" interest rate–income "combinations which generate external equilibrium" (203–4, fig. 1). Wrightsman then combined his construct with IS–LM and added a full employment line (F) to his analysis (206, fig. 2). He went on to illustrate various combinations of fiscal and monetary policy that enabled the economy to converge "at full employment with external equilibrium" (207). Wrightsman's 1970 "IS-LM-EE" framework, however, did not "catch on" either with the profession or pedagogically. Rather, it was Branson's 1972 textbook version of IS-LM-BP that came to "rule the roost."

As Wrightsman did before him, Branson (1972, 305, fig. 15-2) constructed the "BP line" in four-quadrant space. He said that "to determine whether any given internal equilibrium . . . point determined by the intersection of the IS and LM curves will yield a balance-of-payments surplus or deficit, we can simply superimpose the BP line on the IS-LM diagram" (305–6). Branson then analyzed the price effect on balance of payments equilibrium, again using a four-quadrant diagram (307, fig. 15-4). What is important to recall here is that, again, as with Wrightsman, Branson's 1972 IS-LM-BP diagrammatic analysis is for fixed exchange rates only. While he analyzed the case of exchange rate flexibility in equational terms, he did not deal with the case of perfect capital mobility at all. It is not surprising, therefore, that while he cited Mundell's 1960 *QJE* paper and 1962 *IMF Staff Papers* article, he does not mention Fleming's 1962 model or Mundell's 1963 *Canadian Journal* paper in his textbook.

Niehans's 1975 Critique and the Niehans-Dornbusch Nexus

In his note in the 1975 issue of the *Journal of International Economics*, Niehans challenged the results of Mundell, Krueger (1965), and E. Sohmen (1967) on the "efficacy of monetary policy in stabilizing domestic output" under flexible rates (Niehans 1975, 275). Interestingly enough, in his note, Niehans did not mention Fleming's 1962 model. Rather, he utilized "a Keynesian model for an open economy similar to that used by Sohmen" (277) and then analyzed the implications of the dynamic assumptions of his proposed model. His primary result was "the paradox of a possible contractive effect of monetary expansion" in the case of flexible rates (279). As he put it, under certain conditions this model predicted that "monetary policy loses all of its effect on output under flexible rates, and there is even an extreme range in which its effect is perverse" (280). Niehans concluded that "the principal benefit of flexibility should not be looked for in the short-run effects of monetary policy and stabilizing output and employment, but rather in its long-term effects on price trends" (281).

The fact of the matter is that the differential efficacy of monetary versus fiscal policy under flexible rates had appeared as early as Sohmen's MIT PhD thesis (1958, 74–82) and his 1961 book (83–90, 123–24). Sohmen's (1958, 75) approach to the relative efficacy of fiscal and monetary policies under alternate exchange rate regimes—that is, his assertion regarding, as he put it, the "automatic mechanism" and "forceful booster to domestic national income" emanating from expansionary monetary policy under flexible rates, and the "different leverage of monetary policy under fixed and flexible exchange rates"—was the result of his discovery of this "independently" of Mundell (1967, 521 n. 1). This was a clear case of independent multiple discovery rather than "cross-fertilization" (Patinkin 1983; Young 1987), as there was minimal contact between Sohmen and Mundell during the early stages of their respective careers, according to Mundell (1999; 2002, 13–14), who also could not recall noticing Sohmen's early result.

A year later, in his paper "The Theory of Flexible Exchange Rate Regimes and Macroeconomic Policy," Dornbusch (1976a, 255) took up the question raised by Niehans regarding "the effectiveness of monetary policy under flexible rates." In this paper, Dornbusch presented a model in exchange rate–price space but did not link the works of Mundell he cited (Mundell 1964, 1968) to Fleming's paper (1962). In other words, Dornbusch's proposed Mundell-Fleming model does not appear in this paper at all.

Dornbusch's next paper, published in the *Journal of International Economics* and titled "Exchange Rate Expectations and Monetary Policy" (1976b), was a direct outcome of Niehans 1975. As Dornbusch (1976b, 231) wrote,

> The purpose of this paper is to reassess the effects of monetary policy under flexible exchange rates and to give attention to the details of the short-run adjustment process. The paper is stimulated by a recent study of Niehans (1975). . . . the Niehans conclusions are of importance because they run counter to the established Mundell-Fleming view that monetary policy is most effective under flexible rates with capital mobility, and that a monetary expansion under these conditions will lead to an expansion in output and employment, and that it will cause a trade surplus and capital outflow.

This is the first time that Dornbusch puts Mundell's analysis and Fleming's 1962 model together, albeit in exchange rate–income space, "following," as he puts it, "Mundell (1968)" (233). He then considers "the modification to the Mundell-Fleming model that arises from exchange rate expectations, or the endogeneity, in the short run of the domestic interest rate" (235). In this paper, the first in which Dornbusch uses the term "Mundell-Fleming," he presents not only his version of what he calls the "Mundell-Fleming model" but also his notion of "Mundell-Fleming equilibrium" as convergence, over time, to the point "where actual and expected exchange rates are equal" (232, 236). In this context, Dornbusch also talks about "the Mundell-Fleming treatment of the goods market," the "Mundell-Fleming prediction," the "Mundell-Fleming long-run position," and the "long-run Mundell-Fleming equilibrium" (239, 241–43). As in his *Scandinavian Journal of Economics* paper (1976a), Dornbusch cites Niehans. But strangely, neither Krueger's model (1965) nor Sohmen's model (1967)—which formed the basis for Niehans's analysis, according to his own account (1975, 277), both of which Niehans cites—are cited by Dornbusch in either paper.

Dornbusch on Mundell and Fleming and
"Mundell-Fleming," 1976–80

In two subsequent papers published in 1976, Dornbusch further refined his proposed "Mundell-Fleming model," emphasizing its connection with flexible rates and the efficacy of monetary policy. For example, in his *JPE* paper titled "Expectations and Exchange Rate Dynamics," Dornbusch (1976c, 1170 n. 13, 1173) not only talked about the "Mundell-Fleming model" and "Mundell-Fleming results" but also coined the term "Mundell-Fleming world." In Dornbusch's next article, with Krugman, titled "Flexible Exchange Rates in the Short Run" and published in *Brookings Papers* (1976), they define the Mundell-Fleming model as a flexible rate model. As they put it, "The Mundell-Fleming approach to macroeconomics under flexible rates emphasizes interdependence and capital mobility" (548). This definition antedates an identical one in Dornbusch's later textbook, *Open Economy Macroeconomics* (1980). In their paper, Dornbusch and Krugman (1976, 542–43) formally develop a two-country Mundell-Fleming model. Interestingly enough, their model is similar to that proposed by Metzler (1942), albeit with flexible rates, but they only refer to the 1950 Laursen-Metzler paper.

In his survey article "Exchange Rate Economics: Where Do We Stand?" published in *Brookings Papers*, Dornbusch (1980a, 152) described what he called "the traditional Mundell-Fleming model," which, as he put it, "remains, with some adaptations, the backbone of macroeconomic models of the exchange rate." In this context, he referred to his "forthcoming" textbook, *Open Economy Macroeconomics*, "for an exposition" (152). He then outlined the characteristics of what he called "an extended Mundell-Fleming model" that included "rational expectations . . . and full employment" (152–53).

In chapter 10 of *Open Economy Macroeconomics* (1980b), Dornbusch presented an open economy version of IS-LM with fixed exchange rates and perfect capital mobility but did not call this the "Mundell-Fleming model," choosing instead to refer to Fleming's 1962 paper and Mundell's 1968 book *International Economics* as the "seminal work" on which the "literature . . . developed during the '60s" (1980b, 176). He then examined, at the beginning of the next chapter ("Flexible Exchange Rates and Capital Mobility"), what he called "the *Mundell-Fleming model*—the flexible rate version of the standard IS-LM model with output demand determined and prices taken as given" (193; emphasis in the original). He presented the differential effects of monetary versus fiscal expansion in this model, where the latter "leads to full crowding out through a deterioration in the trade balance," saying, "these conclusions oppose those reached for the fixed exchange rate model in Chapter 10" (193). Dornbusch then developed "the basic macroeconomic model of flexible exchange rates under conditions of perfect capital mobility. The model is a direct extension of the IS-LM model." And it is this model, and this model alone, that Dornbusch called "the Mundell-Fleming model" (194).

Why, then, did IS-LM-BP, and its Mundell-Fleming variant, come to "rule the roost"? First, IS-LM-BP provided a mathematical and geometric framework for both policy analysis and pedagogy. Second, it presented a standardized geometric framework for policy analysis and especially teaching, which is lacking in the Swan-Salter-Meade-Corden framework. Third, IS-LM-BP is a generalized and standardized model composed of equations and a singular core diagram encompassing numerous policy prescriptions and regimes, and thus can be easily used for pedagogical purposes, in comparison to alternatives such as the Polak-IMF and Johnsonian–monetary approach frameworks. Moreover, the generalized IS-LM-BP framework, which encompasses the flexible rate Mundell-Fleming model with perfect capital mobility, exhibits similar "plasticity" to its closed economy counterpart. This has enabled it to also undergo a similar metamorphosis into augmented forms (Darity and Young 1995; Young and Zilberfarb 2000). The generality of the IS-LM-BP framework not only enabled it to encompass the opposite conclusions, as Dornbusch put it, of fixed and flexible rate models with imperfect and perfect capital mobility, but enabled the development of two-country models (e.g., Mundell 1964; Dornbusch 1980b, 199–202) and "extended Mundell-Fleming" models that include rational expectations, long-run neoclassical features, and exchange rate dynamics of *Mundell-Dornbusch* vintage (Dornbusch 1980a, 152–57; 1980b, 202–13). But the development of these models is another story.

References

Argy, V. 1969. Monetary Variables and the Balance of Payments. *IMF Staff Papers* 16:267–88.
Blejer, M., M. Khan, and P. Masson. 1995. Early Contributions of Staff Papers to International Economics. *IMF Staff Papers* 42:707–33.
Boughton, J. 2003. On the Origins of the Fleming-Mundell Model. *IMF Staff Papers* 50:1–9.
Boyer, R. 2002. Reflections on the Mundell-Fleming Model on Its Fortieth Anniversary. In *Money, Markets, and Mobility: Celebrating the Ideas of Robert A. Mundell*, edited by T. Courchene. Ontario: McGill-Queens University Press.
———. 2003. Letter to Warren Young, 10 February.
Boyer, R., and W. Young. Forthcoming. *Open Economy Macromodels: Origins, Developments, and Debates*. London: Routledge.
Branson, W. 1972. *Macroeconomic Theory and Policy*. New York: Harper and Row.
Caves, R., and H. Johnson, eds. 1968. *Readings in International Economics*. Homewood, Ill.: Irwin.
Corden, M. 1960. The Geometric Representation of Policies to Attain Internal and External Balance. *Review of Economic Studies* 28:1–22.
Darity, W., and W. Young. 1995. IS-LM: An Inquest. *HOPE* 27:1–41.
Dornbusch, R. 1971. Notes on Growth and the Balance of Payments. *Canadian Journal of Economics* 4:389–95.
———. 1973a. Currency Depreciation, Hoarding, and Relative Prices. *Journal of Political Economy* 81:893–915.
———. 1973b. Devaluation, Money, and Non-Traded Goods. *American Economic Review* 63:871–80.
———. 1974. Real and Monetary Aspects of the Effects of Exchange Rate Changes. In *National Monetary Policies and the International Financial System*, edited by R. Aliber. Chicago: University of Chicago Press.
———. 1975a. Alternative Price Stabilization Rules and the Effects of Exchange Rate Changes. *Manchester School* 43.3:275–92.
———. 1975b. Exchange Rates and Fiscal Policy in a Popular Model of International Trade. *American Economic Review* 65:859–71.
———. 1976a. The Theory of Flexible Exchange Rate Regimes and Macroeconomic Policy. *Scandinavian Journal of Economics* 78:255–75.

————. 1976b. Exchange Rate Expectations and Monetary Policy. *Journal of International Economics* 6:231–44.

————. 1976c. Expectations and Exchange Rate Dynamics. *Journal of Political Economy* 84:1161–76.

————. 1980a. Exchange Rate Economics: Where Do We Stand? *Brookings Papers on Economic Activity* 1:143–85.

————. 1980b. *Open Economy Macroeconomics*. New York: Basic Books.

————. 2000. Robert A. Mundell's Nobel Memorial Prize in Economics. *Scandinavian Journal of Economics* 102:199–210.

Dornbusch, R., and P. Krugman. 1976. Flexible Exchange Rates in the Short Run. *Brookings Papers on Economic Activity* 3:537–75.

Fischer, S. 1987. 1944, 1963, and 1985. In *Macroeconomics and Finance: Essays in Honor of Franco Modigliani*, edited by R. Dornbusch, S. Fischer, and J. Bossons. Cambridge: MIT Press.

Flanders, J. 1989. *International Monetary Economics, 1870–1960*. Cambridge: Cambridge University Press.

Fleming, J. 1962. Domestic Financial Policies under Fixed and under Floating Exchange Rates. *IMF Staff Papers* 9:369–79.

————. 1963. Developments in the International Payments System. *IMF Staff Papers* 10:461–84.

————. 1968. Targets and Instruments. *IMF Staff Papers* 15:387–404.

————. 1978. *Essays on Economic Policy*. New York: Columbia University Press.

Frenkel, J., and H. Johnson, eds. 1976. *The Monetary Approach to the Balance of Payments*. London: Allen and Unwin.

Haberler, G. [1937] 1941. *Prosperity and Depression*. 3rd ed. Geneva: League of Nations.

Haberler, G., L. Metzler, and R. Triffin. 1947. *International Monetary Policies*. Washington, D.C.: Board of Governors, Federal Reserve System.

Harrod, R. 1933. *International Economics*. Cambridge: Cambridge University Press.

————. 1936. *The Trade Cycle: An Essay*. Oxford: Clarendon.

Hemming, M., and M. Corden. 1958. Import Restriction as an Instrument of Balance of Payments Policy. *Economic Journal* 68:483–510.

Hicks, J. 1939. *Value and Capital*. Oxford: Clarendon.

Hume, D. [1752] 1970. Of the Balance of Trade. In *David Hume: Writings on Economics*, edited by E. Rotwein. Madison: University of Wisconsin Press.

Isard, P. 1995. *Exchange Rate Economics*. Cambridge: Cambridge University Press.

Johnson, H. [1958] 1968. Towards a General Theory of the Balance of Payments. In Caves and Johnson 1968.

Kenen, P. 1985. Macroeconomic Theory and Policy: How the Closed Economy Was Opened. In vol. 2 of *Handbook of International Economics*, edited by R. Jones and P. Kenen. Amsterdam: North Holland.

Keynes, J. M. 1936. *The General Theory of Employment, Interest, and Money*. London: Macmillan.

Kindleberger, C. 1937. *International Short-Term Capital Movements*. New York: Columbia University Press.

Krueger, A. 1965. The Impact of Alternative Government Policies under Varying Exchange Systems. *Quarterly Journal of Economics* 79:195–208.

Kuska, E. 1978. On the Almost Total Inadequacy of Keynesian Balance-of-Payments Theory. *American Economic Review* 68:659–70.

Laursen, S., and L. Metzler. 1950. Flexible Exchange Rates and the Theory of Employment. *Review of Economics and Statistics* 32:281–99.

Machlup, F. 1943. *International Trade and the National Income Multiplier*. Philadelphia: Blakiston.

McKinnon, R. 1981. The Exchange Rate and Macroeconomic Policy: Changing Postwar Perceptions. *Journal of Economic Literature* 19:531–57.

Meade, J. E. 1936. *An Introduction to Economic Analysis and Policy*. Oxford: Oxford University Press.

———. 1949. A Geometrical Representation of Balance of Payments Policy. *Economica*, n.s., 16:304–20.

———. 1951a. *The Balance of Payments*. Oxford: Oxford University Press.

———. 1951b. *The Balance of Payments: Mathematical Supplement*. Oxford: Oxford University Press.

———. 1952. *A Geometry of International Trade*. London: Allen and Unwin.

Metzler, L. 1942. Underemployment Equilibrium in International Trade. *Econometrica* 10:97–112.

———. 1951. Wealth, Saving, and the Rate of Interest. *Journal of Political Economy* 59:93–116.

———. 1968. The Process of International Adjustment under Conditions of Full Employment: A Keynesian View. In Caves and Johnson 1968.

Michaely, M. 1968. The Impact of Alternative Government Policies under Varying Exchange Systems: Comment. *Quarterly Journal of Economics* 82:508–10.

Modigliani, F. 1944. Liquidity Preference and the Theory of Interest and Money. *Econometrica* 12:45–88.

———. 1987. Comments on "1944, 1963, and 1985" by S. Fischer. In *Macroeconomics and Finance: Essays in Honor of Franco Modigliani*, edited by R. Dornbusch, S. Fischer, and J. Bossons. Cambridge: MIT Press.

Mosak, J. 1944. *General Equilibrium Theory in International Trade*. Bloomington: Indiana University Press.

Mundell, R. 1960. The Monetary Dynamics of International Adjustment under Fixed and Flexible Exchange Rates. *Quarterly Journal of Economics* 74:227–57.

———. 1961a. The International Disequilibrium System. *Kyklos* 14:153–72.

———. 1961b. Flexible Exchange Rates and Employment Policy. *Canadian Journal of Economics and Political Science* 27:509–17.

———. 1962. The Appropriate Use of Monetary and Fiscal Policy for Internal and External Stability. *IMF Staff Papers* 9:70–77.

———. 1963. Capital Mobility and Stabilization Policy under Fixed and Flexible Exchange Rates. *Canadian Journal of Economics and Political Science* 29:475–85.

———. 1964. A Reply: Capital Mobility and Size. *Canadian Journal of Economics and Political Science* 30:421–31.

———. 1968. *International Economics*. New York: Macmillan.

———. 1971. *Monetary Theory: Inflation, Interest, and Growth in the World Economy*. Pacific Palisades, Calif.: Goodyear.

———. 1999. Letter to Warren Young, 3 August.

———. 2001. On the History of the Mundell-Fleming Model. *IMF Staff Papers* 47 (special issue): 215–27.

———. 2002. Notes on the Development of the International Macroeconomic Model. In *The Open Economy Macromodel: Past, Present, and Future*, edited by A. Arnon and W. Young. Boston: Kluwer Academic Publishers.

———. 2003. Letter to Warren Young, 22 January.

Niehans, J. 1975. Some Doubts about the Efficacy of Monetary Policy under Flexible Exchange Rates. *Journal of International Economics* 5:275–82.

Nurkse, R. 1947. Domestic and International Equilibrium. In *Equilibrium and Growth in the World Economy: Essays of Ragnar Nurkse*, edited by G. Haberler and R. Stern. Cambridge: Harvard University Press.

Patinkin, D. 1956. *Money, Interest, and Prices*. Evanston, Ill.: Row, Peterson.

———. 1983. Multiple Discoveries and the Central Message. *American Journal of Sociology* 89.2:306–23.

Plessner, Y. 2002. Discussion of Polak 2002. In *The Open Economy Macromodel: Past, Present, and Future*, edited by A. Arnon and W. Young. Boston: Kluwer Academic Publishers.

Polak, J. 1957. Monetary Analysis of Income Formation and Payments Problems. *IMF Staff Papers* 6:1–50.

———. 1978. Commemorations. In *Essays on Economic Policy*, by J. M. Fleming. New York: Columbia University Press.

———. 1998. The IMF Monetary Model at 40. *Economic Modelling* 15:395–410.

———. 2002. The Two Monetary Approaches to the Balance of Payments: Keynesian and Johnsonian. In *The Open Economy Macromodel: Past, Present, and Future*, edited by A. Arnon and W. Young. Boston: Kluwer Academic Publishers.

Polak, J., and V. Argy. 1971. Credit Policy and the Balance of Payments. *IMF Staff Papers* 16:1–24.

Rhomberg, R. 1964. A Model of the Canadian Economy under Fixed and Fluctuating Exchange Rates. *Journal of Political Economy* 72:1–31.

Salter, W. 1959. Internal and External Balance: The Role of Price and Expenditure Effects. *Economic Record* 35:226–38.

Salvatore, D. 1987. *International Economics*. 2nd ed. New York: Macmillan.

Samuelson, P. 1942. The Foundations of Analytical Economics: The Operational Significance of Economic Theory. Unpublished manuscript.

———. [1947] 1958. *Foundations of Economic Analysis*. Cambridge: Harvard University Press.

Sohmen, E. 1958. The Economics of Flexible Exchanges. PhD diss., MIT.

————. 1961. *Flexible Exchange Rates*. Chicago: University of Chicago Press.

————. 1967. Fiscal and Monetary Policies under Alternative Exchange-Rate Systems. *Quarterly Journal of Economics* 81:515–23.

Swan, T. 1960. Economic Control in a Dependent Economy. *Economic Record* 36:51–66.

————. [1950] 1963. Longer Run Problems of the Balance of Payments. In *The Australian Economy: A Volume of Readings*, edited by H. Arndt and M. Corden. Melbourne: Chesire.

————. [1955] 1968. Longer Run Problems of the Balance of Payments. In Caves and Johnson 1968.

Takayama, A. 1969. The Effects of Fiscal and Monetary Policies under Flexible and Fixed Exchange Rates. *Canadian Journal of Economics* 2:190–209.

Wilson, R. 1931. *Capital Imports and the Terms of Trade*. Melbourne: Melbourne University Press.

Wrightsman, D. 1970. *IS*, *LM*, and External Equilibrium: A Graphical Analysis. *American Economic Review* 60.1:203–8.

Young, W. 1987. *Interpreting Mr. Keynes: The IS-LM Enigma*. Boulder, Colo.: Westview.

————. 1989. *Harrod and His Trade Cycle Group*. New York: New York University Press.

————. 1991. The Early Reactions to *Value and Capital*: Critics, Critiques, and Correspondence in Comparative Perspective. *Review of Political Economy* 3:289–308.

Young, W., and B. Zilberfarb, eds. 2000. *IS-LM and Modern Macroeconomics*. Boston: Kluwer Academic Publishers.

James Tobin and the Transformation of the IS-LM Model

Robert W. Dimand

Transforming IS-LM

James Tobin, one of the second generation of American "Old Keynesians" (Tobin [1992] 1996, 1993), played a leading role in the transformation of IS-LM from a model with simple equations for the money market and the flow of investment into a modeling framework with a much more fully developed treatment of asset markets and investment, and mounted a spirited defense of this approach against new classical critiques. After taking part as a student and postdoctoral fellow in Alvin Hansen's reformulation of IS-LM, Tobin spent his career focused on replacing the money market equilibrium equation and the investment function of the IS-LM model with what he termed "a general equilibrium approach to monetary theory" (the title of Tobin's 1969 contribution to the inaugural issue of the *Journal of Money, Credit, and Banking*), replacing "the interest rate" with a menu of asset returns and paying attention to stock-flow dynamics. This was a general equilibrium approach in the sense that equilibria in the various markets for stocks of assets were linked by the adding-up constraint on wealth (the demands for individual assets must add up to total wealth). Failure to impose the wealth constraint in earlier models led to "pitfalls in financial model building" (Brainard and Tobin 1968). Tobin's approach involved optimization in

I am grateful for helpful comments from participants at the 2003 *HOPE* conference, two anonymous referees, and Perry Mehrling.

deriving, for instance, the Allais-Baumol-Tobin square root rule for transactions demand for money and in the mean-variance analysis of portfolio balance (given a quadratic loss function or a normal distribution of returns). However, his approach was not general equilibrium in the new classical (or equilibrium business cycle) sense of continuous clearing of goods, labor, and asset markets linked by the budget constraints of optimizing representative agents (a modeling strategy against which Tobin argued vigorously).

In his Nobel lecture, Tobin ([1982] 1996, 24) held that

> Hicks's "IS-LM" version of Keynesian and classical theories has been especially influential, reaching not just professional economists but, as the standard macromodel of textbooks, also generations of college students. Its simple apparatus is the trained intuition of many of us when we confront questions of policy and analysis, whatever more elaborate methods we may employ in further study. But the framework has a number of defects that have limited its usefulness and subjected it to attack. In this lecture I wish to describe an alternative framework, which tries to repair some of those effects. At the same time, I shall argue, the major conclusions of the Keynes-Hicks apparatus remain intact.

In keeping with his emphasis on a vector of asset prices rather than a single interest rate, Tobin modeled investment as a function of q, the ratio of the market value of corporate assets to the replacement cost of the underlying capital stock (with adjustment costs allowing q to differ from one). Tobin's attention to asset stocks and adding-up constraints (related to the work of Alan Blinder and Robert Solow [1973, 1974]) had implications throughout the IS-LM framework. Tobin used his extended IS-LM framework to expound "Old Keynesian" concerns about macroeconomic stabilization in his Yrjö Jahnsson Lectures on asset accumulation and economic activity (1980), while the Backus et al. 1980 "model of U.S. financial and nonfinancial economic behavior" illustrates how Tobin's approach translated into more formal modeling, and Tobin ([1992] 1996, 1993) defended the continued usefulness of the American Keynesian approach. Beyond reformulating the components of the IS and LM equilibrium conditions (the consumption, investment, money demand, and money supply functions), Tobin also reworked the graphic presentation of IS-LM when that suited his exposition: figures 1 to 5 of the discussion of real balance effects in Tobin 1980, 14–17, drew IS and

LM curves in interest rate (r) and price level (p) space, for given real national product Y and nominal stock M (contrary to occasional monetarist statements that IS-LM is inherently a fixed-price framework), while figures 6 and 7 reverted to the traditional (r, Y) space.

Present at the Creation of American Keynesianism

Alvin Hansen, through his books (1949, 1953) and his (and John H. Williams's) fiscal policy seminar at Harvard's Graduate School of Public Administration (now the Kennedy School of Government), was so influential in introducing the IS-LM representation of Keynes's *General Theory* into North American economics that the IS-LM diagram became known as the "Hicks-Hansen diagram" (see Young 1987, 115–21, on Hansen's role in the institutionalization of IS-LM; Tobin 1976 on Hansen's seminar; and Samuelson's interview in Colander and Landreth 1996, 164, for an example of the use of the term *Hicks-Hansen diagram*). While Hicks (1937) used his SILL diagram to offer "a suggested interpretation" of Keynes, Hansen presented IS-LM as the only valid representation of the *General Theory*. Hansen (1949, 71 n), in his book's only mention of Hicks,[1] acknowledged that "the analysis given in this chapter is based on Keynes's *General Theory*; but heavy reliance is placed upon the brilliant work [1937] of J. R. Hicks." Hansen had not always been an admirer of Keynes. A severe critic of the "fundamental equations" of Keynes's *Treatise on Money*, Hansen had also reviewed the *General Theory* unfavorably in the *Journal of Political Economy* (deleting the most hostile sections of the review when reprinting it in Hansen 1938). Reminiscing in 1972 about his early days as a Keynesian, Hansen recalled that even John Maurice Clark "wasn't really intellectually friendly to Keynesian economics" (Colander and Landreth 1996, 104). However, Hansen had written to Clark in 1934 that "your analysis still follows too much along the Keynes lines" of *The Means to Prosperity*. "Keynes' analysis I regard as definitely wrong" (Hansen to Clark, 8 August 1934, in appendix to Fiorito 2001, 31). After Hansen moved to Harvard in September 1937, contact with Keynesian students stimulated Hansen's rethinking his view of the *General Theory*.

---

1. In contrast, the index to Hansen 1953 has thirteen entries for Hicks, suggesting that Hansen made a closer study of Hicks's writings between 1949 and 1953.

One of those Keynesian students, and the one with the most influence on the IS-LM framework of Hansen 1949, was James Tobin. When Tobin was an eighteen-year-old Harvard sophomore taking principles of economics (Ec A) in 1936, his tutor Spencer Pollard (a graduate student who was also teaching Tobin's principles section) "decided that for tutorial he and I, mainly I, should read 'this new book from England. They say it may be important.' So I plunged in, being too young and ignorant to know that I was too young and ignorant" to begin studying economics with the *General Theory* (Tobin 1988, 662). Apart from Seymour Harris, editor of the Economics Handbooks Series in which Hansen 1949 appeared, Tobin (then a junior fellow at Harvard, 1947–50) was the only person thanked for prepublication reading and comments (Hansen 1949, vi). Hansen (1949, 168 n), when citing Tobin (1947–48), stated, "I have relied heavily upon his analysis." Tobin (1947–48), using IS and LM curves and the underlying equations, showed that Clark Warburton's protomonetarist argument for monetary policy rather than fiscal policy rested on an unstated implicit assumption of the interest inelasticity demand for cash balances (Warburton 1945), and demurred from William Fellner's (1946) belief that demand for cash balances was not very interest elastic. Hansen (1949, 59) also cited Tobin (1947–48) for a "more sophisticated view" (i.e., more sophisticated than the "naïve quantity theory of money") of how an increase in cash balances increases investment by lowering the interest rate. Expanding on this discussion, Hansen (1953, 148–51) introduced "a new 'sophisticated' curve which I shall label LIS" that incorporated the liquidity preference, saving, and investment-demand functions to show the relationship between the interest rate and the desired amount of money L (in i, L space, rather than the i, Y space of the IS and LM curves),[2] when account is taken of the effect of the interest rate on the level of income (along the IS curve) and hence on the transactions demand for money. In "The Modern Theory of Wages and Employment," Hansen (1949, 126 n) referred to "the exceptionally able statement by James Tobin in *The New Economics*, edited by S. E. Harris [1947]." Tobin was present at the creation of the mainstream American Keynesian IS-LM framework at the Harvard of Hansen and Harris, and the more technical parts of Hansen 1949 explicitly relied

2. While Hansen drew IS and LM in interest and real income space, Hicks had drawn IS and LL in interest and nominal income space, with capital goods and consumption goods aggregated only in nominal terms. See Ingo Barens in Young and Zilberfarb 2000 and DeVroey 2000.

on Tobin (1947–48).[3] Tobin eventually wrote a companion volume in the same series. In 1949 Seymour Harris invited Joseph Schumpeter (Tobin's dissertation adviser) to cover the theory of money and banking (in the same Economic Handbook Series as Hansen 1949) with a manuscript already under contract to McGraw-Hill since 1946, but that spot in the series was finally filled by Tobin in 1998.[4]

The IS-LM portions of Hansen 1949 and 1953, built around diagrams and equations, were more formal than was usual for Hansen—and it was these more formal IS-LM sections that became the most influential portions of the books and perhaps the most influential of any of Hansen's writings. Other current or former participants in Hansen's fiscal policy seminar were formalizing aspects of American Keynesian macroeconomics in other ways at the time, such as Paul Samuelson (a Harvard junior fellow in 1937–40) on multiplier-accelerator interaction and on the 45-degree Keynesian cross-diagram (writing up the latter for Hansen's Festschrift in 1948), Richard Goodwin on the nonlinear accelerator and the persistence of business cycles, or William Salant on the balanced budget multiplier (see Samuelson's interview in Colander and Landreth 1996, 166), but IS-LM reached Hansen (1949) by way of Tobin (1947–48), and then the IS-LM discussion in Hansen's *Guide to Keynes* (1953) was based on Hansen 1949.

Tobin recalled that "there wasn't much Walras at Harvard then, until Hicks finally came out with *Value and Capital* [1939]" (Shiller 1999, 870) and that he "attended as an undergraduate a course on general equilibrium theory with Schumpeter as teacher and people such as Paul Samuelson, Lloyd Metzler, and R. G. D. Allen as students. As you know, Hicks, Allen and Samuelson basically imported general equilibrium theory from the Continent into Anglo-Saxon economics" (Klamer 1984, 100).[5] Since Tobin graduated in 1939, these recollections, taken together,

---

3. The papers by Roy Harrod and James Meade, presented to the same Econometric Society session in Oxford in September 1936 as Hicks 1937 and outlining similar systems of equations (Young 1987), were known at Harvard and reprinted in Harris 1947, immediately following Tobin's chapter, but did not offer any of the diagrammatic analysis that was taken up by Tobin (1947–48) and Hansen (1949).

4. Parts of Schumpeter's unfinished manuscript, originally to have been published by Springer in 1930, appeared long after his death as Schumpeter 1970, 1991 (see Messori 1997). After Schumpeter's death, Tobin was invited by Harris to write the money and banking volume for the Economic Handbook Series. Although he began drafting it during a sabbatical in Geneva in 1958, it appeared four decades later as Tobin and Golub 1998.

5. Yale's first doctoral dissertation in economics, Irving Fisher's *Mathematical Investigations in the Theory of Value and Prices* (1892), was an earlier importation of general equilibrium

suggest that Tobin studied Hicks's general equilibrium theorizing as soon as *Value and Capital* was published, in the company of Hicks's sometime coauthor Allen and of Samuelson, then completing the dissertation that became his *Foundations of Economic Analysis* (1947), and that this study prepared Tobin to introduce Hansen to Hicks (Hicks 1937). Although Tobin was an enthusiastic Keynesian, his undergraduate thesis (which was the basis for his first article, Tobin 1941, and his chapter in Harris 1947) rejected Keynes's proof that reductions in money wage rates cannot reduce unemployment, on the grounds that Keynes was assuming that people act differently as wage earners (subject to what Irving Fisher termed "money illusion") from how they behave as consumers. In this undergraduate thesis supervised by Wassily Leontief, Tobin followed Leontief (1936), who labeled money illusion in the labor supply schedule the "fundamental assumption" of Keynes's system. Tobin's acceptance in 1947 of money illusion as a realistic assumption stands in contrast to his later view (e.g., Tobin 1972) and presumably reflects the influence of Leontief on Tobin's undergraduate thesis. Later, Tobin (1972) recognized and accepted the argument of Keynes (1936, chap. 2) that workers could quite rationally (without any money illusion mistaking money wage changes for real wage changes) resist money wage reductions as unsynchronized contracts expire, because such money wage cuts alter relative wages, while a price level increase would reduce the purchasing power of all wages at the same time. Tobin was sympathetic to the formalization of this staggered-contracts approach by John Taylor (1980) (author's recollection of a graduate course on money and finance taught by Tobin and Taylor in 1979–80, when Taylor was visiting Yale). The publications resulting from Tobin's undergraduate thesis are significant in showing his long-standing concern with the rationality of the assumed behavior underlying Keynesian economics.

Revising the IS Curve

Although Tobin is best known as a monetary economist and for the q theory of investment, he wrote his Harvard doctoral dissertation (accepted in 1947) on the other building block of the IS curve, the consumption function. When he contributed to the *International Encyclopedia of the Social Sciences* two decades later, he did so as an expert on the

---

analysis into North America, but had been forgotten and was not cited by either Hicks (1939) or Samuelson (1947).

consumption function. Responding to theories of consumption advanced by James Duesenberry in his Harvard dissertation and by Dorothy Stahl Brady and Rose Director Friedman in a National Bureau of Economic Research conference volume, Tobin (1951) presented empirical evidence that absolute income (as in Keynes 1936) performed better than relative income in explaining consumption. However, he advocated including wealth as well as absolute income in the consumption function, to better explain cross-section data. Tobin (1951) argued that differences in saving propensities between white and black households in the same city reflected differences in household wealth. The inclusion of wealth as an argument in the consumption function was a step toward subsequent consumption theories (Milton Friedman's permanent income hypothesis and the Modigliani-Brumberg-Ando life-cycle hypothesis) and also toward rediscovery of Irving Fisher's (1907, 409) two-period optimal consumption smoothing diagram relating consumption to the present discounted value of expected lifetime income, given perfect credit markets. Given that Tobin's 1947 dissertation added wealth as an argument in the consumption function, it is striking that Hansen (1949) included wealth as an argument in the consumption, investment, and money demand functions of his IS-LM model (an innovation noted by Darity and Young 1995, 27).[6] However, rather than continuing to take a leading role in formulating new theories of the consumption function, Tobin's interest in analyzing data on consumption decisions (e.g., for automobiles, where for many households spending in a given year would be zero) led him in the later 1950s to the latent variable method for estimating limited dependent variable models (where the dependent variable is continuous over strictly positive values but zero for a nontrivial portion of the population) that Arthur Goldberger labeled the Tobit analysis (Shiller 1999, 873, 876–77).

Tobin's dissertation contributed to the development of models linking consumption to the present discounted value of expected lifetime after-tax income. Tobin (1980, lecture 3) was critical of Robert Barro's debt neutrality (or Ricardian equivalence) proposition that, given the level of government spending, lump-sum tax cuts have no effect on the position of the IS curve, an implication of combining such a forward-looking theory of consumption with additional strong assumptions. Tobin objected

6. Hansen (1949) also included an accelerator effect in the investment function, perhaps influenced by Samuelson's work on multiplier-accelerator interaction, but his diagrammatic presentation reverted to a simpler model without wealth or accelerator effects.

particularly to the unrealism of the assumption of perfect credit markets (no liquidity constraints or credit rationing), which holds that consumers can borrow against expected future earnings at the same interest rate that they would receive on their savings. If these interest rates differed, a consumer whose intertemporal indifference curve was tangent to the kink in the intertemporal consumption possibility frontier would have consumption determined by current after-tax income, a return to Keynes's simple absolute-income consumption function and a retreat from the Fisherian approach to which Tobin's 1947 dissertation had contributed.

Tobin's most famous contribution to economics was the q theory of investment (Brainard and Tobin 1968; Tobin 1969; Tobin and Brainard 1977; Purvis 1982), which related net investment to q, the ratio of the market value of equity to the replacement cost of the capital stock underlying the equity. The name suggests an affinity to the Q (either windfall profits or expected above-normal returns, depending on the passage one cites) that drove investment decisions in Keynes's *Treatise on Money* (1930), which in turn owed its name to Marshall's quasi rents, but Tobin did not recall choosing the symbol q for that reason. When the economy has its desired capital stock, q would equal one, and gross investment would just cover depreciation. If q exceeds one, entrepreneurs can make a profit by adding to their capital stock and issuing equity, selling the new equity for the present discounted value of the expected stream of earnings from the additional capital stock. Hayashi (1982) offered a neoclassical reinterpretation of q, in which deviations of q from one are explained by adjustment costs. Tobin, however, insisted that Hayashi's q is a shadow price of an optimal program solution, whereas the Tobin-Brainard q is an observable market variable, "a datum for individual agents, created by monetary policy interacting with the economy, a datum to which individuals and firm respond in their investments" (Shiller 1999, 887–88). Tobin's goal was to subsume both the investment function underlying the IS curve and the money demand and money supply functions underlying the LM curve into a more general theory of asset accumulation.

Microeconomic Foundations of the LM Curve

James Tobin's most widely reprinted articles (e.g., Tobin 1956, 1958) were part of his intensive effort to ground the LM curve (money market equilibrium) in the optimizing behavior of rational agents. Keynes

(1936) wrote the demand for real money balances (liquidity preference, measured in wage-units) as a function of income (because of the transactions motive for holding money) and the interest rate (because of the speculative motive). Despite his overall sympathy for Keynes's *General Theory*, Tobin was dissatisfied with Keynes's treatment of both transactions and speculative motives. He did not consider that Keynes had explained why people hold moneys and near-moneys even though other marketable assets have higher yields, or why the demand for moneys and near-moneys is empirically observed to vary inversely with those yields. Tobin ([1983] 1996, 165) recalled: "The reason for my dissatisfaction was that Keynes's 'speculative motive' for money demand seemed, in modern parlance, to violate the canons of rational expectations."[7] As Tobin interpreted Keynes, Keynes assumed that an agent must hold the same expectation of short-term returns on all assets the agent chooses to hold. Otherwise, the agent would wish to shift his or her portfolio entirely out of the lower-yielding assets into the highest-yielding asset. Money and low-yield short securities are thus held by those agents who expect capital losses on long-term bonds (because of an increase in interest rates) sufficient that their expected net short-term yields on bonds would be no higher than on money and near-moneys. Tobin ([1983] 1996, 166) accepted that many financiers in the 1930s might have continued to regard the higher interest rates of the 1920s as normal, but "eventually expectations must accord with experience." A reduction in current interest rates could induce expectations of a future rise in interest rates (reversion to normal levels), "but clearly if Keynes's speculators had, individually or in aggregate, unbiased expectations, there would be no justification for a liquidity preference function with negative sensitivity to the current rate of interest."

Tobin (1958) reformulated the demand for money as an asset, Keynes's speculative motive for holding money, as the behavior of risk-averse investors toward risk (as distinct from fundamental Keynesian or Knightian uncertainty). Investors have preferences over the distribution of returns to their overall portfolios, rather than individual assets. Money and highly liquid short securities such as treasury bills (near-moneys) differ from other assets not only in expected return (zero nominal return on narrowly defined money, lower nominal returns on treasury bills and interest-bearing bank deposits than on other assets) but also in risk (with

---

7. As an anonymous referee points out, this criticism could also have been directed against the assumption of money illusion in Tobin's chapter in Harris 1947, discussed above.

money as a riskless asset in nominal terms or, allowing for changes in the purchasing power of money, a less risky asset in real terms). While Keynes's liquidity preference theory implied that each agent would own only one asset (see Bernstein 1992, 48, for a quotation from Keynes against portfolio diversification),[8] Tobin's investors would hold a mix of money and other assets. As Tobin ([1982] 1996, 173) emphasized, "John R. Hicks' 1935 article has been an inspiration and challenge to me and many other monetary economists" (see Maes 1991). In addition to Hicks (1935), Harry Markowitz (1952, 1959) strongly influenced Tobin's approach. Markowitz, who spent the 1955–56 academic year at Yale at the Cowles Foundation turning his 1955 Chicago dissertation on selection of an optimal portfolio of risky assets (which Milton Friedman had proposed rejecting as not economics) into a Cowles monograph (Markowitz 1959; see also Bernstein 1992 on Friedman's view of Markowitz's thesis). The Cowles Commission had moved from the University of Chicago to Yale in 1955 (changing its name to the Cowles Foundation for Research in Economics) when Tobin became its director (after he declined to move to Chicago). Tobin (1958, 85 n. 1) noted that "Markowitz's main interest is prescription of rules of rational behaviour for investors; the main concern of this paper is the implications for economic theory, mainly comparative statics, that can be derived from assuming that investors do in fact follow such rules." Tobin (1958) also differed from Markowitz (1952) in showing that, if there is a riskless asset, the division of the portfolio between risky and riskless assets and Markowitz's optimal diversification of the risky part of the portfolio among different risky assets are two separate decisions. There is an optimal portfolio of risky assets, which will be the same for all investors. Each investor's degree of risk aversion then determines the fraction of the investor's wealth to be invested in that optimal portfolio of risky assets, with the remainder invested in the riskless asset. This remained a purely theoretical result, unused by financial practitioners, until 1961, when William Sharpe (writing a UCLA doctoral dissertation unofficially supervised by Markowitz)

8. See Bernstein 1992, 46–49, for similar advocacy of portfolio concentration by John Burr Williams and Gerald Loeb, leading authorities on portfolio investment whose books first appeared in the 1930s (that by Williams as a Harvard doctoral dissertation). Ivo Maes (1991, 10) notes that Paul Chambers (1934) had a graph of indifference curves between risk and return similar to Tobin 1958, 152, "but the risk under consideration is different. Tobin is concerned about capital gains or losses, something which is impossible in Chambers' stationary state. Chambers is concerned about uncertain future payments."

discovered that one need only determine how each stock covaried with the market index, not with every other stock, reducing the computing time for a single run of a simplified Tobin-Markowitz model from thirty-three minutes to thirty seconds (Harrison 1997, 177).

To be a strict representation of the maximization of expected utility, Tobin's mean-variance diagram for portfolio choice required either that asset returns are normally distributed (so that the distribution of returns has only two parameters) or that investors have quadratic utility functions (so that the investors care only about the first two moments of the distribution) (see Tobin 1984). When Karl Borch and Martin Feldstein objected in 1969 that Tobin's two-parameter mean-variance analysis was only an approximation, Tobin argued that it improved on the previously prevailing one-parameter approximation (expected return plus a constant, unexplained risk premium). Given that investors in Tobin 1958 know the correct probability distributions for asset returns, Tobin later reflected that "my theory of liquidity preference as behavior towards risk was built on a rational expectations model long before the terminology" (Shiller 1999, 878).

The treatment of money in Tobin 1958 as one of many assets, each having a distribution of returns with some particular mean and variance, was the basis of the "general equilibrium approach to monetary theory" of Tobin 1969, in which a vector of market-clearing asset prices (and hence asset returns) is determined by the whole range of asset supplies and demands, providing a channel through which open market operations changing the relative supplies of money and bonds affect the cost of capital (Tobin and Brainard 1977). Work in this approach by Tobin and his associates at the Cowles Foundation, most notably his doctoral student and then colleague William Brainard, was gathered in three Cowles Foundation monographs (Hester and Tobin 1967a, 1967b, 1967c; for example, Tobin 1958 was reprinted in Hester and Tobin 1967a). While the post-1955 Cowles Foundation provided an institutional base for Tobin and his collaborators, Tobin and Robert Shiller were at pains to emphasize in Colander 1999 that Cowles was not the same as the "Yale school" (or Tobin school) of monetary economics: many or most Cowles researchers worked in non-Keynesian macroeconomics (Fellner 1976) or in econometrics, game theory, or mathematical general equilibrium theory.

Keynes's presentation of the transactions motive for holding money offered no reason for an inverse relation between money demand and interest (even though Fisher 1930, 216, had already stated the marginal opportunity cost of holding money), and simply posited a direct relation between liquidity preference and income, with no derivation of how much money should be held for a given rate of spending. Independently of each other (and of any knowledge of Allais 1947; see Baumol and Tobin 1989), William J. Baumol (1952) and Tobin (1956) derived the transactions demand for money from the need to use money (the generally accepted medium of exchange) as means of payment and the existence of transactions costs of converting funds from interest-bearing assets into money. Optimizing agents would choose to hold the average level of money balances that minimized the costs of cost management, balancing higher transactions costs (from lower average money balances and consequently more transactions between bonds and money) against foregone interest (from higher average money balances and consequently lower average bond holdings). Assuming that all income would be spent at a steady rate during a pay period, Maurice Allais (1947, 238–41; translated in Baumol and Tobin 1989), Baumol (1952), and Tobin (1956) solved for the optimal number of transactions between bonds and money per pay period. The resulting square root rule, already familiar in the literature on optimal inventories, related optimal holdings of nominal money balances directly to the square root of nominal income and nominal transactions costs, and inversely to the square root of the nominal interest rate (neglecting the constraint that the number of transactions be an integer). Baumol (1952), on the basis of information from Thomson M. Whitin, noted the independent formulation of the square root rule for optimal inventories by a half-dozen authors between 1925 and 1927.[9]

Tobin also reworked the other building block of the LM curve, the money supply, developing a simple model of a commercial banking firm, based on a bank's precautionary demand for safe liquid assets (both primary reserves and secondary reserves). While "endogenous money" in some post-Keynesian writing has come to mean a perfectly elastic money supply at a fixed interest rate set by the central bank ("horizontalism"), Tobin (1982; Tobin and Golub 1998, chap. 7) linked reserves to deposits through the optimizing portfolio choices of banks facing risk. The publication dates are misleading. According to Tobin and Golub (1998, xxiii),

9. F. Y. Edgeworth (1888) derived a square root rule for optimal levels of bank reserves against deposits, but in a different context (randomness in withdrawals of deposits) more relevant to Keynes's precautionary motive for holding money. Knut Wicksell ([1898] 1962, 57–58) echoed Edgeworth's analysis.

"Chapter 7 was published in Tobin [1982] virtually as it had been circulating in draft," as part of a manuscript drafted between 1958 and 1960 but put aside when Tobin joined the President's Council of Economic Advisers in 1961.

Tobin (1969) pulled together his work on the components of LM, together with the q theory of investment first presented in Brainard and Tobin 1968. Tobin ([1982] 1996, 45) reflected in his Nobel lecture that in 1969, "I tried to generalize the stock equilibrium of asset prices and quantities to a larger collection of assets while winding up nonetheless with a single LM locus to be juxtaposed with an IS locus. This condensation, I now recognize, is not in general attainable. The major points of the 1969 paper did not depend on this feature, but the blending of stock adjustments and savings flows advocated in this lecture seems to me a preferable approach." The problem identified by Tobin ([1982] 1996) is that the equations underlying the LM curve concern the asset prices that induce wealth owners, constrained by the net worth created by past savings (revalued at current asset prices), to hold the existing stocks of assets (also predetermined, apart from open market operations of the monetary authority). The saving function underlying the IS curve gives the flow of additions to accumulated wealth, but not how wealth owners wish to distribute that accumulation across alternative assets. In particular, Tobin wished to extend the standard textbook IS-LM framework to track how investment, government deficits, and international capital flows affect asset stocks. Making such extensions still led to "conventional macroeconomic results, qualitatively the same as comparable conclusions of IS-LM apparatus. Note, however, that—contrary to the classical Mundell conclusion that monetary policies work and fiscal policies do not in a regime of floating exchange rates—expansionary policies of both kinds are here effective" (Tobin [1982] 1996, 49; see also Tobin 1980, 76–77, and especially Tobin and de Macedo 1980).

Backus et al. 1980, Backus and Purvis 1980, Purvis 1978, Smith and Brainard 1976, Tobin and Buiter 1976, 1980, and Tobin and de Macedo 1980 together represent a major effort to implement simplified prototype models of the integrated stock-flow modeling advocated in Tobin [1982] 1996. Referring to this project, Tobin (1980, 95) wrote, "Although models of this type in some sense 'vindicate' IS/LM analysis, this is not their sole or principal purpose. Their richer structural detail permits the analysis of policies and exogenous shocks for which more primitive and more highly aggregated models are ill-suited. The vector of endogenous variables is also larger, and in particular effects on financial prices and quantities can be traced."

Appropriately, Douglas Purvis (1980) rebutted the claim of Karl Brunner and Allan Meltzer (in Stein 1976) that the multiasset nature of their models set them apart from Tobin-style models. Indeed, Brunner (1971, 168 n. 5, 173 n. 17), in a review article on Hester and Tobin 1967a, 1967b, and 1967c, twice stressed the consistency of the Tobin-Brainard and Brunner-Meltzer money-supply theories, as well as repeatedly and emphatically acknowledging the valuable contribution of "Yale" portfolio analysis to monetary theory (see also Meltzer 1989). Stanley Fischer (1988, 1 n. 1) finds that "Brunner and Meltzer's basic analytic model [in Stein 1976] is not dissimilar to Tobin's (1969) three asset model."

Notwithstanding this similarity, Brunner (1971, 169–70) criticized "Yale" for treating the use of money as a medium of exchange as something to be taken for granted, rather than derived from rigorous microeconomic foundations. In a witticism celebrated by David Laidler (1991, 651–53), Brunner (1971, 168–69) described the work of Tobin and his associates as "a remarkable combination of Schmoller and Walras" that offered both "elegant syntactical exercises" of portfolio optimization with uncertain empirical content and "skilful manipulation of large masses of data" to the neglect of "the middle range where analysis emerges in the form of explicitly constructed empirical hypotheses with a definitely assessable content." Tobin's associate Gary Smith (1989, 1692–93) also expresses this problem of combining the theory of portfolio optimization, implying many explanatory variables in asset demand functions, with available data: "Because of the strong intercorrelations among the available data, the implementation of the Yale approach is inevitably plagued by severe multicollinearity problems. While monetarism is too simple, the Yale approach is too complex. Some [e.g., Owen 1986] accept the high standard deviations and low t-values, observing that the data are not adequate for answering the questions asked. Some researchers try to get more precise estimates by using exclusion restrictions; others have tried more flexible Bayesian procedures for incorporating prior information" (e.g., Smith and Brainard 1976).

The modeling effort of Tobin and his associates was not sustained, perhaps because of the enormous funding and data requirements of such a modeling approach (and also because of the early deaths of Douglas Purvis and Arthur Okun, leading macroeconomists whose work was close to Tobin's).[10] When computing costs plummeted in later years, fashions in macroeconomics had changed. Shiller (1999, 888) posed the question, "So what happened to your general equilibrium approach to monetary theory? It seemed to be a movement for a while, right? Here at Yale a lot of people were doing this, and I haven't heard about such work lately," to which Tobin replied only, "Well, people would rather do the other thing because it's easier." The fact that other forms of computable general equilibrium, numerical general equilibrium, or applied general equilibrium modeling continued as a flourishing cottage industry (using the fixed point algorithm of Tobin's Yale and Cowles colleague Herbert Scarf), although equally subject to the Lucas (1976) critique (that models estimated with data generated under a particular policy regime may change if the policy is changed), is consistent with this explanation for the disappearance of Tobin-style general equilibrium modeling.

An Old Keynesian Counterattacks

Like Tobin, other leading American Keynesians constructed optimizing foundations for particular building blocks of the IS-LM framework (although Tobin was unusual in working on all of consumption, investment, money demand, money supply, and international payments). Franco Modigliani, a pioneer in adapting Hicks's two-sector IS-LM model into a one-sector model and shifting its focus from the liquidity trap to nominal wage rigidity (Modigliani 1944; De Vroey 2000), is a notable example for the life-cycle hypothesis of consumption and saving. Thomas Sargent acknowledged, "When you go back and look at the history of macroeconomics since the '30s, there's an underlying effort to build more and more optimizing theory underneath the decision rules of Keynesian economics, such as in the consumption function, the portfolio schedule, and the investment schedule," but dismissed these as "essentially partial equilibrium exercises which were then put together at the end" as in the Brookings model of 1965 (Klamer 1984, 65–66). Tobin, however, took a different kind of "general equilibrium approach to monetary theory" (1969), linking asset markets through the adding-up constraint for wealth, rather than through optimization by a representative agent (or, in the case of overlapping generations models, two representative agents). Brainard and Tobin (1968) criticized models, such as the

10. See Tobin's "A Final Comment" (Tobin 1983), concerning Okun's (1981) posthumously published *Prices and Quantities: A Macroeconomic Analysis*.

Federal Reserve–MIT–Penn or MIT-Penn-SSRC (FMP or MPS) model of Modigliani and Albert Ando, which omitted the adding-up constraint for wealth and failed to include all asset markets, often implying implausible demand elasticities for the omitted asset market (cf. Tobin in Shiller 1999, 877). Even though Walras's law implied that the equilibrium condition for one market was redundant, it would be better to include all asset markets and make wealth explicitly the sum of asset values.

Tobin's modeling approach paid careful attention not only to this adding-up constraint but also to the government budget constraint and its implications for the dynamics of asset stocks. But, as Shiller (1999, 888) told Tobin, "you . . . had general equilibrium in a sense different from what we think now." Tobin's general equilibrium was not the general equilibrium of equilibrium business cycle theory (either the monetary misperceptions variant, such as Lucas 1981a, or real business cycles), which links markets through the optimization of representative agents subject to budget constraints. Tobin rejected continuous market clearing, denied that faster adjustment necessarily implies greater stability, and objected to representative agent models as an arbitrary evasion of coordination problems. He refused to identify general equilibrium modeling with a single representative agent acting optimally in all markets at all times. He was equally unimpressed with the overlapping generations extension of representative agent models (anticipated by Allais 1947), which provides a rigorous justification for a positive value of fiat value— provided that one assumes that no other stores of value exist and that the number of time periods is infinite (see Tobin in Colander 1999, 124, on Judgment Day and the existence of money, and Tobin's comments on overlapping generations models in Kareken and Wallace 1980).

Tobin's version of general equilibrium stressed the consistency of stock-flow relationships and the interrelationships of asset markets through the adding-up constraint on wealth. As Smith (1989, 1692) observed, "Tobin sometimes integrates household consumption-saving and portfolio-allocation decisions, essentially taking the Yale approach back one step, from wealth allocation to income allocation. It can be taken back another step by allowing the labor supply decision to be part of the integrated framework. However, institutional constraints and labor market disequilibria often make labor income predetermined in the short run," so Tobin refused to take that additional step.

Representative agent models exclude considerations of distribution or coordination, since the economy is presented as a number of identical agents. Since agents are identical, they do not exchange with each other in equilibrium, and the equilibrium values of variables are those values that lead representative agents not to trade (see Kirman 1992 and Hartley 1997). Walrasian general equilibrium analysis did not permit agents to trade at other than equilibrium prices, but in representative agent models they don't trade at equilibrium prices either. Increased unemployment in a representative agent model means a bit more leisure for everyone, rather than some people becoming completely unemployed. In a real business cycle model, with no misperceptions, such increased unemployment would reflect either a preference shock increasing the taste for leisure or a technology shock making household production more productive relative to paid employment. Such a view brings to mind Dennis Robertson's 1930 "attempt to convince the Macmillan Committee that mass unemployment was attributable to the satiation of human wants . . . a satiation that should have produced a general reduction in working hours but unfortunately and inexplicably operated instead differentially to reduce the working hours of a substantial part of the population to absolute zero" (Harry Johnson in Johnson and Johnson 1978, 210, 187).

John Geweke (1985) argues that the assumptions needed for consistent aggregation to a representative agent model are at least as heroic and arbitrary as those underlying the aggregate functions of Keynesian economics. Hugo Sonnenschein (1972), Gerard Debreu (1974), and Rolf Mantel (1976) showed that the standard assumptions about individual agents, such as strict convexity and monotonic preferences, are not sufficient for uniqueness and stability of equilibrium. That would require assumptions about how individuals are related to each other, such as identical preferences—which is just what is implied by arbitrarily assuming the existence of a representative agent (see Kirman 1992). Standard assumptions about preferences, endowments, and technology imply no more than Walras's law and continuity for aggregate excess demand functions (Rizvi 1997). Tobin recognized no need to accept that new classical models were based on consistent microeconomic foundations that yield unique and stable equilibria. Tobin (1975) argued that even a model with a unique full-employment equilibrium could be unstable for large negative demand shocks. If the claim to firmer microeconomic foundations was rejected, the case for new classical economics rested on empirical claims, and Tobin accepted the finding of his Cowles colleague

Ray Fair (1979) that new classical models were no better at out of sample forecasting (see also Mishkin 1983).

Tobin ([1992] 1996, 25) insisted that "it is not true that only an arbitrary and gratuitous assumption of complete rigidity, converting nominal demand shocks into real demand shocks, brings into play Keynes's multipliers and other demand-determining processes (including the IS-LM curves taught to generations of college students). Any degree of stickiness that prevents complete instantaneous price adjustment has the same qualitative implications."[11] It is possible to construct models with nominal stickiness in which anticipated aggregate demand shifts are nonetheless neutral (e.g., McCallum 1979), but it is uncommon. Tobin argued for sluggish adjustment (on behavioral grounds, as well as an optimizing response to adjustment costs) and invoked Okun 1981 as providing a microeconomic justification for such sluggish adjustment, based on monopolistic competition (see Tobin's concluding remarks in Tobin 1983).

Tobin (1975; 1980, lecture 1) went beyond this to argue that faster adjustment of wages and prices might even be destabilizing (as in Keynes 1936, chap. 19, and Fisher 1933).[12] Falling prices are not the same as lower prices. The Pigou-Haberler real balance effect might show that, in comparative statics, a lower price level is associated with a higher level of aggregate demand even if a liquidity trap (because of the higher real value of outside money, the monetary base that is part of net wealth, which affects consumption). However, expected deflation lowers the opportunity cost of holding real money balances, and so raises real interest rates. Unanticipated deflation raises the real value of inside nominal debt, which vastly exceeds the amount of outside money. The effect of a transfer of wealth from debtors to creditors (who presumably became creditors and debtors because of differing propensities to spend) and

11. Tobin made a similar claim to the middle ground in his debate with Friedman (in Gordon 1974), in which he argued that the validity of the Keynesian-Hicksian approach did not depend on the slopes of IS and LM, provided that the IS curve is not horizontal and the LM curve is not vertical. He did not have to defend the usefulness of IS-LM on that occasion, because Friedman had for once used IS-LM to expound his approach, hoping to improve communication with his critics.

12. Tobin (1997, 12–13), "writing as J. M. Keynes" for a "second edition" to mark the sixtieth anniversary of the *General Theory*, had Keynes write, "In Chapter 19 I emphasized the negative effects of increasing debt burdens, and Professor Fisher has made a convincing case that debt burdens augmented by deflation exacerbated the Great Depression in the United States. I also agree with Professor Fisher that, whatever may be the effects of lowering the level of money-wages and prices, the process of moving to a lower level is counterproductive. Expectations of deflation are equivalent to an increase in interest rates."

of higher risk premia in real interest rates because of increased risk of bankruptcy could swamp the Pigou-Haberler real balance effect, so that money wage cuts and price deflation (resulting from an excess supply of labor) could further reduce real aggregate demand, moving the economy further away from full employment. Real aggregate demand depends on both the price level and the rate of change of the price level. Speed of price adjustment plausibly increases the further the economy is from full-employment equilibrium. Tobin ([1992] 1996, 1993) cited De Long and Summers 1986 and Chadha 1989 in support of his argument that increased price flexibility need not be stabilizing, and that instability was more likely the further a demand shock took the economy away from full-employment equilibrium. An economy could be self-stabilizing for small demand shocks, but not for large demand shocks (hence government intervention could be needed for stabilization in the face of large shocks, as in the 1930s). Tobin invoked the finding by Shiller (1989) that financial markets fluctuate excessively. Tobin ([1992] 1996, 1993) did not, however, cite R. A. Driskill and Stephen Sheffrin (1986), who reached the opposite conclusion that, within their model, increasing price flexibility would be stabilizing. Unfortunately, Lucas (1981b) concentrated primarily on the fairness or otherwise of the presentation of new classical economics as "Monetarism, Mark II" in lecture 2 of Tobin 1980, rather than on the stability questions raised in lecture 1, so debate on this issue has never been fully joined.

Conclusion

Opening the final lecture ("Portfolio Choice and Asset Accumulation") of his Yrjö Jahnsson Lectures, Tobin (1980, 73) announced that he would "be particularly concerned with the Keynesian model and the famous IS/LM formalization of it by Sir John Hicks. . . . I shall consider critically its possible interpretations, some objections to them raised by others, and some of my own. Yet I want to begin by saying that I do not think the apparatus is discredited. I still believe that, carefully used and taught, it is a powerful instrument for understanding our economies and the impacts of policies upon them." At the end of the lecture, Tobin (94) offered "one major general conclusion, namely the robustness of the standard results of Hicksian IS/LM analysis. They survive in these models in which time, flows, and stocks are more precisely and satisfactorily modeled, in which time is allowed for flows to affect the stocks of government liabilities and of other assets too, in which the menu of distinct assets is as large as desired." Tobin transformed the IS-LM analysis (which he had helped Hansen introduce into North America) by introducing wealth as an argument in the consumption function, formulating the q theory of investment, proposing optimizing decision rules for portfolio choice (both for money demand in a multiasset setting and, through portfolio choices by banks, for money supply), linking asset markets through the adding-up constraint for wealth, and treating investment, international capital flows, and government budget deficits as changes in stocks of assets (and, in Tobin 1955, with an extension to long-run growth theory, a year before the better-known articles of Robert Solow and Trevor Swan), but he did so within the spirit of the IS-LM framework, continuing to view it as a useful and powerful instrument. Many of the changes that Tobin made to the framework inherited from Hicks 1937 were in the spirit of Hicks 1935, treating money as one of many assets, and Hicks 1939, through which Tobin first encountered general equilibrium. Tobin's concern for stock-flow consistency, adding-up constraints, and portfolio optimization never led him to accept the uniqueness and stability of classical full-employment equilibrium. His disequilibrium dynamic interpretation of Keynes (enriched by the deft-deflation process of Fisher 1933) led Tobin (1997, 20) to conclude that "given the non-linearities of the relevant equations, the system may be stable in the neighbourhood of equilibrium but unstable to large displacements," so the economy is self-adjusting in normal times but requires active stabilization policy (as formulated in an IS-LM framework) to respond to major demand shocks, as in the Great Depression.

References

Allais, Maurice. 1947. *Économie et intérêt*. Paris: Imprimerie Nationale.

Backus, David, William C. Brainard, Gary Smith, and James Tobin. 1980. A Model of U.S. Financial and Nonfinancial Economic Behavior. *Journal of Money, Credit, and Banking* 12.2:259–93.

Backus, David, and Douglas D. Purvis. 1980. An Integrated Model of Household Flow-of-Funds Allocations. *Journal of Money, Credit, and Banking* 12.2:400–421.

Baumol, William J. 1952.The Transactions Demand for Cash: An Inventory Theoretic Approach. *Quarterly Journal of Economics* 66:545–56.

Baumol, William J., and James Tobin. 1989. The Optimal Cash Balance Proposition: Maurice Allais's Priority. *Journal of Economic Literature* 27.3:1160–62.

Bernstein, Peter L. 1992. *Capital Ideas: The Improbable Origins of Modern Wall Street.* New York: Free Press.

Blinder, Alan S., and Robert M. Solow. 1973. Does Fiscal Policy Matter? *Journal of Public Economics* 2:318–37.

———. 1974. Analytical Foundations of Fiscal Policy. In *The Economics of Public Finance*, by Alan S. Blinder, Robert M. Solow, George F. Break, Peter O. Steiner, and Dick Netzer. Washington, D.C.: Brookings Institution.

Brainard, William C., and James Tobin. 1968. Pitfalls in Financial Model Building. *American Economic Review* 58.2:99–122.

Brunner, Karl. 1971. "Yale" and Money. *Journal of Finance* 26.1:165–74.

Chadha, Binky. 1989. Is Increased Price Inflexibility Stabilizing? *Journal of Money, Credit, and Banking* 21.4:481–97.

Chambers, Stanley Paul. 1934. Fluctuations in Capital and the Demand for Money. *Review of Economic Studies* 2.1:38–50.

Colander, David C. 1999. Conversations with James Tobin and Robert Shiller on the "Yale Tradition" in Macroeconomics. *Macroeconomic Dynamics* 3.1:116–43.

Colander, David C., and Harry Landreth. 1996. *The Coming of Keynesianism to America: Conversations with the Founders of Keynesian Economics.* Cheltenham, U.K.: Edward Elgar.

Darity, William, Jr., and Warren Young. 1995. IS-LM: An Inquest. *HOPE* 27.1:1–41.

Debreu, Gerard. 1974. Excess Demand Functions. *Journal of Mathematical Economics* 1.1:15–23.

De Long, J. Bradford, and Lawrence H. Summers. 1986. Is Increased Price Flexibility Stabilizing? *American Economic Review* 76.5:1031–44.

De Vroey, Michel. 2000. IS-LM à la Hicks versus IS-LM à la Modigliani. *HOPE* 32.2:293–316.

Driskill, R. A., and Stephen M. Sheffrin. 1986. Is Price Flexibility Destabilizing? *American Economic Review* 76.4:802–7.

Edgeworth, Francis Ysidro. 1888. The Mathematical Theory of Banking. *Journal of the Royal Statistical Society* 51.1:113–27.

Fair, Ray C. 1979. An Analysis of the Accuracy of Four Macroeconometric Models. *Journal of Political Economy* 87:701–19.

Fellner, William. 1946. *Monetary Policies and Full Employment.* Berkeley: University of California Press.

———. 1976. *Towards a Reconstruction of Macroeconomics.* Washington, D.C.: American Enterprise Institute for Public Policy Research.

Fiorito, Luca. 2001. John Maurice Clark's Contribution to the Genesis of the Multiplier Analysis. *History of Economic Ideas* 9.2:7–37.

Fischer, Stanley. [1988] 1991. Recent Developments in Macroeconomics. In vol. 1 of *Surveys in Economics*, edited by Andrew J. Oswald. Oxford: Blackwell for the Royal Economic Society.

Fisher, Irving. 1892. *Mathematical Investigations in the Theory of Value and Prices.* Hartford, Conn.: Transactions of the Connecticut Academy of Sciences. In vol. 1 of Fisher 1997.

———. 1907. *The Rate of Interest*. New York: Macmillan. In vol. 3 of Fisher 1997.

———. 1930. *The Theory of Interest*. New York: Macmillan. In vol. 9 of Fisher 1997.

———. 1933. The Debt-Deflation Theory of Great Depressions. *Econometrica* 1.3:337–57. In vol. 10 of Fisher 1997.

———. 1997. *The Works of Irving Fisher*. 14 vols. Edited by William J. Barber, assisted by Robert W. Dimand and Kevin Foster; consulting editor, James Tobin. London: Pickering & Chatto.

Geweke, John. 1985. Macroeconometric Modeling and the Theory of Representative Agents. *American Economic Review: Papers and Proceedings* 75.2:206–10.

Gordon, Robert J., ed. 1974. *Milton Friedman's Monetary Framework: A Debate with His Critics*. Chicago: University of Chicago Press.

Hansen, Alvin H. 1938. *Full Recovery or Stagnation?* New York: Norton.

———. 1949. *Monetary Theory and Fiscal Policy*. New York: McGraw-Hill.

———. 1953. *A Guide to Keynes*. New York: McGraw-Hill.

Harris, Seymour E., ed. 1947. *The New Economics: Keynes' Influence on Theory and Public Policy*. New York: Alfred A. Knopf.

Harrison, Paul. 1997. A History of an Intellectual Arbitrage: The Evolution of Financial Economics. In *New Economics and Its History*, edited by John B. Davis. *HOPE* 29 (supplement): 172–87.

Hartley, James E. 1997. *The Representative Agent in Macroeconomics*. London: Routledge.

Hayashi, Fumio. 1982. Tobin's Marginal and Average q: A Neoclassical Interpretation. *Econometrica* 50.1:215–24.

Hester, Donald D., and James Tobin, eds. 1967a. *Risk Aversion and Portfolio Choice*. Cowles Foundation Monograph 19. New York: John Wiley.

———. 1967b. *Studies of Portfolio Behavior*. Cowles Foundation Monograph 20. New York: John Wiley.

———. 1967c. *Financial Markets and Economic Activity*. Cowles Foundation Monograph 21. New York: John Wiley.

Hicks, John R. 1935. A Suggestion for Simplifying the Theory of Money. *Economica*, n.s., 2.1:1–19.

———. 1937. Mr. Keynes and the "Classics": A Suggested Interpretation. *Econometrica* 5.2:147–59.

———. 1939. *Value and Capital*. Oxford: Clarendon.

Johnson, Elizabeth S., and Harry G. Johnson. 1978. *The Shadow of Keynes*. Chicago: University of Chicago Press.

Kareken, John H., and Neil A. Wallace, eds. 1980. *Models of Monetary Economies*. Minneapolis: Federal Reserve Bank of Minneapolis.

Keynes, John Maynard. 1930. *A Treatise on Money*. 2 vols. London: Macmillan.

———. 1933. *The Means to Prosperity*. New York: Harcourt Brace.

———. 1936. *The General Theory of Employment, Interest, and Money*. London: Macmillan.

Kirman, Alan P. 1992. Whom or What Does the Representative Individual Represent? *Journal of Economic Perspectives* 6.2:117–36.

Klamer, Arjo. 1984. *The New Classical Macroeconomics: Conversations with New Classical Economists and Their Opponents*. Brighton, U.K.: Wheatsheaf Books.

Laidler, David E. W. 1991. Money, Credit, and Banking Lecture: Karl Brunner's Monetary Economics—an Appreciation. *Journal of Money, Credit, and Banking* 23.4:633–58.

Leontief, Wassily W. 1936. The Fundamental Assumption of Mr. Keynes' Monetary Theory of Unemployment. *Quarterly Journal of Economics* 51.2:192–97.

Lucas, Robert E., Jr. 1976. Econometric Policy Evaluation: A Critique. In Lucas 1981a.

———. 1981a. *Studies in Business-Cycle Theory*. Cambridge: MIT Press.

———. 1981b. Tobin and Monetarism: A Review Article. *Journal of Economic Literature* 19.2:558–67.

Maes, Ivo. 1991. On the Origins of Portfolio Theory. *Kyklos* 44.1:3–18.

Mantel, Rolf. 1976. Homothetic Preferences and Community Excess Demand Functions. *Journal of Economic Theory* 12.2:197–201.

Markowitz, Harry M. 1952. Portfolio Selection. *Journal of Finance* 7.1:77–91.

———. 1959. *Portfolio Selection*. New Haven, Conn.: Yale University Press.

McCallum, Bennett T. 1979. A Monetary Policy Ineffectiveness Result in a Model with a Predetermined Price Level. *Economics Letters* 3.1:1–4.

Meltzer, Allan H. 1989. Tobin on Macroeconomic Policy: A Review Essay. *Journal of Monetary Economics* 23.1:159–73.

Messori, Marcello. 1997. The Trials and Misadventures of Schumpeter's Treatise on Money. *HOPE* 29.4:639–73.

Mishkin, Frederic S. 1983. *A Rational Expectations Approach to Macoeconometrics: Testing Policy Ineffectiveness and Efficient-Markets Models*. Chicago: University of Chicago Press for the National Bureau of Economic Research.

Modigliani, Franco. 1944. Liquidity Preference and the Theory of Interest and Money. *Econometrica* 12.1:45–88.

Okun, Arthur M. 1981. *Prices and Quantities: A Macroeconomic Analysis*. Washington, D.C.: Brookings Institution.

Owen, Dorian. 1986. *Money, Wealth, and Expenditure: Integrated Modelling of Consumption and Portfolio Behaviour*. Cambridge: Cambridge University Press.

Purvis, Douglas D. 1978. Dynamic Models of Portfolio Behavior: More on Pitfalls in Financial Model Building. *American Economic Review* 68.3:403–9.

———. 1980. Monetarism: A Review. *Canadian Journal of Economics* 12.1:96–122.

———. 1982. James Tobin's Contributions to Economics. *Scandinavian Journal of Economics* 84.1:61–88.

Rizvi, S. Abu Turab. 1997. Responses to Arbitrariness in Contemporary Economics. In *New Economics and Its History*, edited by John B. Davis. *HOPE* 29 (supplement): 273–88.

Samuelson, Paul A. 1947. *Foundations of Economic Analysis*. Cambridge: Harvard University Press.

Schumpeter, Joseph A. 1970. *Das Wesen des Geldes*. Edited by F. K. Mann. Göttingen: Vandenhoeck & Ruprecht.

———. 1991. Money and Currency. Translated by Arthur W. Marget. *Social Research* 58.3:499–543.

Shiller, Robert J. 1989. *Market Volatility*. Cambridge: MIT Press.

———. 1999. The ET Interview: Professor James Tobin. *Econometric Theory* 15:867–900.

Smith, Gary. 1989. Review of *Money, Wealth, and Expenditure* by Dorian Owen. *Journal of Economic Literature* 27.4:1691–93.

Smith, Gary, and William C. Brainard. 1976. The Value of A Priori Information in Estimating a Financial Model. *Journal of Finance* 31.4:1299–1322.

Sonnenschein, Hugo. 1972. Market Excess Demand Functions. *Econometrica* 40.3:549–63.

Stein, Jerome L., ed. 1976. *Monetarism*. Amsterdam: North-Holland.

Taylor, John. 1980. Aggregate Dynamics and Staggered Contracts. *Journal of Political Economy* 88.1:1–24.

Tobin, James. 1941. A Note on the Money Wage Problem. *Quarterly Journal of Economics* 55:508–16.

———. 1947–48. Liquidity Preference and Monetary Policy. *Review of Economics and Statistics* 29.2:124–31; 30.4:314–17.

———. 1951. Relative Income, Absolute Income, and Saving. In *Money, Trade, and Economic Growth: Essays in Honor of John Henry Williams*. New York: Macmillan.

———. 1955. A Dynamic Aggregative Model. *Journal of Political Economy* 63.2:103–15.

———. 1956. The Interest-Elasticity of Transactions Demand for Cash. *Review of Economics and Statistics* 38:241–47.

———. 1958. Liquidity Preference as Behavior towards Risk. *Review of Economic Studies* 25.1:65–86.

———. 1969. A General Equilibrium Approach to Monetary Theory. *Journal of Money, Credit, and Banking* 1.1:15–29.

———. 1972. Inflation and Unemployment. *American Economic Review* 62.1:1–18.

———. 1975. Keynesian Models of Recession and Depression. *American Economic Review* 65.2:195–202.

———. 1976. Hansen and Public Policy. *Quarterly Journal of Economics* 90.1:32–37.

———. 1980. *Asset Accumulation and Economic Activity*. Chicago: University of Chicago Press.

———. 1982. The Commercial Banking Firm: A Simple Model. *Scandinavian Journal of Economics* 84.4:495–530.

————, ed. 1983. *Macroeconomics, Prices, and Quantities: Essays in Memory of Arthur M. Okun*. Washington, D.C.: Brookings Institution.

————. 1984. A Mean-Variance Approach to Fundamental Variations. Offprint from *Journal of Portfolio Management* (fall): 26–32.

————. 1993. Price Flexibility and Output Stability: An Old Keynesian View. *Journal of Economic Perspectives* 7.1:45–65.

————. [1982] 1996. Money and Finance in the Macroeconomic Process. In vol. 4 of *Essays in Economics*. Cambridge: MIT Press.

————. [1983] 1996. Liquidity Preference, Separation, and Asset Pricing. In vol. 4 of *Essays in Economics*. Cambridge: MIT Press.

————. [1988] 1996. A Revolution Remembered. In vol. 4 of *Essays in Economics*. Cambridge: MIT Press.

————. [1992] 1996. An Old Keynesian Counterattacks. In *Full Employment and Growth: Further Keynesian Essays on Policy*. Cheltenham, U.K.: Edward Elgar.

————. 1997. An Overview of *The General Theory*. In vol. 2 of *A "Second Edition" of The General Theory*, edited by G. C. Harcourt and P. A. Riach. London: Routledge.

Tobin, James, and William C. Brainard. 1977. Asset Markets and the Cost of Capital. In *Economic Progress: Private Values and Public Policy (Essays in Honor of William Fellner)*, edited by Richard Nelson and Bela Balassa. Amsterdam: North-Holland.

Tobin, James, and Willem Buiter. 1976. Long-Run Effects of Fiscal and Monetary Policy on Aggregate Demand. In vol. 1 of *Monetarism: Studies in Monetary Economics*, edited by Jerome Stein. Amsterdam: North-Holland.

————. 1980. Fiscal and Monetary Policies, Capital Formation, and Economic Activity. In *The Government and Capital Formation*, edited by George M. von Furstenberg. Cambridge: Ballinger.

Tobin, James, and Jorge Braga de Macedo. 1980. The Short-Run Macroeconomics of Floating Exchange Rates: An Exposition. In *Flexible Exchange Rates and the Balance of Payments*, edited by John S. Chipman and Charles P. Kindleberger. Amsterdam: North-Holland.

Tobin, James, with Stephen S. Golub. 1998. *Money, Credit, and Capital*. Boston: Irwin/McGraw-Hill.

Warburton, Clark. 1945. The Monetary Theory of Deficit Spending. *Review of Economics and Statistics* 27:74–84.

Wicksell, Knut. [1898] 1962. *Interest and Prices*.Translated by Richard F. Kahn. Reprint, New York: Augustus M. Kelley.

Young, Warren. 1987. *Interpreting Mr Keynes: The IS-LM Enigma*. Boulder, Colo.: Westview.

Young, Warren, and Ben Zion Zilberfarb, eds. 2000. *IS-LM and Modern Macroeconomics*. Boston: Kluwer Academic Publishers.

Patinkin on IS-LM:
An Alternative to Modigliani

Goulven Rubin

Whereas Don Patinkin's contribution to the development of the "neoclassical synthesis" is widely acknowledged (D'Autume 2000; Lucas [1980] 1981; Weintraub 1979), his name is generally forgotten when it comes to the history of IS-LM (e.g., see Darity and Young 1995). The aim of this essay is to fill this gap.

To this end, I compare Patinkin's contribution, especially *Money, Interest, and Prices* (1956), his major work, with that of Franco Modigliani. The representative character of Modigliani's works justifies his choice as the emblematic IS-LM author. Two of his articles need to be considered. The first, a 1944 article, developed the work initiated by John Hicks and set out what became the standard version of IS-LM (De Vroey 2000; Kouri 1986; Leijonhufvud 1994).[1] The second, a 1963 paper, updated the 1944 model. According to William Darity and Warren Young (1995), this updated model is the apex of IS-LM.

Patinkin's originality lies in his analyzing the IS-LM model with a Walrasian methodology. What Patinkin proposed was actually an alternative to Modigliani's version of IS-LM and, for that matter, a superior model. However, although Patinkin's 1956 book exerted an important

I wish to thank Andres Alvarez, Alain Béraud, and Carlo Benetti for helpful discussions. I am especially grateful to Michel De Vroey for his comments and encouragements. Any error or omission remains my responsibility.

1. "The 'income-expenditure theory' criticized in my 1968 book was, of course, basically the mainstream macroeconomics descended from Hicks' 1937 paper via Franco Modigliani's almost equally influential 1944 contribution" (Leijonhufvud 1994, 147).

influence, his model was never considered as an alternative to standard IS-LM.

In section 1, I present Modigliani's 1944 paper. In section 2, I show how Patinkin's method allowed him to develop a superior version of IS-LM. In section 3, I consider the content of Modigliani's 1963 paper in order to assess Patinkin's impact on Modigliani's revisions of his prior model. Finally, I come back to the nature of Patinkin's contribution, showing that it formed a bifurcation in the evolution of IS-LM from 1937 to the 1960s.

In what follows, I use the label *IS-LM* to characterize a set of simplified general equilibrium models sharing a common basic framework. This definition implies that the label *IS-LM* cannot be restricted to fixed-price models. Such restriction is historically inadequate, since Hicks (1937) assumes flexible prices alongside rigid wages. Actually, three subtypes of IS-LM models should be separated: the market-clearing, or "classical" version, with flexible wages and flexible prices; and two unemployment versions, the first with rigid wages and flexible prices and the second with both wages and prices being rigid.

1. Modigliani 1944: An Overview

Modigliani's 1944 paper, "Liquidity Preference and the Theory of Interest and Money," decisively influenced the development of macroeconomics. Its contribution was threefold. First, it recast Hicks's IS-LL model in a new way, allowing for a sharper contrast between its classical and its Keynesian cases. Second, it defended the traditional dichotomy between the real and the monetary sectors and clarified the debate over the determination of the interest rate. Third, it comprised one of the first dynamic analyses of the IS-LM model. I insist on the latter because it reveals a basic defect of Modigliani's approach, the lack of an adequate method to deal with general equilibrium.

IS-LM and the Nature of Keynes's Contribution

Modigliani's article contained two versions of IS-LM, a market-clearing, or classical, version and a Keynesian one. The main difference between them concerned money wages. In the classical model, both wages and prices were flexible; in the Keynesian model, prices were still flexible but money wages were downward rigid. As a result, the Keynesian model comprised two main regimes. If the quantity of money was sufficiently large, wage rigidity was not effective. The Keynesian model behaved like the classical model. If the quantity of money was too low, wage rigidity was effective and the model featured unemployment.

As stressed by Michel De Vroey (2000), Modigliani's contribution represented a crucial step in the evolution from Hicks's 1937 "Mr. Keynes and the 'Classics'" to the received interpretation of IS-LM. In Hicks 1937, both the classical and the Keynesian models included exogenous wages. The Keynesian theory differed from the classical only when the money demand became infinite, that is, in the liquidity trap case. Hence Hicks concluded that the Keynesian theory was the "economics of depression" instead of a general theory. In contrast, according to Modigliani, Keynes's theory was truly "general," for the Keynesian model included the classical model as a particular case. Moreover, Modigliani (1944, 65) claimed that the key aspect of the Keynesian theory was the assumption of downward wage rigidity rather than liquidity preference, for only wage rigidity was sufficient to generate an unemployment equilibrium:

> It is usually considered as one of the most important achievements of the Keynesian theory that it explains the consistency of economic equilibrium with the presence of involuntary unemployment. It is, however, not sufficiently recognized that, except in a limiting case to be considered later, this result is due entirely to the assumption of "rigid wages" and not to the Keynesian liquidity preference.

In Modigliani's view, the liquidity trap was only a part of the Keynesian theory. It was an important result, for it showed that the market-clearing model could be deprived of any equilibrium solution: "The very mechanism that tends to bring about full-employment equilibrium in a system with 'flexible' wages" could "break down" (74). Nevertheless, this was only an extreme case.[2]

---

2. It should be noted that there is a gap between Modigliani's definition of the liquidity trap and the trap as derived from his mathematical model. This is the consequence of an error in the formulation of the first versions of IS-LM. Hicks and Modigliani's models determine a money income instead of a real income. Consequently, the aggregate demand curve in their models is of a hyperbolic form ($X^D = Y/P$). This means that, contrary to Modigliani's statement (our quotation from 1944, 74), if wages are flexible, his model always has a full-employment equilibrium.

The Defense of the Traditional Dichotomy and
the Determination of the Interest Rate

In "Say's Law: A Restatement and Criticism" (1942), Oskar Lange combined Walras's law and a specific definition of Say's law to show that the level of money prices was indeterminate in the classical theory of prices.[3] In his 1944 article, Modigliani challenged this criticism of the traditional dichotomy of real and monetary economics. According to Modigliani (1944, 69), Say's law was not an attribute of the classical system. Rather, the hallmark of the classics was their view that "all the supply and demand functions [except the ones for money] must be homogeneous of zero degree, if people behave rationally" (46). In accordance with the traditional approach, the equations concerning the goods markets determined relative prices, while a monetary equation of the form $M = kPX$ determined the price level. This defense of the traditional dichotomy was reflected in the 1944 market-clearing model (67–68, 71). The savings and investment functions were assumed to be homogeneous of degree zero with respect to money prices. This allowed Modigliani to multiply money income by $1/W$ in each function to obtain the equilibrium condition:

$$S(r, PX/W) = I(r, PX/W) \tag{1}$$

Since the equilibrium condition for the labor market and the production function determined the level of output X and the real wage W/P, this equation determined the rate of interest. The latter being given, the monetary equation determined the money wage, hence the price level:

$$M = L[r, W(PX/W)] \tag{2}$$

This dichotomy also played an important role in Modigliani's contribution to the debate over the determination of the rate of interest because it generated the conclusion that the interest rate depended only on "real factors" as long as wages were flexible (i.e., it was independent of the quantity of money and of money demand). In contrast, whenever wages were rigid, the rate of interest was simultaneously determined by real and monetary factors, that is, by IS and LM.

---

3. Say's law, in Lange's definition, states that the sum in value of all excess demands, except the excess demand for money, is identically nil. Walras's law extends this property to the excess demand for money. If both "laws" are valid, it means that an economic system of n equilibrium conditions comprises only $n - 2$ independent equations for $n - 1$ money prices.

The Formation of the "Monetary Equilibrium" and
the Lack of a General Equilibrium Method

Modigliani called the point of intersection of the IS curve and the LM
curve the "monetary equilibrium." He must be credited for having attempted to account for its formation: "We now finally proceed to consider the process by which the equilibrium of the system is established"
(1944, 60). While this analysis is a noteworthy aspect of Modigliani's
contribution, it has often been neglected.[4] Modigliani's reference was
the Marshallian equilibrium theory, an approach conceived to analyze
the adjustment in time of a single market, not the interaction between
the markets for goods and money.

In the Marshallian approach, a distinction is drawn between the short
period equilibrium and the long period, or normal, equilibrium. In the
short period, the quantity supplied is given and price adjusts until demand equals supply. In the long period, the quantity supplied varies until
no agent wants to modify his behavior. Modigliani (1944, 87) attempted
to apply this conceptual scheme to the IS-LM model, as explicitly stated
in the conclusion of the paper:

> As we have shown in our model the equality of demand and supply
> of loanable funds is the equilibrium condition for the week (or for our
> income period) and determines the equilibrium rate of interest (or sys-
> tem of rates) for the week. It corresponds to the short-run equilibrium
> condition of the Marshallian demand and supply analysis: price equals
> marginal cost. But the stock of money to hold (the supply) tends itself
> to change and thus to push the daily rate towards the level at which
> the flow of money saving equals the flow of money investment. The
> condition (ex ante) saving = (ex ante) investment, corresponds to the
> long-run Marshallian condition (under perfect competition): price =
> average cost including rent.

In order to apply the Marshallian short period equilibrium concept to
the IS-LM model, Modigliani introduced a separation between the transaction demand for money and the speculation demand for money. The
former depended on money income only, the latter on the rate of interest only. Given this separation, Modigliani reformulated the LM relation

---

4. See, for instance, Darity and Young 1995. An exception is offered by P. J. K. Kouri (1986,
313), who notes that "the second contribution of [Modigliani's] article was an explicit analysis
of the short-run dynamics of the Keynesian model."

as $S_a = D_a$ where $S_a \equiv M^s - D_T(Y)$ was the "supply of money to hold" and $D_a \equiv D_a(r)$ was the "demand for money to hold." Moreover, Modigliani defined the adjustment process toward the "monetary equilibrium" as a sequence of "income periods." In each income period, agents decided how to use the income inherited from the preceding period. The variable Y in the behavior functions was given within the income period. As a result, S_a was fixed. Modigliani further assumed that the rate of interest varied until the demand for money D_a equaled the supply S_a. Thereby, the money market equilibrium became tantamount to the Marshallian short-period equilibrium.

As to the "monetary equilibrium," suppose, said Modigliani, that for a given money income, the rate of interest that equilibrates S_a and D_a does not equilibrate savings and investment. A process of adjustment was triggered. The supply of money to hold would change from one period to the other until savings equaled investment. The latter was viewed as tantamount to the Marshallian long-period equilibrium condition.

Unfortunately, Modigliani's use of short-period and long-period equilibrium was beset with ambiguities. First, Modigliani's specific use of the Marshallian method turned the IS schedule into an expression of the state of the money market. That is, LM defined the short-run equilibrium of this market, IS its long-run equilibrium. "For this purpose we must once more revert to the money market which we must, this time, consider in terms of flow rather than in terms of stocks" (1944, 60). So, according to Modigliani, IS reflected the state of the money market in terms of flows.[5]

Conversely, Modigliani never mentioned the goods market in relation to IS. Now, if IS was nothing but a reflection of the money market, IS-LM was no longer a general equilibrium model. Put differently, the "monetary equilibrium" was not the simultaneous equilibrium of two different markets (goods and money), but the equilibrium of a single market (money) in the short run and in the long run.

A second problem facing Modigliani's approach was the discrepancy that arose between his formalization of the mechanism adjusting savings and investment, and his verbal account of it. It comes out very clearly when looking at how Modigliani wrote down the dynamic version of his model in section 10 of his paper:

$$Y_t - Y_{t-1} = I_t(r_t, Y_{t-1}) - S_t(r_t, Y_{t-1}) \tag{3}$$

5. "There are two ways of looking at [the money market]: (a) in terms of flows (*savings and net borrowing*) and (b) in terms of stocks" (1944, 54; emphasis added).

Money income was supposed to diminish discretely as long as savings exceeded investment. However, when describing the formation of the "monetary equilibrium" and in commenting on his dynamic model, Modigliani never referred to this mechanism. To wit, here is how he presented "the process by which the equilibrium of the system is established": "If net savings exceeds net borrowing then, on balance, the supply of money to hold will increase above the level of the previous period, say D_{a0}. But at the old rate of interest (r_0) people will not want to hold extra supply; they will therefore try to purchase securities and thus will lower the rate of interest" (61).

Modigliani's reasoning was globally correct. If savings exceeded investment at the equilibrium rate of interest of period one, the supply of money to hold would exceed the demand of money to hold in period two. The missing link was that Modigliani should have said that excess savings in period one triggered a fall in money income. Consequently, the transaction demand for money declined in period two and S_a increased. Oddly enough, Modigliani never mentioned this mechanism. A possible explanation is that the status of money income as an adjustment variable of the money market was quite difficult to justify.

In short, Modigliani's paper lacked an adequate method to deal with a general equilibrium.

2. Patinkin's *Money, Interest, and Prices*

In *Money, Interest, and Prices* (1956), Patinkin presented two macro models, a market-clearing and a market-nonclearing one, without making clear their relation to IS-LM.[6] Nonetheless, some evidence exists suggesting that they derived from this apparatus. For what concerns the fixed-price model (1956, chap. 13, sec. 4), Patinkin indicated in 1990 that "the interpretation presented in chapter XIII: 4 and XIV: 1 and 3 of the 1956 and subsequent (1965 and 1989) editions of my *Money, Interest and Prices* is essentially that of IS-LM" (1990, 213). In contrast, he never used the label *IS-LM* to characterize his market-clearing model. Yet the titles of the chapters of *Money, Interest, and Prices* in which Patinkin presented his macro models, "The Workings of the Model: Full Employment" and the "Workings of the Model: Involuntary Unemployment," suggest that they were subtypes of a broader apparatus. Moreover,

6. He alludes to IS-LM only once to point to the parallel between one of his diagrams (1956, 226) and Hicks's 1937 diagram.

the idea that the basic structure of Patinkin's "full employment" model was essentially that of IS-LM is supported by this assertion taken from a paper preceding the publication of *Money, Interest, and Prices*: "This model is essentially Keynesian in nature, in so far as its basic components are an aggregate demand function and a liquidity-preference function which depends upon the rate of interest" (1954, 124).

These elements support the claim that Patinkin borrowed the skeleton of his macro models from Hicks and Modigliani. The originality of his contribution stemmed from its outright Walrasian inspiration. The result of this "Walrasation"[7] of IS-LM was a superior apparatus, for, as I now want to show, Patinkin's version of IS-LM was clearer and more consistent than Modigliani's 1944 model.

Patinkin's Method

As the subtitle of *Money, Interest, and Prices* indicated, Patinkin's aim was to integrate "monetary and value theory." This aim was pursued both at the microeconomic level (part 1 of the book) and at the macroeconomic level (part 2), but its meaning differed slightly in each case. At the microeconomic level, the subject of analysis was the Walrasian model of a pure exchange economy. At the macroeconomic level, the subject of analysis was IS-LM, but IS-LM developed and analyzed as if its foundations could be derived from the Walrasian theory. For Patinkin, this attempt to make macroeconomics consistent with the Walrasian theory of prices was a necessary aspect of the "integration of monetary and value theory" because for him IS-LM belonged to monetary theory.[8]

Three basic ideas, all drawn from the Walrasian theory, underlie Patinkin's method. First, a general equilibrium model represented a market system or a set of interrelated markets. This meant that each market should be represented by a set of equations in the model and that each equation of the model should refer to a specific market. In this context, the term *market* simply referred to the fact that a certain good had a demand, a supply, and a price.

Second, goods were demanded and supplied by agents whose behavior was bounded by the discipline of the Walrasian budget constraint.

7. This expression is borrowed from De Vroey 1999a.

8. In Patinkin's language, "monetary theory" comprised the quantity theory of money and Keynes's unemployment theory, hence classical and Keynesian macroeconomics (cf. the title of Patinkin's 1976 essay about the genesis of the *General Theory*: "Keynes' Monetary Thought").

This constraint stated that, prices being given, the value of agents' spendings should always equilibrate the value of their resources. The budget constraint was unique, which meant that each agent decided simultaneously what his or her demands would be on all the markets of the economy. Walras's law, stating that, whatever the vector of prices, the sum in value of all market excess demands was identically equal to zero, could be derived from the aggregation of all budget constraints.

Third, Patinkin considered that assessing the logical existence of general equilibrium was insufficient. The issue of its formation also had to be addressed. This was the role played by the Walrasian *tâtonnement*. The *tâtonnement* was primarily a representation of how "a free market economy finds its way towards the equilibrium position" (1956, 36). In this respect, it implied a set of assumptions (the metaphorical auctioneer, the recontracting assumption) ensuring that it "necessarily brings the economic system to that same set of prices yielded by a direct mathematical solution of the system of excess-demand equations" (378). But *tâtonnement* was also the "method of successive approximation" (32, 152) enabling the theorist to decompose the process of adjustment of the market system. This method was based on the general application of the law of demand. Any disequilibrium on one market triggered an equilibrating variation of the price on this market. Yet it also impinged on the state of other markets. Variations of other prices were induced that would, in turn, react on the initial market.

IS-LM as a Market System

Contrary to Modigliani, Patinkin defined explicitly his model as the representation of a market system. Yet, as is normal in a macroeconomic perspective, the numerous markets of microeconomics were reduced to a small number of representative markets: "In particular we forego microeconomic detail and work instead with an aggregative model which divides all the goods of the economy into four composite categories: labor services, commodities, bonds and money. To each of these categories there corresponds a market, a price, an aggregate demand function and an aggregate supply function" (1956, 125). As a consequence of this general approach, Patinkin replaced the savings-investment equation by an equation relating the demand and the supply for commodities. Admittedly, this modification was minor insofar as both equations were equivalent (chap. 11, sec. 6). Still, it eliminated the ambiguity surrounding

IS in Modigliani's paper. "This decision has been based on the fact that such a concept [savings] is out of place in an analytical framework which views the economy as consisting of a number of goods, each with a price, and each with a market. For savings are clearly not a good, they have no price, and they are not themselves transacted on a market" (186).

Following the same logic, Patinkin introduced explicitly the bonds market in his macroeconomic model. The model then appeared as a system of four equilibrium equations with three unknowns:

$$N^S \left(\frac{W}{P} \right) = N^D \left(\frac{W}{P} \right) \tag{4}$$

$$X_{fe} = F \left(X_{fe}, r, \frac{M}{P} \right) \tag{5}$$

$$B^S \left(X_{fe}, r, \frac{M^F}{P} \right) = B^D \left(X_{fe}, r, \frac{M^H}{P} \right) \tag{6}$$

$$M = P \cdot l^D \left(X_{fe}, r, \frac{M}{P} \right) \tag{7}$$

Next, using Walras's law and a set of simplifying assumptions related to the labor market, Patinkin showed how his four-equations model could be reduced to the interaction between two different markets (goods and bonds or goods and money).

Thereby he was able to avoid Modigliani's tortuous concept of "monetary equilibrium." The general equilibrium of the "full employment" macro model was simply the situation in which prices were such that demand equaled supply on each market. Patinkin used Walras's law to show that the system contained only three independent equations for three unknown variables and explained that he took "this equality between the number of equations and unknowns as justifying the reasonableness of the assumption that this system of equations does have a solution" (152).

Tâtonnement and the "Working" of the Model

The use of Walras's law and of the *tâtonnement* device allowed Patinkin to account verbally for the adjustment process leading to equilibrium in the various versions of the IS-LM model.

The *tâtonnement* method was perfectly appropriate for the analysis of the market-clearing model. Like Modigliani, Patinkin conducted a thought experiment. He defined a situation in which the goods market was in equilibrium but the bonds market was in excess demand. Next, with the help of the law of demand and supply, he showed how this situation resulted in a process of interaction between the two markets. The disequilibrium on the bonds market induced an adjustment of the price for bonds. This adjustment had a stabilizing influence on this market yet a destabilizing influence on the goods market; that is, the rate of interest fell so that aggregate demand for goods rose. This new disequilibrium on the goods market induced a fall of the price level, which had a stabilizing effect on both the goods and the bonds markets. These forces were assumed to bring the system back toward general equilibrium.[9]

Patinkin also used the *tâtonnement* approach for his market nonclearing model. If a disequilibrium on the goods market was assumed to induce a variation of the price level, how could one account for the fact that income became the adjustment variable in the model with unemployment? This was the question addressed in chapter 13 of *Money, Interest, and Prices*. According to him, some impediment on the adjustment of aggregate demand toward its market-clearing level was needed. In these conditions, firms eventually adjusted production, hence income, to the level of aggregate demand whatever the level of real wages. Patinkin (1956, 225) offered a formal representation of this situation in the "extreme" case where prices and wages were "absolutely rigid." The functioning of this model was analyzed just like the functioning of the market-clearing model, using the "*tâtonnement*" method, income replacing the price level as the adjustment variable for the goods market. Patinkin stressed the connection between his analysis and the IS-LM analysis of Hicks and Modigliani, neglecting the fact that in their models only wages were rigid, while both prices and wages were fixed in his own model.[10]

9. Of course, Patinkin did not go far enough in the verbal exposition of his experiment. The first reason for this was that an exhaustive description of the evolution of the varying combinations of forces at work during the adjustment process and of their possible effects on the two markets would rapidly have become too tedious. Hence Patinkin borrowed from Metzler 1951 a graphic apparatus similar to Hicks's IS-LM graphic but designed for the full-employment case. And since this phase diagram hardly provided a proof of stability, in his "mathematical appendix" Patinkin eventually proceeded to analyze algebraically the conditions for stability of a dynamic version of his model.

10. According to Patinkin, the Keynesian theory had to demonstrate that a perfectly competitive system with price and wage flexibility could suffer from chronic unemployment. Hence its

Patinkin's method also clarified the adjustment mechanism of the "rigid wage-cum-flexible price" IS-LM model. In such a framework, the price level was the adjustment variable of X^D and X^S, hence of I and S. An excess demand for goods induced a fall of prices, the real wage increased, and the desired aggregate supply for goods decreased until $X^S = X^D$ (1956, 223–24). This analysis ran counter to Modigliani's claim that income was the adjustment variable for the goods market. This was true only when prices as well as wages were "absolutely rigid."

False Dichotomy, Monetary Illusion, and the Real Balance Effect

Another improvement made by Patinkin was his correction of a contradiction involved in Modigliani's full-employment model, a particular instance of the "false dichotomy" between the real and the monetary sector.

Patinkin (1947, 1949a, 1956) generalized Lange's criticism by showing directly, that is, without reference to Say's law, that the assumption of zero-degree homogeneity was inconsistent with the use of the Cambridgian monetary equation. The key of his demonstration was Walras's law. If all market excess demands, save the excess demand for money, were homogeneous of degree zero with respect to the price level, the excess demand for money should also share this property because of Walras's law. This was in contradiction with the specification of the traditional monetary equation ($M = kPX$), which stated that the excess demand for money was not homogeneous with respect to P. As soon as the IS-LM model was considered as a system of interrelated markets consistent with Walras's law, Patinkin's criticism applied. Modigliani claimed that only the excess demand for money was not homogeneous of degree zero. Therefore, it had to be inferred that the excess demand for bonds was also homogeneous of degree zero. In this case, Modigliani's

---

object was "the dynamic workings of an economy in disequilibrium" (Patinkin 1956, 224; on the origin of this aspect of Patinkin's thought, see Rubin 2002a and 2002b). Obviously, IS-LM was not an appropriate vehicle for this conception. Patinkin thus developed an interpretation of the fixed-price version of IS-LM in accordance with his interpretation of the theory of involuntary unemployment. Either it was a limiting case of the Keynesian theory, as in *Money, Interest, and Prices* (chap. 13, sec. 4), or it was the reflection of the state of an economic system in disequilibrium at a point in time. It was like a snapshot of the economy during its adjustment process. Prices were given but not rigid. They were bound to change under the pressure of disequilibrium on the markets for goods and labor. This last interpretation appeared in later works (Patinkin 1974, 1990a, and 1990b).

monetary equation (equation [6] above) was inconsistent with his equilibrium conditions for the labor and the goods market and with his implicit equation for the bonds market.

Patinkin also provided a solution to the indeterminacy of the price level in the Walrasian model through the introduction of real balances in the excess demand functions. The key concept in this respect was the Walrasian budget constraint. In a monetary economy, agents held money balances. Insofar as they acted in accordance with their budget restraints, any variation of the price level had to affect their expenses. A price increase reduced the real value of their money balance. Therefore, the demands for goods, bonds, and money had to decrease. This real balance effect still existed in the aggregate if money was a net wealth for the economic system as a whole or if the value of money balances was not canceled by the value of some private debts (Patinkin 1948, 550).

Real demand functions were now homogeneous of zero degree with respect to P and M. Therefore the inconsistency affecting Modigliani's classical model disappeared. The classical dichotomy between a real sector and a monetary sector also vanished, yet the neutrality of money could still be demonstrated. In the context of a system with price and wage flexibility and no distribution effects, this result depended only on the absence of monetary illusion (Patinkin 1954, 1956).

The Debate over the Determination of the Rate of Interest

Patinkin's introduction of the bonds market clarified the debate over the determination of the interest rate. For Modigliani, the issue was whether the rate of interest was determined by IS or by LM. Patinkin's general equilibrium approach showed how irrelevant this issue was. The rate of interest was primarily related to the bonds market, since it was the reciprocal of bonds' price. Nonetheless, like all prices, it was generally determined simultaneously by all the equations of the model. Hence the determination of the rate of interest by IS was necessarily due to some special assumptions implicitly made by Modigliani, namely, the absence of real balance effect on the goods market.

The Liquidity Trap

According to Hicks (1937), Lange (1938), and Modigliani (1944), the liquidity trap was the consequence of an infinite money demand. This definition was based on an "individual-experiment," to borrow Patinkin's expression (1956, 15). To check its validity, it was necessary to examine how an isolated agent reacted to a change in the rate of interest. Hicks, Lange, and Modigliani all assumed that when the rate of interest reached a certain value, "individuals'" money demands became infinite. This feature no longer held when the budget constraint was brought into the picture. Assuming that agents respected their budget constraints, an infinite money demand required infinite resources. The only possible source of such infinite resources was an infinite bonds supply: "But an individual who plans an infinite supply of bonds is for some reasons unconcerned with his obligation to make interest payments on these bonds. Hence if the amount supplied is infinite at any positive rate of interest, it must be so at all rates. Under this assumption, it follows that the demand for money would also be infinite at all positive rates" (1956, 149). In other words, Hicks's definition of the liquidity trap amounted to the assumption that agents did not respect their intertemporal budget constraints. Conversely, if this constraint was to hold, the liquidity trap could not be the consequence of an "individual-experiment."

Next, Patinkin showed that this phenomenon could still appear as a "market experiment," that is, as the result of the interaction between different individuals on the marketplace. The form of the demand for bonds was decisive here. Suppose that the aggregate demand for bonds became nil when the rate of interest reached a low value. As soon as this low value was reached, any increase in the money supply could no longer finance an increase in the demand for bonds, for this demand was nil. If, in addition, it was supposed that agents did not spend any additional real balances on the goods market (i.e., if there was no real balance effect on the goods market), then the only effect of this increase would be an increase in money demand. In these conditions, an infinite increase in money supply would finance an infinite increase of money demand (Patinkin 1956, 245–49). This implied that an LM curve built on the assumption of a constant money supply could not present a flat portion. In the (r, X) space, the phenomenon of the liquidity trap would be reflected by the curve expressing the equilibrium condition for the bonds market rather than by the shape of the LM curve. Beyond a certain amount of money supply, this curve would appear as a horizontal straight line and define a minimum rate of interest.

Walras's Law and Unemployment

The final important clarification introduced by Patinkin that I want to discuss concerns the use of Walras's law. The latter was implicitly invoked by Modigliani to justify the exclusion of the bonds market from IS-LM analysis.[11] Yet if this procedure was perfectly correct in the case of a market-clearing model, it became problematic when applied to a model with unemployment. Patinkin was the first to raise this issue in a 1958 paper titled "Liquidity Preference and Loanable Funds: Stock and Flow Analysis."

In this paper, Patinkin analyzed an unemployment equilibrium model based on fixed prices and wages. Unemployment equilibrium meant that the labor market was in excess supply, whereas the markets for goods, bonds, and money were in equilibrium. Such an outcome contradicted Walras's law as defined by Patinkin at the beginning of his paper: "If any $n - 1$ excess-demand equations are satisfied, the remaining one must also be satisfied" (300), hence the remark that "at first sight, then, there would seem to be no place for the operation of Walras' law" (314).

Clearly, such a result was hardly acceptable for Patinkin, since Walras's law was a basic instrument of his analysis of the fixed-price version of IS-LM. For instance, it allowed him to state that "the curve MM [or LM] must, of course, also pass through the points" (1956, 229), the point of intersection of his IS curve and of the curve expressing the locus of all equilibrium in the bonds market. Likewise, in his 1958 paper, Patinkin used Walras's law to show that there was no difference between a theory of interest based on the equation for bonds (a "loanable funds theory") and a theory based on the money equation (a "liquidity preference theory"). In order to extend this conclusion to the case of involuntary unemployment, he had to show that Walras's law applied in this case, too.

Patinkin's escape consisted of modifying the households' budget constraint. Drawing from the idea that in a situation of involuntary unemployment workers' incomes were determined by firms' labor demands, he substituted N^D for N^S in the household budget constraint: "The right-hand side of the household account reflects our assumption that wage earners passively expect to receive whatever employers plan to pay; hence the term N^D appears there as well as on the left-hand side of the

11. "Without the benefit of that crutch, in my 1944 paper I was led in the formal model of section 2, to drop any explicit reference to the bond market–implicitly treated as the redundant one" (Modigliani 1944, 81). In the text preceding this note, the notion of "redundant market" was related to "Walras' law."

business account" (1958, 315). As a result, the aggregation of agents' budget constraints yielded a modified Walras's law that was restricted to three markets: the markets for goods, bonds, and money. This relation could then be used to analyze the unemployment versions of IS-LM.

To conclude this section, my above analysis clearly indicates that Patinkin's model was more consistent than Modigliani's 1944 IS-LM model. In the main, the framework of Patinkin's macro model was basically similar to Modigliani's: a four-market system with the same simplifying assumptions to deal with the labor market; the same treatment of expectations; aggregate demand split in two components, consumption and investment; a liquidity preference function; and a market for bonds. But Patinkin's use of the Walrasian method clarified the properties of the system. Moreover, as seen, it eliminated many of the inconsistencies of Modigliani's article. What remains to be studied is the fate of Patinkin's version of IS-LM.

3. Modigliani's Monetary Mechanism

Modigliani's 1963 article, "The Monetary Mechanism and Its Interaction with Real Phenomena," is an updated version of his 1944 model examining its implications for monetary theory and for economic policy. Modigliani refers to that model as a "Mid-50's model" and says it is "essentially the model that I would have used had I been writing a comparable article at that time (and did actually use in my class lectures)" (1963, 79). My purpose here is to assess Patinkin's influence on Modigliani's revised model.

In the first part of his paper, Modigliani listed five modifications introduced in his 1963 model and distinguishing it from his 1944 model: (1) "explicit reliance on a general equilibrium formulation"; (2) "explicit treatment of the bond market" and introduction of a private banking sector; (3) "improvements in the consumption and investment functions"; (4) "correction of the faulty formulation of the homogeneity properties of the consumption, investment and demand for money functions"; and (5) "use of a more convenient and effective device for expressing the hypothesis of wage rigidity." Patinkin's influence is obvious for several of these modifications. As far as the first is concerned, the "explicit reliance on a general equilibrium formulation" (1963, 80) was a novelty whose definition paraphrased the introduction of chapter 9 of *Money, Interest, and Prices* (1956, 125): "The mid-fifty model is explicitly structured in terms of markets, one for each commodity, with each market in turn described by (a) supply conditions, (b) demand conditions, and (c) clearing of market or equilibrium conditions, of which one is redundant (Walras' law)" (1963, 80–81). Thus, Modigliani adopted Patinkin's idea that a general equilibrium model represented a market system. The "explicit treatment of the bond market" (81) was also borrowed from Patinkin. The same was true for the "correction of the faulty formulation of the homogeneity properties of the consumption, investment, and demand for money functions" (82). The assumption that "the real demand for consumption, investment, and money is homogeneous of zero degree in money income, wealth, and prices" and the fact that "this property is an implication of rational behavior" (82) were the results of Patinkin's investigations.

Modigliani's new formalization of wage rigidity (1963, 82) must also be viewed as an indirect consequence of Patinkin's criticisms. In 1944, Modigliani associated wage rigidity with the assumption of a horizontal supply curve of labor. Patinkin (1947, 1949b, 1956) had shown that this was an unsatisfactory representation of involuntary unemployment, because workers were always "on their supply curve of labor." Modigliani was well aware of this criticism, having read Patinkin's PhD thesis, in which it was already present. Furthermore, Patinkin expressed this criticism in a letter addressed to Modigliani in April 1948.[12] Modigliani's abandonment of the "horizontal supply curve of labor" must thus be interpreted as having been prompted by Patinkin. This explains Modigliani's insistence on the fact that "the difference between this level of employment [determined by N^D] and the potential supply at W_0 is then 'involuntary unemployment' in the Keynesian sense" (1963, 82).

The two modifications not inspired by Patinkin were of more secondary importance. The first was the introduction of a private banking sector in the model. The second consisted in "improvements in the consumption and investment function and in particular more adequate recognition of the role of stocks" (81). The latter "improvements" were the introduction of aggregate labor income NW/P in addition to real income X in the consumption function and the introduction of the stock of capital K_0 in the investment function. Yet both variables were actually neglected in the subsequent analysis. The introduction of a banking sector did not modify the basic structure of the model. Though a useful

12. An analysis of Patinkin's position on this point and of the problems raised by the "horizontal supply curve of labor" is presented in Rubin 2002a.

refinement, it was hardly new in 1963 after Gurley and Shaw 1960 and Patinkin 1961.[13]

In sum, the modifications of the 1944 model resulted in a set of equations nearly identical to the equations of Patinkin's model. There is, however, one topic on which Modigliani refused to accept Patinkin's viewpoint, the issue of the dichotomy between the real and the monetary sector. Modigliani persisted in defending his own definition of this dichotomy. To him, Patinkin's conclusion concerning the neutrality of money was erroneous: "We proceed first to a summary of some implications of the model within the classical framework of price and wage flexibility. Its main justification is the hope of disposing for good of a controversy, connected with the names of Pigou and Patinkin, which has plagued the profession, draining the resources into what strikes me as a largely barren endeavor" (Modigliani 1963, 83).

In terms of these definitions, Patinkin's basic contention could be summarized as follows: "In an economy relying on a token money as a medium of exchange, the dichotomy does not hold, but under certain conditions money will be neutral. . . . It is found that Patinkin's contention is basically unwarranted, although no attempt at rigorous proof is possible here" (84).

To substantiate his claim, Modigliani analyzed three cases. The first was a model with pure bank money or internal money, the second a model with government money and no public debt, and the third a model with public debt. Since in the first case the classical dichotomy was valid and since in the third money was not neutral, Patinkin, he claimed, was wrong. This criticism is hardly convincing, since it actually boils down to a summary of different results that could be derived from Patinkin's model. That money was not neutral when public debt was introduced was explicitly recognized in *Money, Interest, and Prices* (1956, 207). The case of a system with pure bank money was not analyzed in that edition. Distribution effects being absent, a variation of P does not affect the goods market, for the resulting variation in the aggregate value of real money balances is offset by the losses of bank debtors. If, moreover, full employment is assumed, the rate of interest is determined by the condition of equilibrium on the goods market so that "the equilibrium value of the real variables of the system is independent of both the

13. In the first edition of *Money, Interest, and Prices*, Patinkin explicitly excludes the banking sector from his analysis, assuming that money is only composed of government money (cf. 1956, 145, 206 n. 17).

supply and the demand for money" (Modigliani 1963, 84). In this context, Modigliani's definition of the dichotomy proves valid. Moreover, in the absence of real balance effect, the model could contain a liquidity trap. In the second edition of *Money, Interest, and Prices*, Patinkin ([1965] 1972, 331) admitted the logical validity of Modigliani's analysis of the pure bank money case. Nevertheless, he hardly considered it an invalidation of his own conclusions concerning the dichotomy and the neutrality of money. Modigliani showed that, if some of Patinkin's 1956 assumptions were removed, his 1944 conclusions held good. In this sense, his analysis was only an extension of Patinkin's work. However, by Modigliani's own standards, his assumptions were extreme. To get a model with no real balance effect, he had to assume that the economy had no central bank and no public debt. For, like Patinkin and most authors of the neoclassical synthesis, Modigliani considered that money supplied by the government, or by a central bank, and government bonds were net wealth.[14] Obviously, the model he put forward had only a limited utility.[15]

Modigliani's argumentation about dichotomy and the neutrality of money shows that much of his 1963 paper should be viewed as an answer to Patinkin, yet all in all, Modigliani's very efforts to evade Patinkin's conclusions illustrate the rigor and scope of Patinkin's model.

The conclusion can then be drawn that Modigliani's updating of his 1944 model was inspired by *Money, Interest, and Prices*. However, Modigliani stopped short of adopting the Walrasian dimension of Patinkin's approach. In particular, he left aside the Walrasian budget constraint and the *tâtonnement* process.

While mentioning Walras's law, Modigliani was wanting in his consideration of the budget constraints of agents. His analysis of the classical model (1963, 85) suggests that he considered the decisions of each agent as a set of separate optimization programs, each with its specific constraint. Households made a decision concerning their labor supply, then they decided how much of their income to save, and, finally, they determined the level of their demand for money or the composition of

14. Indeed, Modigliani (1987) was very critical about Robert Barro's Ricardian equivalence theorem (Barro 1974). Yet, ironically, this theorem is the strongest argument to support the idea that there is nothing else but "inside money" or that the "pure bank money case" is the general case.

15. To discuss the "role of government monetary and fiscal operation" (1963, sec. 4, 93), Modigliani had to integrate government money and government debt in his model.

their portfolio. This loose treatment of microfoundations hardly differs from his approach in the 1944 paper (48–54). Actually, the latter was more explicit.

No reference to the formation of equilibrium is to be found in the 1963 article. While Modigliani abandoned his 1944 analysis of the short and long periods, he did not adopt the *tâtonnement* method. The way Modigliani uses the word *force* in his paper illustrates the contrast between his approach and Patinkin's. In physics, a force is the cause of movement. By analogy, in *Money, Interest, and Prices*, the "market force" is the pressure an excess demand on one market exerts on the price of this market. This "force" is thus the immediate cause of price variations. It is a precise dynamic concept used to analyze the formation of equilibrium. In Modigliani's 1963 paper, the word *force* carries the same dynamic connotations. Yet its use is actually inappropriate, since the related analysis is purely static: "It may be useful to state in plain English the major forces determining equilibrium in the system described by Model II under the stated assumptions. This mechanism can be summarized roughly as follows . . . " (85). The words *forces* and *mechanism* in this passage seem to announce a dynamic analysis. Yet eventually the "forces determining equilibrium in the system" turn out to refer to the parameters lying behind the equilibrium conditions of Modigliani's model, the "initial stock of capital," the "preferences for current and future consumption as compared with leisure," and so on, rather than to forces in the strict sense. This loose utilization underlines Modigliani's lack of a definite way to deal with the formation of equilibrium. Some isolated fragments of dynamic analysis further illustrate how distant he is from Patinkin in this respect. For instance, when dealing with his market-clearing model with government debt, Modigliani (1963, 87) states that "an increase in the money supply by increasing P and reducing real wealth, will tend to increase saving and reduce the rate of interest to the extent necessary to produce a matching increment in investment." In contrast to Patinkin's *tâtonnement* approach, this piece of analysis implies that the price level is the adjustment variable on the money market (rather than on the goods market), and the rate of interest the adjustment variable on the goods market (rather than on the bonds market). Instead of reasoning in terms of well-defined markets and of behavior functions, Modigliani manipulates rather mechanically, though correctly, his IS and LM equations. A last example of the difference between Modigliani and Patinkin is Modigliani's adoption of a markup pricing (1963, 91). The assumption of markup pricing is clearly incompatible with a *tâtonnement* setting in which agents are assumed to be price takers.

Two points have been made in this section. I have shown that Modigliani's "Mid-50's model" was strongly influenced by Patinkin. However, it must also be realized that Modigliani did not fully rally behind Patinkin's standpoint. In particular, he stopped short of adopting two basic features of the Walrasian approach, the budget constraint and the *tâtonnement* method.

4. A Bifurcation That Was Not Taken

My above analysis runs counter to the standard conception of the history of IS-LM as a steady accumulation of knowledge beginning in 1937 and culminating in the 1960s. Patinkin's general equilibrium method significantly contributed to the advancement of the standard model. However, if the accumulation story were right, Patinkin's model should have replaced Modigliani's 1944 model as the referential version of IS-LM. This did not happen. The right perspective to adopt, then, is Axel Leijonhufvud's, when proposing to consider the history of economics as forming a decision tree.[16] In this perspective, Patinkin's work should be viewed as having opened a methodological bifurcation, proposing a Walrasian way to practice general equilibrium analysis as an alternative to Modigliani's Marshallian way. Yet, oddly enough, that bifurcation was not perceived as such and hence remained unexploited.[17]

An in-depth analysis of Modigliani's 1944 paper shows that his approach was non-Walrasian (in the radical sense of this modifier). True, in the beginning of his article, he referred to the Walrasian system as the "only rigorous procedure" to deal with general equilibrium. Yet he soon discarded it as "cumbersome and not well suited to an essentially literary exposition" (1944, 46). No sign of any Walrasian inspiration is present in the remainder of his article. As seen above, whenever Modigliani faced a difficulty, the solution he proposed was Marshallian. Marshallian traits are less present in the 1963 paper, yet the lack of any reference to the

---

16. "It is useful to think of the history of our subject as forming a decision tree. Major economists force their contemporaries to face choices—choices of what to ask, what to assume, what to regard as evidence and what methods and models to employ—and persuade the profession or some faction of it to follow the choice they make. The path that any particular school has followed traces a sequence of such decisions" (Leijonhufvud 1994, 148).

17. Cf. De Vroey 1999a, 1999b, and this volume.

tâtonnement and to the Walrasian budget constraints suggests he was not more Walrasian than in 1944.[18] In other words, the Walrasian theory was actually alien to Modigliani's IS-LM. These elements are consistent with the fact that IS-LM was a general equilibrium model inspired by the *General Theory* and therefore rooted in the Marshallian school of thought.

In this context, Patinkin's approach marked a breach with Modigliani's conception of IS-LM. Whereas Modigliani developed IS-LM without trying to relate its structure to a fully articulated general equilibrium theory, Patinkin aimed at founding his model in the Walrasian general equilibrium theory. The difference between their respective attempts was more than just a matter of degree. A difference in research programs was involved. The program derived from Modigliani aimed to extend the scope of IS-LM (open economy, Phillips curve, macroeconometric applications) and to deepen the understanding of its components (the consumption function, the investment function, etc.) while keeping them insulated from each other. The emphasis was put on the pragmatic applications of IS-LM. Instead, Patinkin's method called for a synthesis between the macroeconomics inspired by the *General Theory* and the Walrasian theory of price, with the emphasis put on the logical consistency of the general apparatus. As I have shown in section 3, Patinkin was not followed by the economists of his generation. IS-LM did not become the Hicks-Modigliani-Patinkin model, and the research program of the "neoclassical synthesis" remained the Modigliani program.

These remarks are made in hindsight for the protagonists of this story, and, in particular, Patinkin did not see the matter as I do. While Patinkin opened a new bifurcation on the economic theory decision tree, he did it unwittingly. His lack of awareness persisted over time as two subsequent papers, published in 1990, testify to. The most noticeable, presented at a conference for the fiftieth anniversary of Hicks's model (Patinkin 1990a), was titled "In Defence of IS-LM." Patinkin contended that IS-LM was, first, a "valid representation of the *General Theory*" and, second, a "useful analytical construct." Patinkin (1990b) developed the same theme when examining critically various post-Keynesian interpretations of Keynes. These two texts show that Patinkin ranked himself among the promoters of the IS-LM model. Yet, above all, they buttress how much he

---

18. A Marshallian reference appears when Modigliani (1963, 89) states that he derives a "relation between P/W and X, which represents in essence the Marshallian short-run supply function for commodities (short run because K_0 is fixed)."

underestimated the distance between the version of IS-LM in *Money, Interest, and Prices* and the standard version. Only one difference between them is mentioned in these papers, namely, that Modigliani considered a rigid wages-cum-flexible-prices model featuring a "permanent" or "long-run unemployment equilibrium," while his own model was a fixed-price model, the equilibrium of which was interpreted as a "Marshallian short-run unemployment equilibrium" (1990a, 125; 1990b, 213).

Against my above analysis, such an assessment is most surprising. The aspects pertaining to the foundations of IS-LM are now totally neglected. Patinkin ends up assuming that a single framework exists, which could be the vehicle for two distinct interpretations of Keynes, his interpretation in terms of unemployment disequilibrium and Modigliani's interpretation in terms of wage rigidity and unemployment equilibrium. If my above analysis is correct, Patinkin's remark makes no sense. It totally eschews what I view as the main difference between him and Modigliani, confirming that inventors of models can go astray when it comes to putting models in perspective.[19]

Why did Patinkin as well as his contemporaries fail to realize the true nature of his contribution? The fact that IS-LM stemmed from the Marshallian tradition means that it was developed without the help of a fully specified general equilibrium theory. The absence of an identified Marshallian general equilibrium model can then explain why Patinkin did not perceive the Marshallian ascendancy of IS-LM. For him, as a general equilibrium model it was necessarily Walrasian (cf. De Vroey, this volume). Most of his contemporaries were actually of the same opinion (which moreover is still prevailing at present) that any model that was general equilibrium was automatically Walrasian. This was definitely the case for the early promoters of IS-LM. They believed that IS-LM was linked in some way to the Walrasian model, an idea that was explicitly put forward by Lawrence Klein ([1947] 1966, 56–57) in his *Keynesian Revolution*:

---

19. I believe the contention that economists can develop theoretical ideas without fully realizing their implications would not have seemed outrageous to Patinkin, who once wrote that it was "this personal experience of knowing, but not knowing—knowing something, but not realizing its 'obvious' implications for other problems with which I was concurrently dealing until a later point of time, an experience that I have had on other occasions as well—that has strongly influenced my subsequent work in the history of doctrines, especially that dealing with the discovery of the *General Theory*" (1995, 381–82).

A problem which has never been adequately considered by Keynesians is the derivation of a theory in terms of communities of individuals and groups of commodities from a basic theory in terms of individuals and single commodities. In modern economic terminology this is the problem of passing from micro to macro economics, i.e., aggregation. . . . The theories of individual behavior provide a complete set of inter-relationships within the economy; e.g., they give us the demand-and-supply relationships of every commodity in the system. This is the famous Walrasian system of general equilibrium.

This passage introduced Klein's presentation of the components of IS-LM, showing that he considered IS-LM as a simplified version of the Walrasian system. The same view appears in Lange's founding contribution, "The Rate of Interest and the Optimum Propensity to Consume," which stated that the equation $Y = C + I$ corresponded "to the sum of the budget equations in the Walrasian system" (1938, 22–23). Modigliani's reference to the Walrasian system as the "only rigorous procedure" to "set up a system of equations describing the relation between the variable to be analyzed" on page 46 of his 1944 paper is a further example. However, all these economists hardly went further than these general statements, remaining unaware of the non-Walrasian character of their macro models. Only Patinkin systematically attempted to relate IS-LM and the Walrasian model. However, he overlooked the fact that the Walrasian foundation he was so eager to keep was absent from the other models.

5. Conclusion

I have shown that Patinkin's model is superior to Modigliani's 1944 IS-LM model. Modigliani lacked an adequate method to deal with general equilibrium. In contrast, because of his Walrasian approach, Patinkin was able to complete, to correct, and to clarify the IS-LM model. However, in spite of its superiority, Patinkin's Walrasian recasting of the IS-LM did not replace Modigliani's model as the referential version of IS-LM. *Money, Interest, and Prices* played an important role in the teaching of economics at the graduate level, but when it came to textbooks, Modigliani's 1944 model prevailed (cf. Branson 1979 or Sargent 1987).

The fate of Patinkin's model becomes intelligible when considered from the viewpoint of Leijonhufvud's conception of history as forming a decision tree. In the history of IS-LM, Patinkin's work marked a methodological bifurcation, opening a route departing from the original conception of IS-LM associated with Hicks and Modigliani and which was Marshallian in spirit. Unfortunately, Patinkin himself did not realize the true nature of his contribution.

If Patinkin's option had no sequel in the 1960s, the route he opened was taken up later. In the 1970s, "disequilibrium" theorists (e.g., Barro and Grossman 1971) returned to the task of constructing a Keynesian model starting from the Walrasian model. This attempt was short-lived, as it was dethroned by the new classical revolution that marked the real takeoff of a purely Walrasian macroeconomics. The connection between this new bifurcation in the history of macroeconomics and Patinkin's work shall be the subject of further research.

References

Barro, R. J. 1974. Are Governments' Bonds Net Wealth? *Journal of Political Economy* 82:1095–117.

Barro, R. J., and H. I. Grossman. 1971. A General Disequilibrium Model of Income and Employment. *American Economic Review* 61:82–93.

Branson, W. H. 1979. *Macroeconomic Theory and Policy*. 2nd ed. New York: Harper & Row.

Darity, W., and W. Young. 1995. IS-LM: An Inquest. *HOPE* 27:1–41.

D'Autume, A. 2000. L'essor de la macroéconomie. In *La nouvelle histoire de la pensée économique*, edited by A. Béraud and G. Faccarello. Paris: La Découverte.

De Vroey, M. 1999a. Keynes and the Marshall-Walras Divide. *Journal of the History of Economic Thought* 21:117–36.

———. 1999b. The Marshallian Market and the Walrasian Economy: Two Incompatible Bedfellows. *Scottish Journal of Political Economy* 46:319–38.

———. 2000. IS-LM à la Hicks versus IS-LM à la Modigliani. *HOPE* 32:293–316.

Gurley, J. G., and E. S. Shaw. 1960. *Money in a Theory of Finance*. Washington, D.C.: Brookings Institution.

Hicks, J. 1937. Mr. Keynes and the "Classics": A Suggested Interpretation. *Econometrica* 5:147–59.

Klein, L. [1947] 1966. *The Keynesian Revolution*. 2nd ed. New York: Macmillan.

Kouri, P. J. K. 1986. Franco Modigliani's Contribution to Economics. *Scandinavian Journal of Economics* 88:335–53.

Lange, O. 1938. The Rate of Interest and the Optimum Propensity to Consume. *Economica* 5:12–32.

———. 1942. Say's Law: A Restatement and Criticism. In *Studies in Mathematical Economics and Econometrics*, edited by O. Lange, F. McIntyre, and T. O. Yntema. Chicago: University of Chicago Press.

Leijonhufvud, A. 1994. Hicks, Keynes, and Marshall. In *The Legacy of Hicks: His Contributions to Economic Analysis*, edited by H. Hagemann and O. F. Hamouda. London: Routledge.

Lucas, R. E., Jr. [1980] 1981. Methods and Problems in Business Cycle Theory. In *Studies in Business Cycle Theory*. Cambridge: MIT Press.

Metzler, L. A. 1951. Wealth, Saving, and the Rate of Interest. *Journal of Political Economy* 59:93–116.

Modigliani, F. 1944. Liquidity Preference and the Theory of Interest and Money. *Econometrica* 12:45–88.

————. 1963. The Monetary Mechanism and Its Interaction with Real Phenomena. *Review of Economics and Statistics* 45.1 (part 2, supplement): 79–107.

————. 1987. Comments on "1944, 1963, and 1985." In *Macroeconomics and Finance: Essays in Honor of Franco Modigliani*, edited by R. Dornbusch, S. Fisher, and J. Bossons. Cambridge: MIT Press.

Patinkin, D. 1947. *On the Consistency of Economic Models: A Theory of Involuntary Unemployment*. PhD diss., University of Chicago.

————. 1947–48. Correspondence with Franco Modigliani. Box DPP29, Don Patinkin Papers. Rare Book, Manuscript, and Special Collections Library, Duke University.

————. 1948. Price Flexibility and Full Employment. *American Economic Review* 38:543–64.

————. 1949a. The Indeterminacy of Absolute Prices in Classical Economic Theory. *Econometrica* 17:1–27.

————. 1949b. Involuntary Unemployment and the Keynesian Supply Function. *Economic Journal* 59:361–83.

————. 1954. Keynesian Economics and the Quantity Theory. In *Post Keynesian Economics*, edited by K. K. Kurihara. New Brunswick, N.J: Rutgers University Press.

————. 1956. *Money, Interest, and Prices*. Evanston, Ill.: Row, Peterson.

————. 1958. Liquidity Preference and Loanable Funds: Stocks and Flow Analysis. *Economica* 25:300–318.

————. 1961. Financial Intermediaries and the Logical Structure of Monetary Theory: A Review Article. *American Economic Review* 51:95–116.

————. [1965] 1972. *La monnaie, l'intérêt et les prix*. Paris: Presses Universitaires de France.

————. 1974. The Role of the "Liquidity Trap" in Keynesian Economics. *Banca Nazionale del Lavoro Quarterly Review* 108:3–11.

————. 1976. Keynes' Monetary Thought: A Study of Its Development. *HOPE* 8.1:1–150.

————. 1990a. In Defense of IS-LM. *Banca Nazionale del Lavoro Quarterly Review* 43:119–31.

————. 1990b. On Different Interpretations of the *General Theory*. *Journal of Monetary Economics* 26:205–43.

―――. 1995. The Training of an Economist. *Banca Nazionale del Lavoro Quarterly Review* 195:359–95.

Rubin, G. 2002a. From Equilibrium to Disequilibrium: The Genesis of Don Patinkin's Interpretation of the Keynesian Theory. *European Journal of History of Economic Thought* 9:205–25.

―――. 2002b. La contribution de Don Patinkin à la "synthèse néoclassique": Genèse et portée. PhD diss., University of Paris X-Nanterre.

Sargent, T. J. 1987. *Macroeconomic Theory*. 2nd ed. San Diego: Academic Press.

Weintraub, E. R. 1979. *Microfoundations*. Cambridge: Cambridge University Press.

IS-LM and Monetarism

Michael D. Bordo and Anna J. Schwartz

Monetarism is the name that the late Professor Karl Brunner of the University of Rochester gave in 1968 to propositions about the relation between money and other economic variables such as income, prices, interest rates—propositions that Keynesian economists of that date and earlier denied. Specifically, monetarists regarded the relation between money balances and nominal income as a strong one, and Keynesians regarded it as a weak one. Even the view of inflation as a monetary phenomenon, a core monetarist proposition, to many Keynesians before 1970 was unacceptable.[1] There is no canon, however, that one can consult to establish the orthodox monetarist position. Proponents of monetarism all accept the quantity theory of money as the explanation of inflation and deflation, although they differ on the importance of selected building blocks of the approach.[2]

Although there is no canon of monetarist views, two principal spokesmen for monetarism can be named. They are Milton Friedman, on the one hand, and, on the other, the team of Karl Brunner and Allan Meltzer,

For helpful comments we thank Allan Meltzer and participants at the 2003 *HOPE* conference.

1. See Bronfenbrenner and Holzman 1963 for a nonmonetarist survey of inflation theory. Johnson (1971, 7) refers to inflation as "the issue Keynesian theory was least well designed to deal with."

2. According to Mayer (1978) there are twelve characteristic monetarist propositions, but he suggests that readers may choose to add or delete items from his list. Purvis lists eight as most basic but adds that "one can believe some without believing others" (1980, 98). David Laidler (1981) discusses four key characteristics of monetarism. Kevin Hoover (1988, 10) identifies two criteria as defining monetarists.

even if their individual versions are not invariably identical. It is their views that we explore in later sections of our essay.

Our task is to study elements of the IS-LM model that the above-mentioned spokesmen rejected. First developed by John Hicks in 1937, the IS-LM model was an attempt to portray the central ideas of Keynes's *General Theory* in contrast to the classical paradigm. The model was widely adopted in teaching macroeconomics in the decades that followed. Section 1 describes equilibrium in the investment and savings market and in the money market as defined by the IS-LM model, and the evolution of the model since the 1960s.

Section 2 presents Friedman's alternative analysis of macroeconomics between 1956 and 1970. He contrasted it with the Keynesian version, describing the basic differences between the two. If IS-LM is the distillation of the *General Theory*, it suited Friedman better to confront the source rather than the distillation. His objections to the IS-LM model, however, are implicit, since he never directly stated what they were. The *General Theory* and IS-LM simply did not express his own conception of how the macroeconomy functioned. His description of the features of the economy that he regarded as crucial was expressed in a language inconsistent with the language most economists used to explain an explicit model like IS-LM. So there was no engagement with the IS-LM model when Friedman presented his views. This observation must be qualified in one respect. In an essay responding to the charge that the omission of an interest rate variable in his study of velocity (1959) implied that money was divorced from the real sector, Friedman (1966) introduced Hicks's IS-LM analysis. It is not necessary for our purpose to report his use of different versions of the analysis to defend the view that inclusion of the interest rate in the demand for money equation is neither a necessary nor a sufficient condition for the divorce of money from the real sector.

While Friedman did not explicitly state the reasons that he generally chose not to use the IS-LM model to discuss his rejection of Keynesianism, we can summarize one or another aspect of the views that he challenged in his publications. It is interesting, nevertheless, that he lectured on IS-LM in the graduate course in macroeconomics that he taught for the first time in 1967, evidently to acquaint his students with the language that he customarily spurned in his analytic work. In 1970, however (published 1974), in an effort to facilitate communication with his critics, Friedman phrased his arguments in terms of IS-LM. The effort proved unsuccessful. Friedman (2001) later concluded, "It was really a waste, I think, trying to reconcile the Keynesian thinking with the monetarist thinking." Friedman did not say outright why expressing his views with respect to the IS-LM formulation did not achieve the reconciliation that he sought. His shorthand explanation was that he was a Marshallian, and his opponents were Walrasians. It is possible, however, to note some concrete differences, which we detail below.

In section 3 we turn to the explicit objections to the IS-LM model that Brunner and Meltzer posed at different stages in their treatment of the subject. We discuss an early version and a later version of their dissatisfaction with the model. They sought to amend the model, unlike Friedman, who in the main disregarded it.

In section 4 we conclude by discussing the evolution of the IS-LM model in the decades since it came into common use in the heyday of the monetarist-Keynesian debate. It has survived and prospered as a pedagogical device for undergraduate economics at the intermediate level. The monetarist debate is moribund, but the main tenets of monetarism have been incorporated in the new Keynesian synthesis model that has succeeded IS-LM as the apparatus used for technical and policy discussions.

1. IS-LM from Hicks to Friedman

Hicks ([1937] 1967) synthesized in a simple general equilibrium model the central argument of the *General Theory* and compared it to the position of the classical economists. The model had two markets: the market for goods and the money market.[3] In the goods market, investment is assumed to be a negative function of the interest rate (Keynes's marginal efficiency of capital schedule) and savings a positive function of income (derived from Keynes's marginal propensity to consume) and of the interest rate.[4] The equality of investment and savings clears the market. The solution of these three equations produces the IS curve, a negative relationship in interest rates–nominal income space. A rise in the interest rate reduces investment and, via the multiplier, also income.

3. Hicks (1937) assumes rigid money wages. Also, income is derived from a two-sector model consisting of consumption and investment goods, which in turn are functions of employment in the two sectors.

4. In a more general model, Hicks also includes income in the investment function.

In the money market, Hicks distinguishes the Keynesian demand for money or liquidity preference function—a negative function of the interest rate—from the classical Cambridge cash balance equation where money is solely a positive function of income. In a more general Keynesian model, money demand depends on both income (the transaction demand) and the interest rate (the speculative demand). Money supply is assumed to be fixed by the central bank. From the equality of money demand and supply, the LM curve is derived as a positive function in interest rates–nominal income space. A rise in income increases money demand, which requires a rise in the interest rate to restore equilibrium.

Hicks then uses his apparatus to delineate the salient differences between the Keynesian and classical positions. In his analysis, he maintains the assumption of wage rigidity in both models so that the key difference between the two is the money demand function used, and hence the shape of the LM curve. In the pure Keynesian case, LM is horizontal—interest elastic (absolute liquidity preference). In the pure classical case, it is vertical—interest inelastic. Whether monetary policy can stimulate the economy, then, depends on whether IS intersects LM in the Keynesian (flat) zone of LM to the left of the diagram or the classical (steep) zone to the right.

Hicks's contemporaries (James Meade, Roy Harrod, David Champernowne, W. Brian Reddaway) developed many components of the Hicksian apparatus, but Hicks is remembered because he embedded it in a simple compelling diagram (Darity and Young 1995; De Vroey 2000). Although we always think of Hicks when discussing IS-LM, his model is not the direct antecedent of the popular textbook model commonly used since the 1950s. Hicks's assumption of wage rigidity in both Keynesian and classical models made it difficult to interpret the classical case (De Vroey 2000). Indeed, the model adopted by the textbooks, which Friedman used in his debate with his critics in the early 1970s, was developed by Franco Modigliani (1944). That model of the labor market explicitly distinguished between the Keynesian and classical cases. In the classical case, labor demand and supply are both functions of the real wage, and prices and wages are perfectly flexible, so that full employment and the full-employment level of output are determined. In the Keynesian model the assumption of a rigid money wage leads to a perfectly elastic supply curve for labor, and movements in labor demand lead to movements in employment and output.

For Modigliani the key difference between Keynes and the classics was wage rigidity, which leads to a less-than-full-employment equilibrium. He viewed absolute liquidity preference as a curiosity and not the true hallmark of the Keynesian model.

The Hicks-Modigliani model was then popularized by Alvin Hansen (1953). The simplest textbook version of the 1950s assumed price rigidity and operated in interest rate–real income space. Other popular textbooks of the era (e.g., Dernberg and MacDougal 1960; Ackley 1961) followed the Hansen lead. A more sophisticated extension of the Modigliani model that provided the framework used by Friedman in his 332 course at the University of Chicago in the late 1960s and later appeared in his debate with the critics in the early 1970s is developed in Bailey 1962. In that framework, the classical model with fully flexible wages and prices was elucidated in an IS-LM diagram where the IS and LM curves intersect the full-employment level of output shown as a vertical line and derived from Modigliani's labor market equations. Various Keynesian cases (wage rigidity, absolute liquidity preference, interest inelastic investment and savings) then follow as special cases of the more general model.

2. Friedman Bypasses IS-LM before 1970

Instead of directing his criticisms to the shorthand version of the *General Theory* (1936), represented by IS-LM, Friedman directly attacked the thinking on which the book was based. For Friedman, the gist of Keynes was that money did not matter.[5] Keynes believed that any change in the supply of money in the main would be offset by a change in velocity. Thus he regarded the quantity theory equation in its Cambridge cash balance version, $M = kPY$, to be valid as an identity but useless for policy or for predicting short-run fluctuations in income, which Keynes treated as if there were no difference between nominal and real income.

Each of the Keynesian ideas and Friedman's alternative are presented in the works Friedman published at various dates before 1970, the year he first defined his approach in terms of the IS-LM model. Friedman in turn became the target of criticism by defenders of Keynes. We also review the disputes.

---

5. In fact, Keynes never expressed such a view in these terms. Rather, it was the Keynesians who interpreted him who regarded money in this stark way.

The Liquidity Trap versus
a Stable Demand Function for Money

Friedman's 1956 essay "The Quantity Theory of Money: A Restatement" presented the quantity theory as a theory of the demand for money. To households, money is one kind of asset, one way to hold wealth. To firms, money is a capital good that combined with other sources of productive services yields the products that firms sell. Friedman interprets the theory of the demand for money as a special topic in the theory of capital.

The demand for money by households, like their demand for other consumption services, is dependent on total human and nonhuman wealth (the budget restraint), the expected price of and return on money and alternative forms of wealth, as well as intertemporal rates of substitution, tastes, and preferences of household wealth holders. Friedman distinguishes between real and nominal magnitudes and casts the demand for money by households as a demand for real balances—a function of real variables independent of nominal money values.

A firm's demand to hold more or less money, like its demand for other productive services, depends on the cost of the productive services money yields, the cost of substitute productive services, and the value of the product the productive service yields. Like the household, the firm's demand for money is a demand for real balances and is responsive to rates of return on bonds, equities, and other assets as well as the rate of change of the price level.

From Friedman's viewpoint, the Keynesian distinction between "active balances" and "idle balances," and "transaction balances" and "speculative balances," is irrelevant. Each unit of money renders a variety of services that the household or firm equates at the margin.

According to Friedman, three issues account for the difference of opinion between someone who is and someone who is not a quantity theorist. The first issue is that a quantity theorist accepts the empirical hypothesis that the demand for money is highly stable, more so than the consumption function that Keynes offered as an alternative. The quantity theorist assigns a key role to the demand for money in determining such variables as the level of nominal income or of prices. Rejection of the quantity theory has been based on the assertion that the demand for money is unstable and that it is not possible to specify a limited number of variables on which that demand depends.

A second issue is that the quantity theorist regards the supply of money as affected by factors other than those affecting the demand for money.

A third issue is that Keynes asserts that under conditions of underemployment, when interest rates are positive but low, a liquidity trap exists such that the demand for money becomes infinitely elastic. Changes in the real supply of money then have no effect at all.

Of all the commentators on Friedman's restatement of the quantity theory, Don Patinkin (1969, 1972) offered the most critical appraisal. He did so not on grounds that its substance was flawed but for three incidental shortcomings. One, it was an improper representation of the traditional quantity theory. Two, it was a misinterpretation of doctrinal history, of the shift from the transaction approach to the income version, to the cash balance version of the quantity theory and the Keynesian income-expenditure approach. Finally, in Patinkin's view, Friedman should have acknowledged that his analysis was far closer in its conceptual framework to Keynes's liquidity preference theory than to that of the quantity theory. Friedman denies each of Patinkin's strictures, particularly the one that terms Friedman's formulation of the demand for money a riff on Keynes's liquidity preference theory.

Testing the Keynesian Multiplier versus
the Velocity of Money

Friedman's 1963 study "The Relative Stability of Monetary Velocity and the Investment Multiplier in the United States, 1897–1958" (written with David J. Meiselman) predicts consumption expenditures in the United States for the six decades since 1897, using annual data, and for a shorter period, using quarterly data. Two equations represent the competing hypotheses, one with the stock of money as the independent variable, the other with Keynes's definition of investment, that is, autonomous expenditures. Three comparisons were reported, one in real terms, one in nominal terms (a price variable was added to each equation), and a multiple regression with both autonomous expenditures and stock of money as independent variables in the same equation. The relative accuracy of forecasts of consumption predicted by the two competing hypotheses was the issue. The correlation coefficient for the full period for the money equation was 0.98, and for the autonomous expenditure equation, 0.76. Results for subperiods were similar. The multiple regressions with both autonomous expenditures and money as independent variables in the same equation that showed a partial correlation of consumption with autonomous expenditures were interpreted as reflecting a correlation between money and autonomous expenditures. Friedman and Meiselman (1963, 187) conclude that the simple version of the income-expenditure theory is "almost completely useless as a description of stable empirical relationships."

Early on, three articles appeared attacking the work: Ando and Modigliani 1965, DePrano and Mayer 1965, and Hester 1964. Albert Ando and Modigliani dismiss the tests as meaningless for either the prediction or control of income. Their reason is that the independent variables are not shown to be exogenous to the system, and that the competing means of stabilization are parts of the single Keynesian general equilibrium system. They maintain that tests they perform substituting for actual money data a measure of money that is the maximum that can be created, given the supply of reserves excluding borrowed reserves, confirm the Keynesian position that the interaction of monetary and real forces determines income, and that after eliminating trend the contribution of money supply to income fluctuation was at most slightly over one-third. Michael DePrano and Thomas Mayer find specification errors in the models and conclude that both autonomous expenditures and money are of roughly equal importance. Donald Hester labels Friedman and Meiselman's finding false because their definition of income excludes tax-financed government expenditure; their use of net rather than gross private domestic expenditure biases the correlation coefficient for autonomous expenditure toward zero; and in the period from 1930 to 1958, the autonomous expenditure theory outperformed the quantity theory.

Friedman and Meiselman, in answer to their critics, note that focusing on overarching theories and theoretical models is not the way to discriminate between empirically verifiable and unverifiable hypotheses. They decry the absence of an unambiguous criterion of the most useful empirical counterpart for autonomous expenditure, as there is about the counterpart for money. Because the critics omit some components of income for the income-expenditure calculations, their results are incorrect, according to Friedman and Meiselman.

Keynesian Investment versus
Money Stock in Business Cycle Fluctuations

Friedman's 1963 conference paper "Money and Business Cycles" (written with Anna J. Schwartz) is divided into two parts. The first part reports factual evidence on the behavior of money during National Bureau of Economic Research business cycles from 1867 to 1961. We do not summarize that evidence at this juncture. It is reported below in the comments of the critics on individual findings about the behavior of money.

The first part ends with a statement concerning the Keynesian position, which regards the rate of cyclical expansion or contraction as fairly rigidly determined by the rise or fall in investment or autonomous expenditure, with this link far more crucial than any link with the contemporary behavior of the money stock. The statement is followed by an assessment of the relative roles of money and investment by correlating (1) the variability of annual changes in money with the variability in annual changes in consumption, and (2) the variability of annual changes in investment with the variability of annual changes in consumption. The synchronous correlation coefficients are consistently higher, both for the period as a whole and for the period since 1899 (when income figures require less interpolation) for money-consumption variability than they are for investment-consumption variability. These results are the same as for the Friedman-Meiselman study, though, derived by a different methodology, from first differences of logarithms and moving standard deviations of the first differences. For a given stock of money, these results suggest that there is no systematic relationship at all between autonomous expenditures and consumption.

The second part of the conference paper presents interpretations of the factual evidence.

The factual evidence shows that the stock of money displays a consistent cyclical behavior, which is closely related to the cyclical behavior of the economy, but is not decisive about the direction of influence. One relevant factor cited in the paper is that, despite substantial changes in arrangements determining the quantity of money over the period, the changes have not altered the relation between business changes and monetary changes. More convincing evidence that money plays an important independent part cited next is the historical record of major economic fluctuations, including deep depressions, substantial inflations, and a few long-continued movements in one direction. These events justify two generalizations. First, disturbances in the rate of growth of the money stock in every case are accompanied by changes in money income and prices in the same direction and of appreciable magnitude, and there are no comparable disturbances in the rate of growth of the money stock unaccompanied by changes in money income and prices.

Second, the changes in the stock of money can generally be attributed to specific historical circumstances that are not attributable to contemporary changes in money income and prices. The consistent relation between money and income must reflect an influence running from money to business. The demonstration that the major changes in the stock of money have been attributable to a variety of sources connected directly neither with contemporary nor earlier business developments contradicts an explanation of the one-to-one relation between monetary change and major economic change as a relation running from economic change to money. Hence appreciable changes in the rate of growth of the money stock are a necessary and sufficient condition for appreciable changes in the rate of growth of money income. This is true, it is argued, both for long secular changes and for changes over business cycles. Secular changes in money income produced by a changed secular rate of growth of the money stock are reflected mainly in different price behavior rather than different rates of growth of output. Shorter period changes in the rate of growth of the money stock can exert a considerable influence on the rate of growth of output as well. This is the case for monetary fluctuations as the source of major movements in economic fluctuations.

The case for a monetary explanation of minor economic fluctuations is not nearly so strong, the paper concedes. The view that monetary change is important does not preclude the existence of other factors that affect the course of business or that account for the rhythmical character of business fluctuations. What is needed to explain minor movements is a specification of the distribution of the random disturbances impinging on the economy and a specification of the systematic disturbances that can be introduced into it as well as the reaction mechanism of the economy. That explanation is not yet at hand.

The paper includes a theory that accounts for the observed tendency of cyclical fluctuations in income to be wider in amplitude than cyclical fluctuations in money. The theory yielded an independent statistical estimate of the ratio of the percentage change in income to the associated percentage change in the stock of money of 1.84. The directly observed ratio was 2.0.

The paper concludes with a sketch of the transmission mechanism that could explain how monetary changes produce cyclical fluctuations in income. The mechanism emphasizes adjustment of stocks to flows, with money playing a key role as a component of the stock of assets. Balance sheet adjustments are important. Money's effects are transmitted through a wider channel than the interest rate on financial assets. It includes prices of sources of services of durable and semidurable consumer and producer goods as well as the prices of the goods that yield a flow of services.

Two discussants of the paper were critical. Hyman Minsky argued that the paper failed to make a convincing case that monetary changes fully explain observed business cycles. He would agree only with a proposition that there should be fuller integration of monetary phenomena into the basically income-expenditure models. For Arthur Okun, the estimate of the money multiplier effect on national income of an increase in money was unbelievable, given the much smaller estimated combined multiplier-accelerator effects on national income of fiscal action comparable in size to the monetary increase. He faulted the paper for the larger estimate of the leverage of money as the consequence of associating the demand for money with *permanent* income that varies from year to year by an estimated one-third as much as aggregate measured income. By then assuming that demand for and supply of money are equilibrated by changes in *measured* income, it follows that a change in the money supply must induce magnified income changes. Okun also challenged the view of money as a luxury good, with a long-run income elasticity of the demand estimated as 1.8. (In a 1982 study of trends by Friedman and Schwartz, this estimate of the long-run income elasticity of the demand for real money balances was lowered to allow for growth of financial sophistication in the United States before 1903.) With respect to the transmission mechanism the paper described, Okun expressed surprise that it was similar to the one he visualized.

The third discussant, Clark Warburton, gave generally favorable comments.

Complementing and amplifying the cyclical evidence was historical evidence that Friedman and Schwartz (1963b) provided in *A Monetary History of the United States, 1867–1960*. Written within the framework of the quantity theory although without an explicit model, the history documented a close relationship between money and nominal income and the price level. It also documented the short-run relationship between changes in money and changes in real income, revealed most dramatically in episodes of deep recessions, especially the Great Depression of 1929–33. In addition, institutional evidence identified independent sources of monetary changes such as wartime fiat money issues and gold discoveries (see Lucas 1994, Miron 1994, and Summers 1991).

Keynesian Fiscal versus Friedman Monetary Policy

In "Monetary vs. Fiscal Policy: A Dialogue" (Friedman and Heller 1969), Heller argued that the issue was not which policy contributed more to economic stabilization, since Keynesian economics assigned an important role to both. The issues were twofold: whether only money matters, disregarding interest rates and credit availability, and whether the Fed should have discretion or be bound by a rule. On fiscal policy, the issues again were twofold: how much budget cuts or tax changes contributed to stabilization, and whether there should be rigid rules or discretion to modify procedures for cutting or boosting taxes. Money was resurrected by the Accord of 1951, but was threatened by Friedman's money-supply peg. Heller addressed eight questions for Friedman to answer before money was given dominance over fiscal policy. He pleaded for joint efforts to develop a more complete model to ascertain why the economy worked far better than it did before active fiscal and monetary policy came into play. Heller then argued for the potency and effectiveness of fiscal policy and for continued and expanded use of discretionary policy.

Friedman's response to Heller was that money matters a great deal for nominal income and prices in the long run and has an important effect on fluctuations in nominal and real income in the short run. Money does not matter, however, over the long run for real magnitudes. The real wealth of a society depends on its institutional structure; the abilities, initiatives, and driving force of its people; investment potentialities; and technology. How many dollars the output will be valued at is the issue for which money matters. Both fiscal and monetary policy have been oversold because the fine-tuning of both has been oversold. Friedman contended that we have the ability to avoid extreme fluctuations and to correct past mistakes, but we do not know enough to fine-tune to eliminate minor fluctuations. We know there is a close relation on average between monetary changes and nominal income changes, but the relation is not precise enough to predict from changes in money in one quarter what's going to happen one or two quarters later. That is the reason Friedman favored a rule.

With respect to fiscal policy, according to Friedman, the state of the government budget matters for many things, but by itself it has no significant effect on the course of nominal income, on inflation or deflation, or on cyclical fluctuations. The influence of fiscal policy needs to be separated from the influence of monetary policy, since changes in both occur at the same time. Friedman formulated two questions: What happens if monetary policy is held constant and fiscal policy is changed? What happens if fiscal policy is held constant and monetary policy is changed?

He answered the questions by noting that fiscal policy can change without a change in monetary policy. For example, the government can borrow from the market to finance a tax cut, in which case interest rates but not money supply will be affected. Alternatively, the government can finance a tax cut by printing money to cover the deficit. The essence of the claim for the potency of fiscal policy, Friedman argued, is that it doesn't matter how a tax cut is financed.

Fiscal policy could be potent if indirect effects were strong, but no statistical empirical evidence supported Heller's assertion that the 1964 tax cut by itself was expansionary. That assertion ignores what monetary policy was doing at the same time. The same observation applies to the assertion that the 1966 surtax was contractionary.

According to Friedman, statistical evidence is available on the relative potency of fiscal and monetary policy. He cited his study of monetary and fiscal magnitudes during three war periods. It demonstrates that it was monetary, not fiscal, magnitudes that explain wartime price behavior. In Friedman and Meiselman's study, monetary effects on income outperformed autonomous expenditure, the Keynesian driving variable, in their effects on income. The St. Louis study by Leonall Andersen and Jerry Jordan (1968) confirmed that the response of economic activity from 1952 to 1968 was larger, more predictable, and faster for money than for fiscal variables.

Friedman challenged proponents of the importance of fiscal effects for inflation and the price level to offer evidence to support their assertions.

Heller replied that Keynesians use complete models of the economy rather than one-equation systems to formulate more interesting questions than the simple one of whether fiscal or monetary policy is paramount. His view was that one cannot test and measure the effects of policy on the economy without a correctly specified model. The models show that fiscal policy matters a great deal.

In Friedman's rebuttal, he denied the Keynesian position that tax increases or expenditure decreases were equivalent and that they are an effective stabilization device. Since he regarded the U.S. federal government budget as excessive, he favored expenditure decreases, rather than tax increases. Friedman concluded by answering some of the eight questions about money that Heller posed in his opening statement.

In the foregoing studies the debate between Keynesians and monetarists was joined. Although the discussion touched on different relationships embodied in the IS-LM model and the roles of monetary and fiscal policy, they were not spelled out in terms of a general equilibrium model. One reason that Friedman preferred single equations rather than testing general equilibrium models was his long-standing position that he was a Marshallian. That meant focusing on particular problems of economic analysis, using theory as "an engine for the discovery of concrete truth." In this approach, hypotheses need to be tested by the accuracy of their predictions. Friedman's regard for Marshall as his lodestar appears most succinctly in his essay "The Marshallian Demand Curve": "The important distinction between the conceptions of economic theory implicit in Marshall and Walras lies in the purpose for which the theory is constructed and used. To Marshall—to repeat an expression quoted earlier—economic theory is 'an engine for the discovery of concrete truth'" ([1949] 1953, 90–91). Economic theory, in this view, has two intermingled roles: to provide "systematic and organized methods of reasoning" about economic problems; to provide a body of substantive hypotheses, based on factual evidence, about the "manner of action of causes." In both roles the test of the theory is its value in explaining facts, in predicting the consequences of changes in the economic environment.

Friedman explicitly rejected the alternative Walrasian paradigm of "general equilibrium" that emphasizes the realism of its assumptions and is characterized by "abstractness, generality, and mathematical elegance."[6] His critique of the Walrasian approach also appears in "The Marshallian Demand Curve." Again, we quote his words:

Abstractness, generality, mathematical elegance—these are all secondary, themselves to be judged by the test of application. The counting of equations and unknowns is a check on the completeness of reasoning, the beginning of analysis, not an end in itself. . . . Abstractness, generality, and mathematical elegance have in some measure become ends in themselves, criteria by which to judge economic theory. Facts are to be described, not explained. Theory is to be tested by the

6. For an extensive discussion of these methodological issues, see Hirsch and De Marchi 1990, Hammond 1996, and Blaug 1992.

accuracy of its "assumptions" as photographic descriptions of reality, not by the correctness of the predictions that can be derived from it. (91)

Friedman had tried to establish the validity of his work in monetary economics by presenting statistical findings, historical evidence, and econometric results, but his efforts had not succeeded. His opponents did not confront him with conflicting empirical evidence. Instead, his critics, who were not exclusively Keynesians, charged that monetarists relied on a black box instead of providing a credible explanation of how monetary policy was transmitted to the real economy. They said that there was no underlying theoretical model of the economic structure corresponding to Friedman's empirical findings. A persistent complaint was that Friedman had not demonstrated the exogeneity of money.[7] In general, the critics found that identification problems marred Friedman's formulations. Moreover, statistical correlation was all that accounted for the importance he claimed for money.

A critique by James Tobin (1970) was particularly effective in buttressing opposition to Friedman's treatment of money. To dispute the use of timing patterns as a basis for the claim that monetary actions preceded income changes, Tobin constructed models that produced simulated patterns of money and income. The Keynesian model has money leading income, although money does not determine income. The monetary model has money lagging income in time, yet money determines income.[8]

Friedman was frustrated by the fact that he and his critics were talking past one another. They were Walrasians, he was a Marshallian. That for Friedman accounted for the communication failure. The solution, Friedman thought, was to encompass both the quantity theory and the income-expenditure theory in one model that included explicit terms for IS and LM. This was the monetary framework that he presented in 1970.

Robert Gordon (1974) invited four critics to assess Friedman's attempt to communicate across doctrinal differences. The critics did not appreciate that Friedman was trying to provide a framework in order to discriminate between alternative hypotheses. In acknowledging that $Y = kA$ and $Y = vM$, he offered the Keynesian model as a particular case

7. Opponents of Friedman did not address his argument that a variable could be exogenous in some contexts and endogenous in others, depending on the issue.

8. Tobin's critique essentially condemned Friedman's work because it lacked an explicit model that specified cause and effect relations before undertaking measurement and estimation. See Hammond 1996, 138.

and the quantity theory model as an alternative case of a more general model that he specified, but he was unsuccessful in closing the model. In retrospect, Friedman concluded that his attempt to reconcile the quantity theory with the income-expenditure theory was a waste of time.[9] Expressing monetarist analysis in IS-LM terms did not clarify the issues dividing Marshallians and Walrasians.

Jerome Stein organized a conference at Brown University in 1974 to try once more to sort out the differences between Friedman and his critics. Douglas Purvis (1980), commenting on the subjects the conference considered, thought the major issue should have been whether stabilization policies were desirable. Disagreement centers on alternative theories of the causes of unemployment. IS-LM treats deficient aggregate demand as the primary cause. Recent emphasis, however, is on aggregate supply. Differences in theories of aggregate supply and the determinants of output are the issue the Brown conference neglected.

The Brown attempt at reconciling monetarist and Keynesian views was futile.[10] For the critics, monetarism lacked a broad theoretical foundation. For Friedman, different theories were appropriate for different problems. Carving up a broad issue into smaller parts that could be studied empirically produced more precise results than a big structural model with hundreds of equations. The division between the opposing sides seemed more acute when lined up as Marshallians versus Walrasians than as monetarists versus Keynesians.

Friedman did not win adherents to his advocacy of Marshallian methodology, even among those sympathetic to monetarist tenets. The profession at large embraced the Walrasian general equilibrium approach.

3. Brunner and Meltzer Elaborate the IS-LM Model

The definitive statement by Karl Brunner and Allan Meltzer concerning the problems they perceived with IS-LM is contained in the second of the four Raffaele Mattioli Foundation Lectures they gave in Milan at Bocconi University in August 1988 (published in 1993). (Earlier versions of

9. Purvis (1980) notes that despite dissatisfaction with IS-LM and some of the shortcomings of Keynesian conventional wisdom, the alternative Friedman offered of "virtual constant full employment" had little appeal.

10. For an attempt at such a reconciliation, see the papers by Tobin (1981) and Laidler (1981) in the *Economic Journal*.

the model in the lecture appeared in Brunner and Meltzer 1972, 1976.) Their approach is in the tradition of Walras, with an emphasis on the existence of general equilibrium.

The coauthors describe IS-LM with the addition of the Phillips curve as a model of stock-flow interactions consisting of two equations, the equilibrium conditions for the asset and output or income markets.

IS: $y = f(i, M/p)$

LM: $M/p = g(i, y)$

M is predetermined or given, p is either given or obtained from the Phillips curve. Other variables may be added.

The coauthors review early uses of IS-LM by Keynesian economists. Some treated money as a substitute for bonds or financial assets only. Until the 1950s the monetary mechanism was viewed as sensitive to the system's interest elasticities, which contrasted with more reliable, direct effects of fiscal policy. Interest rates were interpreted as borrowing costs borrowers paid to finance investment projects, but studies reported that borrowing costs were trivial. The upshot was that the interest elasticity of aggregate demand was negligible, and the IS line relatively steep. Hence stabilization policy had to rely on fiscal policy, and the role of monetary policy was to keep borrowing costs low.

In the late 1950s, the concerns of IS-LM users shifted. Monetary policy effects were concentrated on the housing market where borrowing costs were important, but politics limited the use of monetary policy to keeping interest rates low.

Other users of IS-LM recognized that money is a substitute for the whole spectrum of both financial and real assets. One interpretation was that bonds and real capital have identical rates of return, so financial markets have to keep the two returns identical. This assumes active financial markets. However, relations between money, income, and prices exist with primitive or nonexistent financial markets. Further, the coauthors demur, portfolio adjustments are delayed by transactions and information costs. Also, risk distributions for all real and financial assets are not always and everywhere identical. Accordingly, bonds and capital are not always perfect substitutes.

The coauthors believe that neither the interpretation of money as a substitute for bonds only or as a substitute for a full range of assets includes analysis of main aspects of financial markets and of portfolio allocations affecting the relation of money to income and prices. IS-LM has no markets for credit or bank loan rationing. Shocks affecting the credit markets are treated as shocks to the demand for money. The two sets of shocks have different consequences. Income effects on loan demand and on the credit market in the IS-LM model must also be treated as a shift in the demand for money. IS-LM analysis cannot accommodate intermediation and disintermediation and their effect on transmission of monetary and real impulses. Deregulation is outside the scope of IS-LM.

For these reasons Brunner and Meltzer regard the analysis of monetary policy in the IS-LM framework as deficient. A single interest rate misrepresents the problem central banks confront and may mislead them to believe that they control interest rates. It is not possible to understand the effects of permanent and transitory shocks as well as real and nominal shocks on the relation between rates for different maturities and on real and financial assets within the IS-LM framework.

Brunner and Meltzer proceed to elaborate the framework. They add a credit market and introduce three assets: base money, government debt, and real capital. They are less than perfect substitutes in portfolios. Money differs from the other two assets because of its services in a world of uncertainty. The public may hold the three assets or exchange securities for loans from financial institutions. These institutions determine separate rates for each liability they offer in response to market conditions. The coauthors specify the equilibrium conditions of the credit market and money market, respectively. They set up a model with the government budget constraint, an aggregate supply function, and an aggregate demand function that involves solving for equilibrium in the goods and asset markets. Equilibrium in the money and credit markets involves the banking system, money supply, and credit demand multipliers. The authors' papers on permanent and transitory changes are further departures from the IS-LM framework.

The core of the Brunner and Meltzer model is its emphasis on disaggregated asset markets. Rudiger Dornbusch (1976) questions the value added of disaggregated asset markets and the manner in which the model translates monetary and fiscal actions into changes in prices and output. The transmission channels in the aggregate demand function involve interest rate and wealth effects. Dornbusch discounts the authors' claim that their model provides a more pervasive adjustment mechanism than in Keynesian models. Finally, he questions the extent to which the Brunner and Meltzer model qualifies as monetarist.

Purvis (1980) finds the multiasset feature in Brunner and Meltzer's work to be an important departure from the IS-LM straitjacket but a "total red herring" as marking its distinction from eclectic Keynesian analysis.

Like Friedman, Brunner and Meltzer always sharply disagreed with the Keynesian approach embodied in the IS-LM paradigm. Unlike Friedman, however, they were not averse to the use of general equilibrium models, like IS-LM. Indeed, as discussed above, much of their work involved improving that model.

4. IS-LM and Monetarists Today

IS-LM has survived all of its criticisms over the years and is alive and well in the intermediate macro textbooks. The reason it is still used is the same reason that it won over its competitors over sixty years ago: it is simple, elegant, and easy to manipulate for expository purposes. However, as Colander (this volume) points out, its use is no longer as the common language for debates among monetary theorists over the issues of high theory as it was thirty years ago, but rather as a classroom device to point out to undergraduates the economic impact of alternative macroeconomic policies. It is also still the workhorse of open economy macroeconomics and the International Monetary Fund in its evaluation of member countries' economic balance (Young and Darity, this volume; Boughton 2002). Finally, it has now been endowed with the legitimacy of microfoundations based on optimizing behavior by households and firms (McCallum and Nelson 1999).

Yet while IS-LM has survived, the monetarist-Keynesian debate that so consumed the profession thirty years ago is moribund. Today, the synthesis that unites theorists and policymakers is the new Keynesian model, which, like IS-LM, is a general equilibrium model with nominal rigidities but also incorporating optimizing microbehavior, rational expectations, and policy rules. Although this model is used to evaluate and conduct monetary policy, it does not actually have money in it or an explicit LM function.

The model has three equations: an IS equation where the output gap (actual less potential GDP) depends on the real interest rate (the nominal rate minus rationally expected inflation); a Phillips curve, which relates the inflation rate to the output gap and to both past inflation and rationally expected future inflation; a policy rule (commonly the Taylor rule), which relates the short-term interest rate (in the United States the federal funds rate), the central bank's policy instrument, to the output gap and the difference between inflation and the central bank's inflation target (Meyer 2001).

Although the model does not have an LM curve in it, one can be added on to identify the amount of money (high-powered money) that the central bank will need to supply when it follows the policy rule, given the shocks that hit the economy (McCallum 1999). However, this fourth equation is not essential for the model.

Yet although money is now missing from the mainstream macro model, the lessons of monetarism have not been ignored. Incorporated in the model are a number of Friedman's main tenets: that inflation is always and everywhere a monetary phenomenon and can be controlled by monetary policy; that monetary policy in the short run has important real effects because of the presence of nominal rigidities or lags in the adjustment of expected to actual inflation, that is, that in the long run the Phillips curve is vertical, as expected inflation adjusts to its actual level; that there is a distinction between nominal and real interest rates embodied in the Fisher equation; and that policy rules are important anchors to stable monetary policy.

Moreover, Brunner and Meltzer, working in the Walrasian tradition, incorporated a number of these tenets into the general equilibrium models that they developed in the 1960s and 1970s. Their work thus served as an important building block to the modern synthesis.

In sum, Friedman's main criticism of Keynes—that money matters (in the long run for inflation and in the short run for output)—has survived and prospered and is at the heart of both the synthesis model and the emphasis today on low inflation as the key policy goal of the world's leading central banks.

References

Ackley, Gardner. 1961. *Macroeconomic Theory*. New York: Macmillan.
Andersen, Leonall, and Jerry L. Jordan. 1968. Monetary and Fiscal Actions: A Test of Their Relative Importance in Economic Stabilization. *Federal Reserve Bank of St. Louis Review* 50:11–23.
Ando, Albert, and Franco Modigliani. 1965. The Relative Stability of Monetary Velocity and the Investment Multiplier. *American Economic Review* 55:693–728.
Bailey, Martin. 1962. *National Income and the Price Level: A Study in Macrotheory*. New York: McGraw-Hill.

Blaug, Mark. 1992. *The Methodology of Economics*. 2nd ed. Cambridge: Cambridge University Press.

Boughton, James. 2002. On the Origin of the Fleming-Mundell Model. *IMF Working Paper* 02/107. Washington, D.C.: International Monetary Fund.

Bronfenbrenner, Martin, and Franklin D. Holzman. 1963. Survey of Inflation Theory. *American Economic Review* 53:593–661.

Brunner, Karl. 1968. The Role of Money and Monetary Policy. *Federal Reserve Bank of St. Louis Review* 50:8–24.

Brunner, Karl, and Allan H. Meltzer. 1972. Money, Debt, and Economic Activity. *Journal of Political Economy* 80:951–77.

———. 1976. An Aggregative Theory for a Closed Economy. In *Monetarism*, edited by Jerome Stein. Amsterdam: North-Holland.

———. 1993. *Money and the Economy Issues in Monetary Analysis*. New York: Cambridge University Press.

Darity, William, Jr., and Warren Young. 1995. IS-LM: An Inquest. *HOPE* 27:1–41.

DePrano, Michael, and Thomas Mayer. 1965. Tests of Relative Importance of Autonomous Expenditures and Money. *American Economic Review* 55:729–52.

Dernberg, Thomas, and Duncan MacDougal. 1960. *Macroeconomics*. New York: McGraw-Hill.

De Vroey, Michel. 2000. IS-LM à la Hicks versus IS-LM à la Modigliani. *HOPE* 32.2:293–316.

Dornbusch, Rudiger. 1976. Comments on Brunner and Meltzer. In *Monetarism*, edited by Jerome Stein. Amsterdam: North-Holland.

Friedman, Milton. [1949] 1953. The Marshallian Demand Curve. In *Essays in Positive Economics*. Chicago: University of Chicago Press.

———. 1956. The Quantity Theory of Money: A Restatement. In *Studies in the Quantity Theory of Money*, edited by Milton Friedman. Chicago: University of Chicago Press.

———. 1959. The Demand for Money: Some Theoretical and Empirical Results. *Journal of Political Economy* 67:327–51.

———. 1966. Interest Rates and the Demand for Money. *Journal of Law and Economics* 9:71–85.

———. 1974. A Theoretical Framework for Monetary Analysis. In Gordon 1974.

———. 2001. Interview by John B. Taylor. *Macroeconomic Dynamics* 5:101–31.

Friedman, Milton, and Walter W. Heller. 1969. *Monetary vs. Fiscal Policy: A Dialogue*. New York: Norton.

Friedman, Milton, and David J. Meiselman. 1963. The Relative Stability of Monetary Velocity and the Investment Multiplier in the United States, 1897–1958. In *Stabilization Policies*. Prepared for the Commission on Money and Credit. Englewood Cliffs, N.J.: Prentice Hall.

Friedman, Milton, and Anna J. Schwartz. 1963a. Money and Business Cycles. *Review of Economics and Statistics* 45.2 (supplement): 32–64.

———. 1963b. *A Monetary History of the United States, 1867–1960*. Princeton, N.J.: Princeton University Press.

————. 1982. *Monetary Trends in the United States and the United Kingdom: Their Relation to Income, Prices, and Interest Rates.* Chicago: University of Chicago Press.

Gordon, Robert J., ed. 1974. *Milton Friedman's Monetary Framework: A Debate with His Critics.* Chicago: University of Chicago Press.

Hammond, J. Daniel. 1996. *Theory and Measurement: Causality Issues in Milton Friedman's Monetary Economics.* New York: Cambridge University Press.

Hansen, Alvin. 1953. *A Guide to Keynes.* New York: McGraw-Hill.

Hester, Donald D. 1964. Keynes and the Quantity Theory: A Comment on the Friedman-Meiselman CMC Paper. *Review of Economics and Statistics* (November): 364–477.

Hicks, John R. [1937] 1967. Mr. Keynes and the "Classics." In *Critical Essays in Monetary Theory.* Oxford: Clarendon.

Hirsch, Abraham, and Neil De Marchi. 1990. *Milton Friedman: Economics in Theory and Practice.* New York: Harvester Wheatsheaf.

Hoover, Kevin D. 1988. *The New Classical Macroeconomics: A Sceptical Inquiry.* Oxford: Blackwell.

Johnson, Harry G. 1971. The Keynesian Revolution and the Monetarist Counter-Revolution. *American Economic Review* 61:1–14.

Keynes, John Maynard. 1936. *The General Theory of Employment, Interest, and Money.* London: Macmillan.

Laidler, David. 1981. Monetarism: An Interpretation and an Assessment. *Economic Journal* 91:49–55.

Lucas, Robert E., Jr. 1994. Review of Milton Friedman and Anna J. Schwartz's *A Monetary History of the United States, 1867–1960. Journal of Monetary Economics* 34.1:5–16.

Mayer, Thomas. 1978. *The Structure of Monetarism.* New York: Norton.

McCallum, Bennett T. 1999. Recent Developments in the Analysis of Monetary Policy Rules. *Federal Reserve Bank of St. Louis Review* (November–December): 3–11.

McCallum, Bennett T., and Edward Nelson. 1999. An Optimizing IS-LM Specification for Monetary Policy and Business Cycle Analysis. *Journal of Money, Credit, and Banking* 31.3:296–315.

Meyer, Laurence H. 2001. Does Money Matter? *Federal Reserve Bank of St. Louis Review* (September–October): 1–15.

Miron, Jeffrey A. 1994. Empirical Methodology in Macroeconomics: Explaining the Success of Friedman and Schwartz's *A Monetary History of the United States, 1867–1960. Journal of Monetary Economics* 34:17–25.

Modigliani, Franco. 1944. Liquidity Preference and the Theory of Interest and Money. *Econometrica* 12:45–88.

Patinkin, Don. 1969. The Chicago Tradition, the Quantity Theory, and Friedman. *Journal of Money, Credit, and Banking* 1:46–70.

————. 1972. Friedman on the Quantity Theory and Keynesian Economics. *Journal of Political Economy* 80 (September–October): 883–905.

Purvis, Douglas D. 1980. Monetarism: A Review. *Canadian Journal of Economics* (February): 96–122.

Summers, Lawrence H. 1991. The Scientific Illusion in Empirical Macroeconomics. *Scandinavian Journal of Economics* 93.2:129–48.

Tobin, James. 1970. Money and Income: Post Hoc Ergo Propter Hoc? *Quarterly Journal of Economics* 84:301–17.

———. 1981. The Monetarist Counter-Revolution Today—an Appraisal. *Economic Journal* 91:29–42.

How Have Monetary Regime Changes Affected the Popularity of IS-LM?

Scott Sumner

> Finally, what emerges clearly from this study of Keynes's views on monetary policy are the close links between theory and policy. For every change in the problem at hand came new proposals growing out of previous theory or, if previous doctrine could not accommodate the new situation, shifts in his theoretical position. This is clearly illustrated (from a Keynesian point of view) by the evolution of Keynes's views under the impact of British (and world) events between 1925 and, say, 1934. This interrelationship was the hallmark of Keynes, the economist.
> —Donald Moggridge and Susan Howson, "Keynes on Monetary Policy, 1910–1946" (1974)

1. Explaining Innovations in Macroeconomic Theory

There are several ways of explaining theoretical innovations in macroeconomics. One is to view the history of macroeconomics as a steady progression from ignorance to enlightenment. Each succeeding model builds on previous theoretical developments in a way that is if not predictable, then at least readily explicable. Others view the field of macroeconomics as endlessly cycling between one conceptual approach and another: classical/Keynesian, demand-side/supply-side, statist/laissez-faire. In many cases these fads are attributed to changes in the underlying macroeconomy. Thus Keynesian economics is often regarded as a "depression model."

I thank Clark Johnson, Kevin Hoover, two anonymous referees, and the participants at the 2003 *HOPE* conference at Duke University for their helpful comments and suggestions.

There is undoubtedly some truth to both perspectives. If one views macroeconomics as a series of technical innovations in areas such as money demand or expectations of inflation, then the optimistic perspective is probably warranted. If, on the other hand, one views macroeconomics in terms of conceptual approaches to stubborn macro problems, then the picture is much less clear. It could be argued that the essence of contemporary "macroeconomics" is what the one hundred top macroeconomists think about issues such as what explains the persistently high unemployment rates in Europe, or why Japan seems to find it so difficult to boost aggregate demand, or what is the relative importance of real and monetary factors in recent U.S. business cycles. These issues remain highly controversial, and the debates have a way of continually reviving discussions from decades, or even centuries, ago.

Academic debate about current macro issues involves much more than just the recitation of findings from time-series regressions. References to events such as the Volcker disinflation or the Great Depression play an important role in theoretical discussions, even at the highest levels of macroeconomics. To be widely persuasive, it's not enough that an economic model is consistent with the key phenomena of interest to macroeconomists, it must also seem consistent with those phenomena. In this essay, I focus on the plausibility of the simplest, and hence most widely understood, versions of IS-LM. My thesis is that the changing popularity of IS-LM (or indeed any macroeconomic framework) has more to do with changes in the external policy environment than with the internal logic of progress within the field of macroeconomic theory.

In the next section, I argue that the IS-LM model is a technical apparatus specifically tailored to a particular conceptual approach to macroeconomics and, more precisely, monetary theory. Furthermore, the model is only likely to prove useful (i.e., persuasive) for economies with a very specific institutional setup. In particular, IS-LM is especially suited to an environment where there are doubts about the effectiveness of monetary policy, and where monetary analysis is based on an interest rate transmission mechanism. And these two factors are related to even more basic structural factors, such as the nature of the monetary regime, and the sophistication or complexity of the economic system. The analysis required to support these hypotheses requires an unconventional mixture of economic history, the history of thought, and monetary theory.

The conference title refers to the "strange persistence" of IS-LM, and if one views macroeconomics as a progression of better and better technical models, then the persistence is indeed strange. I hope to demystify the enduring popularity of the IS-LM approach to macroeconomic issues. To do this, I begin by examining some of the strengths and weaknesses of the IS-LM approach. Then I examine how structural changes in the major industrial economies at first hid, and then exposed, those strengths and weaknesses.

2. Some Strengths and Weaknesses in the IS-LM Approach to Monetary Policy

The IS-LM model as developed by John Hicks (1937), and others, provides a framework for illustrating some of the key ideas of the *General Theory*. Thus it will be useful to begin with a brief discussion of those ideas. Although there are differences of opinion as to the essential components of the Keynesian revolution, any list would probably include the following:

1. An inadequate level of nominal expenditure can result in chronically high levels of unemployment.
2. In a mature capitalist economy, investment expenditures will often fall short of the amount necessary to generate a level of nominal expenditure adequate to maintain full employment.
3. In a depressed economy, monetary policy may be relatively ineffective and fiscal expansion may be required to generate a level of nominal expenditure consistent with full employment.
4. The equation of exchange ($MV = PY$) is not useful; instead, nominal expenditure is best modeled using the expenditure approach, that is, by modeling key components of gross domestic product (GDP) such as consumption and investment.

The preceding list can be partitioned into two groups. Only the first item relates to the interaction between nominal and real variables. It is already widely understood that changing expectations of inflation are a potentially troublesome issue for the sort of simple aggregate supply model that Keynes discusses in the *General Theory*, and I have little to add to that discussion. Keynes's focus on aggregate demand shocks is reflected in the early versions of IS-LM, which are essentially models of nominal expenditure determination, not models of how nominal shocks are partitioned between prices and real output.[1] Thus I focus on items 2,

---

1. To see how changes in nominal expenditure affect real output, an aggregate supply function must be grafted onto the IS-LM model.

3, and 4, which relate to the issues of how nominal expenditure movements can best be explained, controlled, and modeled.

Although the IS-LM model has many applications, most of its really distinctive implications involve its treatment of money. When Hicks first formalized Keynes's insights into the IS-LM apparatus (originally termed *IS-LL*), he noted two key differences from the preceding "classical" tradition, the multiplier equation and the liquidity preference doctrine. While Hicks saw the former as being "a mere simplification, and ultimately insignificant," he also suggested "it is the liquidity preference doctrine which is vital." But even here, Hicks saw continuity with the Marshallian tradition, which also allowed for the possibility that money demand could be influenced by the rate of interest. Finally, Hicks concludes that the "most important thing in Mr. Keynes' book" is the possibility of a flat LM curve, that is, the liquidity trap.[2] It is this special case that allowed Keynes to question the effectiveness of monetary policy and to call for increased public works spending.

One problem with Hicks's interpretation is that in the *General Theory* Keynes ([1936] 1964, 207) indicated that he knew of no previous examples of a complete liquidity trap. So is the Hicksian interpretation unjustified? Milton Friedman (1974, 169) also suggested that "absolute liquidity preference" played a key role in the *General Theory*.[3] In the subsequent analysis, I accept Hicks's model as a valid representation of Keynes's analysis, and more specifically I accept Hicks's and Friedman's assumptions about the importance of the liquidity trap concept to the model presented in the *General Theory*. However, my interpretation is slightly different. Although a major impetus to the development of the IS-LM model was the need to incorporate Keynes's liquidity preference doctrine into the monetary sector, Keynes's real concern was not the pure

2. This is not to argue that Hicks's paper contains the only "correct" IS-LM model. Rather, Hicks's version seems to best represent the views of Keynes and his followers during the 1930s. Michel De Vroey (2000) showed that Franco Modigliani's (1944) later version, which emphasizes wage rigidity instead of the liquidity trap, is probably closer to the spirit of modern Keynesianism. De Vroey (2000, 304) argued that once the concept of an absolute liquidity trap began to seem implausible, "the only bequest from the Keynesian revolution was a rudimentary pragmatic general equilibrium model, the IS-LM apparatus in general, devoid of any specific Keynesian trait."

3. Friedman (1974, 169) suggested: "One consequence of my rereading large parts of the *General Theory* . . . has been to reinforce my view that absolute liquidity preference plays a key role. Time and again when Keynes must face up to precisely what it is that prevents a full-employment equilibrium, his final line of defense is absolute liquidity preference." Mauro Boianovsky (this volume) discusses Hicks's (1937) analysis of the liquidity trap and IS-LM in the context of his later research on monetary economics.

liquidity trap but rather the broader (and vaguer) notion of monetary policy ineffectiveness. Note that throughout the essay I use the term *monetary policy ineffectiveness* in the Keynesian sense in which policy is incapable of affecting prices, aggregate demand, or nominal output, not the modern (new classical) sense where policy is incapable of influencing real output.[4] It is easy to see how people can have differing interpretations of the importance of the liquidity trap in Keynes's analysis. In an earlier paper (1999), I argued that Keynes's doubts about the effectiveness of monetary policy seem to have been linked both to issues of liquidity preference and to practical constraints on monetary policy, but his writings on these issues are often vague and contradictory.

Even if one accepts the preceding interpretation, one might ask how central the concept of monetary policy ineffectiveness is to either the Keynesian revolution or the development of IS-LM. The IS-LM model is used to look at a wide variety of macroeconomic issues, and thus my focus on the "LM" side of the model might seem unduly restrictive. To see why monetary policy ineffectiveness is so important, consider the role that money plays in nominal income determination. Had Keynes thought that monetary policy was capable of controlling nominal income, it seems unlikely that he would have devoted so much time to issues that become tangential under a monetary policy rule targeting nominal GDP (such as fiscal policy, the paradox of thrift, investment instability, etc.). Much of the Keynesian apparatus is set up to examine economies where monetary policy has failed to provide an adequate level of aggregate demand. And one of the most important uses of IS-LM has been to compare the relative effectiveness of monetary and fiscal policy.

A second, and related, characteristic of IS-LM analysis is the highly restrictive transmission mechanism involving money, interest rate, investment, and aggregate demand. Early on, a number of monetarists suggested that a truly "general" theory would be expected to incorporate a wide variety of transmission mechanisms for monetary shocks. And those mechanisms should be operative in even the most primitive economic systems, that is, systems completely lacking a financial system.[5]

4. This is clearly Keynes's concern in the *General Theory*. See, for example, his discussion of money, effective demand, and aggregate supply ([1936] 1964, 298–304).

5. Karl Brunner (1981) argued that "the evidence drawn from inflation (or deflation) experiences of countries with (at best) rudimentary 'money' or capital markets (Turkey, Israel, Belgium, the Netherlands, Korea, South America, and others) is hard to reconcile with a 'Hicksian' substitution pattern. It appears that the 'Hicksian' interpretation expresses a somewhat parochial 'City of London syndrome.'" Brunner's point is important, although one might

Allan Meltzer (1995) and Edward Nelson (2002) argued that monetary policy can affect aggregate spending without necessarily having any effect on interest rates. In a sense, then, IS-LM is a "special theory," which is only applicable to sophisticated economies with well-developed financial systems.[6] The interest rate transmission mechanism also relies on the liquidity effect, a mechanism that requires the existence of sticky prices. If wages and prices are completely flexible, then a one-time increase in the money supply would result in a proportionate increase in the price level, leaving nominal interest rates unchanged.

Furthermore, the simpler versions of IS-LM often ignored expectations of inflation and thus failed to distinguish between real and nominal interest rates. More sophisticated versions of IS-LM do incorporate expectations, but at a significant cost. Robert King (1993) showed that an expansionary monetary policy could easily shift the IS curve by more than the LM curve, resulting in higher interest rates (real and nominal). In fact, a permanent change in the money growth rate produces a set of effects that look very much like an IS shock. This is important because today one of the most important uses of the IS-LM model is to provide a framework for the analysis of monetary policies aimed at macroeconomic stabilization.

Additional problems arise when the IS-LM model is used to compare the relative effectiveness of monetary and fiscal policy. For instance, when the LM curve is relatively elastic, then monetary policy is generally viewed as being less effective than fiscal policy. Yet the term *effectiveness* is often left undefined. One definition would be "cost-effectiveness," that is, which of the two policies can increase aggregate demand by a given amount at the lowest social cost. Fiscal expansion increases government debt, however, whereas monetary expansion produces seigniorage and thus reduces the stock of government debt held by the public. Under this criterion, an expansionary monetary policy would always be the more cost-effective option (for a given increase in nominal income). More commonly, the criterion that economists have in mind is "effectiveness at boosting nominal expenditure." But if cost-effectiveness is not the issue, then a comparison of monetary and fiscal policy

---

easily find even more "primitive" examples in extremely low-income countries, or in earlier epochs of world history.

6. The monetarist-Keynesian debate is beyond the scope of this essay. Michael Bordo and Anna Schwartz (this volume) provide a much more complete analysis of monetarist objections to IS-LM.

effectiveness implicitly presupposes limited resources, or some sort of constraint on policy. Once again, however, under a pure fiat money regime, monetary policy would always come out ahead. There are certainly limits to a government's ability to engage in deficit spending, but no obvious limits to the ability of central banks to print money.

Because an expansionary monetary policy reduces the national debt (and thus the future excess tax burden) but also imposes an inflation tax on money holders, an expansionary monetary policy actually becomes more desirable as it becomes less effective at boosting aggregate demand (and thus prices). In the extreme case of a complete liquidity trap, the optimal policy would be for the central bank to buy up the entire world's stock of wealth. By assumption, this policy would result in no inflation (and would allow for a huge reduction, if not elimination, of the excess burden from ordinary taxes). Although this reductio ad absurdum case is almost inconceivable in the real world, this thought experiment is a useful point of reference when examining how the IS-LM model has been used to analyze the alleged liquidity traps of 1930s America and late-1990s Japan.[7]

As a practical matter, under an inflationary fiat money regime the debate about the relative effectiveness of monetary and fiscal policy becomes essentially meaningless. With high nominal interest rates there isn't even a possibility of a liquidity trap, and with no gold backing for the currency there is essentially no constraint on the central bank's ability to create money. Since fiat money creation is virtually costless, it doesn't really matter how much money must be created to hit a given aggregate demand target, and thus the central bank assumes the (de facto) sole responsibility for nominal expenditure determination.

In section 5, I argue that Keynes never intended the monetary policy ineffectiveness concept to apply to an unconstrained fiat money regime. Rather, he generally assumed (at least implicitly) that monetary policy was at least partially constrained, perhaps by a link to gold.

With all of the preceding disadvantages, it may seem surprising that IS-LM has become the standard textbook model of aggregate demand. But the IS-LM approach also has some enormous pedagogical advantages. Although some students find the derivation of IS-LM a bit difficult

7. Of course, there are many real-world complexities that might overturn this conclusion. Nevertheless, traditional IS-LM analyses of monetary and fiscal policy under a fiat money regime don't even begin to examine the sorts of issues that would allow one to make sense of the term *policy effectiveness*. See Sumner 2003 for a critique of textbook analyses of monetary policy effectiveness.

to follow, it does incorporate several commonsense notions about key macroeconomic relationships. It is also the view implicit in almost all news coverage of macroeconomic issues. Thus, for instance, the IS-LM model provides an easy way to explain to students why the news media view the term *expansionary monetary policy* as being synonymous with *lower interest rates*. Of course, if the problems with IS-LM identified by the monetarists were too glaring, then even the pedagogical advantages in teaching undergraduates would not be sufficient to convince professional macroeconomists to retain the IS-LM framework. I show that the IS-LM approach seems to have reached its greatest popularity when the structure of the financial and monetary system hid its weaknesses and highlighted its perceived strengths.

We have already seen that the simpler versions of IS-LM have problems modeling the monetary policy transmission mechanism in a primitive economy that lacks a well-developed financial system, in an economy where wages and prices are completely flexible, or in an inflationary economy where movements in the nominal and real interest rates are not closely related. And the use of IS-LM to evaluate monetary policy effectiveness seems meaningless in a pure fiat money regime. One might then have expected the IS-LM approach to have thrived during the latter part of the classical gold standard era—say from the 1870s to 1914. In the next several sections we will see why both the initial development of IS-LM, and its subsequent decline in popularity, occurred several decades later than what we might have expected from the preceding analysis.

To summarize, any explanation of the rise and fall of IS-LM must consider two key issues: under what circumstances will interest rate–oriented monetary analysis be preferred to alternative approaches, and under what circumstances will there be doubts regarding the effectiveness of monetary policy. The preceding analysis suggests the IS-LM model would be expected to have its greatest appeal during periods when the economy featured (1) a highly developed financial system and relatively sticky prices; (2) low expectations of inflation, and thus a rough equivalence between real and nominal interest rates; and (3) important constraints on using monetary policy to control aggregate demand (i.e., a commodity standard or a fixed exchange rate regime).

3. Three Approaches to Monetary Economics

All macro models have advantages and disadvantages. Any explanation of the varying popularity of IS-LM needs to consider two issues: First, what are the competing approaches to monetary analysis? And second, under what circumstances will the IS-LM approach be more useful or, more important for our purposes, seem more useful than those alternative approaches? At the risk of oversimplification, one might identify three distinct approaches to monetary economics, a commodity approach, a quantity approach, and an interest rate approach. A widespread acceptance of the third approach was a necessary condition for the general acceptance of IS-LM, but to place that development in a specific historical context we also have to consider the advantages and disadvantages of the first two.

The earliest monetary regimes were commodity standards, and some of the earliest monetary theories were based on value theory. Changes in the supply and demand for the commodity used as a medium of account determined the value (or purchasing power) of that commodity. And changes in the overall price level reflected both changes in the value of the underlying monetary commodity, and changes in the amount of that commodity contained in each monetary unit. For small primitive economies, monetary policy often consisted of little more than the debasement of coins. Important elements of the commodity approach to monetary analysis run through the nineteenth-century banking school, Irving Fisher's "compensated dollar plan," and even the "new monetary economics" of the 1980s.[8]

The quantity approach to monetary analysis goes back at least to the early eighteenth century and can be used to analyze either commodity or fiat money regimes. In this framework, money supply and demand are independent, and an excess cash balance transmission mechanism is employed to explain how changes in the quantity of money affect the price level (or aggregate demand). The quantity approach underlies the monetary analysis of David Hume, the nineteenth-century currency school, the theoretical work of Fisher, and, of course, post–World War II monetarism.

The interest rate approach assumes the existence of a well-developed financial system. Under this approach, changes in the money supply have little or no direct effect on aggregate demand and prices. This approach to monetary economics underlies the work of Knut Wicksell and Keynes, as well as the new Keynesian economics of the 1980s and 1990s. Just as monetarists argue that changes in the gold stock only matter if they

---

8. See, for example, Greenfield and Yeager 1983 for a summary of the new monetary economics.

affect the money supply, Keynesians argue that changes in the money stock affect the economy (if at all) only through changes in the interest rate.

To see why IS-LM arose in the 1930s and declined in the 1970s, we need to examine the compatibility of each of these three approaches with the financial and monetary conditions of various historical periods.

4. Pre-Keynesian Monetary Economics

In an earlier paper (1999), I argued that the Keynesian model was essentially a gold standard model, that is, a model of constrained monetary policy and expectations of near-zero inflation.[9] This raises the question of why IS-LM was not developed earlier than the 1930s. My conjecture is that there were already several well-established monetary theories, and in order for those theories to be dislodged, it would take a set of empirical facts for which existing theory found it difficult to account.

It is hardly surprising that medieval philosophers failed to employ an IS-LM-type apparatus to explain why inflation occurred after the debasement of coinage. And as long as commodities continued to serve as the primary media of exchange, there was no reason to discard monetary theories based on the commodity approach. Over time, however, the role of commodities gradually diminished as first currency notes, and then checks, became the dominant media of exchange. David Glasner (2000) showed that during the nineteenth century the currency school used a quantity theoretic approach to argue that the overissue of paper money, even of gold-backed notes, could lead to inflation.

It is not clear exactly how well-developed a financial system must be in order for the interest rate transmission mechanism to become an important channel of monetary policy. The fact that the liquidity effect was discussed at least as far back as Hume ([1752] 1970) certainly suggests that the Keynesian type of monetary analysis could have preceded the development of quantity theoretic models. The fact that the golden age of the quantity theory predates Keynesian economics may be attributable to ongoing structural changes in the major Western economies.

The interest rate transmission mechanism relies on the liquidity effect, and this requires the existence of sticky prices. At the risk of oversimplification, quantity theorists assume that (onetime) shifts in the

---

9. M. Roberts (1995) also examined the link between the liquidity trap and the gold standard.

supply of money affect prices, not interest rates, whereas Keynesians assume that the nominal interest rate is the best indicator of monetary policy and that a monetary shock will initially affect interest rates. The effect on the price level (if indeed there is any effect) will come at the end of a long and complex transmission mechanism involving interest rate, investment, aggregate demand, real output, and inflation.

Christopher Hanes (1996) provides evidence that price indexes available during the nineteenth century were much more volatile (and procyclical) than those available during recent decades. Part of the difference is that those indexes were more heavily weighted toward crude, unfinished goods, and it is well known that the prices of commodities tend to be far more flexible than those of highly processed consumer goods. But he also found that much of the difference in price flexibility was real. In particular, Hanes showed that between 1889 and 1969 the crude goods/GNP ratio in the United States declined from 27 percent to 6 percent. Thus nineteenth-century economists were looking at price level data that was especially well suited for a quantity theoretic mode of analysis. In fact, even as late as the interwar period, the U.S. (wholesale) price level often showed an astoundingly rapid response to shocks such as the sharp drop in the monetary base during 1920–21, or the dollar devaluation of 1933.[10]

By the close of the classical gold standard era in 1914, the quantity theory of money had become entrenched within academia. Although the price flexibility of that era may have contributed to the popularity of the quantity theory, other factors were beginning to undermine support for the theory. The simplest version of the quantity theory—the view that changes in the money supply cause proportionate changes in the price level—works best when money supply shocks are more important than money demand shocks. Thus the quantity theory was actually not especially well suited for monetary analysis under an international gold standard regime. (During the century preceding World War I the supply of gold grew at roughly the same rate as gold demand.) The quantity theory is better suited to explaining the price level during those periods when the gold stock grew rapidly (such as the sixteenth century), or when convertibility was temporarily suspended and a highly inflationary fiat currency was placed into circulation.

10. The U.S. wholesale price index plunged 41.6 percent between mid-1920 and mid-1921. The WPI soared by 17.9 percent in just the first six months after the April 1933 dollar devaluation, despite record unemployment in the United States.

The later part of the classical gold standard era was, in two respects, ideally suited for the development of IS-LM-type models. Robert Barsky (1987, 9) showed that during this period the price level was approximately a white noise process with a zero trend rate of inflation. Because actual changes in the price level were essentially unforecastable, nominal and (*ex ante*) real interest rates were roughly equivalent. The major industrial economies now had well-developed financial systems, and with expectations of inflation at close to nil, the nominal interest rate could be viewed as a reasonable indicator of monetary policy. The quantity theorists of the nineteenth century were aware of the interest rate transmission mechanism, but decreases in the nominal interest rate were not viewed as being a necessary condition for an expansionary monetary policy to increase the price level.[11] Nevertheless, during the late nineteenth and early twentieth centuries, quantity theorists did begin to distinguish between the monetary theory suitable for a simple cash economy and the type of monetary theory more appropriate to a sophisticated credit economy.

Wicksell (1907) was probably the first to place the interest rate transmission mechanism at the very center of a macroeconomic model. David Laidler (1991, 147) argued that "Wicksell went further than Marshall and Fisher. He postulated that a modern banking system had the capacity to render the velocity of currency a passive variable in the face of real shocks." By making velocity a passive variable, Wicksell took a decisive step toward Keynes's liquidity preference theory. But although the interest rate transmission mechanism was a necessary condition for the development of IS-LM, it was not a sufficient condition.

Motivation for IS-LM also came from the debate over the relative effectiveness of monetary and fiscal policy. During the classical gold standard era the Bank of England was viewed as being a highly effective "conductor of the international orchestra" (Keynes 1930, 2:306–7). Peripheral countries might have occasionally struggled to achieve an adequate level of aggregate demand, but it was not obvious that the issues they faced were easily explained by an IS-LM mode of analysis. For instance, during the 1890s the United States had no central bank at all, and the silver-gold dispute was hardly something that would naturally be

11. This assertion is based on Laidler's (1991, 64–79) analysis of the views of Marshall and Fisher on the monetary transmission mechanism. Although Marshall's views on the interest rate transmission mechanism are somewhat more "Keynesian" than those of Fisher, even Marshall maintains a mechanism by which money can affect prices through the real balance effect.

modeled using an interest rate transmission mechanism. If a bimetallic standard (an expansionary policy) had raised the expected rate of inflation, then nominal interest rates in the United States would have risen above British levels.

World War I and its immediate aftermath produced a number of dramatic inflationary episodes that were easily explained by the quantity theory of money (and its corollaries, purchasing power parity and the Fisher effect). Lars Jonung (1988) reports that by 1920 even Wicksell had reverted to the view that high inflation rates were simply a product of excessive note issue. (As we will see, Keynes's thinking was evolving in a strikingly similar fashion.)

This was also a period of dramatic policy innovations. The United States went from having no central bank in 1913 to ten years later having a central bank that seemed capable of fine-tuning the economy. Under the leadership of Governor Strong, the Federal Reserve was able to achieve approximate price stability after 1922, and thus (at least in the United States) the issue of monetary policy effectiveness remained in the background throughout most of 1920s. By 1929 the development of IS-LM required only one additional factor: a perception of policy impotence at the world's dominant central bank.

5. The Liquidity Trap and IS-LM

One way of looking at the Keynesian revolution of the 1930s is to ask a simple question: Why did Keynes not simply recommend that central banks increase the money supply enough to move the level of nominal expenditure back up to its target level (i.e., a level consistent with full employment)? Many people think they know the answer to this question and would no doubt include a discussion of the relative elasticities of the IS and LM curves. There is support for this viewpoint in Keynes's writings, but there is also a sense in which this answer is profoundly inadequate. To see why, we need to return to the distinction between relatively weak monetary policy and the reductio ad absurdum case of complete monetary policy ineffectiveness, that is, where even extreme monetary expansion has no inflationary effect.[12] For simplicity, I refer to the latter case as an "extreme liquidity trap" (although monetary

12. As far back as 1692, John Locke also used a reductio ad absurdum argument against the hypothesis of complete monetary policy ineffectiveness. The argument involved extreme reductions in the silver content of the pound. See Eltis 1995.

policy ineffectiveness can also be due to investment being unresponsive to changes in the interest rate).

The problem with the standard IS-LM interpretation of Keynes's writings is that there are severe conceptual problems with any attempt to pinpoint exactly how Keynes viewed the problem of monetary policy ineffectiveness. As we saw in section 2, an environment where monetary policy is relatively weak is in some respects an environment where an expansionary monetary policy is most desirable as a stabilization tool. The more assets that a central bank must buy in order to meet a given AD target, the more desirable the use of expansionary monetary policy.

One can also find evidence that Keynes occasionally questioned not just the strength of monetary policy but also even the ability of central banks to hit a given AD target. Is it possible that Keynes did in fact accept the possibility of the extreme liquidity trap? In a previous paper I argued that there are three problems with this interpretation.[13] In the first place, the reductio ad absurdum case seems too far-fetched to be accepted by an economist who was both brilliant and pragmatic. And as noted earlier, even if such a trap emerged, the policy implication would be that the central bank should generate an extremely massive expansion of the money supply—something that Keynes strongly opposed. And, most important, Keynes never seemed to waver from his long-held view that a completely unconstrained fiat money regime was likely to result in very high inflation rates. Yet under an extreme liquidity trap, monetary expansion would generate no inflation.

One possibility is that Keynes's thinking on this question was rigidly compartmentalized. Keynes had studied the post–World War I hyperinflations and knew that throughout history an unanchored fiat money regime usually degenerated into a device for inflationary deficit spending. When Keynes looked at policy issues in the leading industrial economies, however, he implicitly viewed a pure fiat money regime as being both highly implausible and highly undesirable. As a result, there was always an unwritten assumption in his analysis of real-world policy issues, that is, that monetary policy operated (either implicitly or explicitly) under a *constraint*. Throughout most of his career Keynes was opposed to a rigid gold standard, which he called "the worst of all conceivable systems (apart from the abuses of a *fiat* money which has lost all its anchors)" (1930, 1:170). Yet he also asserted that "at all stages of the

13. Sumner 1999 provides a much more detailed analysis of the ideas discussed in this section.

post-war developments the concrete proposals which I have brought forward from time to time have been based on the use of gold as an international standard, whilst discarding it as a rigid national standard" ([1933] 1982, 186). Thus most of Keynes's monetary analysis, including the *General Theory*, involved the implicit assumption that monetary policy had an "anchor," or constraint of some type. Only his analysis specifically tailored to the problems of hyperinflation incorporated the sort of unconstrained fiat money regime that is now a standard assumption in monetary analysis. Next, I briefly summarize some evidence for the view that Keynes's thinking was "compartmentalized" in this way and then explain why the concept of a constrained monetary regime lies at the heart of Keynesian economics.

One indirect piece of evidence for the preceding view comes from Keynes's view of the Fisher effect. Although Keynes was aware that increased expectations of inflation could, in principle, raise nominal interest rates, he viewed that scenario as almost a pathological case—unlikely to occur in a "normal" (i.e., nonhyperinflationary) economy. Keynes's failure to recognize the possibility of a Fisher effect had several consequences for the issue of monetary policy effectiveness. In the *General Theory*, Keynes's argument ([1936] 1964, 306) against the quantity theoretic approach to monetary policy (implicitly) relies on the assumption that a Fisher effect is very unlikely to result from an increase in the money supply. In addition, Meltzer (1988) wondered why Keynes never recommended a policy of maintaining a positive inflation rate. A sufficiently high inflation rate would keep nominal interest rates well above zero, and this would prevent the formation of a liquidity trap. It's a good question, but if Keynes never entertained the possibility of a Fisher effect under normal policies, then he was unlikely to have ever considered Meltzer's solution.

As noted earlier, there is some evidence that (excluding the postwar hyperinflationary episodes) the expected rate of inflation was near zero throughout virtually all of Keynes's life. If the gold standard was the cause of expectations of a stable price level, then it may have indirectly contributed to Keynes's mindset on this issue. Overall, however, Keynes's theoretical writings provide only very slight support for the view that Keynesian economics is implicitly a gold standard model, or even a constrained model of any sort. Rather, it is a close reading of Keynes's views on contemporaneous policy issues that provide the strongest support for this hypothesis.

In the *General Theory*, Keynes provides only one concrete, real-world, example of a possible liquidity trap. This was his brief discussion ([1936] 1964, 207–8) of the spring 1932 open market purchases by the Federal Reserve System. Many contemporaneous observers viewed these purchases as evidence of monetary policy ineffectiveness,[14] but to modern theorists they must appear a very curious example of a liquidity trap. There was profound pessimism as stock prices, commodity prices, and industrial production all fell throughout the period when the Fed was at its most aggressive. Yet it was not a question of monetary expansion failing to boost aggregate demand during the spring of 1932, but rather the Fed failing to expand the money supply, as the effect of open market purchases was mostly offset by a large gold outflow from the United States.[15] The monetary base grew only slightly, and as banking difficulties reduced the money multiplier, the broader monetary aggregates actually declined during the spring. Thus the one liquidity trap episode cited by Keynes is (at least to some extent) an example of the constraints on policy imposed by the classical gold standard, constraints that were well understood by the classical economists.[16]

14. Laidler (1999, 259 n) calls this "one of the key 'stylized facts' underlying the evolution of monetary economics in the 1930s and 1940s."

15. If these gold outflows were caused by the expansionary policy (and we cannot be certain of that), it would be an example of Ben Bernanke's (1995) "multiple monetary equilibria." That is, an expansionary policy stance by a central bank could so reduce confidence that it might actually lead to a reduction in the money supply.

16. Lauchlin Currie ([1934] 1935) was one of the few who understood this fact. Sumner (1997) argued that the radically different interpretations of this episode by Keynes ([1936] 1964), and Friedman and Schwartz (1963), are both unsatisfactory. Friedman and Schwartz point to the upswing in monetary and output statistics in the last half of 1932. But the widespread feeling that monetary policy had failed was mostly based on the extreme declines in stock and commodity markets during the spring of 1932. These declines were attributed to a loss of confidence in the dollar and were associated with widespread gold hoarding (see Sumner 1997, 2004). And these concerns were linked to Fed open market purchases, as well as congressional spending deliberations. The markets seemed to have little faith in the famous 1932 open market purchases. None of this means that Friedman and Schwartz were wrong in their view that the gold standard did not prevent the Fed from doing far more than it did. Perhaps markets were concerned that the Fed and Congress did just enough to disturb confidence, but not enough to promote recovery. But there is also abundant evidence that gold market disturbances weighed on stock and commodity markets at various times during the 1930s. And these periodic crises led everyone from conservative bankers to monetary reformers like Keynes and Fisher to have doubts about monetary policy effectiveness.

This example suggests another possible link between the gold standard and Keynes's views on monetary policy effectiveness. Laidler (1999, 272) noted that during the mid-1930s Keynes had emphasized the restoration of "confidence" over "purely monetary" remedies to depression. I believe that the gold outflow that neutralized the spring 1932 open market purchases was

Unfortunately, outside the *General Theory* one can find examples where Keynes questioned the effectiveness of monetary policy even under less constrained circumstances, such as during the later stages of Roosevelt's dollar depreciation program. To fully understand this episode, we need to briefly compare the views of Keynes with those of Irving Fisher. Frank Steindl (2000) noted that during the early thirties Fisher seemed to move away from a quantity theoretic approach, as he joined Keynes in questioning the effectiveness of the Fed's 1932 open market purchases. But Robert Dimand (2000) convincingly demonstrated that Fisher soon readopted many of his long-standing views on monetary policy. If the constraints associated with the gold standard led Fisher to question his belief in the effectiveness of monetary policy during 1932, then the (limited) success of Roosevelt's dollar depreciation program of 1933 helped Fisher regain confidence in the power of monetary policy.

Like many other prominent interwar macroeconomists, Fisher (1920) believed that price level stabilization should be the goal of monetary policy. His most famous proposal was the "compensated dollar plan," under which the price of gold would be periodically adjusted in (inverse) proportion to changes in the price level. The proposal was certainly not Keynesian in character; it wasn't even obviously linked to Fisher's quantity theoretic work. It is probably best viewed in terms of the commodity approach to money, inasmuch as it was being sold as a proposal to stabilize the purchasing power of a given nominal value of gold. Fisher understood that his proposal represented an abandonment of the gold standard and that the vestigial link to gold was only a marketing device to reassure those who viewed fiat money as dangerously radical.

Keynes initially welcomed President Roosevelt's decision to let the dollar depreciate during 1933. The decision was consistent with his long-standing opposition to a rigid gold standard. But he actually preferred a more flexible link to gold (as under Bretton Woods) and opposed further depreciation once gold had reached about $28 an ounce in mid-1933. When Roosevelt adopted a gold-buying program quite similar to Fisher's compensated dollar plan in the fall of 1933 and began to aggressively push the price of gold higher as a way to boost the price level, Keynes became a vociferous critic of U.S. monetary policy. In a scathing *New York Times* piece written in late 1933, Keynes criticized the Roosevelt policy as being ineffective and also as being based on a discredited economic

---

triggered by just such a loss of confidence. Of course, under an unconstrained monetary regime this sort of deflationary currency crisis would never arise in the first place.

theory.[17] Because the policy was developed by Roosevelt's economic adviser Professor George Warren (a committed supporter of Fisher's plan), contemporaneous observers presumably would have recognized Keynes's criticisms as being at least partially directed at Irving Fisher.

It would be difficult to disentangle all of the possible motives for Keynes's attack. He probably saw through the symbolic link to gold and correctly recognized the scheme as pure fiat money. As noted earlier, Keynes had suggested that a fiat money regime was even worse than a rigid gold standard. In addition, his *New York Times* critique alluded to the negative effect this plan could have on the European economies, including Britain.[18] And finally, it is worth noting that in 1933 Keynes was beginning to develop a new approach to monetary economics that could hardly have been any more different from the thinking of Warren and Fisher.[19]

Just three weeks after the *Times* piece, Roosevelt finally did agree to refix the dollar to gold (at $35 an ounce), and Keynes congratulated Roosevelt for rejecting the advice of the "extreme inflationists" (see Keynes [1934] 1982, 312). Whatever one thinks of the preceding analysis, this comment would seem to be quite revealing. In one short statement, Keynes seems to both accept the positive danger that a pure fiat regime could lead to high inflation, even in the severely depressed economy of 1933, and also suggest that Keynes opposed Fisherine policies in 1933 because they were potentially too inflationary. (This just three weeks after denying that a dollar devaluation policy could succeed in reflating the U.S. economy!) Obviously, there are many ways to reconcile Keynes's contradictory comments on this episode, but I would suggest that the "compartmentalization" approach discussed earlier is the most promising. Keynes saw a modest depreciation (of the type actually implemented) as being of only limited effectiveness, and perhaps (because of its destabilization of investor confidence) even a bit counterproductive. On the other hand, Keynes saw that if this plan were followed to its logical conclusion, then the potential for dollar depreciation would

17. See the *New York Times*, 31 December 1933, 2XX.

18. Fisher had little direct influence on Roosevelt, but Warren's plan was clearly influenced by Fisher. Sumner 2001 provides a detailed examination of the gold-buying program.

19. Elsewhere I have argued that, in the absence of the National Industrial Recovery Act, Warren's plan would have led to almost complete economic recovery by late 1934. If this had occurred, one has to wonder how both the structure of the *General Theory*, and its reception in America, might have differed.

be unlimited, and he may have feared the inflationary consequences of such an open-ended policy regime.

Even if one accepts the preceding interpretation of Keynes's contradictory statements on monetary policy effectiveness, one might still question how central this issue was to the broader Keynesian revolution. For instance, that revolution included a change in orientation from the quantity equation–based monetary approach to nominal expenditure determination, to the multiplier-based expenditure approach. And it also centered on issues such as investment instability, the paradox of thrift, and the possibilities for fiscal stabilization policies—all issues easier to visualize from a Keynesian expenditure approach. Nevertheless, the monetary policy effectiveness question indirectly influences all of these issues.

Consider the following thought experiment. Suppose we are operating under a fiat money regime and that (discretionary) monetary policy is used to target aggregate nominal expenditure. Also assume that that monetary policy is at least somewhat effective, that is, we are not in an extreme liquidity trap. In that case it is difficult to see how any of the preceding factors (investment shocks, changes in the marginal propensity to save, or fiscal policy) could affect the anticipated level of aggregate demand. Monetary policymakers would simply readjust the money supply growth rate to offset the anticipated effect of the specific nonmonetary shock. At best, a feeble version of Keynesianism could have inhabited the interstices left by the lags in monetary policy.[20] But in the *General Theory* it was issues like the long-run imbalance between savings and investment that seemed most to concern Keynes, not short-run policy lags. It is hard to see how Keynes's Depression-era theories could have gained much traction under a regime where monetary policymakers targeted nominal expenditure. Without some (at least implied) constraint on monetary policy, the *General Theory* simply makes no sense.

Thus far, we have seen that Keynes's views during the 1930s reflected the world in which he lived. If so, then it ought to be possible to trace out the development of his thinking in terms of the ongoing monetary

20. And even this caveat would not apply if the nominal income targeting regime was efficient in the sense discussed by Robert Hall and N. Gregory Mankiw (1994) and Lars Svensson (1997), that is, policy targeted the public's expectation of future nominal income (or prices), rather than current nominal income. It is interesting to note that as far back as 1923, Keynes advocated a policy similar to that of Svensson, when he suggested policymakers should try to prevent future changes in the price level, not simply react to past changes.

developments in the Western world. Although a complete analysis of this topic is far beyond the scope of this essay, a few observations from 1911, 1923, 1930, and 1933 will provide some support for the preceding analysis.

In a review of Fisher's first major work on the quantity theory of money, Keynes (1911) suggested that Fisher's explanation of the money supply transmission mechanism was inadequate. Keynes suggested that the initial effect must come through an interest rate transmission mechanism, a view he would hold, with one notable exception, throughout his entire career.

The one exception occurred in 1923, after the relatively stable pre-war gold standard had collapsed, and many countries were in the midst of hyperinflationary episodes. Not surprisingly, in the *Tract on Monetary Reform* Keynes focused almost entirely on the subject of price level instability, but what is surprising is that he used a strikingly quantity theoretic mode of analysis. This is not to say that he employed any simplistic assumptions about velocity being constant, but rather that in his analysis he employed an "excess cash balance" approach where interest rates played only a minor role. More important, he assumed that even if velocity were to change, central bankers could still ensure price level stability through offsetting adjustments in the quantity of currency notes (or by changing reserve requirements).[21]

By 1930 the international gold standard had been restored, and George Tavlas (1981) showed that in the *Treatise on Money* Keynes replaced the earlier analysis of currency notes and the price level with a new approach based on interest rates and investment. Then in 1932 and 1933 Keynes made a number of statements in which he expressed doubts about the efficacy of monetary policy. By the time the *General Theory* was published in 1936, there were signs of a return to inflation in the United States and Britain. But Keynes actually developed its key concepts several years earlier, and this work certainly reflects the sense of pessimism about monetary policy that was so widespread during 1932–33. Finally,

---

21. Keynes (1923, 81–82) even suggests how events turned his thinking in a more quantity theoretic direction: "On the other hand a large change in *n* [i.e., money], which rubs away the initial friction, and especially a change in *n* due to causes which set up a general expectation of a further change in the same direction, may produce a *more* than proportionate effect on *p*. After the . . . narratives of catastrophic inflation given in Chapter II, it is scarcely necessary to illustrate this further,—it is a matter more readily understood than it was ten years ago." (Note that Keynes dropped this transmission mechanism soon after the hyperinflationary episodes ended.)

in late 1937 there was a return to deflation, rising excess reserve ratios, and near-zero nominal interest rates, ideal conditions for the widespread acceptance (in America) of Keynes's message.

We have already seen that when Hicks began formalizing Keynes's theories, the concept of monetary policy ineffectiveness lay at the center of that effort. This raises a difficult question: If IS-LM is a model where monetary policy is constrained, then why did this theory gain ground after 1937, just as all of the major countries were abandoning the gold standard? In the next section we will see that reports of the death of the gold standard were greatly exaggerated.

6. Was Bretton Woods a Commodity Standard?

There are at least three commonly cited criteria for adherence to an international gold standard. The central bank must peg the currency to gold at a fixed nominal price, the currency must be freely convertible into gold, and the central bank must adhere to the "rules of the game," usually interpreted as maintaining a stable ratio between currency in circulation and gold reserves. In standard theoretical models of the gold standard such as Barro 1979, however, there is really only one sine qua non requirement—a fixed price of gold. This is what assures the inverse relationship between the price level and the value (i.e., purchasing power) of gold, which is the essence of all theoretical models of the gold standard. Before the United States left the gold standard in 1933, two of these three rules were adhered to, including the essential one. For several years after the United States repegged the dollar in 1934, two of the three rules were adhered to, again including the essential fixed price of gold. The difference was that prior to 1933, the United States did allow dollars to be freely converted into gold, but did not even come close to adhering to the rules of the game. After 1934, something close to the opposite situation prevailed—the dollar was not (domestically) convertible into gold—but Friedman and Schwartz (1963) showed that for the remainder of the 1930s changes in the monetary base were highly correlated with changes in the size of the government's monetary gold stock. It is not at all obvious which of the two systems is better characterized by the term *gold standard regime*.

One might argue that the official price of $35 dollars an ounce meant nothing if dollars could not be freely converted into gold. But as long as gold remained at $35 in the (free) world market, the fact that Americans could not legally own gold was of only slightly more consequence than if Belgians had not been legally allowed to purchase the metal. Although the New Deal era, World War II, and Bretton Woods are a quite heterogeneous set of policy regimes, they are unified in one respect. The dollar remained at $35 an ounce. In fact, the dollar price of gold was only adjusted once during the entire period 1879–1968.

Because the dollar-gold peg was so long lasting, most contemporaneous observers overlooked its implications. They had known virtually nothing else. Instead, they focused on the momentous changes occurring during this period. In hindsight, however, we can see that several of the key components of the classical gold standard never completely faded away during the 1934–68 era. For instance, although not as restrictive as the classical gold standard, Bretton Woods still placed important constraints on the ability of European central banks to pursue independent monetary policies.

Even in the United States, where policy flexibility was somewhat greater, the expected rate of inflation remained relatively low (with the possible exception of World War II and Korea—and war years were always viewed as an anomaly). One difference, however, must be acknowledged; unlike the classical gold standard, during the Bretton Woods era there was a slight positive trend in the price level. The extraordinary changes of the 1930s and 1940s had led to a dramatic economizing of the world's monetary gold reserves. This drop in gold demand reduced the value of gold and allowed for a gradual rise in the price level during the early postwar decades.[22] Even so, Klein (1975, 472) argued that "even as late as 1964 firm expectations must have been held that a long-term monetary policy necessary to maintain foreign convertibility of the dollar at $35/oz. would be followed," and that therefore expectations of inflation were quite low. If we make the reasonable assumption that the expected inflation rate generally stayed in the 0 percent to 2 percent range under Bretton Woods, then there were no insurmountable barriers associated with using movements in nominal interest rates as a proxy for real interest rate movements.

The issue of policy constraints is not so easily resolved. Sumner (2004) argued that the constraints imposed by the gold standard contributed to the severity of the 1937–38 recession in the United States.[23]

22. See McCallum 2002, 73, for a discussion of this issue. Base velocity also increased, and this further contributed to the positive trend in prices.

23. In late 1937, a loss of confidence (similar to the spring 1932 episode) led to renewed gold hoarding and a sharp reduction in U.S. monetary growth.

It is less clear that the gold standard was an important constraint on post-war policymakers. But as long as the dollar-gold peg held, and the inflation rate stayed relatively low, then there was no obvious crisis calling for a reappraisal of the by then well-established IS-LM model. After inflation began accelerating in the late 1960s, however, proponents of the IS-LM approach seemed to become more and more like Ptolemaic astronomers faced with the invention of the telescope, as a wealth of new empirical findings required ever more complex explanations.

7. The Great Inflation and the Decline of IS-LM

A recent article by Olivier Blanchard (2000) presents an optimistic picture of steady, and impressive, progress in twentieth-century macroeconomics. In the introduction, I suggested that this view depended on whether one focused on technical developments or on a conceptual understanding of real-world problems. For instance, Roger Backhouse and David Laidler (this volume) showed that interwar macroeconomic theorists provided a wealth of astute analysis in their relatively nontechnical models. Here I would like to suggest that, at a conceptual level, the biggest changes between the interwar and modern periods have been a set of interrelated theoretical developments generated by the switch from the gold standard to an unconstrained fiat money regime.[24] Before examining the effect of post–Bretton Woods inflation on IS-LM, it will be helpful to briefly look at a related postwar development, the natural rate hypothesis.

Irving Fisher (and to a lesser extent David Hume)[25] came up with something very close to the natural rate hypothesis. In Fisher's (1923) early version of the Phillips curve, a change in the price level causes a temporary change in output and employment, but in the long run, output returns to its original level. From a modern perspective, the flaw in Fisher's model is that a permanent increase in the inflation rate would generate a permanent increase in output. But recall that Fisher lived during a period where the expected inflation rate was generally close to zero.

24. This analysis closely parallels Robert Mundell's (2000) survey of twentieth-century monetary history from the perspective of the changing role of gold. Mundell's analysis of how these events affected Keynesian economics, however, differs somewhat from the interpretation provided here.

25. In discussing the Phillips curve issue, Friedman (1975, 177) argued, "As I see it, we have advanced beyond Hume in two respects only: first, we now have a more secure grasp on the quantitative magnitudes involved; second, we have gone one derivative beyond Hume."

Either one had a commodity money regime with the price level following a random walk, or a temporary fiat regime with such extreme inflation that a Phillips curve type of analysis would be rejected out of hand. And Fisher did not recommend trying to exploit the Phillips curve as a way to boost output—further evidence that he implicitly understood the long-run implications of switching to an inflationary fiat money regime.

When policymakers finally rediscovered the Phillips curve and began to manipulate it, several notable events occurred in rapid succession. First, the gold standard had to be replaced with a fiat money regime. Ignore the official date of 1971; the actual demise of Bretton Woods occurred in 1968 when the dollar price of gold finally rose above the level of $35 an ounce. Although this was just the beginning of the "Great Inflation" (1968–82), some farsighted observers already saw the implications of this policy switch. E. S. Phelps (1967) and Friedman (1968) developed natural rate models in the late 1960s, and then others began to develop models that distinguished between anticipated and unanticipated monetary shocks. It then became clear that what had previously been viewed as the stable parameters of Phillips curve models were not, in fact, policy invariant. This line of analysis culminated in the famous "Lucas critique" (1976). It would be hard to deny that this set of theoretical innovations grew out of the failed attempts to manipulate the Phillips curve. If so, then one could view all of these related developments as representing the economic profession's attempt to come to terms with the new fiat money regime.[26]

Others have already noted the intellectual revolution created by lofty theoretical innovations in the area of rational expectations. I would like to focus on a set of more mundane concerns; how did the Great Inflation affect the Keynesian economics of nominal expenditure determination? Even without the rational expectations revolution, the high inflation rates of 1968–82 greatly reduced the pedagogical attractiveness of IS-LM. For instance, by the late 1970s the interest rate had become virtually useless as an indicator of monetary policy. Nominal interest rates were high, and yet money supply and inflation rate data suggested policy was quite expansionary. Real interest rates were probably fairly low, but expected inflation is difficult to measure.

26. This is not to deny that purely theoretical considerations might have contributed to Friedman and E. S. Phelps's insights, but surely the Great Inflation contributed to the widespread acceptance of their analysis and the subsequent explosion of research in that area.

The high nominal interest rates of the post–Bretton Woods era also reduced the attractiveness of the liquidity trap concept. In essence, the world's central banks implemented Meltzer's solution to the Keynesian liquidity trap. Even worse for the Keynesians, inflation rates varied dramatically from country to country. There is a highly suggestive table in Barro's (1994) intermediate macro textbook that shows rates of change in money, prices, and real output, by country, over several decades (including the Great Inflation). Although changes in velocity are not included in the table, the money growth rates are so highly variable between countries, and yet so obviously correlated with the respective inflation rates, that there is no way to look at this sort of data set without immediately visualizing something like the quantity approach to money. Conversely, it would seem difficult to analyze this type of data using models in which the quantity of money plays no role. As Friedman (1975, 176) observed almost three decades ago, "Double-digit inflation and double-digit interest rates, not the elegance of theoretical reasoning or the overwhelming persuasiveness of serried masses of statistics massaged through modern computers, explain the rediscovery of money."

Another reason why high inflation rates are so destructive to the simpler IS-LM models is that once inflation reaches very high levels, it begins to dominate any plausible movement in real output. Keynes assumed that depressions were caused by an insufficiency of nominal expenditure. If monetary policy is always capable of generating high inflation, then ipso facto, it is also capable of boosting nominal expenditure. Either depressions are not due to insufficient nominal expenditure (as with a real shock), or if they are, then monetary policy can easily remedy the situation.

As if the preceding problems weren't enough, the monetarists made several shrewd predictions that further boosted their reputation. Fiscal restraint in the United States seemed ineffective at slowing inflation in 1969, and monetary restraint seemed highly effective in the 1980s, despite big budget deficits. Add in Friedman's prescient prediction that the Phillips curve trade-off was only temporary, and it is easy to see why Keynesian economics suffered a crisis in the 1970s and 1980s. Only the perceived failure of the monetarist's preferred money supply targeting system prevented a complete rout of Keynesian economics.

Over time, the new Keynesians were able to acknowledge the effectiveness of monetary policy and regroup around a set of policy proposals that continued to employ a nominal interest rate instrument for monetary policy.[27] And ironically, the very success of monetarist policies in reducing inflation brought interest rates back to levels where the interest rate transmission mechanism again began to seem useful. Nevertheless, even among new Keynesians the question of relative policy effectiveness began to recede into the background. Suddenly, fiscal surpluses were recommended as a way to boost national saving and investment, or meet a looming pension crisis, and the role of stabilization policy was almost completely delegated to monetary policymakers.

The preceding analysis would seem to offer one clear example in support of Blanchard's (2000) view of progress in macroeconomic theory. We now understand the implications of a pure fiat money regime that generates a positive steady state rate of inflation—something that could not be said of the prewar theoreticians. And it seems that one side effect of this revolution in macroeconomic theory was the rapid eclipse of the IS-LM approach to monetary policy. Yet IS-LM has made something of a comeback in recent years, despite the fact that the major industrial countries continue to operate under unconstrained fiat money regimes. Edward Nelson (this volume) shows that these newer IS-LM models are consistent with optimizing behavior. And it is interesting to note that inflation rates have fallen to very low levels in the United States and Europe, and Japan has recently experienced the sort of deflation formerly associated with gold standard regimes. Nevertheless, the revival of the monetary policy effectiveness debate in the context of Japan presents something of a puzzle.[28]

8. Conclusion

We have seen that monetary theory continually evolves to reflect changes in the underlying monetary regime. Each policy regime is faced with a set of issues that are most easily visualized within a particular intellectual

27. The primary differences between the monetarists and the new Keynesians revolved around the issues of which policy instrument is best—money or interest rates—and whether an activist policy (regarding money growth rates) could reduce the severity of the business cycle.

28. A recent textbook by Robert Gordon (2000) uses IS-LM analysis to examine the monetary policy effectiveness issue in the context of Japan. The Bank of Japan seems to have the same "compartmentalization" attitude that I attributed to Keynes—both denying the effectiveness of monetary expansion and worrying about the inflationary consequences of such a policy! (See the *Economist*, 2 June 2001, 74.) Boianovsky (this volume) looks at some recent attempts to develop liquidity trap models applicable to the current situation in Japan.

framework. As simple commodity money regimes evolved into more sophisticated financial systems, first the quantity theory and then the interest rate transmission mechanism became the easiest way to visualize the effect of monetary policy. When during the 1930s the effectiveness of monetary policy itself came into question, the IS-LM framework was able to encompass a set of plausible policy alternatives. And when that framework could no longer account for the stylized facts of the post–Bretton Woods policy regime, IS-LM fell into disfavor. Apart from the Japanese anomaly, where does that leave IS-LM as we enter the twenty-first century? It may be helpful here to consider three different monetary policy regimes, each with a peculiar asymmetry: a monetary base feedback rule, the "Taylor rule," and the international gold standard.

Bennett McCallum (1984) proposed a monetary policy rule where the monetary base would be periodically adjusted to offset fluctuations in base velocity—with the policy goal being stable growth in nominal GDP. The Taylor rule has a broadly similar policy goal but employs a nominal interest rate feedback rule. Above-target price and output growth triggers higher nominal interest rates, and vice versa.

The international gold standard is often thought of as an automatic system where independent monetary policy is an impossibility. This is not an accurate description of the operation of real-world gold standards with large central banks. During the latter part of the international gold standard, monetary policy could be viewed as a change in a central bank's demand for monetary gold stocks. Increases in monetary gold demand reduced the money supply and were deflationary. Decreases in monetary gold demand had the opposite effect.

The preceding three policy regimes all include a specific type of asymmetry. Under a McCallum-type monetary feedback rule, the monetary base cannot fall below zero, but there are no obvious upper limits to monetary expansion. For the Taylor rule, nominal interest rates cannot fall below zero, but again there is no upward limit. And under a gold standard regime, the monetary demand for gold cannot fall below zero, but again there is no obvious upper limit—gold demand is limited only by the fiscal resources of the government making the purchases.

Although all of the preceding asymmetries have a superficial similarity, in practice they have quite different implications. As the famous "pushing on a string" metaphor suggests, doubts about the effectiveness of monetary policy almost always occur with respect to expansionary monetary policy, not contractionary policy. In this context, it is interesting to note that the monetary base feedback rule only has a constraint (if one can call it that) that sets zero as the minimum level for the money stock. In contrast, the asymmetry embedded in the Taylor rule may limit the potential for an expansionary monetary policy. This distinction is, of course, widely understood. It is why monetarists generally don't worry about monetary policy ineffectiveness. What may be less well understood is the similarity between the asymmetries of the Taylor rule and the gold standard.

Because monetary gold stocks cannot fall below zero, there is also an upward limit on the potential expansiveness of the monetary policy of a central bank operating under the constraints of a gold standard regime. Conceptually, the constraints imposed on policy by the Taylor rule have nothing to do with those imposed by a fixed exchange rate regime like the gold standard. But it seems that these constraints may have become mixed up in many people's minds, perhaps to the detriment of monetary theory and policy. Ironically, the IS-LM approach, which is basically a gold standard model, reached its greatest popularity just before the (gold-based) Bretton Woods system was replaced with a set of freely floating fiat currencies.

Beginning in the 1980s, many central banks have been able to create an environment of low and stable inflation. King (1993) showed, however, that even in this environment there are important conceptual problems with the way IS-LM treats expectations, but it at least allowed for a revival of interest rate targeting. Ironically, the success of the Federal Reserve in reducing inflation during the (1979–82) money targeting period helped lay the groundwork for a policy regime based on a modified IS-LM model, with Taylor-type rules for interest rate targeting. Many new Keynesians are still attracted to monetary models where the interest rate is the key indicator of monetary policy. Because monetary policy ineffectiveness is not a particularly attractive concept in a fiat money regime, however, these newer versions of IS-LM may owe more to the work of Wicksell than that of Keynes.[29]

To summarize, the traditional IS-LM model has severe conceptual flaws, particularly in how it treats monetary policy. Yet its powerful pedagogical appeal allows it to remain an important analytic tool during periods when its "commonsense" interpretation seems to conform to events

29. Michael Woodford (2003) refers to his own recent theoretical work as a "neo-Wicksellian framework." Nelson (this volume) provides a good discussion of recent optimizing IS-LM models that eliminate many of the defects identified by King (1993).

in the real world. It is not surprising that any macro model is likely to be most popular when the "issues of the day" are most easily visualized through that framework. In the current low inflation environment, the IS-LM approach still has some appeal. Because it is easy to visualize the effect of monetary policy with an interest rate transmission mechanism, IS-LM continues to be used in many college textbooks, and it also underlies most news analysis of the economy. And the recent events in Japan testify to the enduring appeal of notions of monetary policy ineffectiveness. Unfortunately for the proponents of IS-LM, it is a fragile model, with weaknesses that become apparent whenever one moves very far from the conditions experienced by the major economies during the first two-thirds of the twentieth century.

References

Barro, Robert. 1979. Money and the Price Level under the Gold Standard. *Economic Journal* 89.353:13–33.

———. 1994. *Macroeconomics*. 4th ed. New York: John Wiley.

Barsky, Robert B. 1987. The Fisher Hypothesis and the Forecastability and Persistence of Inflation. *Journal of Monetary Economics* 19.1:3–24.

Bernanke, Ben S. 1995. The Macroeconomics of the Great Depression: A Comparative Approach. *Journal of Money, Credit, and Banking* 27.1:1–28.

Blanchard, Olivier. 2000. What Do We Know about Macroeconomics That Wicksell and Fisher Did Not? *Quarterly Journal of Economics* 115.4:1375–409.

Brunner, Karl. 1981. Understanding the Great Depression. In *The Great Depression Revisited*, edited by Karl Brunner. The Hague: Martinus Nijhoff.

Currie, Lauchlin. [1934] 1935. *The Supply and Control of Money in the United States*. Cambridge: Harvard University Press.

De Vroey, Michel. 2000. IS-LM à la Hicks versus IS-LM à la Modigliani. *HOPE* 32.2:293–316.

Dimand, Robert W. 2000. Irving Fisher and the Quantity Theory of Money: The Last Phase. *Journal of the History of Economic Thought* 22.3:329–48.

Eltis, Walter. 1995. John Locke, the Quantity Theory of Money, and the Establishment of a Sound Currency. In *The Quantity Theory of Money*. Brookfield, Vt.: Edward Elgar.

Fisher, Irving. 1920. *Stabilizing the Dollar: A Plan to Stabilize the Price Level without Fixing Individual Prices*. New York: Macmillan.

———. 1923. The Business Cycle Largely a "Dance of the Dollar." *Journal of the American Statistical Association* 18.144:1024–28.

Friedman, Milton. 1968. The Role of Monetary Policy. *American Economic Review* 58.1:1–17.

————. 1974. Comments on the Critics. In *Milton Friedman's Monetary Framework: A Debate with His Critics*, edited by Robert J. Gordon. Chicago: University of Chicago Press.

————. 1975. Twenty-Five Years after the Rediscovery of Money: What Have We Learned?—a Discussion. *American Economic Review* 65.2:176–79.

Friedman, Milton, and Anna J. Schwartz. 1963. *A Monetary History of the United States: 1867–1960*. Princeton, N.J.: Princeton University Press.

Glasner, David. 2000. Classical Monetary Theory and the Quantity Theory. *HOPE* 32.1:39–59.

Gordon, Robert. 2000. *Macroeconomics*. 8th ed. Reading, Mass.: Addison Wesley Longman.

Greenfield, Robert L., and Leland B. Yeager. 1983. A Laissez-Faire Approach to Monetary Stability. *Journal of Money, Credit, and Banking* 15.3:302–15.

Hall, Robert E., and N. Gregory Mankiw. 1994. Nominal Income Targeting. In *Monetary Policy*, edited by N. Gregory Mankiw. Chicago: University of Chicago Press.

Hanes, Christopher. 1996. Changes in the Cyclical Behavior of Real Wage Rates, 1870–1990. *Journal of Economic History* 54.4:317–37.

Hicks, John R. 1937. Mr. Keynes and the "Classics": A Suggested Interpretation. *Econometrica* 5:147–59.

Hume, David. [1752] 1970. Of Money. In *David Hume: Writings on Economics*, edited by Eugene Rotwein. Madison: University of Wisconsin Press.

Jonung, Lars. 1988. Knut Wicksell's Unpublished Manuscripts—a First Glance. *European Economic Review* 32.2–3:503–11.

Keynes, John M. 1911. Review of Irving Fisher: *The Purchasing Power of Money*. *Economic Journal* 21:393–98.

————. 1923. *A Tract on Monetary Reform*. London: Macmillan.

————. 1930. *A Treatise on Money*. London: Macmillan.

————. [1936] 1964. *The General Theory of Employment, Interest, and Money*. New York: Harcourt, Brace & World.

————. [1933] 1982. *The Collected Writings of John Maynard Keynes*. Vol. 21. Edited by Donald Moggridge. Cambridge: Cambridge University Press.

King, Robert G. 1993. Will the New Keynesian Macroeconomics Resurrect the IS-LM Model? *Journal of Economic Perspectives* 7.1:67–82.

Klein, Benjamin. 1975. Our New Monetary Standard: The Measurement and Effects of Price Uncertainty, 1880–1973. *Economic Inquiry* 13:461–84.

Laidler, David. 1991. *The Golden Age of the Quantity Theory*. Princeton, N.J.: Princeton University Press.

————. 1999. *Fabricating the Keynesian Revolution*. Cambridge: Cambridge University Press.

Lucas, Robert. 1976. Econometric Policy Evaluation: A Critique. *Carnegie-Rochester Conference Series* 1:19–46.

McCallum, Bennett T. 1984. Monetarist Rules in the Light of Recent Experiences. *American Economic Review* 74.2:388–91.

————. 2002. Recent Developments in Monetary Policy Analysis: The Roles of Theory and Evidence. *Federal Reserve Bank of Richmond, Economic Quarterly* 88.1:67–96.

Meltzer, Allan. 1988. *Keynes's Monetary Theory: A Different Interpretation.* Cambridge: Cambridge University Press.

————. 1995. Monetary, Credit, (and Other) Transmission Processes: A Monetarist Perspective. *Journal of Economic Perspectives* 9.4:49–72.

Modigliani, Franco. 1944. Liquidity Preference and the Theory of Interest and Money. *Econometrica* 12.1:45–88.

Moggridge, Donald E., and Susan Howson. 1974. Keynes on Monetary Policy, 1910–1946. *Oxford Economic Papers* 26.2:226–47.

Mundell, Robert A. 2000. A Reconsideration of the Twentieth Century. *American Economic Review* 90.3:327–40.

Nelson, Edward. 2002. Direct Effects of Base Money on Aggregate Demand: Theory and Evidence. *Journal of Monetary Economics* 49.4:687–708.

Phelps, E. S. 1967. Phillips Curves, Expectations of Inflation, and Optimal Unemployment over Time. *Economica* 34.135:254–81.

Roberts, M. 1995. Keynes, the Liquidity Trap, and the Gold Standard: A Possible Application of the Rational Expectations Hypothesis. *Manchester School of Economic and Social Studies* 63.1:82–92.

Steindl, Frank G. 2000. Fisher's Last Stand on the Quantity Theory: The Role of Money in the Recovery. *Journal of the History of Economic Thought* 22.4:493–98.

Sumner, Scott. 1997. News, Financial Markets, and the Collapse of the Gold Standard, 1931–1932. *Research in Economic History* 17:39–84.

————. 1999. The Role of the Gold Standard in Keynesian Monetary Theory. *Economic Inquiry* 37.3:527–40.

————. 2001. Roosevelt, Warren, and the Gold-Buying Program of 1933. *Research in Economic History* 20:135–72.

————. 2003. Does Monetary Policy Become More Desirable as It Becomes Less Effective? *Economics Letters* 88.1:125–28.

————. 2004. Exchange Rate Crises and U.S. Financial Markets during the 1930s. In *Exchange Rate Regimes and Economic Policy in the Twentieth Century*, edited by Ross Catterall and Derek H. Aldcroft. Aldershot, U.K.: Ashgate.

Svensson, Lars E. O. 1997. Inflation Forecast Targeting: Implementing and Monitoring Inflation Targets. *European Economic Review* 41.6:1111–46.

Tavlas, George S. 1981. Keynes on Monetary Theory and Policy: Reply. *Southern Economic Journal* 47.4:1137–42.

Wicksell, Knut. 1907. The Influence of the Rate of Interest on Prices. *Economic Journal* 17.66:213–20.

Woodford, Michael. 2003. *Interest and Prices: Foundations of a Theory of Monetary Policy.* Princeton, N.J.: Princeton University Press.

Money and the Transmission Mechanism in the Optimizing IS-LM Specification

Edward Nelson

Macroeconomic discussions in the 1980s and 1990s frequently concluded that traditional IS-LM analysis was flawed, in ways that made it irreconcilable with modern macroeconomic theory. A. J. Policano (1985, 396), for example, contended that "the current research approach casts serious doubt on models . . . where the IS/LM framework forms the basis of the demand-side," while J. D. Hamilton (1989, 113) characterized modern economic theory as being conducted "in a general equilibrium setting that seems far removed from IS-LM." The last few years, however, have seen significant dissension from these conclusions,[1] with W. Kerr and R. G. King (1996), J. J. Rotemberg and M. Woodford (1997), and Bennett McCallum and Edward Nelson (1999a) offering small-scale macroeconomic models that are grounded in optimizing behavior but are similar in spirit to the IS-LM approach. In particular, my 1999 paper with Bennett McCallum labeled the "optimizing IS-LM specification" a pair of equations for aggregate demand behavior, which we derived from a dynamic stochastic general equilibrium model.

This essay discusses criticisms of the IS-LM framework in the macroeconomic literature of the last forty years and how the modern optimizing

I am grateful to Michael Artis, Jason Buol, Charles Goodhart, Kevin Hoover, Peter Ireland, David Laidler, Bennett McCallum, Allan Meltzer, two anonymous referees, and participants at the 2003 *HOPE* conference for helpful comments and discussions. The views expressed in this essay should not be interpreted as those of the Federal Reserve Bank of St. Louis or the Federal Reserve System.

1. An early dissent was that of Stanley Fischer (1987, 247): "There is no necessary inconsistency between IS-LM type models and maximizing models." See also footnote 6.

version addresses those criticisms. For concreteness, however, I offer the following definition of an IS-LM system, which guides the discussion in the rest of the essay. A macroeconomic analysis follows an IS-LM approach if the model's structure includes two equations (which in general will be both dynamic and stochastic): an equation describing aggregate real spending behavior in terms of financial variables; and a money demand equation relating the real quantity of money demanded to scale and opportunity-cost variables. This definition is sufficiently strict to rule out many macroeconomic systems. True, as Karl Brunner and Allan Meltzer (1993, 78) note, "any system of $n > 2$ equations involving an interest rate and output can be reduced to two equations," one of which describes the demand for output; but my definition of IS-LM requires that an IS relation for total output is presented *explicitly*. I do not require that only a single interest rate appear in the IS equation, but I do exclude analyses where the only description of aggregate demand behavior is as a disaggregated block of equations for separate expenditure categories. Thus none of the following qualify as having IS-LM features by my criterion: textbook models of the Keynesian multiplier that separate consumption from investment spending, highly disaggregated macroeconometric models, and most general equilibrium models.[2]

The emphasis on model structure in this definition also implies that I treat "IS-LM" as a pair of equations intended by their user to be policy invariant (i.e., the elasticities can be held constant while treating alternative monetary policies). These equations are silent on whether prices are sticky, flexible, or fully rigid, and on whether monetary policy uses the nominal interest rate or the nominal money stock as its policy instrument. Those issues depend instead on the specification in the model of the economy's price-adjustment equation (Phillips curve) and of monetary policy behavior. Reduced-form representations for output and money balances obtainable after imposing the assumption of a particular monetary policy rule or price-setting behavior are not IS-LM equations by my criterion.

With this definition in mind, consider the pair of equations regarded by McCallum and Nelson (1999a, 297) as representative of "traditional" IS-LM analysis. Suppressing constants (or, equivalently, regarding real

2. For example, T. J. Sargent's (1987, chap. 2) exposition of the aggregate demand side of the "Keynesian model" as a system of consumption and investment equations would not qualify as IS-LM analysis as defined here, but his subsequent approach of "collapsing [the equations] into a system of two equations in [output] and [interest rates] . . . by substitution" (53) does fall into the IS-LM framework.

variables as expressed in deviations from their steady-state values), these equations are:

$$y_t = b_1 r_t + v_t \tag{1}$$

$$m_t - p_t = c_1 y_t + c_2 R_t + \eta_t, \tag{2}$$

where y_t is log output, m_t is the log nominal money stock, p_t is the log price level, R_t is the nominal short-term interest rate on securities, and r_t is the corresponding real rate:

$$r_t = R_t - E_t \pi_{t+1}, \tag{3}$$

where π_t is the inflation rate (defined as $\pi_t = p_t - p_{t-1}$), and $E_t[\bullet]$ denotes the rational expectation based on period-t information. Finally, v_t and η_t are exogenous disturbances, and the parameters satisfy $b_1 < 0, c_1 > 0, c_2 < 0$. My discussion focuses on cases in which R_t is above zero and accompanied by a value of c_2 that is finite in absolute value. These assumptions ensure that central bank actions that raise the nominal money stock will be effective in expanding nominal aggregate demand. This perspective on IS-LM, which regards the "liquidity trap" only as a degenerate special case rather than the center of the analysis, is, as Michel De Vroey (2000) stresses, very much an inheritance from the development of IS-LM analysis by Franco Modigliani (1944).[3]

McCallum and I argued that formal analysis using a dynamic stochastic general equilibrium model justified a log-linear IS-LM formulation with the money demand equation unchanged from equation (2), and with the IS equation (1) modified to:

$$y_t = b_1 r_t + E_t y_{t+1} + v_t. \tag{4}$$

Other work using optimizing analysis has justified variants of equation (4),[4] but formulation (4) is probably the most commonly used version of the optimizing IS equation in the literature.[5] The recent IS-LM revival

3. Samuelson (1976) argues that such a perspective is "contrary to the view of 1939 Keynesians and the stubborn 1959 view of many English economists." The "stubborn 1959 view" is that of the Radcliffe Committee report (1959), whose position I discuss in detail in section 3.

4. For example, Kerr and King (1996) and Woodford (1996) use variants of equation (4) with no IS shock, while Rotemberg and Woodford (1997) have a more complicated setup in which decision lags matter for spending decisions, implying that the previous period's expectations of variables appear in the IS equation.

5. The usual caveat about deducing the chronology of research from publication dates applies with force to the optimizing IS-LM literature. My 1999 paper with McCallum, for example, was released as an NBER Working Paper in 1997 and circulated in 1996 in manuscript form (with one such version cited in Fuhrer 1997). Both Kerr and King (1996) and McCallum

has followed E. F. Koenig (1989, 1993a, 1993b) in building an aggregate IS equation from the standard Euler optimality condition for consumption that appears in forward-looking models and in stressing that the effect of optimizing behavior is to make current spending decisions depend on expected future output.[6] This is evident from the fact that the only modification of the traditional IS equation (1) produced by the explicit maximizing analysis is the introduction of the $E_t y_{t+1}$ term (with unit coefficient).

The above definitions of the IS-LM framework—traditional and optimizing—have a material effect on the coverage of this essay. My focus on IS-LM as a description of aggregate demand significantly departs from King's (2000) discussion of "the new IS-LM model: language, logic, and limits." King (2000, 48) defines the "new IS-LM model" as the combination of the optimizing IS-LM specification (2)–(4) and a forward-looking "New Keynesian Phillips curve." Accordingly, King's discussion focuses on price-setting behavior in new Keynesian models, and on the policy recommendations that arise from the combined IS-LM/Phillips curve setup. Since my IS-LM definition is silent on the specification of the Phillips curve, a focus on price-setting behavior is not germane to my discussion of the optimizing IS-LM apparatus. And while the policy implications of modern optimizing models form an important issue, almost all of those that King draws from the modern model arise from his *Phillips curve* specification rather than the new aspects of the optimizing IS-LM specification. Therefore, policy recommendations play only a minor role in my discussion of IS-LM in this essay.[7]

---

and Nelson (1999a) give as their source for the derivation of the IS function McCallum 1995, which is composed of 1994 lecture notes.

6. Beside Koenig's contribution, other 1980s work should be noted. G. Fane's (1985) "derivation of the IS-LM model from explicit optimizing behavior," S. R. Aiyagari and M. Gertler's (1985, 41) "intertemporal . . . flexible price IS-LM model," and N. Rankin's (1987, 66) " 'choice-theoretic' IS-LM model" all feature relations labeled *IS-LM* obtained from finite-horizon (overlapping generations) optimizing models. In all cases, the relation labeled *IS* includes endogenous variables beside output and interest rates, and so its applicability is limited mainly to comparative-static exercises.

7. The IS-LM side of a model does have a significant impact on the choice between interest rate and money growth rules, as Poole (1970) showed. But while Poole's analysis has been generalized in several directions—for example, to include a variable price level, an output/output-gap distinction, and interest-rate feedback rules—these extensions mainly involve changes to the aggregate supply and policy-rule specifications, so the advent of the optimizing IS-LM equation does not make a critical difference to Poole's results. One basis on which Brunner and Meltzer (1993) questioned Poole's results, namely, the dependence on the IS-LM's two-asset structure, is related to the discussion in section 3.

My focus is instead on the transmission mechanism in the optimizing IS-LM specification—the role that this aggregate demand specification plays in governing the response of prices and output to monetary policy actions and real shocks—and how this mechanism compares to that in traditional IS-LM work. A convenient way of organizing the analysis is to follow one aspect of the discussion in McCallum and Nelson 1999a. Relative to other discussions of optimizing models for monetary policy, our paper had the distinguishing feature of an explicit comparison of the optimizing IS-LM specification with traditional IS-LM approaches. Our aim was to separate valid from invalid criticisms of older IS-LM work and, in so doing, to obtain a modern version of IS-LM less susceptible to the earlier criticisms. In that light, we considered a list of six key criticisms of traditional IS-LM analysis. With the order rearranged, the six objections to IS-LM in the literature that we contemplated were:

1. IS-LM analysis presumes a fixed, rigid price level.
2. It does not distinguish between real and nominal interest rates.
3. It permits only short-run analysis.
4. It treats the capital stock as fixed.
5. It does not recognize enough distinct assets.
6. It is not derivable from explicit maximizing analysis of rational economic agents.

In our discussion of these criticisms, McCallum's and my coverage of the IS-LM literature was necessarily brief, given the other objectives of our paper. In the present essay, I provide a far more in-depth discussion of each criticism, and a more detailed analysis of the relationship between traditional IS-LM and the optimizing IS-LM specification.[8] On criticisms (1) and (2), discussed in section 1, I examine several issues not covered by McCallum and Nelson 1999a, including the integration of price-level analysis into the IS-LM paradigm. On issues (3) and (4), which are the subject of section 2, I discuss a variety of claims in the literature made about IS-LM dynamics. In section 3, which covers issues (5) and (6), I provide a detailed discussion of the large monetarist literature criticizing IS-LM. This literature was only briefly discussed in McCallum and Nelson 1999a; the analysis here offers a much more thorough treatment of the issue, building on the comparison that I presented

---

8. Because it does not form part of the list that McCallum and I developed, I have little to say about the issue of whether traditional IS-LM analysis accurately reflected Keynes's *General Theory* (on which see, e.g., Patinkin 1990, Darity and Young 1995, and De Vroey 2000).

in Nelson 2003 of the monetarist literature with the optimizing IS-LM approach. I draw conclusions about the merits of the monetarist structure in light of both empirical evidence and modern optimizing macroeconomic theory.

Throughout the essay, my discussion draws on sources not used by McCallum and Nelson, including much archival material not available until recently. For example, several Federal Reserve banks, including Minneapolis, Richmond, and St. Louis, now provide on their Web sites the historical back runs of their working papers and journal publications, including material published during the debates in the 1960s and 1970s on rational expectations, monetarism, and the microfoundations of macroeconomics. This material, which is typically not stored by economics libraries, contains many discussions of IS-LM relevant to this essay. In addition, in discussing the monetarist criticism of IS-LM, I make use of Brunner's position papers during 1973–87 for the Shadow Open Market Committee, many of which were never reprinted in journals or collections. I also draw on contributions by Milton Friedman and Paul Samuelson to magazines like *Newsweek* and the *Economist*. This material supplements the academic debate on monetarist views of the transmission mechanism, and a substantial portion of it has never been reprinted.

1. Objections (1) and (2): "IS-LM analysis presumes a fixed, rigid price level" and "It does not distinguish between real and nominal interest rates"

The first criticism of IS-LM that I discuss, namely that "IS-LM analysis presumes a fixed, rigid price level," has appeared frequently in both textbooks and journals. McCallum and I rejected it as a valid criticism. The basis for this rejection is implicit in the definition of IS-LM that I presented in the introduction. As stressed there and also in J. M. Johannes's (1980) defense of IS-LM, the IS-LM framework describes the *aggregate demand* portion of a macroeconomic model and does not, by itself, constitute a complete model of the behavior of money, output, prices, and the nominal interest rate.

It is true that John Hicks's (1937) original derivation of his "IS-LL" curves was under the assumption of fully rigid nominal wages, while even some modern textbook treatments (e.g., Auerbach and Kotlikoff

1995, 314) give the impression that the derivation of IS and LM relations requires the assumption of a rigid price level. But analysis of the flexible-price (and wage) equilibrium was an important element of the IS-LM analysis of Franco Modigliani (1944), Lloyd Metzler (1951), and Don Patinkin (1951); and, incorporating these developments, sophisticated use of IS and LM equations from the 1950s onward was compatible with various assumptions about price adjustment. The use of IS-LM diagrams, as opposed to equations, may involve more restrictive assumptions, but even so (as I argue in section 2), these restrictions are essentially restrictions on the dynamics of the IS and LM relations rather than assumptions about nominal inflexibility.[9]

The fact that both flexible-price and sticky-price IS-LM variants existed by the 1950s need not necessarily invalidate another allegation made about traditional IS-LM analysis, namely, that "one of the most significant weaknesses of the simple IS-LM framework is that prices and output cannot change simultaneously" (Policano 1977, 233). But again, such a criticism seems misplaced. If valid, it would imply that IS-LM analysis is inconsistent with an upward-sloping aggregate supply curve. Such a curve implies short-run reactions of both prices and output to monetary policy actions and is consistent with both Phillips curve analysis and Lucas 1973–style aggregate supply functions. Since, as argued above, algebraic representations of IS-LM *are* consistent with various Phillips curve specifications, Policano's criticism is invalid for IS-LM *equations*. A. Vercelli (1999, 206) dates the use of Phillips curve specifications in combination with IS-LM to the late 1960s, and an early example is Sargent 1972. Perhaps Policano's criticism is intended more to apply to IS-LM *diagrams*. It is certainly easier to represent models with more than two-period dynamics in difference equations than in diagrams, and I do not advocate the use of IS-LM diagrammatic analysis. But it is notable that Robert Lucas (1973, 327) certainly regarded the "standard IS-LM diagram" as consistent with an upward-sloping aggregate supply curve, and derivations of this have become commonplace in textbooks.[10]

9. The discussion of Solow (1984, 16–18) does appear to presume that some kind of wage-stickiness assumption is necessary in drawing the LM curve. Closer to the spirit of the present treatment is his statement that for analyzing macroeconomic behavior in conditions of variable wages and prices, "IS-LM is . . . only part of the right model" (17).

10. Lucas (1973, 327) noted that an "explicit derivation of the price-output relationship from the IS-LM framework is given by Frederic [actually, Fredric] Raines" in an unpublished 1971 manuscript.

The allegation that the IS-LM specification confuses nominal and real interest rates is closely related to how suitable IS-LM analysis is in situations of a variable price level. The nominal/real rate distinction is one that arises when price-level movements take the form not just of once-and-for-all shifts but of more pervasive movements that lead to fluctuations in the private sector's anticipations of future inflation. It is therefore a distinction essential for the analysis of realistic monetary-policy and price-setting rules. T. Mayer (1972, 541) notes that "the IS-LM diagram fails to distinguish between real and nominal interest rates," but this criticism of the IS-LM diagram does not carry through to algebraic versions of IS-LM, which either in their traditional form of equations (1) and (3) or in the optimizing form of equations (2) and (4) easily allow for the nominal/real rate distinction. Even graphic representations of IS-LM dynamics can be generalized to distinguish between nominal and real interest rates (Bailey 1962; Mundell 1963; Patinkin 1990, 129–32), although the vertical axis must then keep track of two distinct rates.

E. M. Leeper and C. A. Sims (1994, 84) make a more serious allegation than Mayer, arguing that even the algebraic form of IS-LM does not recognize the Fisher relation. Their contention is that "the general equilibrium versions of Keynesian models . . . usually fall back on the IS-LM framework, without even a clear distinction of real and nominal interest rates." It is true that algebraic versions of the IS-LM model appeared in journals well into the late 1970s that held the price level constant both in the short and the long run, and also treated nominal and real interest rates as identical (e.g., Van Order 1978). But the best practice had an "IS-LM framework in which the demand for money balances is affected by nominal interest rates and the demand for goods by real interest rates" (Bean 1983, 813). Even Karl Brunner, a strong critic of the specification of assets in IS-LM analysis (see section 3), acknowledged in 1980 that "standard Keynesian analysis assigns different interest rates to the IS and LM relation" (1980, 11). Not only was such a specification—real rates mattering for output demand, nominal rates for the opportunity cost of holding real money[11]—standard by 1980, it seems to me the only defensible formulation and continues today in the optimizing IS-LM specification.

---

11. I consider in section 3 the important question of whether the only rates in the IS and LM relations should be short-term rates on financial securities.

There is therefore no inconsistency between IS-LM analysis and modeling the price level, inflation, and expected inflation endogenously. While assumptions about wage behavior did underlie the early work of Hicks (1937), IS-LM analysis per se does not rely on restrictive assumptions about wage or price-setting behavior. Accordingly, criticisms that IS-LM analysis presumes a fixed, rigid price level, and does not distinguish between nominal and real interest rates, are invalid. Both best-practice algebraic work with traditional IS-LM equations and the modern optimizing IS-LM specification allow for the price level to be variable and endogenously determined by the interaction of the model's IS-LM block with the monetary policy rule and the Phillips curve.

2. Objections (3) and (4): "It permits only short-run analysis" and "It treats the capital stock as fixed"

Let me first discuss the criticism that IS-LM "permits only short-run analysis." Influenced by the pioneering work of Hicks (1937), which in Robert M. Solow's (1984, 16) words took "the IS and LM curves to refer to a unit period within which the nominal wage could be taken as fixed," some interpreters of the IS-LM framework have regarded it as suitable for analysis of only the short-run effects of policy actions and of private-sector shocks. Vercelli (1999, 210), for example, observes that "the assumption of the short period, typical of first-generation IS-LM models, implies that the model cannot be applied to too long a series of data (exceeding, say, one year)."

As we have seen, however, the presumption that IS-LM analysis relies on an assumption of rigid nominal wages or prices is misplaced. Accordingly, both applications of the traditional IS-LM specification, such as Sargent 1972, and the optimizing IS-LM specification of today, are intended to cover periods during which nominal variables adjust. McCallum and I viewed the optimizing IS-LM specification as "designed for quarterly time series data over sample periods of many years' duration (for example, ten to fifty years)" (1999a, 299) and, consistent with this perspective, later (1999b) estimated the IS-LM system (2) and (4) on U.S. quarterly data for 1955–96. Accompanied by some version of an expectations-augmented Phillips curve, the resulting system has properties that make it reasonable for monetary policy analysis on quarterly data. For example, a permanent, exogenous increase in the nominal money stock leads in these models to effects of monetary policy on output and the real interest rate wearing off over time, but has a permanent and equal percentage effect on nominal money balances and prices.[12]

The distinction between short-run nonneutrality and long-run monetary neutrality is, however, a weak requirement of the IS-LM framework and does not absolve it from criticism on other dynamic grounds. IS-LM could be judged inadequate on criteria that relate to its applicability to intertemporal decisions regarding real resources. James Tobin (1979, 218), for example, argues that "the common IS/LM apparatus" has a "temporary and short-run character," owing to the absence of asset stocks from the IS and LM functions. In his words: "The only precise way to justify the Keynesian procedure is to regard the IS/LM model as determining the values of variables at a point in time. Then this model must be regarded as a slice, in time of measure zero, of a continuous-time dynamic model" (219). A harsher judgment along the same lines has been made by N. A. Wallace (1980, 70), who contends that "the macroeconomic paradigm that flows from Keynes['s] (1936) *General Theory* via Hicks (1937) consist[s] of nothing more than interpreting each term in a time series as the outcome of a separate, static, nonstochastic experiment."

In judging the validity of these criticisms, it is important to distinguish saving and investment decisions. First, consider saving decisions. The traditional IS-LM framework typically builds up to an output-demand equation from a postulated consumption function like equation (7) below. Such a specification typically cannot be justified rigorously from a household problem of utility maximization subject to an intertemporal wealth constraint. Therefore, from the perspective of modern macroeconomics, traditional IS-LM is guilty of inadequate recognition of intertemporal issues. This criticism, however, does not apply to the optimizing IS-LM specification. This specification bases its IS equation on a household consumption Euler equation like equation (8) below. Such a condition arises from an explicit household dynamic optimization problem and so does recognize intertemporal issues rigorously. Accordingly, the optimizing IS equation does not rest on the point-in-time

12. The effect on the nominal interest rate is also temporary but would be permanent if the shock type was changed to one that permanently raises nominal money *growth*. In that case, inflation, anticipated inflation, and (via the Fisher effect) the nominal interest rate would be increased permanently. The framework therefore captures the phenomenon mentioned by King (1993, 77–78).

interpretation given by Tobin above. Instead, it can be used as a description of decades of quarterly data.

Tobin's message that an IS curve *diagram*, plotting output against the real interest rate, entails a suppression of dynamics and does carry through to the optimizing version of the IS curve. To express equation (4) in a two-dimensional diagram, one must suppress not asset stocks but the expectation of future output. A diagrammatic representation must assume that expected output is constant; or, better, the behavior of expected future output should guide the drawing of the slope of the IS curve; or, best of all, the "interest rate" on the vertical axis of the plot should not be the current real short-term rate but instead a long average of current and expected future real short rates.[13] The complications involved, however, reaffirm that for analysis of modern models, difference equations like (4) are more flexible tools than diagrams. Now consider the modeling of investment. Here, Tobin's stress on the absence of asset stocks from the IS equation becomes relevant. While an infinite-horizon optimizing model actually provides justification for the exclusion of explicit asset-stock terms from the consumption equation, investment decisions are another matter. There is an undeniable connection between the physical capital stock and investment, and so, in principle, the capital stock should be a state variable that appears in the economy's aggregate IS equation. Nevertheless, McCallum and Nelson (1999a) argued that, as an approximation, the role of the capital stock can be neglected in deriving an IS equation for monetary policy and business cycle analysis. B. Dupor (2001) criticizes our advocacy of this approximation. After quoting from our argument, Dupor (2001, 107) argues that we miss "the overwhelming rationale for modeling investment—investment is a significant fraction of GDP. The fact that quarterly investment is more than four times as volatile as consumption in the post-war U.S. [data] provides ample motivation for modeling investment!"

Neither of the arguments in the quotation from Dupor's paper justifies his conclusion that investment should be modeled endogenously. First, note that a log-linearized resource constraint for a closed private economy is

$$y_t = s_c c_t + s_i i_t, \tag{5}$$

---

13. Solving equation (4) forward reveals that output can be written as a function of current and expected real short rates if the IS shock is held constant.

where s_c and s_i are steady state shares of consumption and investment in GDP, and c_t and i_t represent log-deviations in the time series of consumption and investment from their trend values. With equation (5) as one building block, several derivations of the traditional IS equation (1) are possible. One approach, as in Martin Bailey's *National Income and the Price Level* (1962, 29–32), is to assume that the consumption function has income as its sole argument, while the assumed investment function has the real interest rate as its sole argument. But an alternative derivation, which is somewhat closer in spirit to the approach underlying the optimizing IS equation (4), is to start from a consumption function like

$$c_t = b_c r_t + b_y y_t + e_{ct}, \tag{6}$$

where $b_c < 0$, $b_y \geq 0$, and e_{ct} is an exogenous term. The IS equation (1) then emerges by postulating that it is valid to model investment as though it is not a separate expenditure category.[14] This amounts to the assumption that $i_t = \gamma c_t + e_{it}$, where $\gamma > 0$ and e_{it} is a stationary exogenous shock process. Note that this assumption neither denies that s_i in equation (5) is large (and so is in complete agreement with the empirical regularity that Dupor argues is the "overwhelming rationale" for modeling investment explicitly), nor that that investment is highly volatile. Furthermore, setting a value of γ greater than 1.0 generates an IS equation that satisfies the property that investment is more volatile than consumption. Such a parameter choice would also imply that investment is more interest elastic than consumption. One could alternatively keep total output at the same interest-elasticity as consumption spending while making investment volatile, by setting γ to unity and the variance of the investment shock e_{it} to a high value.

McCallum and I started instead from the optimization-based consumption equation,

$$c_t = b_c r_t + E_t c_{t+1} + e_{ct}, \tag{7}$$

and proposed a specification of investment behavior slightly more general than that above. Specifically, we proposed $i_t = \gamma c_t + e_{it} + \xi_t$, where ξ_t is an exogenous random walk. Positive values for s_i, γ, and

14. Although not allowed for in Bailey's derivation, the dependence of consumption on the interest rate appeared early in U.S. developments of Keynesian theory; see, for example, Darity and Young 1995, 37, and B. Friedman 1976, 355. McCallum 1989, 78–82, is an example of a textbook presentation that derives a relation like (1) in a manner similar to that described here.

the variances of the e_{it} and ξ_t innovation processes can all be permitted, and all lead—when combined with equations (5) and (7)—to the aggregate IS equation (4). Thus, both in traditional IS-LM analysis and the optimizing version, the restrictions imposed on the treatment of investment are consistent with volatile and cyclical investment behavior. In addition, with the optimizing IS-LM specification, using the household consumption condition to model the whole of private aggregate demand captures the forward-looking nature of investment.

The decision underlying IS-LM analysis not to treat investment completely endogenously is, therefore, perfectly consistent with a recognition of the contribution of investment to aggregate demand fluctuations, and of the interest elastic character of investment. As Tobin (1979) noted, what is being suppressed is not investment variation but, instead, the connection between investment and the capital stock. Such an abstraction, however, seems to be an innocuous assumption for the purposes of monetary policy and business cycle analysis. As McCallum and I observed, the capital stock is empirically an acyclical variable, so it remains valid to treat it as constant (or growing smoothly) even while recognizing that investment is both volatile and cyclical. A typical quarter or year's investment has such a small impact on the total stock of physical capital that the link between the two series can be neglected. None of this is to deny that, in a study of economic growth, recognition of the endogeneity of the capital stock is mandatory. But for the study of monetary policy issues, it seems legitimate to neglect the connections between investment and the supply side in specifying the aggregate demand side of the model while taking potential GDP as an exogenous process that appears in the economy's Phillips curve.

A different criticism of the treatment of dynamics in IS-LM specifications that has appeared in the literature is that IS-LM ignores not the long run but the short run. Such a perspective appears to be the basis for P. H. Hendershott and G. Horwich's (1974, 389) statement that "the IS-LM schedules cannot provide a framework for dynamic analysis because they implicitly assume that total income supplied and demanded are always equal."[15] I would argue, however, that Hendershott and Horwich's criticism is misplaced. An analysis in which the goods market clears every period, or, equivalently, there is continuous intersection of

15. This perspective may also have motivated Modigliani's (1944, 46) statement, prior to presenting his prototype IS-LM analysis, that his model was "concerned with the determinants of equilibrium and not with the explanation of business cycles."

the aggregate demand and aggregate supply curves, in no way implies the absence of dynamics. In the case in which IS-LM is supplemented by an augmented Phillips curve, dynamics—in the sense of protracted deviations of output and the real interest rate from their flexible-price values—*are* present. The fact that aggregate supply equals aggregate demand does not mean that output is equal to potential; on the contrary, output is demand-determined in the short run, with firms hiring whatever inputs are needed to ensure that the amount of output supplied is equal to the quantity demanded. And even in a flexible-price version of the model, where output does equal potential every period, there can be dynamics in the responses of output to real shocks.

Turning to Wallace's objection that IS-LM is nonstochastic, it is seemingly echoed by W. Poole's (1982, 68) statement that "the IS-LM framework is not very convenient for thinking about stochastic issues." But this criticism surely applies more to geometric IS-LM analysis than analysis with equations. Poole 1970 is an example of a stochastic analysis in a traditional IS-LM framework,[16] and many of the restrictions that were part of Poole's setup can be relaxed without sacrificing an analysis of stochastic issues in an IS-LM environment.

I conclude that while a legitimate criticism of older IS-LM analyses was their insufficient and inadequately rigorous dynamics, the current optimizing IS-LM analysis does accurately build in intertemporal considerations. Failing to model the capital stock's behavior, on the other hand, is not a critical shortcoming. As well as having rigorously founded dynamics, the optimizing IS-LM specification can be made explicitly stochastic, allowing standard behavioral interpretations of the IS and LM disturbance terms.

3. Objections (5) and (6): "It does not recognize enough distinct assets" and "It is not derivable from explicit maximizing analysis of rational economic agents"

This section discusses the two features of IS-LM that have been the source of greatest debate in the literature. The representation in traditional IS-LM analysis of all nonmoney assets by a single interest-bearing security has been the subject of scathing criticism by monetarists,

16. Indeed, Patinkin (1990, 126) credits Poole (1970) with "introducing stochastic elements into the IS-LM model."

especially Karl Brunner, who condemned IS-LM's "emasculated representation of financial markets" with its reliance on "the never-never land of a two-asset world."[17] Criticisms of the traditional IS-LM framework on the grounds that it is not based on an optimizing framework have been made by King (1993), J.-P. Danthine (1997), and the authors quoted in the introduction.

Though considered separate criticisms by McCallum and Nelson (1999a), these two criticisms of IS-LM are closely related. The issue of IS-LM's treatment of assets leads naturally to a consideration of whether IS-LM is consistent with the behavior of maximizing private agents; both issues bear on the implications of forward-looking behavior for the specification of the LM function. The microfoundations of the LM function can be the principal focus here, as section 2 has already discussed key aspects of the optimizing foundations of the IS function.[18] The question of whether IS-LM represents enough distinct assets is so intertwined with the "monetarist" criticisms of IS-LM that it is worthwhile to center the discussion in this section on the latter.[19] So I begin by discussing the monetarist critique of IS-LM, then outline the relation of this critique to various Keynesian perspectives, and finally reconsider the monetarist critique in light of more recent empirical work.

As M. Parkin (1979, 435) observed, "Monetarists have for many years been complaining that the IS-LM framework does not adequately capture their views." The key questions are why monetarists viewed the transmission mechanism in the IS-LM specification as inadequate and how their suggested alternative conveyed increased significance on the money stock. Parkin's own assessment of the monetarists' critique was negative: "The trouble has been that they have not known what to write down in its place," and he contended that this state of affairs continued until the mid-1970s. On the surface, such a conclusion is supported by Friedman's (1974, 33) use of "the IS curve of Hicks's famous IS-LM analysis . . . [and] Hicks's LM curve." However, Friedman also noted that "the same symbols can have very different empirical counterparts, so that the algebraic statement can conceal" (29) substantially different views regarding the transmission mechanism. In addition, Friedman

17. The two quotations are from Brunner 1983, 26, and 1969, 271.

18. In particular, replacing equation (1) with the optimizing IS equation (4) can be seen as an acknowledgment of the importance of intertemporal considerations for spending decisions.

19. As Michael Bordo and Anna Schwartz (2003) note, much of the pre-1970 monetarist literature did not discuss IS-LM explicitly, but differences from IS-LM were implicit in the outline of the transmission mechanism.

later (1976, 315–16) clarified his position as follows: "In my attempt to communicate, I have tried for example to present monetarist analysis in IS-LM terms, even though recognizing that this was a cumbrous theoretical structure for this purpose." In fact, the cornerstones of the monetarist critique of IS-LM can be found in the outlines of the transmission mechanism of monetary policy by Brunner, Meltzer, and Friedman and Schwartz in the early 1960s, all of which built on the money demand theory outlined in Friedman 1956.

As to why monetarists thought IS-LM was inadequate, one channel that should be ruled out is that operating through wealth effects, in the sense of the Pigou-Patinkin real balance effect: the stimulus to consumption spending because of the addition to real financial wealth produced by an increase in real base money. Textbook treatments occasionally attribute to Friedman and other monetarists the view that real balance effects are important influences on aggregate demand behavior, and even Patinkin (1974, 131) viewed Friedman's position on the transmission mechanism as "an alternative statement of the real-balance effect." The real balance effect was not, however, emphasized by monetarists. Friedman (1976, 317) stated, "I have never myself thought that wealth effects of changes in the quantity of money, or of price changes which altered the real quantity of money, were of any empirical importance for short-run economic fluctuations,"[20] while Brunner (1973, 523) endorsed the widely accepted view that the "'real balance effect' contributes quite negligibly" to monetary transmission and argued that the monetarist literature had "removed the real balance effect from the central position assigned it by Patinkin's analysis" (Brunner 1970, 5).

Appending the IS-LM framework with a real balance effect therefore does not capture monetarist views.[21] The monetarist position instead implies, as Brunner (1989, 212) put it, a "substitution-based transmission

20. C. Rogers and T. K. Rymes (2000, 79) find it "extraordinary" that Friedman could simultaneously deny the empirical importance of wealth effects, yet endorse them as an escape from a Keynesian liquidity trap. The compatibility of the two positions should become clear below: the Keynesian liquidity trap refers to a case in which the scope for monetary ease via substitution effects has been exhausted; Friedman and other monetarists did not find any historical episode (including the 1930s) where all substitution channels had been exhausted.

21. Two elements of possible confusion should be noted. First, some discussions, including Laidler (1982, 46), use "real balance effect" to describe the monetarist substitution effects discussed presently rather than the Pigou-Patinkin wealth effect. Second, some advocates of these broad substitution effects (e.g., Brunner 1971, 45; Meltzer [1977] 1978, 164) mentioned that those channels involved some effects that could be considered wealth effects, but which were not of the Pigou-Patinkin variety.

mechanism." This mechanism had two parts.[22] The first was the insistence that a broad set of (nominal) asset yields should appear in the money demand, or LM relation (Friedman 1956). According to this view, the relevant opportunity-cost variables in the money demand function are not just the rate on short-term financial securities but—reflecting the many alternatives that households have to holding money—also long-term security yields, equity returns, and the implicit yield on consumer durables. The second part was that a multiplicity of (real) interest rates and asset prices appear in the IS equation, and that "market rates . . . [are] only a small part of the total spectrum of rates that are relevant" (Friedman and Schwartz 1982, 58). Taken together, these positions implied that expansions of the real money stock would be felt in the reaction of many asset yields; and that the behavior of the interest rate on short-term securities would provide an inadequate summary of the reaction of asset prices to changes in monetary policy, and so of the effect of monetary policy actions on aggregate demand.[23]

The theoretical merits of this view of the transmission mechanism rest on the plausibility of Friedman's position that the money demand function should be broad based. His work did not rely on microeconomic foundations, but early discussions of the LM function by users of dynamic general equilibrium models seemed supportive of Friedman's proposal. J. Bryant and N. A. Wallace (1979, 2), for example, argued that "any sensible model of individual behavior would make current portfolio decisions depend on views about the future and, in particular, on views about future fiscal and monetary policy." This suggested that an LM function like (2), which gives real money demand as a function only of current values of real income and the short-term rate, was inconsistent with optimizing behavior.

---

22. Brunner (1970, 4) observes: "The first description of this price-theoretical approach to the transmission mechanism was made almost simultaneously by P. Cagan [1958], Milton Friedman [1961a], James Tobin and myself [1961]." Of these, Cagan's work mainly built on Friedman's 1956 description of the form of the money demand function, rather than discussing the implications for the transmission mechanism of monetary policy. In addition, it should be noted that Brunner and Friedman's most definitive expositions of the transmission mechanism were in their collaborative work: for example, Brunner and Meltzer 1963, 1972, 1993; Friedman and Schwartz 1963, 59–63; 1982. The relation of this work to Tobin's will be discussed shortly.

23. This statement presumes some form of price stickiness in the short run that allows open market operations to affect both the nominal and real values of the money stock in the same direction.

But more detailed work on the money demand function implied by intertemporal choice theory has legitimized the use of the standard LM equation. Using an infinite-horizon optimizing model, Lucas (1988) derived a money demand relation that (in its linearized and stochastic version) takes the form of equation (2) and explicitly rejected the position that asset yields besides the short rate should appear in the function. His analysis did not assume two assets—a vector of financial securities was present, and physical capital could be added to Lucas's model without changing his result. Substitution between money and many other assets is available to the representative household, but optimizing behavior implies that only substitution between money and short-term securities takes place in equilibrium. The reason is as follows. In the standard model, with agents holding money solely for its service of facilitating current transactions, the only relevant opportunity-cost variable is the one-period nominal yield. Arbitrage conditions linking the returns on different types of financial assets, and those on financial and real assets, mean that the one-period yield is accurately summarized by the short-term security rate. The uncovered interest parity relationship, for example, ensures that there is no gain from contemplating holding foreign exchange for one period instead of a one-period domestic security. In light of these considerations, O. J. Blanchard (1997, 191) concluded that a "quite myopic" LM equation like (2) was justifiable even in modern macroeconomic models and that this was "good news" for conventional textbook analysis.

But if this is good news for conventional analysis, it would appear to be bad news for a broad-based view of the transmission of monetary policy. If the LM function does take the form of equation (2), then the only variation in real money balances not associated with current real income and the short-term nominal interest rate is uninteresting noise— the money demand shock. For a given path of the short rate, it is hard to see how any significance could be attached to the money stock under such circumstances. Equivalently, a policy-induced injection of money would (together with some nominal stickiness) tend to stimulate output through its effect on the nominal interest rate, and so on the real short rate. But any spillover of the monetary injection into other yields such as long-term rates and the exchange rate would be summarized by the path of current and expected short-term rates—exemplifying what Brunner (1974, 22) called a "very Keynesian" view of monetary transmission.

The form of the conventional LM function, together with the tight arbitrage relations that underpin both the standard IS-LM framework and modern optimizing models, limits the implications of the specification of the IS function. One could concede that many yields should appear in the appropriately specified IS equation, yet essentially reproduce results from a two-asset IS-LM framework. Indeed, under some interpretations, even the original IS-LM specification recognized a short rate–long rate distinction. Tobin (1961, 35), for example, observed that "the Keynesian interest rate [is] the long-term bond rate" while Brunner's (1980, 11) characterization of the Keynesian IS equation was that "a long-term real rate affects aggregate demand." The material effect of this distinction is, by itself, not great, either in traditional IS-LM analysis or in optimizing models. Before the mid-1970s, the adaptive expectations assumption meant that long-term rates were modeled as a distributed lag of the short rate up to an exogenous risk premium. Rational expectations analysis in macroeconomics instead treats long-term rates as a distributed lead of the expected short rate, but again typically treats the risk premium as exogenous. It then remains the case that any effect of monetary policy on output can be summarized by the path of the short-term interest rate, effectively restoring a two-asset structure.

The above description, however, makes it clear that the central element of the monetarist criticism of IS-LM is not that IS-LM includes an insufficient number of assets but that it treats all nonmoney assets as perfect substitutes. Such an assumption is manifested in the presence of the aforementioned arbitrage conditions between assets. The prevalence of the perfect substitutes assumption in IS-LM is emphasized by the fact that in Metzler's (1951, sec. 3) exposition, the "interest rate" was the return on equities. In criticizing the perfect substitutes assumption, moreover, the monetarists appear to have support from the work of Tobin (e.g., 1961, 1982).

But the similarity of Tobin's and the monetarist critique of IS-LM itself creates a puzzle. On the one hand, it is well known that there is an isomorphism between Brunner and Meltzer's and Tobin's specifications of aggregate demand behavior (Brunner 1971; B. Friedman 1976).[24] On the other hand, Tobin's framework has also been seen as one that lends

24. According to Samuelson (1983, 25): "In 1976 when Professor Benjamin Friedman of Harvard wrote down for the monetarists Karl Brunner and Allen [sic] Meltzer what their model of monetarism was, it turned out not to be qualitatively distinguishable from a James Tobin Keynesian model." In fact, this equivalence had been noted by Brunner five years earlier:

support to analyses inconsistent with the monetarist position regarding the significance of the money stock as an indicator. The most extreme case of this is the Radcliffe Committee's report (1959), which is widely agreed to be diametric to the monetarist position (e.g., Friedman and Schwartz 1982, 207), with even Paul Samuelson (1969, 9) dismissing "the Radcliffe Committee['s] stupid view that money doesn't matter." Yet D. Gowland (1978, 5) argued: "The Radcliffe Report took a generally 'Tobinesque' approach to monetary policy." There thus appears to be a significant anomaly: a common motivation—namely, to enrich the asset specification relative to the IS-LM baseline—has apparently lent support to the monetarist position (that of Brunner-Meltzer and Friedman-Schwartz); a U.S. Keynesian position (Tobin's) that recognizes the importance of monetary policy but downplays the centrality of money; and an extreme Keynesian position that discounts or denies the importance of monetary policy for aggregate demand determination (the Radcliffe view). How can these claims be reconciled, and what are the implications for the validity of IS-LM analysis?

To answer the above questions, it is useful to discuss in turn how each camp—the monetarists, Tobin, and the Radcliffians—viewed the implications of imperfect substitutability of assets. For the monetarists, the important effect was on the formulation of the money demand function. The rationale offered in the monetarist literature for the Friedman (1956) money demand function was the role that money could serve as a safe asset when many alternative assets to money were imperfect substitutes. In strict analogy with commercial banks holding higher cash reserves against their less liquid and more risky assets, households might add to their cash holdings in some proportion when they shifted into riskier (e.g., longer-term) obligations. This is clearest in two quotations, one from Friedman in 1971, the other from Friedman and Schwartz 1982. From the former:

> As market rates rose above the [legal] maxima [on time deposits], time deposits became less attractive than market instruments. Holders of such deposits tried to shift into Treasury bills, commercial paper and the like. But this involved a loss of liquidity, so part of the shift out of time deposits took the form of an increased demand for demand

---

"In spite of the apparent differences in the descriptions, there exist suitable and purely formal manipulations which transform the Brunner-Meltzer frame[work] into the Tobin-Brainard frame[work,] and conversely" (Brunner 1971, 109).

deposits. As a result, during 1969, M1 rose more rapidly than M2. (Friedman [1971] 1972, 60)

If some of the shift to liquid assets described by Friedman takes the form of movement into currency rather than demand deposits, then this prudential behavior puts yields on riskier assets into the demand function for base money. This provides an underpinning for the persistent monetarist theme that base money expansion should have effects on the spread, or "risk premium," between short-term securities and other assets.

The prudential behavior described above was, in turn, part of Friedman and Schwartz's emphasis on what they called the "temporary abode of purchasing power" function of money.[25] They placed more emphasis on this function than on the transactions role of money and described how it led to long-term yields mattering for money demand:

> Money balances are held for a variety of possible contingencies, the timing of some of which, such as recurrent trips to the market, is reasonably predictable, the timing of others, such as emergency needs for ready funds, is highly uncertain. In principle, the whole term structure of yields, for all possible holding periods, is relevant to the quantity of money demanded. (Friedman and Schwartz 1982, 262)

Under this view, money is a reserve both against holding risky assets and for emergency needs, and the result is that many yields, not a single short-term nominal interest rate, appear as opportunity-cost variables in the money demand function.

Both Brunner (1971, 18–19) and Meltzer (1971) objected to Friedman and Schwartz's emphasis on the temporary abode function because it did not constitute a property of money distinct from that already discussed in the literature. Meltzer (1971, 336) in particular noted that in Friedman and Schwartz's (1970) discussion, "the 'temporary abode' soon becomes the 'asset' motive," and, indeed, Friedman and Schwartz (1982, 24) made no bones about the fact that their temporary abode function was simply a relabeling of the asset function. Furthermore, the "contingencies" that Friedman and Schwartz refer to in the above quotation parallel the "reserve against contingencies" used to justify the asset motive in Modigliani 1944, a paper described by Friedman (1977, 12) as "a major element in the so-called monetarist structure."

---

25. See, for example, Friedman 1961b, 263; and Friedman and Schwartz 1970, 106, 125.

.

Despite the differences in language with Friedman and Schwartz, the role of money as a reserve asset was an important part of Brunner and Meltzer's framework. For example, Meltzer (1983, 351) wrote: "Increased uncertainty about the future discourages investment in real assets and encourages people to hold relatively safe assets such as currency, insured bank deposits and short-term debt." Like Friedman, Brunner and Meltzer argued that the returns on physical capital and long-term debt should appear in the money demand function (e.g., Brunner 1969, 271; Meltzer 1963), and, correspondingly, they viewed the risk premia for those assets relative to short-term debt as endogenous and a function of the real stock of money (Brunner 1989, 209; Meltzer 1983).

The broad-based money demand function that emerges in the monetarist view then gives a significant role to the money stock as an indicator. Though critics of the monetarist literature, L. E. Gramley and S. B. Chase ([1965] 1969, 1403) provided an accurate characterization of the role of money stressed by monetarists:

> Central bank actions . . . [affect] money income . . . not because the money stock has been altered, but because financial variables through which the central bank alters the desired stock of money also affect the public's decisions to purchase goods and services. . . . What is required is that movements in the money stock reflect the influence of central bank actions on the prices and yields of financial assets. . . . Changes in the money stock can then serve as a proxy for the more complex set of variables that enter expenditure functions.

Friedman and Schwartz (1970, 126) and Brunner (1969, 273) explicitly endorsed the above characterization of the issue.

Where does Tobin's position fit in? Like the monetarists, Tobin believed that many asset yields mattered for aggregate demand and that an implication of imperfect substitutability between assets was that differences in yields across assets should not be regarded as exogenous "risk premia" but as endogenous variables—in particular, as functions of the relative quantities of assets supplied (Tobin 1961, 29–34; 1982, 179). But despite acknowledging that imperfect substitutability also meant that many asset yields mattered for money demand (Tobin 1961, 32; 1980, 71), Tobin did not regard the indicator role of money as being enhanced by the imperfect substitutability extension. Rather, he stressed that, by putting more arguments into the velocity function, the extension gave more scope for variation in the numerical value of velocity (Tobin 1974,

89) and that it did not put an explicit term involving money into the structure of the IS equation (Tobin 1961, 35). Tobin's acceptance of the Friedman money demand function and of the endogeneity of risk premia means that expansions of the money stock have effects on the differentials between short rates and other asset yields, but he seems to have judged that this effect was minor. Accordingly, he appears to have regarded the disconnection between short-term rates and other yields implied by imperfect substitutability as weakening the effectiveness of monetary policy. There appears to be no other way to rationalize his statement that "more modern theory actually weakens the link of monetary policy to aggregate demand" (1974, 89).

In ascertaining "Radcliffian" views of the transmission mechanism, it is useful to regard these views as represented by two sources: the Radcliffe Committee report itself (1959) and J. C. R. Dow's *Management of the British Economy, 1945–60* (1964). David Laidler (1989a, 1147) judges these the two foremost products of U.K. postwar Keynesian economics. The Radcliffe Committee stated that "the structure of interest rates . . . [is] the centerpiece of the monetary mechanism"—in itself, a position not different from the monetarist view of transmission. But any connection with monetarism was broken by its view (1959, 133) that the velocity of circulation could be "stretched" without limit. Such a view gave no prospect of uncovering a systematic relationship between real money demand and opportunity-cost variables, and so denied the monetarist position that money could be a good proxy for the output-relevant spectrum of yields.

Like Tobin and the monetarists, the Radcliffians also stressed the importance of imperfect substitutability between assets. But, even more so than Tobin, they took imperfect substitutability to imply that monetary policy became ineffective. For one thing, the Radcliffe Committee report viewed real aggregate demand as highly inelastic with respect to the short-term real interest rates over which central banks had most influence (1959, 174; Laidler 1989b, 23). Imperfect substitutability between assets then broke the link between short-term security rates and the returns on physical assets, further reducing the potency of monetary policy. The possibility, stressed by the monetarists, that monetary expansion could affect the risk premium between assets was not explored, in keeping with the Radcliffian denial of a well-defined LM function.

Dow's (1964) analysis reached some flawed conclusions about the implications of imperfect substitution between assets. Regarding the conventional interest rate channel of monetary policy, Dow (1964, 314) did acknowledge that a lowering of market interest rates would encourage increased investment in new capital goods relative to the use of the existing physical capital stock. But he appeared to believe that this channel was shut off by the existence of firm-specific capital and the absence of an organized market for secondhand capital goods (319). As D. R. Hodgman (1971, 772) noted, Dow's conclusion was flawed because the existence of firm-specific capital does not prevent intertemporal considerations, and hence interest rates, from being relevant for a firm's investment decision. In addition, Dow (1964, 300) argued that if short-term securities and physical assets became perfect substitutes, monetary policy would lose any influence on real rates on securities, the latter being driven entirely by real factors. In fact, price flexibility, not perfect substitutability of assets, would produce this result. Provided that the Phillips curve specification is one that allows some protracted effects of monetary policy on real variables, then monetary policy can influence the real rate when bonds and capital are perfect substitutes (as they are in the baseline optimizing IS-LM specification).

Writing out the following three-asset model can bring out the different positions of the standard IS-LM specification, the monetarists, Tobin, and the Radcliffe Committee report. Time subscripts and shock terms are suppressed to emphasize that specialized versions of the model would include leads or lags of each variable.

$$y = d(r, z, \ldots) \text{(IS function)} \tag{8}$$

$$p = p(y, \ldots) \text{(Price-adjustment equation)} \tag{9}$$

$$R = f(r, \pi) \text{(Fisher equation for short rates)} \tag{10}$$

$$Z = g(z, \pi) \text{(Fisher equation for third asset)} \tag{11}$$

$$m - p = L(y, R, Z) \text{(Money demand equation)} \tag{12}$$

$$z = h(r, \varsigma(m - p, \ldots)) \text{(Asset arbitrage condition)} \tag{13}$$

The model would be completed by a policy rule for m or R and the identity linking the price level p and inflation π. The model layout is similar to Brunner and Meltzer 1972, 415, with the IS equation depending on two distinct real asset yields—here, the real short rate, r, and a second yield, z. The model features a Phillips curve–style price-adjustment equation; Fisher equations to generate nominal yields from real yields;

and two asset-market equilibrium conditions: the money demand function (depending on both nominal yields), and an arbitrage condition linking the real returns z and r. In Brunner-Meltzer and Tobin's work, the third asset was capital, but one does not need a model with capital for a third asset to be relevant. Other candidates for z include the real long-term bond rate or the real exchange rate. The ς variable in equation (13) is a risk premium, the part of z variation that cannot be accounted for by the path of r.

The baseline IS-LM specification (both in its traditional and optimizing form) treats the risk premium between the asset yields as constant or exogenous, and so claims that ς is not, in fact, dependent on real balances $m - p$. Correspondingly, the second nominal yield Z is absent from the money demand function. The whole model then collapses into a two-asset system with the single real interest rate r.

Monetarists stressed the importance of both the dependence of the risk premium ς on $m - p$ and, consistent with this, money demand on the nominal yield Z. Candidates for z include the real long-term bond rate and the real exchange rate. If z is a vector of yields, many of which are hard to observe directly, the monetarists would emphasize the role of monetary growth or real balances as a summary of the behavior of the yields, r and z, that matter for aggregate demand.[26]

Tobin's position, like the monetarists, emphasized the presence of a second asset in the IS equation, and the importance of the wedge ς between the two asset yields. However, in downplaying the role of money, he stressed that $m - p$ does not appear directly in the IS equation and instead tended to focus attention on asset yields that appear in the IS equation across a variety of specifications of the asset structure. Tobin (1961, 35) claimed that, in models with capital, Tobin's q had such a robust or "strategic" role.

In addition, Tobin's position that imperfect substitutability weakens the impact of monetary policy amounts to the claim that the dependence of the risk premium ς on $m - p$ can be neglected. With aggregate demand depending on two yields, and the scope for monetary policy to affect the second yield existing only through policy's effect on r, one can rationalize Tobin's conclusions that "the major conclusions of the

---

26. Meyer (1980, 463) criticizes monetarists as hypocritical for arguing that monetary policy acts through relative-price adjustments, yet elsewhere arguing for putting money directly in econometric models of expenditure. But this criticism misses the point that it is money's role as a stand-in for unobservable yields that justifies its inclusion in econometric equations.

Keynes-Hicks apparatus remain intact" (1982, 172) and that "I have never understood how Brunner and Meltzer could derive monetarist conclusions . . . from multi-asset models" (1980, 69). Such a view might also account for what Brunner (1983, 49) complained was "Tobin's usual lapse into a [two]-asset equation system when discussing output-money interaction." And indeed Tobin and W. Buiter do seem guilty of the double standard attributed to them by Brunner: despite arguing that two-asset models are "strictly for classroom use only" (1980, 90) and not appropriate for analyzing the macroeconomic effects of fiscal policy, they were satisfied in their 1976 paper to evaluate monetarist arguments using a two-asset model. The two positions can be made consistent if Tobin believed that while variations in asset supplies were in general important sources of risk premia variation, the partial derivatives of risk premia with respect to movements in real base money were very small.

Like the monetarist and Tobinesque views, the U.K. Keynesian or Radcliffian position emphasized the importance of asset prices besides the short rate in aggregate demand determination, and so the importance of z variation. Relative to the other positions, it treated the dependence of output on short rates, for given z, as extremely weak. The behavior of z, in turn, is dominated, according to this view, by the risk-premium term ς. The relation between real money balances and other variables is judged loose and unreliable, implying that it is not useful either to think of ς as being dependent on $m - p$ or to use a money demand function to understand variation in money balances. With the most important asset prices in the IS function effectively disconnected from central bank actions, and with aggregate demand depending weakly, if at all, on the central bank's interest rate policy instrument, the scope for monetary policy to control total spending is virtually dismissed in the Radcliffian view.

The two-asset baseline embodied in IS-LM has, therefore, been criticized by three distinct schools, but only one of these, the monetarist school, has claimed that the restrictive asset specification understates the effectiveness of monetary policy. What are the merits of the monetarist critique of IS-LM, in light of the evolution of macroeconomics and empirical evidence over the last quarter century? A first observation is that several studies have obtained, on quarterly data for countries like the United States and the United Kingdom, correctly signed and statistically significant estimates of the interest elasticity b_1 in the optimizing IS equation (4). In that sense, the two-asset approximation implied by the IS-LM baseline appears reasonable for some purposes, provided that forward-looking behavior of agents is modeled appropriately. But it is a natural extension of the baseline IS equation, and consistent with the maintenance of the optimizing-agents paradigm, to expand the menu of asset prices that matter for aggregate demand determination.

Such an extension, however, would not fully validate the monetarist critique, because it would not necessarily convey on money an enhanced indicator role. A key question, then, is what evidence there is to support the monetarists' position on money as an index of yield variation. Brunner and Meltzer's (1993, 81) appeal on this score to the observation that risk premia differ across assets does not automatically support the monetarist view, because variable interest differentials are consistent with a purely nonmonetary view of risk premia.

More decisive evidence on the monetarist view instead could take two forms. The first is whether real money balances contain information about output not contained in real short-term interest rates. As I discuss in detail elsewhere (Nelson 2003), standard modern models, of which the optimizing IS-LM specification is part, imply that money should have no predictive power for output, given real interest rates. But real money base growth does have such predictive power—suggesting that money does have value as an index of the variation in yields that drive aggregate demand. This, in turn, is testimony to the empirical importance of a Friedman-style money demand function, and so an example of where modern analysis could benefit from drawing on earlier theory.

The second form of evidence is from direct estimation of money demand functions. R. G. Anderson and R. H. Rasche (2001) find that the behavior of U.S. money base velocity in the twentieth century is better accounted for by the long-term nominal interest rate than the short-term rate.[27] Taken together with the well-known problems with modeling long-term interest rates as a function of current and expected short rates, a plausible interpretation of their finding is that the long-term rate enters the money demand function in its own right, not just as a proxy for the path of short rates. And, if the estimated money demand relation is a structural relationship, it would imply that changes in the monetary base have implications for the behavior of long-term rates—implications not captured in the expected path of short-term interest rates. The risk premium, in other words, is a function of the real money stock, in line with Friedman and Schwartz's and Brunner and Meltzer's analysis.

27. This follows earlier work by Meltzer (1963).

To sum up, the shift from an ad hoc to an optimizing version of IS-LM does not make IS-LM analysis completely immune from the criticism that it recognizes too few distinct assets. This criticism has been voiced in different contexts by monetarists, by Tobin, and by Radcliffian U.K. Keynesians. These schools have disagreed on the implications of recognizing multiple assets, but the existing empirical evidence appears to support an important claim of the monetarists: the IS-LM framework tends to understate the value of money as an indicator for monetary policy.

4. Conclusion

This essay has discussed criticisms of the IS-LM framework in the macroeconomic literature of the last forty years, with the emphasis on how the modern optimizing version of IS-LM addresses those criticisms. The current version of IS-LM is consistent with dynamic, stochastic general equilibrium analysis, and so addresses concerns voiced by Tobin, Wallace, and others about the applicability of IS-LM to environments where intertemporal considerations and uncertainty are important. Like best-practice traditional IS-LM analysis, the optimizing IS-LM specification also allows for an endogenously determined price level and for the distinction between nominal and real interest rates. On the issue of asset-market specification, however, the optimizing version of IS-LM may have adopted too restrictive a position. The baseline optimizing IS-LM specification recognizes only two distinct assets, tending to understate the value of money as an indicator for monetary policy. This shortcoming formed an important basis for the monetarist critique of traditional IS-LM. A priority for future work on the optimizing IS-LM framework is to take account of this critique and recognize the need for more asset yields in both the IS and the money demand function.

References

Aiyagari, S. R., and M. Gertler. 1985. The Backing of Government Bonds and Monetarism. *Journal of Monetary Economics* 16:19–44.
Anderson, R. G., and R. H. Rasche. 2001. The Remarkable Stability of Monetary Base Velocity in the United States, 1919–1999. Federal Reserve Bank of St. Louis Working Paper no. 2001–08.
Auerbach, A. J., and L. J. Kotlikoff. 1995. *Macroeconomics: An Integrated Approach*. Cincinnati: South-Western College.

Bailey, M. J. 1962. *National Income and the Price Level*. New York: McGraw Hill.

Bean, C. R. 1983. Targeting Nominal Income: An Appraisal. *Economic Journal* 93:806–19.

Blanchard, O. J. 1997. *Macroeconomics*. Upper Saddle River, N.J.: Prentice Hall.

Bordo, M. D., and A. J. Schwartz. 2003. IS-LM and Monetarism. NBER Working Paper no. 9713.

Brunner, K. 1961. Some Major Problems in Monetary Theory. *American Economic Review (Papers and Proceedings)* 51:47–56.

————. 1969. Monetary Analysis and Federal Reserve Policy. In *Targets and Indicators of Monetary Policy*, edited by K. Brunner. San Francisco: Chandler.

————. 1970. The "Monetarist Revolution" in Monetary Theory. *Weltwirtschaftliches Archiv* 105:1–30.

————. 1971. A Survey of Selected Issues in Monetary Theory. *Swiss Journal of Economics and Statistics* 107:1–146.

————. 1973. A Diagrammatic Exposition of the Money Supply Process. *Swiss Journal of Economics and Statistics* 109:481–533.

————. 1974. Monetary Growth and Monetary Policy. Shadow Open Market Committee Position Paper, 8 March.

————. 1980. The Control of Monetary Aggregates. In *Controlling Monetary Aggregates III*. Proceedings of a conference held at Melvin Village, New Hampshire. Boston: Federal Reserve Bank of Boston.

————. 1983. Has Monetarism Failed? *Cato Journal* 3:23–62.

————. 1989. *The Disarray in Macroeconomics*. In *Monetary Economics in the 1980s*, edited by F. Capie and G. E. Wood. London: Macmillan.

Brunner, K., and A. H. Meltzer. 1963. Predicting Velocity: Implications for Theory and Policy. *Journal of Finance* 18:319–54.

————. 1972. Money, Debt, and Economic Activity. *Journal of Political Economy* 80:951–77.

————. 1993. *Money and the Economy: Issues in Monetary Analysis*. Cambridge: Cambridge University Press.

Bryant, J., and N. A. Wallace. 1979. Monetary Policy in the Presence of a Stochastic Deficit. Federal Reserve Bank of Minneapolis Staff Report no. 42.

Cagan, P. 1958. Why Do We Use Money in Open Market Operations? *Journal of Political Economy* 66:34–46.

Danthine, J.-P. 1997. In Search of a Successor to IS-LM. *Oxford Review of Economic Policy* 13:135–44.

Darity, W., Jr., and W. Young. 1995. IS-LM: An Inquest. *HOPE* 27:1–41.

De Vroey, M. 2000. IS-LM à la Hicks versus IS-LM à la Modigliani. *HOPE* 32:293–316.

Dow, J. C. R. 1964. *The Management of the British Economy, 1945–60*. Cambridge: Cambridge University Press.

Dupor, B. 2001. Investment and Interest Rate Policy. *Journal of Economic Theory* 98:85–113.

Fane, G. 1985. A Derivation of the IS-LM Model from Explicit Optimizing Behavior. *Journal of Macroeconomics* 7:493–508.

Fischer, S. 1987. 1944, 1963, and 1985. In *Macroeconomics and Finance: Essays in Honor of Franco Modigliani*, edited by R. Dornbusch, S. Fischer, and J. Bossons. Cambridge: MIT Press.

Friedman, B. M. 1976. The Theoretical Nondebate about Monetarism. *Kredit und Kapital* 9:347–67.

Friedman, M. 1956. The Quantity Theory of Money: A Restatement. In *Studies in the Quantity Theory of Money*, edited by M. Friedman. Chicago: University of Chicago Press.

———. 1961a. The Lag in Effect of Monetary Policy. *Journal of Political Economy* 69:447–66.

———. 1961b. The Demand for Money. *Proceedings of the American Philosophical Society* 105:259–64.

———. [1971] 1972. Money—Tight or Easy? In *An Economist's Protest*. New York: Thomas Horton.

———. 1974. A Theoretical Framework for Monetary Analysis. In *Milton Friedman's Monetary Framework: A Debate with His Critics*, edited by R. J. Gordon. Chicago: University of Chicago Press.

———. 1976. Comments on Tobin and Buiter. In *Monetarism*, edited by J. L. Stein. Amsterdam: North-Holland.

———. 1977. Discussion of "The Monetarist Controversy." *Federal Reserve Bank of San Francisco Economic Review* 3.1 (supplement): 12–19.

Friedman, M., and A. J. Schwartz. 1963. Money and Business Cycles. *Review of Economics and Statistics* 45:32–64.

———. 1970. *Monetary Statistics of the United States*. New York: Columbia University Press.

———. 1982. Monetary Trends in the United States and the United Kingdom: Their Relation to Income, Prices, and Interest Rates, 1867–1975. Chicago: University of Chicago Press.

Fuhrer, J. C. 1997. Towards a Compact, Empirically-Verified Rational Expectations Model for Monetary Policy Analysis. *Carnegie-Rochester Conference Series on Public Policy* 47:197–230.

Gowland, D. 1978. Monetary Policy and Credit Control: The U.K. Experience. London: Croom Helm.

Gramley, L. E., and S. B. Chase. [1965] 1969. Time Deposits in Monetary Analysis. In *Targets and Indicators of Monetary Policy*, edited by K. Brunner. San Francisco: Chandler.

Hamilton, J. D. 1989. Book Review: *Money in Historical Perspective*. *Journal of Economic Literature* 27:112–14.

Hendershott, P. H., and G. Horwich. 1974. IS/LM as a Dynamic Framework. In *Trade, Stability, and Macroeconomics: Essays in Honor of Lloyd A. Metzler*, edited by G. Horwich and P. Samuelson. New York: Academic Press.

Hicks, J. R. 1937. Mr. Keynes and the "Classics": A Suggested Interpretation. *Econometrica* 5:147–59.

Hodgman, D. R. 1971. British Techniques of Monetary Policy: A Critical Review. *Journal of Money, Credit, and Banking* 3:760–79.

Johannes, J. M. 1980. In Defense of the Venerable IS-LM Framework. *Journal of Economic Issues* 14:207–10.

Kerr, W., and R. G. King. 1996. Limits on Interest Rate Rules in the IS Model. *Federal Reserve Bank of Richmond Economic Quarterly* 82:47–75.

Keynes, J. M. 1936. *The General Theory of Employment, Interest, and Money.* London: Macmillan.

King, R. G. 1993. Will the New Keynesian Macroeconomics Resurrect the IS-LM Model? *Journal of Economic Perspectives* 7:67–82.

———. 2000. The New IS-LM Model: Language, Logic, and Limits. *Federal Reserve Bank of Richmond Economic Quarterly* 86:45–103.

Koenig, E. F. 1989. A Simple Optimizing Alternative to Traditional IS-LM Analysis. Manuscript, Federal Reserve Bank of Dallas.

———. 1993a. Rethinking the IS in IS-LM: Adapting Keynesian Tools to Non-Keynesian Economies, Part 1. *Federal Reserve Bank of Dallas Economic Review* 78:33–49.

———. 1993b. Rethinking the IS in IS-LM: Adapting Keynesian Tools to Non-Keynesian Economies, Part 2. *Federal Reserve Bank of Dallas Economic Review* 78:17–35.

Laidler, D. 1982. *Monetarist Perspectives.* Oxford: Philip Allan.

———. 1989a. Dow and Saville's *Critique of Monetary Policy*—A Review Essay. *Journal of Economic Literature* 27:1147–59.

———. 1989b. Radcliffe, the Quantity Theory, and Monetarism. In *Money, Trade, and Payments: Essays in Honour of Dennis Coppock*, edited by D. Cobham, R. Harrington, and G. Zis. Manchester: Manchester University Press.

Leeper, E. M., and C. A. Sims. 1994. Toward a Modern Macroeconomic Model Usable for Policy Analysis. *NBER Macroeconomics Annual* 9:81–118.

Lucas, R. E., Jr. 1973. Some International Evidence on Output-Inflation Tradeoffs. *American Economic Review* 63:326–34.

———. 1988. Money Demand in the United States: A Quantitative Review. *Carnegie-Rochester Conference Series on Public Policy* 29:137–67.

Mayer, T. 1972. The Federal Reserve's Policy Procedures: A Review of a Federal Reserve Study and an Ensuing Conference. *Journal of Money, Credit, and Banking* 4:529–50.

McCallum, B. T. 1989. *Monetary Economics.* New York: Macmillan.

———. 1995. *Topics in Monetary Theory and Policy: Lectures at the Institute for Advanced Studies, Vienna, April 1994.* Manuscript, Carnegie Mellon University.

McCallum, B. T., and E. Nelson. 1999a. An Optimizing IS-LM Specification for Monetary Policy and Business Cycle Analysis. *Journal of Money, Credit, and Banking* 31:296–316.

———. 1999b. Performance of Operational Policy Rules in an Estimated Semi-Classical Structural Model. In *Monetary Policy Rules*, edited by J. B. Taylor. Chicago: University of Chicago Press.

Meltzer, A. H. 1963. The Demand for Money: The Evidence from the Time Series. *Journal of Political Economy* 71:219–46.

———. 1971. Book Review: *Monetary Statistics of the United States. Journal of Business* 44:335–37.

———. [1977] 1978. Monetarist, Keynesian, and Quantity Theories. Reprinted in *The Structure of Monetarism*, by T. Mayer et al. New York: Norton.

———. 1983. Present and Future in an Uncertain World. In *Legislation for Alternative Targets for Monetary Policy*. Hearings before Subcommittee on Domestic Monetary Policy Committee on Banking, Finance, and Urban Affairs, 98th Congress. Washington, D.C.: Government Printing Office.

Metzler, L. A. 1951. Wealth, Saving, and the Rate of Interest. *Journal of Political Economy* 59:93–116.

Meyer, L. H. 1980. *Macroeconomics: A Model Building Approach.* Cincinnati: South-Western Publishing.

Modigliani, F. 1944. Liquidity Preference and the Theory of Interest and Money. *Econometrica* 12:45–88.

Mundell, R. A. 1963. Inflation and Real Interest. *Journal of Political Economy* 71:280–83.

Nelson, E. 2003. The Future of Monetary Aggregates in Monetary Policy Analysis. *Journal of Monetary Economics* 50:1029–59.

Parkin, M. 1979. Book Review: *Monetarism. Journal of Political Economy* 87:432–36.

Patinkin, D. 1951. Price Flexibility and Full Employment. In *Readings in Monetary Theory*, edited by F. A. Lutz and L. W. Mints. Philadelphia: Blakiston.

———. 1974. Friedman on the Quantity Theory and Keynesian Economics. In *Milton Friedman's Monetary Framework: A Debate with His Critics*, edited by R. J. Gordon. Chicago: University of Chicago Press.

———. 1990. In Defense of IS-LM. *Banca Nazionale del Lavoro Quarterly Review* 172:119–34.

Policano, A. J. 1977. Book Review: *Money, Information, and Uncertainty. Journal of Political Economy* 85:231–35.

———. 1985. The Current State of Macroeconomics: A View from the Textbooks. *Journal of Monetary Economics* 15:389–97.

Poole, W. 1970. Optimal Choice of Monetary Policy Instruments in a Simple Stochastic Macro Model. *Quarterly Journal of Economics* 84:197–216.

———. 1982. Discussion: Monetary Targeting in a Zero-Balance World. In *Interest Rate Deregulation and Monetary Policy*. San Francisco: Federal Reserve Bank of San Francisco.

Radcliffe Committee. 1959. Report of the Committee on the Working of the Monetary System. London: HMSO.

Rankin, N. 1987. Disequilibrium and the Welfare-Maximising Levels of Government Spending, Taxation, and Debt. *Economic Journal* 97:65–85.

Rogers, C., and T. K. Rymes. 2000. On Money in IS/LM and AD/AS Models. In *IS-LM and Modern Macroeconomics*, edited by W. Young and B. Z. Zilberfarb. Boston: Kluwer Academic Press.

Rotemberg, J. J., and M. Woodford. 1997. An Optimization-Based Econometric Framework for the Evaluation of Monetary Policy. *NBER Macroeconomics Annual* 12:297–346.

Samuelson, P. A. 1969. The Role of Money in National Economic Policy. In *Controlling Monetary Aggregates*. Proceedings of the monetary conference held on Nantucket Island, 8–10 June. Boston: Federal Reserve Bank of Boston.

————. 1976. Milton Friedman. *Newsweek,* 25 October, 41.

————. 1983. Sympathy from the Other Cambridge. *Economist,* 25 June, 21–25.

Sargent, T. J. 1972. Anticipated Inflation and the Nominal Rate of Interest. *Quarterly Journal of Economics* 86:212–25.

————. 1987. *Macroeconomic Theory.* 2nd ed. New York: Academic Press.

Solow, R. M. 1984. Mr Hicks and the Classics. *Oxford Economic Papers* 36 (supplement): 13–25.

Tobin, J. 1961. Money, Capital, and Other Stores of Value. *American Economic Review (Papers and Proceedings)* 51:26–37.

————. 1974. Friedman's Theoretical Framework. In *Milton Friedman's Monetary Framework: A Debate with His Critics*, edited by R. J. Gordon. Chicago: University of Chicago Press.

————. 1979. Deficit Spending and Crowding Out in Shorter and Longer Runs. In *Theory for Economic Efficiency: Essays in Honor of Abba P. Lerner*, edited by H. I. Greenfield, A. M. Levenson, W. Hamovitch, and E. Rotwein. Cambridge: MIT Press.

————. 1980. Discussion: The Control of Monetary Aggregates. In *Controlling Monetary Aggregates III*. Proceedings of a conference held at Melvin Village, New Hampshire. Boston: Federal Reserve Bank of Boston.

————. 1982. Money and Finance in the Macroeconomic Process. *Journal of Money, Credit, and Banking* 14:171–204.

Tobin, J., and W. Buiter. 1976. Long-Run Effects of Fiscal and Monetary Policy on Aggregate Demand. In *Monetarism*, edited by J. L. Stein. Amsterdam: North-Holland.

————. 1980. Fiscal and Monetary Policies, Capital Formation, and Economic Activity. In *The Government and Capital Formation*, edited by G. M. von Furstenberg. Cambridge, Mass.: Ballinger.

Van Order, R. 1978. On the Bias in Estimates of the Effects of Monetary and Fiscal Policy. *Review of Economics and Statistics* 60:304–6.

Vercelli, A. 1999. The Evolution of IS-LM Models: Empirical Evidence and Theoretical Presuppositions. *Journal of Economic Methodology* 6:199–219.

Wallace, N. A. 1980. The Overlapping Generations Model of Fiat Money. In *Models of Monetary Economies*, edited by J. H. Kareken and N. A. Wallace. Minneapolis: Federal Reserve Bank of Minneapolis.

Woodford, M. 1996. Control of the Public Debt: A Requirement for Price Stability? NBER Working Paper no. 5684.

The Strange Persistence of the IS-LM Model

David Colander

Why has the IS-LM model persisted? In this essay I consider that question, along with the related, and in some ways more interesting, question of how the use of the IS-LM model has changed over time. I begin with some general issues about the persistence of IS-LM and how its treatment has changed, presenting some bibliometric evidence about the appearance of IS-LM in the literature over the last forty years. Then I look specifically at how the treatment of IS-LM has evolved from the 1960s until today, comparing a 1960s intermediate macro text with a modern intermediate text. Finally, I relate that discussion to some thoughts about the future of the IS-LM model.

Some General Comments on the Persistence of IS-LM

IS-LM analysis is a creature of pedagogy, and to understand its persistence one must understand the nature of economic pedagogy in the intermediate macro course, where the IS-LM model predominates. Since just about every economics student takes intermediate macro, just about every economist has taken intermediate macro, and so as long as IS-LM continues to be used in that course, IS-LM will retain its central role in rough-and-ready discussions of macro policy. IS-LM provides a common framework (the "trained intuition") that economists can use to discuss macro policy, as suggested by James Tobin (1980), Robert Solow (1984), and others.

To say that the IS-LM model has persisted is not to say that its use has remained the same or that it currently plays a central role in advanced discussions of macroeconomic policy and theory. In the 1960s, it did play a significant role in both theoretical and empirical discussions of macro, but that is no longer true, which means that the model's use has changed considerably over the last forty or fifty years. Today IS-LM has a limited range of applicability. For example, it does not appear in the principles texts, whereas back in the 1960s it could be found in some high-level principles texts and in appendixes to others. Even the AE/AP building block of the IS-LM model is disappearing from the intro texts and is being replaced with the AS/AD model.[1]

Another example of its limited range is that modern theoretical debates in top journals make little reference to the IS-LM model. For example, in the two-volume *Handbook of Macroeconomics* (Taylor and Woodford 1999), the term *IS-LM* is hardly mentioned, and no discussion of policy or theoretical issues is centered on it. Similarly, other than sometimes being referenced in a review of intermediate macro, graduate courses in macro at top schools seldom mention this model.[2]

There are attempts to translate modern work into the IS-LM framework, such as we see in the work of Bennett McCallum and Edward Nelson (1999), Tack Yun (1996), or Richard Clarida, Jordi Gali, and Mark Gertler (1999). But the foundation of their models is in dynamic general equilibrium theory, and the translation into IS-LM is not central to their analysis. The translation is done simply to give policy-oriented economists a way to relate their conclusions to an IS-LM framework. It is the underlying dynamic general equilibrium model, and not the translation of that debate into the IS-LM model, that is central to modern theoretical debates.[3]

1. An interesting aspect of this development is that, technically, the AS/AD model is derivative of the IS-LM model. Earlier, the AE/AP multiplier model, a building block for IS-LM, dominated the principles texts, and thus the IS-LM intermediate macro model was an extension of the model learned in principles. Today, the multiplier model is absent from many principles books, and AS/AD analysis has become a stand-alone analysis.

2. At Princeton, for instance, it does not appear in recent graduate macro syllabi. At Harvard, the professor who provided the overview told me he lectured on it briefly, but otherwise it went unmentioned. Informal discussion with professors at other schools suggests that this is the rule at top schools.

3. In their work, they show that in these dynamic general equilibrium models, given assumptions of nominal rigidities, it is possible to derive a temporary negative relationship between output and interest rates that can be called an "IS" curve. They close the model not with a traditional LM curve but instead with a specification of nominal interest rates; however, that

The current situation is in marked contrast to the 1960s when both policy debates and theoretical debates were centered on the IS-LM model. In the 1960s, what one learned in intermediate macro provided a foundation for what one learned in upper-level and graduate courses. IS-LM was the end of the line—providing a synthesis of the Keynesian and classical models, which were central to the policy debates and higher theoretical work in economics. Since one learned IS-LM in the intermediate course, there was no quantum jump between intermediate and advanced work in macro. For example, in 1965 Duncan Foley, based on a senior seminar in macro he did at Swarthmore, exempted out of the graduate macro course at Yale (Foley 2002).

As late as the mid-1970s, IS-LM remained the foundation of the graduate course. For example, in my first graduate course in macro in 1971, we had a new Stanford graduate as a professor, and we studied matrix IS-LM models where significant disaggregation was allowed but the IS-LM structure was maintained. So IS-LM was still the core structure being taught. Today that has changed; the discussion of the multimarket goods and money market equilibria gets far less emphasis, and instead IS-LM is used for little else than a handy framework for discussing policy. So IS-LM has persisted, but its role has changed substantially.

In the 1960s, the IS-LM model was not only a stepping-stone to theoretical macro, it was also a stepping-stone to empirical macro and the large econometric models that were then the center of advanced macroeconomic forecasting and policy analysis. When students learned IS-LM in the 1960s, they were learning a simple example of the much larger econometric models, which had thousands, rather than tens, of equations, but otherwise had the same structure. Lawrence Klein (2000) nicely presents this pedagogical use of IS-LM and shows how IS-LM would be presented and given empirical content, if it still played that role. He suggests that "systems that are carefully fitted to observed data and capable of generating realistic values are far better for teaching purposes" (158). This is, of course, true, but that is not the way IS-LM is generally taught today, in part because the profession is far more suspicious of large-scale econometric models and the information that can be drawn from them. So IS-LM is still taught, but it is not taught as a theoretical or empirical stepping-stone, as it was in the 1960s and early 1970s.

---

distinction is, in my view, a minor one and can be related to the standard IS-LM model by defining an effective LM curve that incorporates a monetary feedback rule. See Colander and Gamber 2002.

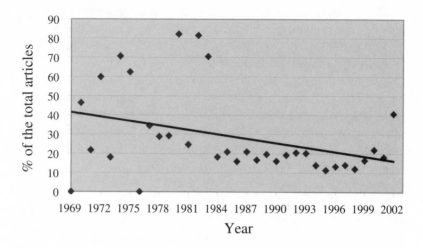

Figure 1   Relative appearance of *IS-LM* (as keyword) in EconLit
Note: $y = -0.0077x + 15.527$. $R^2 = 0.1192$

Bibliometric Evidence

To shed light on the question of how much IS-LM has persisted, I asked a student and a research assistant to conduct a bibliometric study of the appearance of IS-LM in the EconLit database.[4] Specifically, they investigated how often the term *IS-LM* appears in articles from 1969 through 2000.[5] My expectation was that the evidence would show that the relative, and perhaps even the absolute, appearance of articles discussing IS-LM would be falling. The results, as you can see in figure 1, are consistent with the expectation that the relative appearance of the term has been decreasing over time.[6]

4. The paper was done by Fred Wyshak (2002) for my history of economic thought class at Middlebury College. My research assistant was Iqbal Sheikh.
5. The database began in full only in 1969. It contains 332,000 articles and over 400 publications. The number has been growing substantially over time, which is why relative frequency is used. In absolute terms the number of articles on IS-LM has been increasing.
6. The search was of the term *IS-LM* or variations of it found in the title or abstract of one of the included journals. The occurrences were then divided by the total number of articles for the year, giving the relative occurrence. I suspect that the result is an underestimate of the evidence because of a technical aspect of the database. The database represents titles and abstracts of articles. More journals now require abstracts and keywords, and thus in the relevant period there is likely a bias toward finding the searched-for words in the period's later years than in its earlier years. Care should be taken in drawing inferences from this evidence, since the

Table 1 The number and the percentage of articles fitting various approaches

Years	Historical	Pedagogical	Theoretical	Empirical	Total
1970–1980	0	4 (15%)	23 (85%)	0	27 (100%)
1980–2002	19 (16%)	22 (19%)	52 (44%)	25 (21%)	118 (100%)

The bibliometric evidence also tells us something about the changing nature of research on IS-LM. The most articles cited appeared in the *Journal of Macroeconomics*, the *Journal of Economic Education*, and *Economica Internazionale*. Most others appeared in lower-ranked journals. Only four of the journals ranked in the top ten today had IS-LM articles over the entire period, and none of these were recent. This suggests that while IS-LM may remain a research topic, it is not part of the modern core, high-level, research.

Looking further at the nature of research on IS-LM, I went through the list of articles and made an informal classification of them into four categories: theoretical, empirical, pedagogical, and historical, to see if a trend was readily apparent. The results are presented in table 1.

As you can see from the table, in the period from 1970 to 1980 I classified 85 percent of IS-LM articles as theoretical and 15 percent as pedagogical. In the post-1981 period the percentage I classified as theoretical declined to 44 percent, while more articles fell into the historical, pedagogical, and empirical classifications. Also, a significant number of books (not captured in the database) on the history and pedagogy of IS-LM (e.g., Young 1987, Young and Zilberfarb 2000) have been published in the recent period. So it seems that two groups that have played a role in the persistence of IS-LM in the literature are teachers of economics and historians of economic thought.

One surprising finding, shown in the table, is the number of empirical articles on IS-LM in the later period and the lack of empirical articles in the earlier period. Looking specifically at the titles and occurrences of

---

results are highly dependent on the specification of the search. In an original search that did not include some specifications of IS-LM, my student found a slight increase in the percentage of articles on IS-LM; when the additional specifications of IS-LM were added, that increase was eliminated, and a decrease was found. My students did other searches, such as a search of titles in JSTOR, and these showed a stronger downward trend.

those empirical articles, I found that most of them are in foreign journals not included in the earlier-year database. Almost no IS-LM article
classified as empirical appeared in U.S. journals.

My interpretation of this evidence is that core macro theory and empirical work in economics has moved away from the use of IS-LM analysis, but that IS-LM analysis remains a research interest in the history of
economic thought (the publication of essays from this conference likely
will make a big impact on the future data), in pedagogy, and in discussions of macro policy issues outside the theoretical core of the profession. So while IS-LM is still around, its role is fundamentally different
than its role forty years ago. The central theoretical debates have moved
away from the IS-LM model, but IS-LM's pedagogical role as an organizing structure for nonspecialists to think about macro policy has remained.

The Importance of the Intermediate
Macro Course

The question of the persistence of the IS-LM model is in part a question
of why, even as both the lower-level and upper-level consideration of
macro issues change, IS-LM analysis remains in the intermediate macro
course and in similar graduate-level public policy courses and business
school courses.

To answer that question it is necessary to consider what the intermediate macro course is, and is not, designed to do. My first observation
is that today the course is not designed to prepare economics majors to
go on to graduate study. The reasons are simple. Few majors go on to do
graduate work in economics, and many students who take this course are
not majors. For example, at Middlebury College, approximately 150–
175 students take the course each year, and about 1 of those 175 goes on
to graduate work in economics each year. Since only about 60 percent
of the students who take the course are majors, and none of the nonma-
jors go on, that means that about 0.3 percent of the students taking the
course will go on in graduate work in economics.[7] So the course is not
structured for students going into graduate work in economics, but rather

7. The course is required for international politics and economics majors and is recommended for a number of other majors. Many of these students will go on to graduate work—
some in public policy, others in business or law. But they do not tend to go on to PhD programs
in economics.

for a set of students who are primarily interested in macro policy.[8] The course provides those students with insights into some of the workings of the macro economy, as well as an introduction to the debates about growth policies, monetary and fiscal policy, and the problems of balancing long-run and short-run policy.

The nature of the student body is important because students are not learning a macro model as a stepping-stone to theoretical or empirical work. They are using IS-LM as a framework—they care little about the problems with it, or its substantial limitations. They want some basic information about policy and institutions, such as what will likely happen to interest rates and income if monetary policy is expansionary. Despite its many problems, the IS-LM model works for these students. It also works for older (over fifty) teachers such as me, who were taught macro centered on the IS-LM model. This dual support goes a long way toward explaining the persistence of the model in the course.

The Push to Eliminate and Keep IS-LM

If there is a push to eliminate IS-LM from the intermediate course, it comes from professors fresh out of graduate school who are no longer taught the IS-LM model. As graduate students become the teachers, they naturally like to teach what they learned. Thus there is pressure from younger professors to dump IS-LM analysis and to teach a simplified version of what they learned in graduate school. As I discuss below, this pressure has changed how IS-LM is presented in the texts, but has not eliminated it. The reason, in my view, is that the graduate school models students learn are mathematically too sophisticated to present at the intermediate level, and their connection to policy too removed. They require a mathematical sophistication and interest in theory beyond that of most intermediate students.[9] No easy simplification method exists at the moment, and without one, the material can only be presented heuristically.

8. It was only a slightly higher percentage of students who were planning to go on to do graduate work in the 1960s, but at that time there was not such a gap between the undergraduate and graduate courses, and it was possible to expect good undergraduates to understand the articles being read in graduate school. Today, because the technical level of the papers has increased so much, that is generally not the case.

9. Intermediate books such as Barro 1999, which have tried to present a general equilibrium approach more consistent with that taught in graduate school, have not done well in the market. Barro's book was initially published by a textbook publisher, but it was taken over by MIT Press because sales were below the minimum cutoff of commercial college textbook publishers.

This is not to say that modern issues do not show up in the modern texts. Textbooks like to look modern, and textbook authors are always on the lookout for recent developments, new ideas, and discussions to include that make their book look more up-to-date than the competition. Open any intermediate text and you will see discussions of credibility, time inconsistency, rational expectations, real business cycles, and inflation targeting. But these discussions are primarily verbal presentations and have not replaced the core IS-LM structure for presentations of monetary and fiscal policy.

Why not structure an economics text with verbal, rather than geometric, presentations? Economists are not trained in verbal analysis, and exams are much easier to structure relative to a specific model that the students can handle. Questions about geometric models have the advantage of being right or wrong, and thus easily tested; since grading is an important aspect of the course, anything that can reduce conflict and make the grading process easier creates pressure to keep it.

As older professors retire and are replaced by younger and differently trained professors, the pressure to eliminate IS-LM will intensify. But I suspect IS-LM will remain. One reason is inertia. A pedagogical model can only be replaced by another pedagogical model. For the intermediate-level student, IS-LM is a nice pedagogical model; the level of math is about right, so that it challenges students—but not too much. It gives students something to learn that seems to have applications to policy and has, at least in the model, right or wrong answers.

A second pressure to maintain the IS-LM model derives from the fact that it looks similar to a supply and demand model: it has an upward-sloping curve and a downward-sloping curve. For some reason this gives students comfort. A third reason is that it provides nice graphic representations of crowding out, monetary policy, and fiscal policy. A fourth reason is its testability; it provides a wealth of "right or wrong" test questions. A final reason is that its elegance hides much of the underlying reasoning, allowing use of the model without a deep understanding of what does lie beneath. It can be used to talk about policy even if the students do not fully understand the underlying story of interactions of multiple markets being pushed toward equilibrium.

The pressure from younger professors who have not studied IS-LM in graduate school has, however, made a difference in the way IS-LM is presented. Because younger professors are often not familiar with the technical foundations of the curves, the technical presentation of the model has become cursory. Intricacies of dynamics, slopes of curves, or connections of IS-LM issues to earlier debates are no longer presented in the texts, since the younger professors are not trained in them. What this means is that, often, the problems with IS-LM do not become part of what is taught. For example, the fact that the IS curve refers to real interest rates and the LM curve refers to nominal interest rates is seldom discussed. Similarly, the instability of the curves as expectations change, or the problem of interpreting interest rates as differential interest rates of short-term and long-term financial assets, gets little discussion. Instead, IS-LM is now presented in an almost mechanistic way; it is a model that shows the effects of monetary and fiscal policy on interest rates and real output.

A Comparison of Two Texts

One way to see how the presentation of IS-LM analysis has changed is to compare the presentation in the texts back in the 1960s with the presentation in a recent book. In this section I do that, comparing the treatment of the IS-LM model in Gardner Ackley's 1961 book with the treatment in Gregory Mankiw's 2003 book.

The Ackley Text

In the 1960s Gardner Ackley's *Macroeconomic Theory* was the leading book of its day.[10] It was 596 pages long and was seen as accompanying Keynes's *General Theory*. Ackley writes in the preface that he has his students purchase the *General Theory* and that he assigns seven chapters from it. He also states that significant readings from the "vast post-Keynesian literature [are] also assigned" (iii). This is consistent with my recollection of the situation in the 1960s; I remember receiving a multiple-page reading list of articles to accompany the text. The list included numerous, fairly recent, articles developing topics that the text discussed. This connection of the text to the literature conveyed the sense, which I believe was the reality at the time, that the text was providing the student an entrée into modern theoretical and policy debates.

---

10. I base this discussion on the third printing in 1968 of the 1961 Collier-Macmillan Student Edition. The fact that an edition could exist for seven years without a major revision is telling both in how the course was stabilized in presentation and the lack of a developed secondhand book market.

The Ackley text is divided into four parts. Part 1, "Concepts and Measurement," consists of four chapters covering basic concepts, price indexes, and national income accounting, the latter covered in much more depth than it is today. The first three chapters in part 2 are on classical macroeconomics, Say's law, the quantity theory, full-employment equilibrium, the effect of rigid wages, and the savings investment approach to the determination of the interest rate. The fourth chapter in part 2 is a summary that combines the issues discussed in the previous chapters into a model of seven equations, a production function ($y = y(N)$), the profit maximization condition ($dy/dN = W/P$), the supply of labor ($N = N(W/P)$) and the quantity theory ($M = lPy$), the savings function ($s = s(r)$), the investment function ($I = I(r)$), and equilibrium in the capital market ($s = i$) (157). These are the key equations in the model, and Ackley states that "a set of equations either identical with or closely resembling these has frequently been used to represent the 'Classical' in contrast to the 'Keynesian' system." In this chapter he points out that the first four equations are separable from the last three saving-investment equations. He then expands the quantity theory to include the loanable funds theory, which ties the two sets of equations together, at least in the short run. He concludes that chapter with a discussion of how, in "modern macro," fiscal policy is central.

Part 3, "Keynesian Macroeconomics," consists of seven chapters, although the seventh is actually a summary chapter comparing the classical and Keynesian models. This part begins with a discussion of liquidity preference and how there can be an inconsistency between saving and investment. These issues are presented as qualifications to the classical model that were first suggested by Keynes. Finally, it discusses wage and price inflexibility, which is presented as part of classical thought. The next four chapters turn to the consumption function model and the multiplier, which are presented as relevant when there is some constraint preventing the achievement of full employment. The short run, long run, and lags are discussed in these chapters, and there is a fair amount of material on empirical evidence. Ackley concludes that the basic Keynesian thesis that consumption is a stable function of income is tentatively accepted (308).

Chapter 13 is a discussion of multipliers, and an algebraic multiplier model with government is developed. Chapter 14 summarizes the Keynesian model and is the first and last time the IS-LM model is used. (He calls it the Hicks-Hansen diagram.) In this chapter, the IS and LM curves are developed in two ways: by adding a consumption function and speculative demand for money to the classical model; and from the simple Keynesian model, adding the necessary relationships involving wages and prices, labor, money, and the interest rate. There are a total of three complete IS-LM diagrams in the entire book.

Soon after presenting the IS-LM model, Ackley gives an alternative to IS-LM—a four-quadrant diagram, which is similar to diagrams he had used in the presentation of the classical model. He justifies this alternative model as follows:

> The Hicks-Hansen diagram has elegant simplicity that appeals to many. It has the disadvantage, however, that most of the "works" are out of sight. This means that we need to use another diagram (or an extra mental calculation) to determine the effect of a displacement of the equilibrium on the other variables of our system. Likewise, it means that if we wish to consider the effect of a change in some one of the functions which lie behind the IS or LM curve, we need another diagram (or mental process) to determine how the assumed shift will affect the IS or LM curve. Other less elegant apparatus is possible, which exposes more of the relationships to view. (372)

Chapter 15 is the central chapter of the book. It consists of a comparison and evaluation of the classical and Keynesian models, which are both reduced to a set of equations (403). The differences between the models are that the Keynesian model has a speculative demand for money, rigid wages, and saving determined by income, whereas in the classical model savings is determined by the interest rate. Later in the chapter he blends the two models together, specifying money as a function of both income and interest rates and saving as a function of both interest rates and income. This leaves the rigid nominal wages in the Keynesian model as the only difference between the Keynesian and classical models. Chapter 15 is the end of the core presentation, and the remainder of the book, part 4, covers selected topics such as inflation, investment growth, and the relationship between micro and macro.

The Mankiw Text

In the early 2000s, Gregory Mankiw's *Macroeconomics* is the leading book in the field. The book, 514 pages long, is divided into six parts. In the preface he states that his four objectives are (1) to balance short-run and long-run issues; (2) to integrate Keynesian and classical theories; (3) to present macro using a variety of simple models; and (4) to emphasize that macroeconomics is an empirical discipline. These are both similar to and different from Ackley's goals. One major difference is that the Keynesian supplement that Ackley mentioned in his preface is not in Mankiw's book, and in many ways, for Mankiw, Keynes is simply a diversion. He writes: "Although Keynes's General Theory provides the foundation for much of our current understanding of economic fluctuations, it is important to remember that Classical economics provides the right answers to many fundamental questions" (xxiii).

A second difference is that Mankiw focuses on multiple models that are not combined into a complete model, whereas Ackley focuses on the development of a complete model. The various parts of Ackley's book are meant to lead to the synthesis presented in his chapter 15. Mankiw's book has no grand synthesis. In the introductory chapter, he writes, "The field of macroeconomics is like a Swiss army knife—a set of complementary but distinct tools that can be applied in different ways in different circumstances" (11). For Ackley, macro was more a single-bladed knife and the chapters are all developing the components of that knife.

Part 1 in Mankiw consists of only two chapters and has far less discussion of the broader issues or national income accounting than were found in Ackley. Part 2, "Classical Theory: The Economy in the Long Run," is a discussion in which Mankiw states that the economy in the long run involves a time horizon of at least several years. The discussion consists of a chapter on a production function, the components of demand, and the general accounting relationships inherent in a general equilibrium model with flexible prices. While the chapter presents a consumption function and a marginal propensity to consume, it makes no use of them in the determination of equilibrium. The discussion of aggregate equilibrium instead consists of specifying accounting identities that essentially state that if output remains constant, government purchases must crowd out private expenditures. Thus fiscal policy is presented as altering the allocation of output among alternative uses, not as the central policy tool of macro, as it was in the Ackley book.

Chapter 4 introduces the quantity theory and a discussion of inflation. Chapter 5 is on the open economy issues, such as trade and exchange rates, and their relation to the real economy; chapter 6 covers unemployment, focusing primarily on steady state rather than cyclical unemployment. Part 3 consists of two chapters that present economic growth, starting with the neoclassical growth model and then progressing up through new growth theory.

Part 4 provides the first introduction to the subject that in the large majority of Ackley's book provides the focus—short-run stabilization. It consists of five chapters: "Introduction to Economic Fluctuations," "Aggregate Demand I," "Aggregate Demand II," "Aggregate Demand in the Open Economy," and "Aggregate Supply." Mankiw begins with aggregate supply and demand, the latter determined from the quantity theory with fixed velocity. Aggregate supply is presented as vertical in the long run and horizontal in the short run because of price stickiness. The short-run supply is not related to a production function.

Chapter 10, "Aggregate Demand I," presents the foundations of what much of Ackley's book was about. First, the multiplier model is developed in seven pages and then related to the IS curve. The LM curve is then quickly developed from the supply and demand for money. These two curves are then put together as the model that determines the aggregate demand curve (which is a quite different aggregate demand curve than was found in the previous chapter). This new aggregate demand curve, combined with an aggregate supply curve analysis, which he develops in chapter 13, gives Mankiw a model of aggregate supply and demand, which is his core model for explaining short-run economic fluctuations.

Chapter 11, "Aggregate Demand II," uses the IS-LM model to talk about policy, fiscal and monetary. The algebra of IS-LM is briefly presented in an appendix. Chapter 12 discusses open economy issues in reference to the IS-LM model for the case of a small open economy where international markets set interest rates. Chapter 13 develops three alternative models of aggregate supply. Mankiw does not use any of these models to formally close the system as Ackley did, but instead informally puts them together with an aggregate supply curve to close the system.

Parts 5 and 6 tie up loose ends. Part 5 discusses macroeconomic policy debates. Chapter 14 raises issues being discussed in the current theoretical literature: credibility, time inconsistency, inflation targeting, and rules and discretion. Chapter 15 discusses government debt. Part 6 covers microeconomic foundations to macroeconomics, raising issues in consumption, investment, money supply and demand, and advances in business cycle theory.

Differing Treatments of the IS-LM Model

As should be clear from the above discussion, there are substantial differences in the way Ackley and Mankiw use the IS-LM model. In Ackley, IS-LM is an elegant summary of what he has presented before. While IS-LM is used as the model, much of the presentation is about the development and thinking behind that model. It is the ideas behind IS-LM, not the model itself, that Ackley is interested in. He even states that a problem with the IS-LM model is that it hides important elements of the reasoning. Ackley did not give IS-LM much focus because, in its elegance, it tended to hide the ideas that he considers the most important. Consistent with this use of IS-LM, there is no entry in the index for IS-LM or its components, and there are only three complete IS-LM diagrams in the entire book. IS-LM appears in only one chapter, even though the majority of the book is about the short run, and there it is supplemented by an alternative geometric exposition that "exposes more of the relationships to view" (372).

For Mankiw, IS-LM serves a fundamentally different role. It is not meant to synthesize the ideas he has presented earlier, but instead is a subsidiary model of the AS/AD model, useful for handling discussions of monetary and fiscal policy with a fixed price level. But, ironically, in this new role IS-LM gains prominence. Instead of being relegated to one chapter, as it is in Ackley, it shows up significantly in three chapters. The IS curve, the LM curve, and the IS-LM model all have significant entries in the index, and there are twenty-eight complete IS-LM diagrams, compared with the three in Ackley. This is the case even though Mankiw gives much less focus to short-run stabilization issues than did Ackley.

In sum, IS-LM for Ackley is simply a minor expositional tool used as one way to convey multimarket equilibrium, and the components that built it up are discussed at length. The ideas behind the model, not the model, are what is important. For Mankiw, and for modern texts generally, far less discussion goes to the components of IS-LM. Instead, the IS-LM model becomes primarily a tool for discussing policy.

This change in the use of IS-LM reflects the change in the goal of the intermediate course discussed above. Ackley's text was designed for a much more consciously theoretical course in which learning the model connected the reader to the modern theoretical literature. Thus its title: *Macroeconomic Theory*. That is not the case with Mankiw's text. Since the upper-level macro theory is far less unified, he presents multiple models and does not unite them in a grand synthesis model. Hence his text and most other modern intermediate macro texts are no longer called Macroeconomic Theory, but *Macroeconomics*. In modern books, the IS-LM model is not used to connect to the theoretical literature, but is instead used as a convenient focus for the discussion of short-run policy. Because the modern course focuses heavily on policy, ironically, that means that the IS-LM model is given more, not less, emphasis in Mankiw.

Recognizing this difference suggests that we must be clear about what aspect of IS-LM analysis is persisting. The theoretical focus on the analysis of the goods and the money (and the hidden bond market) that underlies the individual curves has not persisted. That discussion, while still there, has been significantly reduced. What has persisted is the particular graphic technique of looking at multimarket equilibrium in equilibrium space and using the curves in that model to discuss monetary and fiscal policy. Today, one does not see the four-quadrant diagram in any major intermediate macro text, but one sees the IS-LM diagram in every one of them.

The way in which the IS-LM model is used today suggests that one reason that the particular IS-LM graphic technique is so persistent is that its elegance allows it to be used in a rough-and-ready fashion, in which the underlying model is less important than whether some underlying model exists that gives the upward- and downward-sloping curves needed to close the model and determine equilibrium. If correct, this suggests that IS-LM has remained central to the teaching of macroeconomics because of its chameleon-like nature, which has allowed it to evolve from a simplified description of the model economists thought described the economy—a simplified econometric model—to a pedagogical crutch that is not descriptive of theory but is instead a convenient totem on which to hang discussions of monetary policy, fiscal policy, and their interactions.

Its elegance allows a clouding over of the theoretical issues and underpinnings of the model. I suspect that it is for that same reason that the AS/AD model has gained such wide acceptance at the introductory level. With IS-LM, there is an upward-sloping curve and a downward-sloping curve, and it is possible to do exercises involving shifts in both curves and the effects of various monetary and fiscal policies.

IS-LM in the Future

The future of IS-LM is very much tied to the future of macro. Because of its chameleon-like nature and ambiguous elegance, it can continue to exist in a variety of alternative scenarios, but not in all. Perhaps the most fertile environment for IS-LM is the one I believe most likely in the near term—an environment in which economists generally accept that IS-LM is loosely consistent with a dynamic general equilibrium model and that, given appropriate nominal rigidities, an inverse relationship between short-run goods market equilibrium and real interest rates is possible. Add to that an assumption that monetary authorities can choose a real interest rate in the short run, and one has a foundation for an IS-LM-type model. Within that environment, the future of IS-LM as a pedagogical device for rough-and-ready discussions of stabilization policy seems assured not because of its strength but because of the lack of an alternative.

In the more distant future, I see macro coalescing as a field whose foundation is in the study of complex systems. By that I mean that macro variables will be seen as following from interrelationships that include nonlinear dynamic relationships. These complex relationships make noncontextual microfoundations for the curves impossible to derive. The reason is that these microeconomic foundations have such complex interrelationships that they are analytically intractable. If this change takes place, it will bring with it a significant change in the way macro problems and policy are thought about. Instead of macro theory being the study of infinitely bright individuals operating in an information-rich environment as it is now, it will become the study of reasonably bright and adaptable individuals operating in information-poor environments.

This change in focus will significantly affect the way we see macro phenomena relating to theory. In large part, the study of macro relationships will turn to the study of sophisticated statistical techniques that will search for possibly exploitable, temporary patterns in the data, and to agent-based simulations that will relate the patterns to broad general deductive laws—such as the law of one price—that loosely underlie our general analytic understanding of the economy. This alternative approach will eliminate the standard analytic foundation for the IS-LM model, as well as the new dynamic general equilibrium approach with nominal rigidities foundation. However, as I have suggested in Colander 2000, it will not necessarily eliminate the IS-LM model, since, even in this framework, it is still possible to view the IS-LM model as capturing temporary patterns. The difference is that IS-LM will become a historical model expressing first-order changes in variables centered on the existing institutional base; it will not be an independent model of the entire economy outside an institutional context. The equilibrium it determines is only in reference to a historically determined starting point.

While it is possible for IS-LM to remain in this complex-system future, it is, in my view, unlikely. As the work in macro becomes more dependent on data extraction and agent-based simulation, the pedagogy of macro will change. It will focus more and more on standard simulations and statistical techniques that pull information from data. As it does so, the teaching of it will move from the printed page to the computer where dynamic models and simulations will be the standard techniques. Within this computer environment the two-dimensional elegance of IS-LM will no longer be a virtue, and IS-LM will fade away, along with the intermediate macro texts that gave it its lifeblood.

References

Ackley, Gardner. [1961] 1968. *Macroeconomic Theory*. Collier-Macmillan Student Edition, 3rd printing. New York: Macmillan.

Barro, Robert. 1998. *Macroeconomics*. 5th ed. Cambridge: MIT Press.

Clarida, Richard, Jordi Gali, and Mark Gertler. 1999. The Science of Monetary Policy: A New Keynesian Perspective. *Journal of Economic Literature* 37 (December): 1661–1707.

Colander, David. 2000. Post Walrasian Macroeconomics and IS-LM Analysis. In Young and Zilberfarb 2000.

Colander, David, and Edward Gamber. 2002. *Macroeconomics*. Upper Saddle River, N.J.: Prentice Hall.

Foley, Duncan. Interview. Forthcoming. In *The Changing Face of Economics: Interviews with Cutting Edge Economists*, edited by David Colander, Barkley Rosser, and Richard Holt. Ann Arbor: University of Michigan Press.

Klein, Lawrence. 2000. The IS-LM Model: Its Role in Macroeconomics. In Young and Zilberfarb 2000.

Mankiw, N. Gregory. 2003. *Macroeconomics*. 5th ed. New York: Worth Publishers.

McCallum, Bennett, and Edward Nelson. 1999. An Optimizing IS-LM Specification for Monetary Policy and Business Cycle Analysis. *Journal of Money, Credit, and Banking* 31:296–316.

Solow, Robert. 1984. Mr Hicks and the Classics. *Oxford Economic Papers* 36 (supplement): 13–25.

Taylor, John, and Michael Woodford. 1999. *Handbook of Macroeconomics*. Amsterdam: North-Holland.

Tobin, James. 1980. *Asset Accumulation and Economics Activity*. Oxford: Basil Blackwell.

Wyshak, Fred. 2002. IS-LM in the Economics Literature. Unpublished manuscript, Middlebury College.

Young, Warren. 1987. *Interpreting Mr. Keynes: The IS-LM Enigma*. Cambridge: Polity Press.

Young, Warren, and Ben Zion Zilberfarb. 2000. *IS-LM and Modern Macroeconomics*. Boston: Kluwer Academic.

Yun, Tack. 1996. Nominal Price Rigidity, Money Supply Endogeneity, and Business Cycles. *Journal of Monetary Economics* 37.2–3:345–70.

Contributors

Roger E. Backhouse is professor of the history and philosophy of economics at the University of Birmingham, England. He has published on the history of macroeconomics and the history of economics more generally. His latest book is *The Penguin History of Economics / The Ordinary Business of Life* (2002).

Mauro Boianovsky is associate professor in the Department of Economics at the University of Brasilia, Brazil. He teaches economic methodology and the history of economic thought at the graduate level. He has published a number of articles in professional journals and edited volumes, mostly on the history of macroeconomics and monetary theory.

Michael Bordo is a professor of economics at Rutgers University.

David Colander received his PhD from Columbia University and has been the Christian A. Johnson Distinguished Professor of Economics at Middlebury College, Middlebury, Vermont, since 1982. In 2001–2002 he was the Kelly Professor of Distinguished Teaching at Princeton University. He has authored, coauthored, and edited over thirty-five books and one hundred articles on a wide range of topics. His books have been, or are being, translated into a number of different languages, including Chinese, Bulgarian, Polish, Italian, and Spanish. He has been president of both the Eastern Economic Association and the History of Economics Society and is, or has been, on the editorial boards of numerous journals, including the *Journal of Economic Perspectives* and the *Journal of Economic Education*.

William Darity Jr. is a professor of economics at the University of North Carolina.

Michel De Vroey is professor of economics at the Université catholique de Louvain in Belgium. He has held visiting positions at the Université de Paris, Panthéon-Sorbonne, Duke University, Université de Montréal, and others. His present domain of research is the history of macroeconomics, in which he has published extensively. His book, *Involuntary Unemployment: The Elusive Quest for a Theory*, will be published by Routledge in 2004.

Robert W. Dimand is a professor of economics at Brock University, St. Catharines, Ontario, Canada, holding a Chancellor's Chair for Research Excellence. A graduate of McGill and Yale Universities, he wrote *The Origins of the Keynesian Revolution* (Edward Elgar, 1988), coauthored volume 1 of *A History of Game Theory* (with M. A. Dimand; Routledge, 1996), coedited *A Biographical Dictionary of Women Economists* (with M. A. Dimand and E. L. Forget; Edward Elgar, 2000), and edited *The Origins of Macroeconomics* (10 vols.; Routledge, 2002).

Kevin D. Hoover is professor of economics, University of California, Davis. Educated at the College of William and Mary and Oxford University, he has written extensively in monetary and macroeconomics, economic methodology, and the history of economics. He is the author of *Causality in Macroeconomics* and *The Methodology of Empirical Macroeconomics* (both Cambridge University Press, 2001). He is past president of the History of Economics Society, past chairman of the International Network for Economic Methodology, and an editor of the *Journal of Economic Methodology*.

David Laidler is Bank of Montreal Professor of Economics at the University of Western Ontario, London, Canada, where he has taught since 1975. He has been concerned with monetary economics and its history throughout his career, more recently taking a particular interest in developments over the period 1870–1940, which form the subject of his two books, *The Golden Age of the Quantity Theory* (Philip Allan, 1991) and *Fabricating the Keynesian Revolution* (Cambridge University Press, 1999).

Robert E. Lucas Jr. is a professor of economics at the University of Chicago. He was awarded the Nobel Prize in 1995.

Edward Nelson received a bachelor's degree in economics from Sydney University and a PhD in economics from Carnegie Mellon University. He worked at the Bank of England from 1998 to 2003, serving as a research advisor to the Bank of England's Monetary Policy Committee from 2000 to 2003. Since June 2003 he has been a research officer at the Federal Reserve Bank of St. Louis. His research interests are macroeconomics and monetary economics, and his research papers have covered such topics as inflation dynamics; the relationship between IS-LM and modern dynamic general equilibrium theory; the role of money in the transmission mechanism of monetary policy; the relationship between the exchange rate and inflation; the measurement of the output gap and the natural interest rate; and the role of policymakers in the stagflation of the 1970s.

Goulven Rubin is Maître de Conférence at the University of Paris VIII Saint-Denis and a member of PHARE (Pôle d'Histoire de l'Analyse et des Représentations Économiques). He received his PhD in 2002 from the University of Paris X-Nanterre; his thesis was titled "The Contribution of Don Patinkin to the Neoclassical Synthesis: Genesis and Scope."

Anna Schwartz is a research associate with the National Bureau of Economic Research.

Scott Sumner received a BA in economics from the University of Wisconsin, and an MA and PhD in economics from the University of Chicago. Since 1982 he has taught undergraduate and MBA-level economics courses at Bentley College in Waltham, Massachusetts. His research interests include monetary history, monetary theory, and the history of thought. He has recently researched the role of the gold standard in the Great Depression, the role of the gold standard in the development of Keynesian economics, and the advantages of using futures prices as targets of monetary policy.

Warren Young is an associate professor of economics at Bar Ilan University. His books include *Interpreting Mr. Keynes* (1987); *Harrod and His Trade Cycle Group* (1989); *Oxford Economics and Oxford Economists* (with Fred Lee, 1993); *Atomic Energy Costing* (1998); *IS-LM and Modern Macroeconomics* (edited with B. Zilberfarb, 2000); *The Open Economy Macromodel: Past, Present, and Future* (edited with A. Arnon, 2002); *Economics, Economists, and Expectations* (with W. Darity and R. Leeson, 2004); and *Open Economy Macromodels: Origins, Development, and Debates* (with R. Boyer, forthcoming). He has published papers in *HOPE* and other journals. His current research focuses on the history of open economy and real business cycle models and the economics of energy and regulation. He is also book review editor, *European Journal of Political Economy*.

Index